Supervision
Georgia J. Kosmoski, Ph.D.

Stylex Publishing Co., Inc.
529 East Maple Lane
Mequon, WI 53092 USA
Phone: (414) 241-8347; Fax: (414) 241-8348; Email: stylex@execpc.com
World Wide Web: http://www.execpc.com/~stylex

Copyright ©1997 by **Stylex Publishing Co., Inc.**
First Printing

Printed in the United States of America

Title: **Supervision**
ISBN 1-878016-15-6

Includes illustrations, bibliographies, index, software.

Available from:

Stylex Publishing Co., Inc.
529 East Maple Lane
Mequon, WI 53092 USA
(414) 241-8347

All rights reserved. No parts of this book may be reproduced in any form whatsoever, by photograph, mimeograph, computerized scanning, photocopying, production of overhead transparencies, production of slides, or by any other means, by broadcast or transmission via modem, airwaves, or closed circuit, by translation into any kind of language, or by recording electronically or otherwise, without permission in writing from the publisher, Stylex Publishing Co., Inc., except by reviewers, who may quote brief passages in critical articles and reviews.

Production of overhead transparencies, slides, charts, or any video reproduction of any part of this book is prohibited except by previous permission from Stylex. Such permission is often available upon classroom adoption. Stylex Publishing Company makes available many transparency masters for university, college, and training usage.

Dedication

Effective supervisors are rarely praised, frequently maligned, and most often taken for granted. Yet research has proven that they are the essential lynch pin of quality schools. This text is dedicated to those extraordinary school supervisors whose expertise, creativity, and tireless efforts facilitate and positively shape the teaching/learning process in our public schools. These dedicated educators serve as the inspiration for this book. A special thank you is extended to my fellow writers who generously shared their skills and knowledge with all of us. A grateful acknowledgment is offered to the faculty, administration, and students at GSU; and especially to Jeffrey S. Kaiser, Sandi Estep; and Laurin Moore who provided patience, direction, and much needed support.

Author Profiles

Dr. Georgia J. Kosmoski is a professor of Educational Administration at Governors State University, University Park, Illinois. She is University Coordinator for the Governors State University Beginning Administrators Program. Her research interests include needs and characteristics of beginning administrators, female administrators, the relationship between self-esteem and student and staff success, and, naturally, effective school supervision.

Dr. Kosmoski has been a public school educator for more than twenty years. First as an elementary classroom teacher and then as a school administrator, she has worked directly with students and teachers in a wide variety of settings. Advancing through ranks from teacher to assistant principal, and principal, she has worked in several inner city schools as well as a number of suburban buildings. Constituents were multiethnic and ranged from lower to upper socio-economic class. Dr. Kosmoski has supervised special needs programs for gifted, learning disabled, and physically challenged pupils.

Dr. Kosmoski earned a Ph.D. in School Administration and a Ph.D. in Curriculum and Instruction from Purdue University, West Lafayette, Indiana. Since that time, she has published regularly and has presented at numerous national association conferences including ASCD, AASA, and AERA.

Dr. Kosmoski explains that she was driven to write this text because of her belief in the importance of school principals. In agreement with *effective school research*, she insists that principals, serving as supervisors of teachers, have the greatest impact upon school performance. *No other individuals will so affect the success or failure of an educational program. Student learning is directly dependent on the quality of performance of school supervisors. Supervisors have an awesome responsibility and a great opportunity to serve.*

Dr. Jeffrey S. Kaiser received his Ph.D. with Distinction from The State University of New York at Buffalo. He is University Professor of Educational Administration at Governors State University in University Park, Illinois where he is twice recipient of the university's *Award for Academic Excellence*. He is an internationally known author of articles for professional journals and is author of textbooks and software for Prentice-Hall, Macmillan, Stylex and the Telelearning Corporation. Dr. Kaiser, now listed in *Who's Who in the World*, has lectured in Australia, New Zealand, Canada, and the United States. He has conducted training programs for administrators from more than a hundred school districts and has conducted management training programs for Rexnord, Kearney & Trecker, Miller Brewing Company, Jacobsen/Textron, General Motors/Delco, and many others.

Dr. Barbara A. Murray is Assistant Professor of Educational Leadership at The University of Central Florida, Orlando. She has been a district superintendent, and a principal at the high school, junior high school, and middle school levels. Before her appointment with the University of Central Florida, she served as a member of the governor's Indiana Task Force for Secondary Education and Vice President for the Joint Education Services for Special Education. Dr. Murray is Associate Editor of the Florida School Law Quarterly which is published by the University of Central Florida Center for Law and Justice in Education and the Florida Association of School Administrators.

Dr. George E. Pawlas is an Assistant Professor in the Educational Leadership Department at the University of Central Florida. He has served as an elementary school principal in Ohio, South Carolina, and Georgia. Dr. Pawlas has published numerous articles in educational journals and made many presentations at national professional conferences. He has co-authored two of the Phi Delta Kappa New Principals handbooks. He is author of *The School Administrator's Guide to School-Community Relations* and is author of two chapters in Jeffrey S. Kaiser's *The 21st Century Principal.* Dr. Pawlas is a member of the Council of Professors of Instructional Supervision (COPIS).

Preface

I hesitated when Ginger (Georgia J. Kosmoski) asked me to write the preface to her new book. She was the expert on educational supervision. I was not. My expertise on the subject comes largely from work with managers in industry. Surely she should be the one to write the preface to what was going to be the newest work in a growing specialty in education.

Ginger was kind enough to give me a few days to think about it. I took the first two days to agonize about how to turn down the honor. Then, when my fear subsided, I thought more sensibly about the field of supervision in general. It was obvious that the supervision of people in business and in education is the most important factor in their productivity and performance. Poor supervision accounts for more corporate bankruptcies and more failing schools than any other component of leadership. And, since uneducated educational administrators are just as notorious for destroying teacher motivation as are their counterparts in industry, I guessed I could manage the preface.

Administrators and managers with negative attitudes and inadequate skills have always been more likely to fall into destructive and autocratic behavior patterns. Those who abdicate their supervisory responsibilities are just as guilty as those who abuse them. There is hardly a retiree on earth who cannot tell hours of stories about horrible bosses who were power hungry, ignorant, or just plain nasty. If those bosses directed their hunger, ignorance, or nastiness toward their own bosses, their would be no stories to tell. They would have been fired. But of course, poor supervisors usually direct their own inadequacies toward their subordinates. It is always easier to fail the powerless.

While human behavior remains quite static over time, our understanding of its nature grows. Aside from classics such as Machiavelli's *The Prince* and Plato's *Republic*, pre-twentieth century literature is largely silent on the subject of supervision. The classics focus on tenets and precepts in philosophical pursuits of truth. None describe mechanisms for implementation of philosophy. Until the twentieth century, little was available to the neophyte manager or administrator in structuring the job of supervision. Early attempts at defining the field were limited to designing structures for watching, telling, and evaluating subordinates. Only recently, toward the turn of the twenty-first century, has the field of supervision emphasized the team approach toward subordinate development.

This team approach is not an abdication of leadership. Instead, it is an awareness of the heightened performance that can be inherent in pluralistic-collegial problem solving. Collegial pluralism is not merely the country-club management orientation of a relationship-motivated leader. It is a model of management that strongly embraces the need for structure in interpersonal goal-related relations. It is that structure which is the back bone of this textbook.

Ginger has spent the past two years making sense out of the seemingly disparate pieces of the field of supervision. To that extent, she has presented us with its first formal structure. In Part I *The Nature of School Supervision*, the field is placed in its American and its human context. Part II, *Improving Instruction* contains the suggested structures for helping teachers plan instruction, evaluate student performance, and manage their classrooms. Part II culminates with a presentation of the most current models of clinical supervision and the methods for their implementation. Part III, *Evaluation, Curriculum, and Staff Development* places the methods of implementation from Part II within the cultural context of Part I. Barbara Murray examines the legal aspects of supervision, I present a model and methodology for appraising subordinate administrator performance, and Ginger looks at the supervisory role in curriculum and staff development.

The cover of this textbook was designed with Ginger's last chapter in mind. The future of schools in America is up for grabs. There is a real possibility that continued decreases in funding will result in increases in privatization. With that may come difficulties associated with lack of funds, and exciting challenges that come with increasing competition and entrepreneurship in a technological milieu. The next century will bring with it great growth in the understanding of pedagogy. The new delivery systems for teaching, supervising, and evaluating will offer an exciting chance for continuous quality improvement in the way we administer our schools and the way we supervise our teachers and administrators.

Jeffrey S. Kaiser, Ph.D.

CONTENTS

Dedication..*iii*
Author Profiles ....*iv*
Preface ....*vi*

Part I: The Nature of School Supervision... 1

Chapter 1. Supervision: An American Perspective *Georgia J. Kosmoski* 3
Understanding History 3
Historical Perspective... 3
Modern Perspective... 11
Supervision Defined... 12
Types of Supervision.. 14
Supervisory Tasks 15
Supervision Models.. 16
Styles of Supervision.. 21
Selecting a Supervision Style 22
Contingency Leadership.. 22
Situational Leadership 22
The Need for Supervision.. 23
Barriers to Quality Supervision 24
Future Ramifications... 28
Principles and Practices for Success 28
Summary 28
Case Problem: *Remediate Bitterman* 29
Case Problem: *Is Marvin Ready?* 29
References 30

Chapter 2. People and Supervision *Barbara A. Murray* 33
The Social Science of Supervision... 33
Adult Lifespan Development.. 35
Personality Styles.. 39
Perceptions, Platforms, and Prejudiced Behavior.. 39
The Learning Process... 43
Behaviorism.. 43
Social Learning Theory... 43
Cognitive Theory 44
Motivation 44
Leadership.. 48
Power and Authority 51
Leading in a Diverse Environment.. 55

-viii-

The Diverse Workforce 60
Supervision of Certified and Noncertified Personnel............................ 60
Principles and Practices for Success 62
Summary 63
Case Problem: *Mrs. Baker*.. 63
References... 64

Part II: Improving Instruction 69

Chapter 3. Supervision and Teacher Planning *Georgia J. Kosmoski* 71
Encouraging Teachers to Plan.. 71
Planning, Implementation, and Evaluation.. 67
Teacher Effectiveness... 72
Macro and Micro Planning 75
Planning: The Initial Phase of the Instructional Process 76
Planning: The Act of Instructional Design 77
One Model for Instructional Design 78
Additional Planning Considerations 84
Writing and Organizing Instructional Plans 86
Positive Supervisory Practices 86
Principles and Practices for Success 89
Summary 90
Case Problem: *So Fresh!* 90
Case Problem: *More of the Same*... 91
References... 91

Chapter 4. Observing Instruction *Barbara A. Murray* 95
Artistic and Scientific Approaches to Teaching 95
Model for Supervising Instruction... 96
Developing the Supervisor-Teacher Relationship 97
Recognition of Educational Beliefs and Platforms 98
Planning and Developing Goals and Objectives................................. 100
Methods of Instructional Delivery 105
Inquiry and Discovery... 106
Individualized Instruction 107
Effective Teaching Strategies 112
Measurement and Evaluation of Student Progress 117
Teacher and Student Evaluation.. 118
Understanding Student Differences 122
Understanding Teacher Differences... 125
Implications for Supervision 126
Principles and Practices for Success 129
Summary 129

Case Problem: *Judy Timmons*.. 130
References 131

Chapter 5. Helping Teachers with Student Evaluation *Georgia J. Kosmoski*.............. **137**
The Need for Student Assessment 137
National Assessment Initiatives 138
Test Criteria: Reliability, Validity, and Usability............................... 139
Reliability 139
Validity.. 140
Usability 140
Types of Tests... 141
Standardized and Nonstandardized Tests 141
Norm-referenced and Criteria-referenced Tests 143
Teacher-made Tests 146
Performance Assessment... 150
Performance Characteristics.. 150
Test Administration Practices 151
Giving Students Feedback... 152
Test Anxiety 153
Supervision Practices to Improve Testing Climate............................ 154
Technology to Facilitate Accessible Information 155
Testing and Special Education 157
Principles and Practices for Success 158
Summary 159
Case Problem: *Finding Waldo*... 160
Case Problem: *New Broom Sweeps In* 161
References 161

Chapter 6. Helping Teachers to Manage Classrooms *George E. Pawlas* **165**
Are Discipline Problems All that Serious? 165
Organizing the Classroom 166
Classroom Climate.. 166
Academic Climate 167
High Standards 167
Orderly Environment... 168
Expectations for Success 169
Kounin's Techniques 171
Withitness... 171
Overlapping... 171
Smoothness... 172
Momentum 172
Group Alerting 172
Concepts of Behavior 173

Attention.. 173
Power.. 173
Revenge 173
Avoidance of Failure.. 174
Discipline Profiles.. 174
Roles and Responsibilities of Supervisors 176
Principles and Practices for Success 176
Summary 177
Case Problem: *Effective Mentoring* 178
References... 178

Chapter 7. Clinical Supervision *Georgia J. Kosmoski* 181
Introduction 181
Clinical Supervision Defined... 181
Identified Components 183
Three Models of Clinical Supervision 184
The Goldhammer Model 184
The Cogan Model 187
The Acheson and Gall Model.. 188
Stumbling Blocks to Successful Clinical Supervision 190
Implementing Clinical Supervision in the School................................ 192
The Supervisor's Readiness... 192
Preparing the Staff 193
Practices for a Successful Preobservation Conference 195
Practices for a Successful Observation 198
Practices for a Successful Postobservation Conference....................... 200
Principles and Practices for Success 202
Summary 202
Case Problem: *Newfangled Ideas* 204
Case Problem: *Out of Step*.. 204
Case Problem: *Perplexed Professor*... 204
References... 205

Part III: Evaluation, Curriculum, And Staff Development........................ 207

Chapter 8. Supervision, Evaluation, and the Law *Barbara A. Murray* 209
Understanding Evaluation.. 209
Resolving Conflict Between Supervision and Evaluation 212
The Influence of Collective Bargaining 213
The Bargaining Process 215
Past Practice and Unfair Labor Practices 217
The Grievance Procedure 221
Teacher Strikes 222

Constitutional Legal Constraints 225
Freedom of Expression.. 225
Academic Freedom 227
Freedom from Prior Restraint.. 227
Freedom of Association.. 228
Right to Privacy 228
Right to Personal Appearance 229
Due Process 229
Contractual Constraints 231
Friction-reducing Methods 232
A Model for Documenting the Observation 233
Positive Translation 234
Positive Statement.. 234
Principles and Practices for Success 236
Summary 236
Case Problem: *Mrs. Anderson* 236
References 237

Chapter 9. Appraising Administrator Performance *Jeffrey S. Kaiser* **239**
Introduction.. 239
Teacher vs. Administrator Appraisal of Performance 240
Problems with Performance Appraisals... 242
Supervisor Preparation for Appraising a Subordinate's Performance 243
Gathering Data 244
Assessing Performance 244
Listing the Points to be Discussed 244
Preparing the Subordinate.. 245
The Performance Appraisal Meeting.. 246
Establishing Rapport.. 247
Discussing Performance... 248
Recommendations for Future Action 260
Closing the Meeting... 261
Other Important Points 262
External Assessment... 262
Principles and Practices for Success 263
Summary 263
Case Problem: *Martin Mobile's Decision*... 263
References 264

Chapter 10. Supervision and Curriculum *Georgia J. Kosmoski*.. **265**
Curriculum Management... 265
Curriculum Defined 265
The Community's Perception of Curriculum...259

-xii-

Specialists' Perception of Curriculum 266
Planned and Unplanned Curriculum 267
A Working Definition of Curriculum 268
The Renewed Dilemma 268
Curricular Roles of the Supervisor 270
Supervision and Curriculum Development 271
The Curriculum Development Process 272
Philosophy of Education Screen 272
The Needs Assessment Screen 274
Goals and Objectives 275
Content 280
Methodology 281
Evaluation 281
Supervision and Curriculum Implementation 281
Supervision and the Evaluation of Curriculum 282
Influences on Curriculum Decisions 283
Spheres of Power 283
Background 288
Political Conflicts 288
Principles and Practices for Success 289
Summary 290
Case Problem: *Dusty Chalk* 290
Case Problem: *A Class Act* 291
References 291

Chapter 11. Supervision and Staff Development *Georgia J. Kosmoski* **295**
Staff Development: A Supervision Function 295
Staff Development Defined 296
The Need for Staff Development 297
Who Benefits from Staff Development 298
Where Does Staff Development Occur? 299
Functions of Staff Development 300
The Role of the Supervisor 301
Characteristics of Effective Staff Development Programs 302
One Staff Development Model 303
Collegiality 304
Staff Development Planning 304
The Planning Team 304
Identifying and Prioritizing Staff Needs 305
Topic Selection 305
Developing a Master Plan 305
Scheduling 307
Selecting a Provider 308

Other Planning Considerations: Cost and Incentives..309
Providing the Staff Development Program 309
Indicators of an Effective Program..309
Adult Learning..310
Common Implementation Formats 311
Evaluation/Application/Reevaluation 312
Principles and Practices for Success..314
Summary..315
Case Problem: *Della Gate's Staff Development Program*.....................................315
Case Problem: *To the Rescue*..316
References 316

Chapter 12. Future Schools and Supervisors *Georgia J. Kosmoski*................... **319**
Supervisors and Vision 319
Schools and Change..321
Schools in 2010..323
School Organization Changes...324
School Autonomy and Accountability...324
Competition and Entrepreneurship...325
Increased Collegiality and Leadership Role Shifting 326
Curricular Changes 327
A Safe And Drug Free Environment 327
A Technology Explosion..329
Curriculum to Meet Social Needs 332
Re-examining the Sacred Cows 333
Exclusive Subordinate Examination 335
Major Additional Changes..336
Closing Thoughts..337
Principles and Practices for Success..338
Summary..338
Case Problem: *Crystal Ball*...339
References 340

Index 345

-xiv-

Part I
The Nature of School Supervision

Supervision
Georgia J. Kosmoski

Chapter 1

SUPERVISION: AN AMERICAN PERSPECTIVE
Georgia J. Kosmoski

Understanding History

The political, religious, economic, and industrial changes in the history of America have affected the development of school supervision. As with most key elements of education, school supervision is a product of both the present and the past. The changing perception of teacher evaluation dramatically illustrates this point. In the early stages of the development of education in America, evaluation was perceived as the task of monitoring and judging the quality of teacher adherence to predetermined standards. However, by the late 1960s, it was suggested that evaluation be viewed as the task of providing teachers with a plan for improvement (Goldhammer, 1969; and Cogan, M., 1973).

**Questions to answer
after studying this chapter**

✔ How has school supervision developed in America?

✔ Why is this important?

✔ How can modern supervision be defined?

✔ What are the two major types of supervision?

✔ What supervisory tasks comprise the two types of supervision?

✔ What are some of the most used contemporary supervisory models?

✔ Why is there a need for supervision in schools?

✔ What internal and external barriers to implementation of supervision must be confronted?

By the 1990s, most public school teacher evaluation processes combined both of these views. Evaluation is now thought to have a judgmental portion and a corrective, prescriptive feedback portion designed to improve instruction.

Historical Perspective

The broad periods of historical development in education and, more specifically, in educational supervision are outlined in Figure 1-1.

Prior to the establishment of organized schools in America, our children learned at home. Parents or tutors providing the instruction for these young charges were their own supervisors. Initially, there was no perceived need for formalized supervisory duties or structure. However, very early on, people recognized the need for more inclusive and uniform education.

4 Chapter 1 *Supervision: An American Perspective*

Major Time Periods of Educational Supervision			
Period	**Purpose**	**Leaders**	**Supervisors**
1600—1700 Early settlements	• Monitor • Inspect	• Pilgrims	• Selectmen (Clergy, Businessmen, Parents)
1700—1800 Colonial	• Monitor • Inspect • Improve instruction	• Horace Mann • Henry Barnard • Committee of 10	• Selectmen
1800—1930 Industrial revolution Scientific Bureaucratic	• Efficiency • Productivity • Improve instruction	• F. Taylor • M. Weber • H. Fayol	• Superintendents • Central office administrators, • Principals
1950—Present Many models coexist simultaneously	• Improve instruction & productivity • Monitor • Inspect	• T. Sergiovanni • Goodlad • Acheson & Gall • Campbell • Daresh	• Principals • School-based supervisors • Central office administrators • Peers • Self

Figure 1-1

To save the children from Satan, *the Old Deluder*, the Commonwealth of Massachusetts passed the famous Old Deluder Satan Act of 1647. This law required communities of fifty families or more to provide the young with instruction in reading and writing, and communities of one hundred or more families to establish grammar schools. This provided the next generation with an education to protect them from the wiles of the devil. Elected school committeemen and selectmen (most often influential businessmen, parents, and clergy) provided supervision for these newly established schools. These colonial supervisors used a strict authoritative and autocratic style to enforce compliance with stipulated rules, requirements, and curriculum. *Selectmen* would visit their community's classroom to insure that the teacher followed required rules and prescribed practices. Any infraction could result in the teacher's dismissal (Oliva, 1993).

During the eighteenth century, the colonial population and the number of schools grew rapidly. Schools began to offer boys a broader range of subjects. In 1751, the Benjamin Franklin Philadelphia Academy opened and provided its students with a more diverse curriculum than that of the earlier grammar schools. With the increased number of schools and the expanded curriculum, selectmen found supervision a difficult job at best.

The phenomenon of universal public education arose in the nineteenth century. For the first time states funded free schooling for both boys and girls. Led by courageous and dynamic leaders such as Horace Mann, the Massachusetts State Board of Education Secretary, and Henry Barnard, the first secretary for the Connecticut State Board of Education, public education made significant strides.

In 1821, Boston opened the first public high school and only six years later the state of Massachusetts passed a law requiring the creation of free high schools in all communities of 500 families or more. The famous Kalamazoo Case in Michigan (1874) upheld the right of communities to tax their citizens for secondary education. Normal schools were established to train the teachers who would staff these grammar and high schools.

Theodore Kowalski and Ulrich Reitzug (1993) explained that the exploding number of students, newly created public schools, and innovative programs of this century required a different form of supervision. Selectmen, committeemen, parents, and clergy proved ill prepared for the requirements of the task of supervision.

Trained professional supervisors began to appear. These specialists, whose duties were to inspect and oversee a number of schools within their jurisdiction, were the first superintendents. The improvement of instruction became an added responsibility of these men. By the end of the century, school principals and central office supervisors were hired to aid the superintendent with ever-growing duties.

Teachers' lives were regulated and austere. At first glimpse, the accompanying charts appear humorous (Figure 1-2: 1872 Teachers Rules, and Figure 1-3: 1915 Rules for Teachers). However, closer inspection provides insight into the practices and conditions of the time. Each list is autocratic, authoritarian, and punitive, suggesting that American education in 1900 ascribed to many of the principles of the bureaucratic management model.

The *Industrial Revolution* occurred in the late nineteenth and early twentieth centuries. Productivity and efficiency were paramount to government, industry, business, social organizations, and schools. To achieve efficiency in production, two major ideologies or philosophies became prominent in American organizations. The first was Frederick Taylor's concept of *scientific management* (Kaiser, 1993). For education, the principles of scientific management were interpreted to mean that teaching was a science rather than an art. Therefore, teaching could be examined, dissected, ordered, and objectively evaluated. Teachers were the "tools" used by the supervisor to deliver the "product," or education.

1872 Teachers' Rules

1. Teachers each day will fill lamps & clean chimneys.

2. Each teacher will bring a bucket of water & scuttle of coal for the day's session.

3. Make your pens carefully. You may whittle nibs to the individual taste of pupils.

4. Men teachers may take one evening each week for courting purposes, or two evenings a week if they go to church regularly.

5. After ten hours in school, the teachers may spend the remaining time reading the bible or other good books.

6. Women teachers who marry or engage in unseemly conduct will be dismissed.

7. Every teacher should lay aside from each pay a goodly sum of their earnings for their benefit during their declining years so that they will not become a burden to society.

8. Any teacher who smokes, uses liquor in any form, frequents pool halls, or gets shaven in a barber shop will give good reason to suspect their worth, intention, integrity, and honesty.

9. The teacher who performs his labor faithfully and without fault for five years will be given an increase of five cents per week in their pay, providing the board of education approves.

Old Time Print Shop, Ozark Folk Center, Mountain View, Arkansas 72560

Figure 1-2

1915 Rules for Teachers

1. You will not marry during the term of your contract.
2. You are not to keep company with men.
3. You must be home between the hours of 8 P.M. and 6 A.M. unless attending a school function.
4. You may not loiter downtown in icecream stores.
5. You may not travel beyond the city limits unless you have the permission of the chairman of the board.
6. You may not ride in a carriage or automobile with any man unless he is your father or brother.
7. You may not smoke cigarettes.
8. You may not dress in bright colors.
9. You may under no circumstances dye your hair.
10. You must wear at least two petticoats.
11. Your dresses may not be any shorter than two inches above the ankle.
12. To keep the school room neat and clean you must:
    Sweep the floor at least once daily;
    Scrub the floor at least once a week with hot, soapy water;
    Clean the blackboards at least once a day and
    Start the fire at 7 A.M. so the room will be warm by 8 A.M.

Old Time Print Shop, Ozark Folk Center, Mountain View, Arkansas 72560

Figure 1-3

8 Chapter 1 *Supervision: An American Perspective*

A second ideology that affected American organizations was Max Weber's bureaucratic management of organizations. Weber theorized that this was the ideal model for any organization whose goal was to achieve efficiency and productivity. It provided the organization with structure and a hierarchy of personnel. The chief executive officer (CEO) was at the apex or top of the hierarchy and held the most power, authority, and responsibility. The lowliest worker was at the base of the hierarchy with the least power and authority. *Max Weber defined organizations in terms of hierarchical structures where all power flows from superordinates to subordinates* (Kaiser, p. 11, 1993).

Weber's bureaucratic management is the most appropriate bureaucratic model describing the early part of the twentieth century. School superintendents are seen at the top of ladders with varying numbers of central office supervisors on the next rungs. They are followed by building principals, principal's assistants (if necessary), teachers, support staff, and finally, on the bottom rung, students.

When this was the model of choice, the immediate supervisor oversaw the subordinate below and so on down the chain of command. The superintendent or the superintendent's designee supervised the central office staff and the building administrators. The building administrators supervised the teachers and support staff. The teachers, in turn, supervised the students. Supervision was characterized as the authoritative "handing down" of curriculum and instruction to teachers from above. The purpose of supervision was to inspect, monitor, and to improve productivity—teaching and learning. Refer to Figure 1-4 for a *Bureaucratic Management Model for Schools*.

Expanding on Weber's bureaucratic management model, Henri Fayol identified five basic management functions: planning, organizing, commanding, coordinating, and controlling. He suggested that all managers perform these tasks and held that the managers who performed them well would be successful. Fayol identified fourteen guiding principles to aid managers in the execution of these five basic functions (Gulick & Urwick, 1937).

By mid-century, Fayol's functions and principles were generally accepted and practiced throughout the American educational system. Many school districts today expect their employees, both managers and workers, to adhere to and practice this organizational model. See Figure 1.5, Fayol's *Five Basic Functions and Fourteen Principles of Management* (Gulick & Urwick, 1937).

Chapter 1 *Supervision: An American Perspective* 9

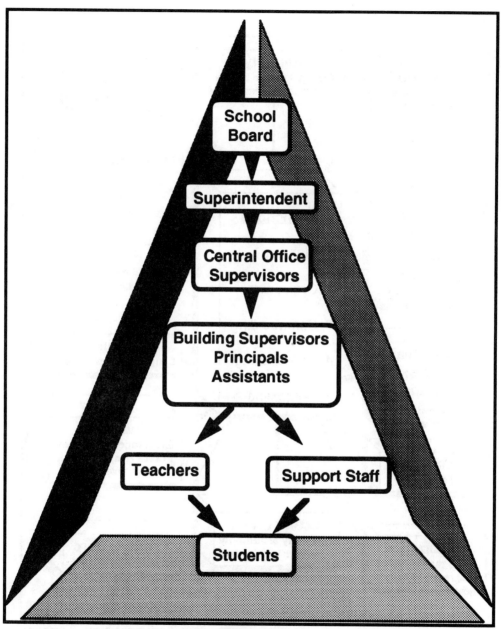

Figure 1-4
Bureaucratic Management Model for Schools

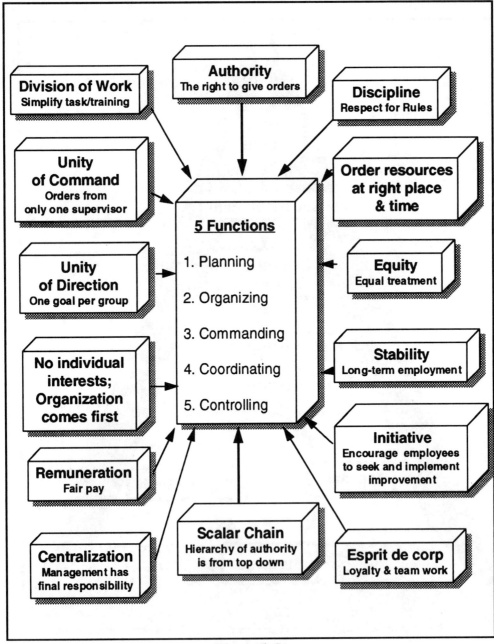

Figure 1-5
Fayol's Five Basic Functions and Fourteen Principles of Management

Although the bureaucratic management model was practiced in most organizations by the middle of the twentieth century, a new concept of administrative organization emerged. This ideology was known as the *human resources*, or *human relations*, or *democratic*, or *collegial*, or *pluralistic* model. Leaders included Mary Parker Follett, Elton Mayo, Ronald Lippitt, Kurt Lewin, and Warren Bennis. This supervision model stressed democratic ideals, collegial approaches, and individual personal worth. Authority, duties, and responsibilities moved horizontally, rather than the strictly downward direction of the bureaucratic model (Kaiser, 1993). Educational supervision became a partnership between the supervisor and the teacher. Supervisors recognized the need for teacher involvement, ownership, and collaboration to successfully improve instruction and student success. Interpersonal skills, sensitivity, supportive techniques, knowledge of the individual, and group dynamics were prized.

Modern Perspective

Today, no one perspective of supervision dominates American education. Rather, the individual supervisor selects the orientation best suited to and consistent with his or her own basic personal philosophy and intrinsic set of values. The selected supervisory orientation is then practiced within the existing organizational view. The two orientations may be in complete harmony or may coexist as two distinct and opposing philosophies.

After making a personal choice, the supervisor must remain faithful to the chosen orientation. Nothing is more damaging to the effectiveness of supervision then a hypocritical supervisor who claims to believe in a particular model, and then displays behaviors diametrically opposed to that perspective. Too often teachers rightfully complain that the supervisor is inconsistent and not genuine. Although most teachers would probably be unhappy with a supervisor who believed in the inspection view, it would be preferable to one who espoused to be a human relations proponent but was in actuality an inspector "in human relations clothing".

Most supervisors in the 1990s ascribe to the basic tenets of the human relations philosophy of supervision. They believe that it is effective and desirable in most cases. Yet, it is also true that no one orientation is best in every situation or for every individual. For example, if a teacher is reported as incompetent or dangerously irresponsible, the supervisor needs to determine the facts. The task may be highly distasteful to the supervisor; but it is necessary to scrutinize or "inspect" the teacher's behavior.

Or, a neophyte supervisor, grounded in human relations, can find that the previous administrator was a strong supporter of the bureaucratic or authoritative view. An immediate switch to a human relations management approach can traumatize an entire organization. The sensitive and knowledgeable supervisor finds a slow and gradual shift from the bureaucratic to the human relations orientation more desirable and effective (Daresh, 1989).

12 Chapter 1 *Supervision: An American Perspective*

Tanner and Tanner (1987) cautioned that an individual supervisor might hold a different and conflicting perspective from that of immediate superiors or the organization. Many school districts operate by top-down management and are characterized as *kingdoms* where the superintendent is the undisputed sovereign dispensing truth as edicts. Yet in such districts, democratic supervision, collaboration, peer coaching, and cooperative curriculum development still exist. The literature is filled with cases where human resource practices occur within the existing bureaucratic and scientific structure.

Where conflicting philosophies exist, successful supervision is only possible if the supervisor remains true to the tenets and behaviors of the chosen model. This supervisor must be candid and forthright when expressing differences with superiors from the outset. If the superiors and the organization willingly accept and value, rather than only tolerate a difference in view, the human relations oriented supervisor may be effective. Contrarily, if the supervisor hides, suppresses, or is pressured into abandoning a desired philosophy, the supervision process will likely fail.

Supervision Defined

Today, the term supervision has numerous credible definitions. Specialists have not agreed upon how to interpret this sweeping and global term. Many narrowed the meaning of supervision by describing only particular aspects. Oliva (1993) noted that these experts offered specific definitions for clinical supervision, developmental supervision, peer supervision, etc., yet did not agree upon a commonly held perception of supervision.

The diversity and disagreement on a definition for supervision is best illustrated by examining a number of existing definitions. Each definition focuses on one or more aspects or characteristics inherent to the process of supervision.

- Mosher and Purpel (1972) described the difficulty as follows:

  The difficulty of defining supervision in relation to education also stems, in large part, from unsolved theoretical problems about teaching. Quite simply, we lack sufficient understanding of the process of teaching. Our theories of learning are inadequate, the criteria for measuring teaching effectiveness are imprecise, and deep disagreement exists about what knowledge - that is, what curriculum - is most valuable to teach.. When we have achieved more understanding of "what" and "how" to teach, and with "special effects" on students, we will be much less vague about the supervision of these processes.

- Sergiovanni and Starratt (1988) stated,

  Supervision . . . can be viewed as a process component of a variety of administrative and supervisory roles or as a label to categorize roles the primary responsibility of which is the improvement of instruction.

  This pragmatic definition recognizes that individuals often perform multiple roles simultaneously. Sergiovanni and Starratt suggested that supervisory and administrative duties, not only coexist, but remain separate and distinct.

- Acheson and Gall (1992) promoted an alternative definition where supervision is:

  interactive rather than directive, democratic rather than authoritarian, teacher-centered rather than supervisor-centered.

  By stressing the collegial nature of supervision, Acheson and Gall highlighted an essential characteristic of clinical supervision.

- Robert Krey and Peter Burke (1989) described supervision in the following manner:

  Supervision is instructional leadership that relates perspectives to behavior, clarifies purposes, contributes to and supports organizational actions, coordinates interactions, provides for maintenance and improvement of the instructional program, and assesses goal achievements.

  As they equated supervision with instructional leadership, Krey and Burke emphasized that supervision encompasses a multitude of functions. They pointed out the wide scope of supervision.

- Simple and straightforward, Campbell, Corbally, and Nystrand (1983) stated:

  Supervision—appraisal of personnel performance.

  This definition suggests that people are the focal point of supervision. The judgmental nature of supervision was underscored.

- Jane Franseth (1961) also stressed the collegial nature of supervision and wrote as follows:

  Today, supervision is generally seen as leadership that encourages a continuous involvement of all school personnel in a cooperative attempt to achieve the most effective school program.

14 Chapter 1 *Supervision: An American Perspective*

Franseth's definition emphasized the cooperative nature of this process. She viewed supervision as leadership and school effectiveness as the overriding purpose of this process.

- After examining these definitions of supervision, it becomes clear that the term is elusive and convoluted. Each definition was predicated on the author's personal perspective and educational philosophy. With many philosophies existing simultaneously today, it is no wonder that there are so many diverse, cogent, and plausible definitions for educational supervision. Yet, to successfully examine this topic, a working definition must be formulated so as to provide a frame of reference for subsequent discussion. Drawing from the common elements or threads found in the definitions examined and relying upon principles found in human relations philosophy, supervision for the purposes of this text will be defined as follows:

> *Supervision is that leadership process whose ultimate purpose is to improve instruction, and thereby facilitate and promote successful student learning.*

Types of Supervision

There are two major types or areas of supervision—general and clinical (Cogan, 1973). Both are important to supervisors in their roles as instructional leaders. *General supervision* is the broad task that encompasses all that goes on outside of the classroom while clinical supervision deals with the tasks that occur within the classroom.

Some activities included in general supervision are providing a positive school environment, arranging for professional development for support staff, scheduling, and allocating program facilities. When a middle school principal ensures a clean safe building, insists upon on-time staff attendance, or replaces a disabled school bus, that principal is engaged in general supervision.

Clinical supervision is a more specific level of supervision where the supervisor, working directly with the teacher, focuses on the improvement of instruction. Improvement is accomplished by active modification of the instruction itself, or through the promotion of the teacher's professional growth. One illustration of clinical supervision is the supervisor regularly visiting the classroom, actively observing, and then sharing those observations with the teacher to help the teacher improve instruction. Likewise, when a high school science department chairperson arranges for one of the science teachers to attend a workshop on integrated learning, the chairperson is practicing clinical supervision.

Supervisory Tasks

Another way to analyze supervision is to examine the specific tasks associated with this leadership behavior. Numerous supervision specialists, starting with Burton in 1922, compiled task lists. One of the most thorough and encompassing lists for the modern supervisor was formulated by Ben Harris (1985). He divided ten tasks into three classes: preliminary tasks—those performed prior to actual instruction by the teacher; developmental tasks—those which should directly improve instruction; and operational tasks—those which deal with facilitating the operation. See Figure 1-6, Supervision: Types and Tasks. The ten tasks enumerated by Harris are as follows:

Preliminary tasks:

1. *Developing curriculum.* This includes the design of what is to be taught. Methodology, sequence, guides, standards, evaluations, and time-lines for units, courses, and programs comprise this task.

2. *Providing staff.* This task provides adequate staff with appropriate qualifications and competencies. Recruiting, hiring, assigning, and removing staff are also included.

3. *Providing facilities.* This task includes designing, remodeling, and equipping facilities so as to meet the needs and requirements of particular forms of instruction.

Developmental tasks:

4. *Arranging for in-service education.* This provides instruction-related learning experiences for staff.

5. *Evaluating instruction.* This task includes the joint planning and implementation necessary for gathering meaningful data, analysis, interpretation, and decision-making for the purpose of improving instruction.

Operational tasks:

6. *Organizing for instruction.* Scheduling and grouping people, materials, and facilities so that instruction may occur.

7. *Providing materials.* Selecting and securing the appropriate materials to ensure proper instruction for the required curriculum.

16 Chapter 1 *Supervision: An American Perspective*

8. *Orienting new staff.* Providing staff with the basic information necessary to perform their duties and responsibilities. This includes acquainting both neophytes and veterans with facilities, procedures, community developments, and organizational developments.

9. *Relating special pupil services.* Coordinating services for students to support the appropriate learning opportunities. This involves developing and interpreting policies, determining priorities, defining relationships between service personnel, and monitoring individual student and school instructional goals.

10. *Developing public relations.* Promoting and providing the free flow of information between the school and the community. Enhancing community involvement in instructional matters.

These ten tasks may be grouped into Cogan's (1973) two types of supervision. All preliminary and operational tasks would be classified as general supervision. The developmental tasks would be classified at the clinical supervision level. As with the types of supervision, these ten tasks are interrelated, exist simultaneously, and must be seriously considered by the successful supervisor. Review Figure 1-6, Supervision: Types and Tasks.

Supervision: Types and Tasks		
Type	General	Clinical
Task	Preliminary	Operational	Developmental
	Develop curriculum	Organize instruction	Arrange in-service
	Provide staff	Provide materials	Evaluate instruction
	Provide facilities	Orient new staff	
		Relate special pupil services	
		Develop public relations	
		Cogan, M. (1973) and Harris B. (1985)	

Figure 1-6

Supervision Models

Successful supervisors select and implement the appropriate supervision model that best fits their own orientation, the situation, and the needs of the teachers. A supervisor might choose from a number of specific models to implement a given perspective or supervisory task. Some widely utilized models are *human resource, clinical, developmental,* and *collegial.*

Chapter 1 *Supervision: An American Perspective* **17**

Human Resources Supervision

The human resources model emerged in the 1960s. Also referred to as the human relations model, this model was the product of such specialists as Bennis, McGregor, and Argyris. It attempted to humanize the bureaucratic scientific management orientation. Sergiovanni and Starratt (1988) and Oliva (1993) pointed out that three basic characteristics must be present for this model to be implemented. These essential characteristics are:

1. Supervision should center on the human beings involved in the process. These people are responsible, active, and growing beings.

2. Supervision is both personal as well as grounded within educational tradition.

3. Supervision may only be exercised within the context of organizational dynamics (group and individual).

Clinical Supervision

Widely accepted as a successful model for supervision, clinical supervision focuses on *classroom behavior for the improvement of instruction and demands that within a positive general supervisory climate, a strong, dynamic relationship exists between the teacher and the supervisor* (Kaiser, 1993). Pioneers who shaped modern clinical supervision include Goldhammer (1969), Cogan (1973), Mosher and Purpel (1972), and Acheson and Gall (1992). Although these specialists disagreed upon the exact formula for obtaining effective results, they did agree upon three basic steps within the process:

1. *The Preobservation Conference.* The preobservation conference sets the agreement between the teacher and the supervisor. It establishes content, ground rules, plans, timing, and mechanics for the forthcoming observation.

2. *Observation.* Observation occurs when the supervisor comes into the teacher's classroom to gather data by clinically observing and objectively recording the the behaviors of the teacher and the students during a lesson.

3. *Postobservation Conference.* The postobservation conference occurs when the supervisor and teacher analyze and interpret, either separately or together, the gathered data for the purpose of prescribing a course of action for improvement and growth.

18 Chapter 1 *Supervision: An American Perspective*

A number of supervision models compatible with classic clinical supervision have been implemented by supervisors throughout America. Among the noteworthy models is scientific supervision developed by Russell and Hunter (1980). This model suggested that supervision, and subsequently teacher evaluation, is based on the frequency a teacher engages in nine identifiable teaching activities. The more frequent the activities the more effective the instruction. These activities are diagnosis, anticipatory set, perceived purpose, learning opportunities, modeling, checking for understanding, guided practice, and independent practice.

Another model compatible with clinical supervision was Eisner's (1982) artistic supervision model. This model is a holistic approach that allows the supervisor to rely on his or her own perception, sensitivity, and acquired knowledge when working with and evaluating teachers. Teaching is considered an ever-changing art, and supervision is viewed as fluid and flexible. Critics suggest that this model is so broad and subjective that the supervisor should combine it with an approach that is more measurable and specific (Kaiser, 1993).

Developmental Supervision

Carl Glickman (1990) described developmental supervision as the

glue for effective, fully functioning school supervision. Glue is not glamorous; neither is supervision. When glue is doing its work properly - for example, by keeping a chair together - it goes largely unnoticed; so does supervision when a school is functioning well. Glue does get attention when the legs of a chair collapse, just as supervision does when a school fragments or fails. With success, both glue and supervision are taken for granted; with failure they both are held responsible. This is as it should be: Teachers are in the forefront of successful instruction; supervision is in the background, providing support, knowledge, and skills that enable teachers to succeed. When improved instruction and school success do not materialize, supervision should shoulder the responsibility for not permitting teachers to be successful.

The developmental model views supervision as a supportive process where the individual characteristics or differences of those supervised, namely teachers, and the basic beliefs or orientations of the supervisor are key ingredients. The effectiveness of the supervision is predicated on how well the supervisor's orientation matches the teacher's characteristics. Glickman (1981) suggested that teacher characteristics are the result of levels of abstraction (the ability of the teacher to think abstractly) and commitment (the level of dedication to the profession). These characteristics combine to produce four basic types of teacher:

1. *Professional*—with high abstraction and high commitment

2. *Unfocused worker*—with low abstraction and high commitment

3. *Analytical observer*—with high abstraction and low commitment

4. *Teacher dropout*—with low abstraction and low commitment

The identifiable orientations of supervisors include *nondirective, collaborative,* and *directive*. Nondirective supervisors serve as facilitators or guides to teachers who take responsibility for their own improvement. Observable behaviors of the nondirective supervisor would include listening, clarifying, encouraging, and presenting (i.e., expressing only a limited number of personal opinions to aid the teacher). This orientation is successful with the professional teacher and the unfocused worker.

The collaborative orientation views the improvement of instruction as a joint responsibility of the teacher and the supervisor. This supervisor would demonstrate problem solving, negotiating, and demonstrating behaviors when interacting with the teacher. Glickman suggests that the collaborative orientation would be effective with the teacher who is an analytical observer.

The third orientation, directive, is described as controlling and negative. This belief system claims that the teacher has little knowledge and is incapable of making satisfactory decisions. A supervisor with this orientation assumes responsibility for the improvement of instruction. The directive supervisor would use the behaviors of directing, standardizing, and reinforcing. Directive orientation is recommended for use with the teacher dropout.

Collegial Supervision

Numerous forms of collegial or collaborative supervision were developed and implemented in the 1980s (Kosmoski, 1994; Glatthorn, 1984; and Redfern, 1980). Generally, they are models with nontraditional supervisors who, acting within a supervisor-teacher partnership, encourage, guide, and facilitate. The focus of collegial supervision is the improvement of instruction by supervisors who do not necessarily have evaluation responsibilities. Some examples are *mentoring,* where an experienced master teacher assists a novice; *peer coaching,* where two experienced teachers share expertise; *cohort groups,* where tenured teachers with similar assignments jointly assume supervisory responsibilities for each other; and *teacher rotation,* where teachers take turns performing supervisory tasks (Sacken, 1994). These and other possibilities will be discussed in greater detail in Chapter 12. For an overview of these models refer to Figure 1-7, A Comparison of Operational Models of School Supervision.

20 Chapter 1 *Supervision: An American Perspective*

Comparison of Operational Models of School Supervision				
Model	**Focus**	**Characteristics**	**Participants**	**Prominent Specialists**
Human Resources	Centers on people involved	• Personal • Active • Responsive • Encourages growth	• Supervisor • Teacher	• Benis • McGregor • Argyris
Clinical	Classroom behavior	• Collegial • Use concrete observational data • Continuous process	• Supervisor • Teacher	• Goldhammer • Cogan • Acheson & Gall • Eisner • Russell-Hunter
Developmental	Match teacher & supervisor style to improve performance	The use of specific supervisory behaviors to support identified teacher type	• Supervisor • Teacher	• Glickman
Collegial	Collaborative to improve instruction	• Partnership between teacher & often non-traditional supervisor • Evaluation eliminated	• Teacher • Mentor • Peers • Building-based Supervisors	• Sergiovanni • Oliva • Yerkes • Austin

Figure 1-7

Styles of Supervision

Lewin, Lippitt, and White (1939) identified three leadership styles that may be appropriately applied to the school supervisor. These styles are autocratic, democratic, and laissez faire. See Figure 1-8, Two Styles of Supervision.

- The *autocratic* supervisor closely monitors the teacher and the teacher's performance, fosters competition between staff, rewards success, and punishes poor performance.

- Supervisors who utilize the *democratic* style give teachers more responsibility for their own actions and involve teachers in the decision-making process. The collegial and collaborative nature of the relationship between the teacher and the supervisor is emphasized.

- Employing the *laissez faire* style, the supervisor avoids contact with the teacher. Little guidance, direction, or support would be provided. This is often referred to as *supervision by avoidance*.

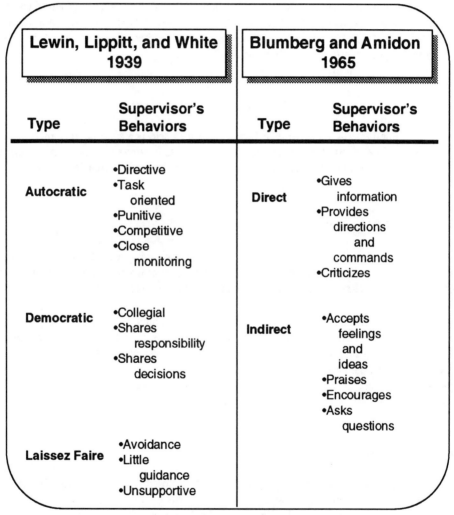

**Figure 1-8
Two Styles of Supervision**

22 Chapter 1 *Supervision: An American Perspective*

In 1965, Blumberg and Amidon theorized a second method for identifying supervisory styles. They suggested that supervisory style or behaviors could be categorized as *direct* and *indirect*. Using direct style, the supervisor consistently demonstrates the behaviors of giving information, providing directions and commands, and criticizing personnel. Whereas, the supervisor who utilized the indirect style regularly displays the behaviors of accepting feelings and ideas, praising and encouraging, and asking questions. After studying a large group of teachers as they reacted to various supervisors, Blumberg and Amidon found that supervisors who emphasized indirect behaviors tended to receive higher ratings from the teachers. They concluded that teachers favor indirect style. Refer to Styles of Supervision, Figure 1-8.

Selecting a Supervision Style

A natural question that arises is how a supervisor selects a style. Models used to explain which style would be most effective and appropriate include *contingency leadership* as suggested by Fiedler (1976) and *situational leadership* as suggested by Hersey and Blanchard (1972).

Contingency Leadership

In contingency leadership, Fiedler theorized that style is predicated or contingent upon the three organizational factors of *leader-member relations, task structure,* and *position power*. He suggests that these factors interact to determine the appropriate style.

Leader-member relations refers to the type and quality of the relationship that exists between the supervisor and the subordinate, usually the teacher. Task structure is the degree of structure that is inherent within the tasks of the subordinate. Although teaching is generally viewed as having little structure, this may vary based upon the organizational model, imposed regulations, and specific assignments. The third factor, position power, refers to the real or perceived power possessed by the supervisor within the organization.

Situational Leadership

In situational leadership, Hersey and Blanchard posed a second method for selecting a supervisory style. They suggested that the level of maturity of the staff should determine which style is most appropriate. Maturation and style should match. If a staff is at a high level of maturity, the supervisor should choose a more indirect style. Whereas, if the staff is at a low level of maturity, the supervisor should select a more direct or authoritarian style.

Chapter 1 *Supervision: An American Perspective* **23**

The Need for Supervision

Critics believe that the need and desirability of supervision in the school has passed. They argue that teachers are professionals and therefore find no reason for *snoopervision* to exist. Rather, they insist that teachers should be allowed the freedom and autonomy to practice their profession without interference. Obviously, these individuals have a narrow and negative perspective. If, however, supervision is viewed as a process designed to improve instruction, its value and need is self-evident. Many arguments may be made to justify the need for supervision within our school districts. Four of these follow.

Humans are natural learners. Teachers are human, and therefore, learners. All learners, including teachers, have the right to skillful assistance in the pursuit of knowledge and understanding. It is suggested that effective supervision provides teachers with the skillful assistance necessary to help them learn and grow. From the beginning student teacher to the veteran on remediation, supervision should have a positive impact (Gorton, 1987).

For the preservice teacher, supervision serves as the vehicle to help the individual overcome insecurities, learn appropriate teacher roles, and practice specific behaviors. The competent or master teacher also needs appropriate supervision. For these teachers, supervision provides a process where they may expand their strategies and instructional techniques. It helps them solve new problems, meet new challenges, and face new situations. The teacher on probationary status needs supervision since this process provides the support the teacher needs to move from probation to a satisfactory state. Left alone, the probationary teacher might find the task of improvement impossible.

Sergiovanni and Starrett (1988) pointed out that supervision and teacher effectiveness are directly linked. A growing body of research clearly demonstrates that good supervision assists teachers to develop classroom skills proven to positively relate to increased student achievement. Meaningful staff development programs and solid evaluation procedures are two supervisory activities proven to influence teacher effectiveness and, in turn, student achievement.

Supervision is frequently viewed as an avenue to motivate teachers and a method to allow them to attain satisfaction from their work. Hackman and Oldham (1976) identified three psychological states critical in determining a person's job satisfaction and motivation. They are:

- The state of experienced meaningfulness—where individuals perceive their work as worthwhile or important to the process or organization.

- The state of experienced responsibility—where individuals believe that they are personally responsible and accountable for outcomes.

24 Chapter 1 *Supervision: An American Perspective*

- The state of knowledge of the results—where individuals are able to determine on a regular basis that their work is satisfactory.

Supervision facilitates the existence of all of these states for teachers. When the organization and the supervisor prioritize improvement of instruction, it implies to the teacher that the work of instruction is highly valued, meaningful, and worthwhile. The use of a collegial or human resource model of supervision implies that teachers are accountable for classroom behaviors and must assume responsibility for their actions. Supervision performed on a regular schedule affords teachers an opportunity to analyze job performance and attain personal satisfaction.

Lunenberg and Ornstein (1991) argued the need for supervision from the professional development perspective. They suggested that to fulfill personnel's potential is to give them the opportunity to learn new skills and develop their abilities to the fullest. Supervision, by its very nature, allows teachers to do just that.

Barriers to Quality Supervision

Quality supervision is faced with numerous difficulties and challenges. While facilitating improvement of instruction, the supervisor will encounter problems in and out of the school. Difficulties within the school are internal barriers and those out of school are external barriers.

<u>Internal Barriers</u>

Numerous roadblocks within the classroom make supervision difficult, if not impossible. Six potential difficulties will be examined.

1. *Lack of trust.* A healthy positive relationship between teacher and supervisor is based on trust. If trust is lacking, meaningful supervision is lost. Trust must be built. This process of "trust building" requires time, patience, and effort from all involved parties. If a teacher experienced a negative supervision relationship in the past, often she or he does not wish to be involved in any future supervision encounter. The supervisor has little recourse but to remain patient and consistent, knowing full well that the value of the supervision is suspect at the onset of the relationship. However, if the supervisor continues to be trustworthy, open, and supportive of the teacher, the teacher will slowly begin to trust. The establishment of trust should generate a climate for quality supervision.

2. *Teacher opposition* to a given supervisory style is often a threat to successful supervision. When hostility exists productivity is diminished. Since style is a matter of

Chapter 1 *Supervision: An American Perspective* **25**

choice the supervisor should select a style to match the needs of the teacher. Frequent open communication between the teacher and the supervisor regarding style preference, along with a willingness to compromise and work collegially, usually remedies this potential difficulty.

3. *Teacher personality* may serve as a deterrent to successful supervision. Because of personalities, teachers might find it difficult or undesirable to work cooperatively, accept suggestions, or recognize the need for improvement. Supervisor can not change personality, but may work patiently and tactfully within the existing limitations and parameters.

4. *Participant misperception* may be a fourth barrier to productive supervision within the classroom in the situation where the teacher, the supervisor, or both, perceive supervision as identical or equal to evaluation. By so doing, supervision becomes judgmental and threatening to the teacher. To equate supervision with evaluation is to corrupt the very essence of this process. Most often the school supervisor is also the teacher's evaluator. In this case, the supervisor needs to deliberately separate the two processes in his or her own mind. The supervisor must understand that evaluation is only one phase in the overall supervision picture. Evaluation honestly reports the current status or condition of classroom instruction. It is the task of closure in one supervision cycle. The supervisor must internalize this concept and convey its essence to the teacher. Again, trust is a key element necessary to overcome this difficulty.

5. Successful supervision also must confront the potential problem of *negative attitudes* and selfish motives. When the supervisor harbors these traits irreparable damage occurs to the process of supervision. If the supervisor has a hidden personal agenda or views supervision as a vehicle for personal glorification or advancement, the activity is tainted. To avoid this trap, the wise supervisor should adopt the reflective practice of regularly examining personal focus and motivation. For supervision to succeed, the teacher's needs, not the needs of the supervisor, are paramount.

6. Finally, the inept or *unprepared supervisor* is a major barrier to good supervision in the classroom. A supervisor unfamiliar with proven supervisory techniques and strategies, will perform poorly or will slide into "supervision by avoidance." The committed supervisor learns and continues to stay abreast of successful supervisory practices (Acheson & Gall, 1991).

External Barriers

Along with the difficulties encountered in the classroom, the supervisor must grapple with outside forces that threaten the quality of the supervision process. Three of the most powerful and frustrating problems facing supervision are *inadequate funding*, *legal and contractual constraints*, and *insufficient time*.

26 Chapter 1 *Supervision: An American Perspective*

One need not search long to find evidence of shrinking educational funding. Reports in the local newspaper, professional journals, and prime time television news specials clearly relate the pullback of federal, state, local, and private financial support for our schools. Paralleling this event is the increase in cost of materials and services. This condition directly and dramatically affects the ability to provide quality supervision. All the crucial supervisory tasks identified by Harris (1985) are directly or indirectly impaired by the lack of adequate funding. Those tasks most directly affected are providing staff, facilities, and materials. The quality and frequency of in-service education, curriculum development, new staff orientation, special pupil services, and the development and maintenance of a viable public relations program are directly tied to financial support. Even the evaluation of instruction within the classroom and the organizing necessary to ensure instruction are indirectly affected by the shrinking dollar. Lack of funds limits the number of supervisors hired to provide these services.

There appears to be no one realistic solution to the money crunch for school supervisors. Yet, they are expected to get more done with less. Although the individual practitioner can do very little to increase the flow of money from conventional sources and has no control of rising costs, some alternative financial sources are available. Examples include public and private grants, school-business partnerships, and the pooling of human and material resources between schools and districts. No single source will cure this crisis, but by tapping a combination of sources, the astute supervisor increases the possibility for successful supervision. The school supervisor is urged to aggressively seek out and utilize these and other unconventional monetary sources.

The supervision process is subject to legal and contractual constraints. Teachers and supervisors, alike, must live and function within the guidelines of existing federal regulations, state laws and codes, district policies, and employment contracts. In some instances these controls limit choice or directly oppose a supervision model, strategy, or practice. One example of legal limitations is *building-based curriculum development*. A school staff chooses to implement a series of teacher-made tests to measure student growth in mathematics. Simultaneously, the state mandates that all pupils complete the state mathematics achievement examination. Obviously, school supervisors cannot disregard state regulations, yet supervisors may guide staff in dual implementation. The key elements necessary when dealing with these constraints or restrictions are awareness of their existence, acceptance of the situation, and creative execution within the given framework.

A third obstacle to school supervision is the lack of time. With fewer funds available the school supervisor and the teacher have additional duties imposed upon them. The time remains the same but the work demands increase. The teacher may no longer have the luxury of a full-time classroom aide and must assume many clerical responsibilities previously delegated. The middle school principal finds that she must personally build student schedules after the district is forced to eliminate an assistant principal position. One suggestion for handling diminished time is to prioritize tasks (Shipman et al., 1983). By listing, in order of importance, those tasks that will positively promote success, the supervisor will be able to determine how best to budget time for a given task. For additional suggestions in good time management practices consult Mackenzie (1972).

Although there are many internal and external barriers to instituting sound supervision practices within a school, they are not insurmountable. It is better to be aware of the difficulties and tackle them in a proactive fashion than to remain ignorant or unconcerned. Successful supervision is not easily implemented. However, it is a process essential to school success. (See Figure 1-9 Internal and External Barriers to Effective Supervision).

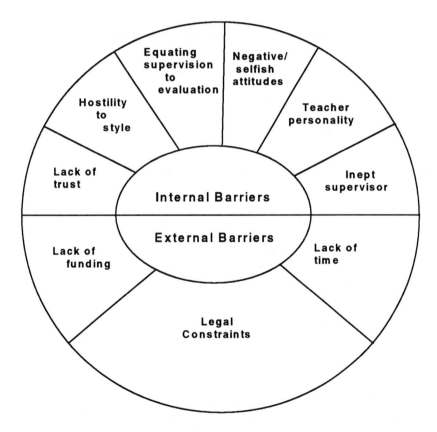

**Figure 1-9
Internal and External Barriers to Effective Supervision**

28 Chapter 1 *Supervision: An American Perspective*

Future Ramifications

Chapter 12 thoroughly examines trends, predictive practices, and possible innovations expected for the twenty-first century. Areas of change include accepted models, compatible styles, and tools for execution. The foremost innovation predicted is the development of new models to meet the needs of teachers who instruct an ever changing and expanding student population. For all levels of the organization, supervisors will formulate styles, techniques, and methods to match and enhance these new models (Hallinger & Murphy, 1982). More technology will be utilized to accomplish supervisory tasks in a timely and efficient manner.

Principles and Practices for Success

- Understand the history of supervision in America and how it affects the present.

- Clarify a personal philosophy of supervision.

- Develop a working definition of school supervision.

- Identify and adopt the supervision model that best matches the individual's belief system and personality.

- Select the supervisory style that best serves the chosen model and teacher needs.

- Prioritize supervisory tasks to achieve effectiveness.

- Recognize the need for quality supervision.

- Identify those barriers to successful supervision for a given setting.

Summary

This chapter studied the historical development of school supervision in America and how it shaped much of our present thought and accepted philosophy. Various definitions, implications, and ramifications of school supervision were reviewed. For purposes of clarity and consistency in this textbook, a working definition was formulated: *School supervision is the leadership process whose ultimate purpose is to improve instruction and thereby facilitate and promote successful student learning.*

Chapter 1 *Supervision: An American Perspective* **29**

Supervision models and their essential components were described. It was strongly suggested that no one model is appropriate or effective for all individuals or circumstances. Rather, supervisors should select a model to fit the people and the situation. An overview of the types, styles, and tasks of supervision was provided. The importance of effective supervision was discussed. The chapter concluded with a review of the internal and exterior barriers the supervisor must face in order to develop and implement a viable and effective supervisory program. Note: Sections entitled *Questions, Principles and Practices for Success,* and *Case Study* will accompany subsequent chapters to guide the adult learner.

Case Problem: *Remediate Bitterman*

It is May 15th. Mrs. Mary Truewell feels she is doing a fine job in her initial year as the principal of Sunny Day Elementary School. Sunny Day School is one of four elementary schools in a pleasant small town district. This morning Mary met with her superintendent in a one-on-one meeting and she was given an assignment that now makes her apprehensive and distressed. Her superintendent explained that Joe Smart, principal of a second elementary school within the district, found it necessary to place Jake Bitterman, fifth grade teacher, on a remediation plan for next year. The superintendent continued and told Mary that Jake exercised his right from the teacher's contract and requested that she, Mary, be appointed his supervisor and evaluator for the coming remediation, probationary status, period. Mrs. Truewell was shocked and confused. The superintendent profusely assured Mary that he had "all the confidence in the world" that she would handle this assignment well. He concluded the meeting by urging Mary to ask for any assistance she might require and insisted that she keep him abreast of all developments throughout the forthcoming school year.

As Mary Truewell sat at her desk that same evening, she realized that this was no small or unimportant task. Her mind was filled with a million questions that needed to be resolved. She wondered what information she should gather and where she would find it. What supervisory model, orientation, and style would be best for this situation? Which supervisory tasks should take priority? Why? What problems or hurdles could she anticipate and be prepared to handle?

What suggestions would you give Mary? How would you advise her to proceed? Be specific in your responses. Justify your course of action with concrete examples.

Case Problem: *Is Marvin Ready?*

Marvin Ready is one of two remaining candidates for the position of principal at Progress Central High School. He had done his homework by gathering information about the school and district. While preparing for this interview, Marvin learned that the district is engaged in restructuring, shared decision-making, and strategic planning.

30 Chapter 1 *Supervision: An American Perspective*

It is 8:15 p.m. and he is doing well in the final interview with the Progress School Board. After looking at her prepared list of questions, Laura Prophett, School Board President, asks Marvin to share his thoughts on school supervision and to include his preference of style, and what he believes are the most important tasks of this process.

Put yourself in Marvin's place and answer Laura Prophett's questions.

References

1872 teachers rules. Mountain View, AR: Old Time Print Shop, Ozark Folk Center.

1915 rules for teachers. Mountain View, AR: Old Time Print Shop, Ozark Folk Center.

Acheson, K. A., & Gall, M. D. (1992). *Techniques in the clinical supervision of teachers* (3rd ed.). New York: Longman.

Blumberg, A., & Amidon, E. (1965). Teacher perceptions of supervisor - teacher interaction. *Administrators Notebook, 14*, 1-8.

Burton, W. H. (1922). *Supervision and the improvement of teaching*. New York: D. Appleton-Century.

Campbell, R. F., Corbally, J. E., & Nystrand, R. O. (1983). *Introduction to educational administration* (6th ed.). Boston: Allyn and Bacon.

Cogan, M. (1973). *Clinical supervision*. Boston: Houghton Mifflin.

Daresh, J. C. (1989). *Supervision as a proactive process*. New York: Longman.

Eisner, E. (1982). An artistic approach to supervision. In Thomas Sergiovanni (Ed.), *Supervision of teaching*. Alexandria, VA: Association for Supervision and Curriculum Development.

Fiedler, F. (1976). The leadership game: Matching the man to the situation. *Organizational Dynamics, 4*, (3).

Franseth, J. (1961). *Supervision as leadership*. Evanston, IL: Row, Peterson.

Glatthorn, A. (1984). *Differentiated supervision*. Alexandria, VA: Association for Supervision and Curriculum Development.

Glickman, C. D. (1981). *Developmental supervision: Alternative practices for helping teachers to improve*. Alexandria, VA: Association for Supervision and Curriculum Development.

Glickman, C. D. (1990). *Supervision of instruction: A developmental approach* (2nd ed.). Boston: Allyn and Bacon.

Goldhammer, R. (1969). *Clinical supervision*. New York: Holt, Rinehart, and Winston.

Gorton, R. (1987). *School leadership and administration: Important concepts, case studies, and simulations* (3rd ed.). Dubuque, IA: Wm. C. Brown Publishers.

Gulick, L., & Urwick, L. (1937). *Papers on the science of administration*. New York: Institute of Public Administration, Columbia University.

Hackman, J. R., & Oldham, G. (1976). Motivation through the design of work: Test of a theory. *Organizational Behavior and Human Performance, 16,* 250 -279.

Hallinger, P., & Murphy, J. (1982). The superintendent's role in promoting instructional leadership. *Administrator's notebook, 30.*

Harris, B. M. (1985). *Supervisory behavior in education* (3rd ed.). Englewood Cliffs, NJ: Prentice-Hall.

Hersey, P., & Blanchard, K. (1972). *Management of organizational behavior* (2nd ed.). Englewood Cliffs, NJ: Prentice-Hall.

Kaiser, J. S. (1993). *Educational administration* (2nd ed.). Mequon, WI: Stylex.

Kosmoski, G. J. (1994). Initiation of the beginning administrators program at Governors State University. *Ad Prof: The Illinois Counsel of Professors of Educational Administration,* 5, (2).

Kowalski, T. J., & Reitzug, U. C. (1993). *Contemporary school administration: An introduction.* New York: Longman.

Krey, R., & Burke, P. (1989). *A design for instructional supervision.* Springfield, IL: Charles C. Thomas.

Lewin, K., Lippitt, R., & White, R. K. (1939). Patterns of aggressive behavior in experimentally created social climates. *Journal of Social Psychology, 10,* 271-299.

Lunenburg, F. C., & Ornstein, A. C. (1991). *Educational administration: Concepts and practices.* Belmont, CA: Wadsworth.

Mackenzie, R. A. (1972). *The time trap.* New York: McGraw-Hill.

Mosher, R. L., & Purpel, D. E. (1972). *Supervision: The reluctant profession.* Boston: Houghton Mifflin.

Oliva, P. F. (1993). *Supervision for today's schools* (2nd. ed.). New York: Longman.

Redfern, G. B. (1980). *Evaluating teachers and administrators: A performance objective model.* Boulder, CO: Westview.

Russell, D., & Hunter, M. (1980). *Planning for effective instruction.* Los Angeles: University Elementary School.

Sacken, D. (1994). No more principals! *Phi Delta Kappan, 75,* 664-670.

Sergiovanni, T. J., & Starratt, R. J. (1988). *Supervision: Human perspectives* (4th ed.). New York: McGraw Hill.

Shipman, N. J., Martin, J. B., McKay, A. B., & Anastas, R. E. (1983). *Effective time management techniques for school administrators.* Englewood Cliffs, NJ: Prentice-Hall.

Tanner, D., & Tanner, L. (1987). *Supervision in education: Problems and practices.* New York: Macmillan.

Chapter 2

PEOPLE AND SUPERVISION
Barbara A. Murray

The Social Science of Supervision

The behaviors of the supervisors and persons being supervised are studied from the perspective of human behavior theory in the social sciences. This includes lifespan development, behaviorism, motivation, and behavior in educational organizations. Questions important to supervisors include: Why do people behave the way they do? What effect does the individual's behavior have upon the organization's achievement? What supervisory behavior will prove to be the most effective in fulfilling the needs of the members of the educational organization? The study of supervisory behavior goes beyond the mere memorization of theories. It must apply those theories to specific situations and their respective outcomes.

**Questions to answer
after studying this chapter**

✔ What social science knowledge is necessary to the process of developing supervisory skills?

✔ Why is it important to understand human behavior?

✔ What traits characterize effective supervisors?

✔ What personnel need to be supervised?

✔ Who should supervise?

✔ What are the different practices for supervising instructional, other certified, and noncertified personnel?

✔ What is the impact of a global society upon supervision?

The complexity and time constraints placed upon the modern educational organization require supervisory behavior to be well planned and executed. There is no future for the "supervise like you were supervised," "knee-jerk," or "trial-and-error" supervisor. One plan for identifying appropriate supervisory behavior is shown in Figure 2-1. Step one includes the study and thorough understanding of behavioral theory and its practical application.

The second step includes observing the situation from many perspectives to omit bias from the final action. Step three diagnoses the situation from a framework of theory. The supervisor must combine the events of the situation and related theory to reduce the possibility of any supervisory behavior error. The fourth step adds a practical dimension by considering those behavioral practices that have proven successful in similar situations. Step five develops a plan for appropriate behavior that can be supported primarily by theory with proof from practice. The sixth step engages in planned behavior and assesses the effectiveness of the behavior and develops strategies for further improvement.

Supervisory Behavior Plan	
Step 1	Study Behavior Theory
Step 2	Observe Situation and Analyze Using Multiple Perspectives
Step 3	Diagnose Situation Using Theoretical Framework
Step 4	Add Perspective from Successful Supervisory Practices
Step 5	Develop Plan from Theory and Practice
Step 6	Implement Plan and Evaluate Effectiveness

Figure 2-1

Supervision specialists have used numerous frameworks to study supervisory behavior. Sergiovanni and Starratt (1993) used theory, practice and hunches as a foundation for supervisory behavior. Often supervision has been studied from a technical skill orientation. This approach is narrow and focuses on task driven supervisory activities that do not include a theoretical framework and are not usually designed by those assigned to the supervisory positions (Alfonso, Firth & Neville, 1981). Other approaches to supervision include the study of conceptual skills and human relations (Gibson, 1990).

One supervisory behavior model includes organizational goals, teacher needs, supervisory behavior, teacher behavior, and student behavior (Alfonso, Firth & Neville, 1981). Figure 2-2 expands the model to include a more global view of supervision that parallels current trends toward school-based management. The school-based model suggests that supervision encompasses a broader range of school members included in the decision process.

Regardless of which orientation is selected, supervisors should understand the behavioral concepts of adult lifespan development, attitude formation, adult learning, motivation, behavioral theory, leadership, communication, change, and group process. It is essential for the aspiring supervisor to develop a clear understanding of the practical applications of each.

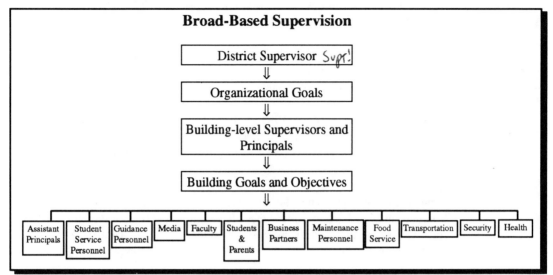

Figure 2-2

Adult Lifespan Development

Adult lifespan development is concerned with the identification and description of an individual's life events which, when analyzed, tend to explain the differences in behavior among adults. For example, an adult who grew up during the depression years and who experienced few of life's conveniences is likely to possess beliefs and exhibit behaviors that are different from those of a younger adult growing up during a more affluent era. Baltes, Reese and Lipsitt (1980) described lifespan as a change process which is best understood as a chain of life events. While most lifespan psychologists insist that a biological model is not appropriate, age-specific research is considered a valuable contribution. Lerner and Ryff (p. 10, 1978) support this contention with the following statement: *Age is little more than a marker variable along which other experiences occur.*

Erik Erikson (1959, 1963, 1968) proposed a model with eight stages of development from infancy throughout adulthood. This model, unlike those that place emphasis upon biological development, emphasizes the importance of life experiences, social interaction and culture. Erikson delineated each stage of life as an event or conflict which, when experienced in a positive way, provides the foundation for healthy growth. Each of the eight Erikson stages is described below.

Stage 1. Infancy—The conflict is basic trust versus basic mistrust. Social interaction is provided primarily by the mother. The interactive

36 Chapter 2 *People and Supervision*

relationship of the infant with society engenders in both parties the quality of hope and a world that is consistent and predictable.

Stage 2. Early Childhood—The conflict is between the development of autonomy versus shame and doubt. This stage is decisive for the future ratio of dependence to independence.

Stage 3. Play Age—The conflict in stage three is between initiative versus guilt. *Play* in this stage is defined as the acting out of roles for the purpose of developing self-confidence to pursue goals without guilt or fear of punishment.

Stage 4. School Age—The conflict is that of industry versus inferiority. Conflict tends to lead to competence. It is important that during this stage the person experiences success to develop feelings of competence rather than inferiority.

Stage 5. Adolescence—The conflict during adolescence is identity versus role confusion. Persons seek to fulfill personal potentialities while upholding beliefs and values earlier learned. People pay particular attention to career choice during this phase. Development of a sense of belonging to society occurs.

Stage 6. Young Adulthood—The conflict in stage six is intimacy versus isolation. The emphasis is to develop lasting personal relationships whereby one's identity involves a shared purpose which surpasses earlier stages more concerned with superficial relationships that place emphasis upon oneself.

Stage 7. Adulthood—The major conflict of this stage is *generativity* versus *stagnation*. This stage, also described as middle or mature adulthood, emphasizes the need for generativity defined *as creativity, productivity, and caring for the next generation.* While many adults fulfill this need through offspring, others engage in activities which may include career leadership roles with the intention of accepting responsibility for the growth of the new generation. The adult who has not developed a sense of *generativity* or productivity will lose interest and stagnate.

Stage 8. Maturity—The conflict during maturity or old age is ego integrity versus despair. Adults with ego integrity draw from life experiences such as heritage, culture, adolescence, and adulthood to establish a sense of order that will give meaning to life and a feeling of contentment. They have a feeling of satisfaction towards their achievement and life in general. Adults dissatisfied with their life's course will feel despair.

Fuller (1969) and Cohen (1983, 1982) found that older teachers focused their concerns toward helping students learn. Younger teachers reflected a greater concern for self acceptance by students and parents, evaluations by superiors, and establishment of their identities.

Havighurst (1974) defined the developmental task, closely paralleling Erikson's stages.

> *A developmental task is a task which arises at or about a certain period in the life of the individual, successful achievement of which leads to happiness and to success with later tasks, while failure leads to unhappiness in the individual, disapproval by the society, and difficulty with later tasks.* (p. 2)

Havighurst (1972) further described the young adult stage, ages 18-30, in the following manner. *Of all the periods of life, early adulthood is the fullest of teachable moments and the emptiest of efforts to teach* (p. 83). It is important to note that this is the age group from which the majority of persons entering the field of teaching is drawn.

Schein (1978) delineated career steps within the field of business into ten stages which include preservice training, midcareer crisis, and late career fulfillment. Each has implications for supervising both certified and noncertified staff within the field of education. Osteen (1994) found preservice field experiences, such as student teaching, to be generally unrealistic and were, therefore, not providing proper experiences necessary for entering the field of teaching. Teachers, like business employees, experience a midcareer crisis, or a 7-12 year plateau. This can be identified when teacher behavior reflects an unusual reduction in motivation, creativity, and general excitement for the field of education. This plateau can also lead to absenteeism and lack of participation in school-related activities outside the classroom.

This group presents an important challenge to the supervisor. Its members are knowledgeable and skilled in instructional techniques, but require support to enable them to achieve their higher level needs. Teachers within this group should be recognized as professional experts and regularly called upon to participate in the decision making processes related to policy, practices, and overall operations of the school. A recent study (Osteen, 1994) found that teachers across the United States perceived that they were not being included in the decision making process even though many current school

38 Chapter 2 *People and Supervision*

organizational structures are marketed to be patterned after shared decision models. Figure 2-3 adapts the work of Schein (1978) and Osteen (1994) to the field of education and suggests that teachers experience career steps which begin with an entry level naiveté, accompanied by formal training and conclude with retirement and lifestyle change.

Education Career Stages, Issues and Dissatisfiers				
Age	**Stage**	**Issue**	**Develpmental Tasks**	**Career Dissatisfiers**
18-22	Growth, fantasy and exploration	Identify career placement, degree earning	Identification of one's needs and interests	Inadequate support from administration
20-25	Enter into field of work	Orientation into professional teaching field	Acquiring maximum career information as well as learning the process for securing a job	Insufficient time working directly with students

Generally poor working conditions |
| 22-25 | Basic training | Becoming part of the "fraternity" | Overcoming the insecurities of inexperience and "rookie" treatment | |
| 25-29 | Full membership in early career | Accepting responsibility and fulfilling professional duties. Displaying additional school-related interest and special skills such as sponsorships, groups and coaching | Performing effectively, acquiring tenure, accepting bureaucratic system and subordinate status. Establishing realistic goals | Insufficient time working directly with students

Inadequate support from administration

Poor student motivation

Lack of community support |
| 29-45 | Full membership in mid-career | Movement toward instructional technique specialization and participation in on-going professional development; graduate coursework | Gaining autonomy, assessing organization and career opportunities | Poor student motivation

Inadequate support from administration |

| 29-45 | Midcareer crisis | Assignment v. Status Assessing career selection, comparing personal goals to career goals; seven year plateau syndrome | Feeling of career stagnation. Making choices about present and future | Poor opportunity for professional development

Student discipline problems |
| 35-65 | Late career in non-leadership role | Accepting responsibility for mentoring new generations of teachers. Broaden interest and deepen skills | Enhancing instructional skills as well as interpersonal skills. Accepting responsibility for helping the next generation | Inadequate support from administration

Poor student motivation

Student discipline problems |
35-65	Late career in leadership role	Serving to improve the educational organization and field in general	Becoming more involved with the organization. Balancing personal and career goals	
50-65	Decline and disengagement	Accepting a reduction in power and responsibility	Broadening interests to discover new sources of satisfaction	
55-65	Retirement	Adjusting to change in lifestyle	Maintaining a sense of indentity and self-worth without a job	

Adapted from Schein, Table 4.1 and Osteen

Figure 2-3

Personality Styles

It is clear that teachers, like all persons, may not be classified into a single group possessing identical behavior or personality characteristics. Kiersey and Bates (1984) developed a tool for distinguishing temperament patterns into four pairs of preferences and a variety of types. The Kiersey and Bates assessment is based upon the Myers-Briggs Type Indicator (Myers, 1962) test drawn from the work of Jung (1924, 1971) and has significance in education in that it enables one to establish an accurate portrait of one's own tendencies toward certain behavior as well as to understand the tendencies of others. It identifies: extroversion (E), introversion (I), sensation (S), intuition (N), thinking (T), feeling (F), perceiving (P) and judging (I). To be effective, the supervisor's self awareness and awareness of others is portentous for understanding, appreciating, predicting, and rewarding behavior.

40 Chapter 2 *People and Supervision*

    A study by the Center for Applications of Psychological Type, (Macdaid, 1988) suggested that school principals were most commonly ESTJ which is further described as those who manage by walking around, maintain frequent contact with others, and are *doers*, not merely *talkers*. Furthermore these *principal types* were more likely to recognize details, analyze causes and effects, and use practical solutions to support outcomes. Finally, they were control oriented, logical, objective, and maintained an efficient task-oriented focus. Other school personnel are described in Figure 2-4.

School Personnel Type Tendencies

Index Log		Index	Personnel
		ISTJ	School Principals
Introversion	(I)		School Bus Drivers
Extroversion	(E)		
Sensing	(S)	ISFJ	School Bus Drivers
Intuition	(N)		Teachers: Grades 1-12
Thinking	(T)		Teachers: Preschool
Feeling	(F)		Teachers' Aides
Judging	(J)		School Nurses
Perceiving	(P)		Clerical Supervisors
		INFJ	Media Specialists
			Education Consultants
			Teachers
		ISFP	School Nurses
			School Bookkeepers
			Clerical Supervisors
		ENFP	Teachers: Art & Music
			Counselors
			Psychologists
		ESTJ	School Principals
			Teachers: Vocational
		ESFJ	Teachers: Grades 1-12
			Student Personnel Administrators
		ENFJ	Teachers
			Counselors

Adapted from *Ten Most Chosen Careers*, Developed by Gerald P. Macdaid, Copyright 1988 Center for Application of Psychological Types

Figure 2-4

Perceptions, Platforms and Prejudiced Behavior

People in organizations engage in behavior based upon how they view and understand a given situation. Such perceptions are influenced by experience, technical knowledge, educational platform and other bias concerns. Generally, no two people will observe and describe a given event in the same way. This can be referred to as the perception field. A supervisor, certified as a science teacher, who is observing another science teacher is more likely to look for specific subject content in addition to effective teaching practices. Also, the individual's status or position within the organization can act as an influencing factor. A supervisor in charge of an entire elementary grade level will perceive the distribution of resources differently than will the individual teacher.

Sergiovanni and Starratt (1993) separated technical knowledge into a *floor of beliefs* known as the educator's platform which provides the foundation for the individual's teaching behaviors. Such platforms include: (a) basic competency, (b) schooling the social drama platform, (c) human growth platform, (d) democratic socialization platform, (e) the critical awareness platform, (f) an ecological platform. The educator's platform is flexible with no specific right or wrong but merely represents the educator's perceptions specific to the general aim and process of education. While the classroom teacher's platform is focused upon instruction, that of the supervisor is more closely aimed at the purpose and process of supervision. The effective supervisor must decide whether to supervise to improve performance and skills as a clinician or coach, or to view supervision as a part of due process by which to rid the education field of incompetence.

Misinterpreted information which alters perceptions can lead to predisposed decisions and can further prejudice behavior. Examples include stereotyping, the self fulfilling prophecy, the halo effect, and projection. Stereotyping occurs when generalizations are made about specified groups and their characteristics. An example of stereotyping is a perception that girls are not successful in math. The self-fulfilling prophecy is a perception that a person will perform only at a level that is expected or previously observed. A coach who has experienced a series of losing seasons will be expected to lose again during the current season. A supervisor who communicates that teachers are not expected to do any extra duty is likely to experience a faculty who does not engage in activity outside instructional time and leaves at the end of the school day with the buses.

The halo effect occurs during an evaluation process when a person is swayed by a particular attribute and therefore gives more attention than it deserves on the overall performance rating (see Chapter 9 for a further definition). A principal who rates a teacher's overall performance highly because the teacher reports to school two hours early and departs two hours late every day would illustrate this point. In this case, the principal views hours at work or *quantity* as the major criterion for determining teacher effectiveness and rates the teacher emphasizing hours worked rather than the *quality* of instruction and learning outcomes.

Projection occurs when one person's feelings are projected on another person. For example, supervisors who disagree with newly introduced curricula might not implement it because of their projected beliefs that *the teachers would not like it*. In this case, it would be similar to *wishful thinking*.

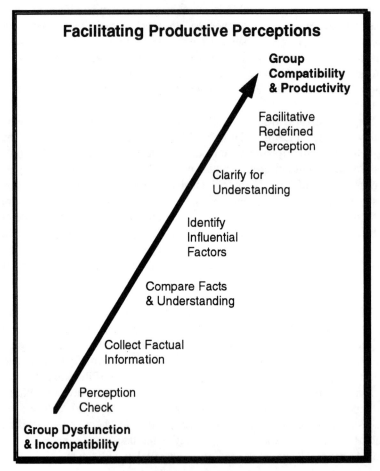

Figure 2-5

While prejudice occurs as a part of human nature, educators should recognize its potential to cause dysfunctional behavior with unproductive consequences. To facilitate productive perceptions and group compatibility that will have a positive effect upon the organization's effectiveness, the strategies described in Figure 2-5 are suggested. Those strategies are: (a) conduct a perception check, (b) collect and communicate factual information, (c) compare the facts with the level of understanding, (d) identify influential factors such as platform, lifespan factors, and preconception, (e) clarify for understanding, and (f) facilitate and revise perception.

The Learning Process

Behaviorism

Behaviorism is defined as the process of learning whereby emphasis is placed upon external influences usually in the form of rewards or other reinforcement. The two approaches to behaviorism include classical and operant conditioning. In classical conditioning, an unconditioned stimulus is applied which results in an unconditioned response, such as in the case of Pavlov's experiment with dogs. A second neutral stimulus is paired and repeated with the unconditioned stimulus, which is followed by a similarly conditioned response. For example, a fire alarm station rings, causing the school occupants to leave their chairs to evacuate the building. When a light is added to the fire alarm station and lighted without the auditory signal, the occupants who see the light will no doubt leave their chairs in a manner conditioned from earlier repeated fire drills.

Operant conditioning expands the focus of classical conditioning to a specific consequence of a behavior; that is, the desirability of the consequence which follows the behavior determines whether the behavior will be repeated. A teacher who receives a university tuition waiver or stipend for supervising a university intern is more likely to repeat the act than if the supervision were overlooked and not rewarded. The understanding of the behavioristic approach and its applicability to supervisory practices is not intended to establish a model of *manipulatory management,* but to better explore motivation which will be discussed later in this chapter.

Social Learning Theory

Rushton (1980) suggested that social development transpires from behavior influenced by classical conditioning, reinforcement, punishment, and observational learning. Bandura (1977) developed a four step model whereby a person must engage in the following steps before imitating a model's behavior: (a) attention, (b) retention, (c) motor reproduction, and (d) motivation.

A supervisor may assign a beginning teacher to observe other teachers considered outstanding in the field. The effective teaching strategies displayed by experienced educators are likely to gain the attention of the beginning teacher who will first consider the importance and relevance of such to his or her own performance. He or she may then retain the information and later imitate it in the classroom. Motivational factors in this case are many and might include greater student interest and achievement, fulfillment of a beginning teacher program, the teacher's formal evaluation, and contract renewal.

44 Chapter 2 *People and Supervision*

The supervisor must understand the importance of motivation in behaviorism and social learning theory. If the reinforcement or motivational factor is not perceived and interpreted by the person being supervised as being either a reward or punishment, the reinforcement will not be effective. People generally will accept that which most closely supports their values and fulfills their needs. The faculty member who is constantly assigned unruly students as a reward for outstanding performance is likely to re-assess the true value of outstanding performance.

Cognitive Theory

Cognitive theory is concerned with the internal mental processes utilized during learning and further suggests that acquired knowledge is proportionate to the perceived value within one's environment. These processes play an important role in how prior knowledge is integrated into current and future events. The adult operating at the highest level of cognition utilizes a wider range of techniques in problem solving, is more flexible and open minded, and approaches problem solving from many perspectives. For example, the design of an interdisciplinary English and United States History curriculum or the development of a school strategic plan involves substantial problem solving and abstract thinking. However, the plan will be better accepted if those involved view the new information as useful.

Motivation

Generally, supervisors in education focus their attention on encouraging others to become productive members of the organization. This encouragement includes support for instructional needs as well as the needs of noncertified staff. The issues involved with motivation are as diverse as the population being served. They concern problems such as salary and assignment equity, control of one's classroom and input into policy making. A real tragedy occurs for students when teachers with little motivation remain on the job, eroding the quality of instruction and overall effectiveness of education.

Needs Theory (Maslow, 1954) identified five needs in hierarchical order ranging from the basic to the highest level. Maslow asserted these needs to be: physiological, safety and security, love and belongingness, esteem and status, and self actualization. According to Maslow, each need is examined in relation to the others and cannot be satisfied until the lower level need has been met. Because Maslow's theory does not distinguish between individual differences the supervisor should exercise caution by recognizing that individuals are not alike and should not be placed into generalized categories.

How can Maslow's theory be applied to the needs of teachers? A teacher who is a recent university graduate entering the field of education for the first time and the teacher with many years of experience who is entering a school district level supervisory position for the first time are likely to experience similar needs. They are both concerned with overcoming the insecurities of new experiences. In addition, both are exposed to groups of new people and, therefore, will be concerned with social activity that will result in their acceptance into the new group. Other examples include personnel members involved in stressors such as marriage and divorce, pregnancy, or children leaving home for college. In short, the perceived priorities in one's life greatly influence needs and motivation.

McClelland (1984) developed a triad of needs which includes: (a) need for achievement, (b) need for affiliation, and (c) need for power. The person who pursues and enjoys supervisory responsibilities is likely to reflect a need for power. McClelland (1961) suggested that persons with a high need for achievement display characteristics that greatly influence the effectiveness of any organization; such as, high levels of energy, expertise, creativity, accepting of responsibility and accountability, risk taking and ability to anticipate outcomes. Teachers who reflect a high need for achievement will be motivated by assignments which enable them to design goal statements, find solutions to problems, and collect data for feedback on their progress.

Herzberg, Mausner, and Snyderman (1959) described two sets of factors affecting worker motivation. The first set, related to working conditions, consists of hygiene factors such as salary, status, contractual obligations, policies and practices. While generally thought to be influential in the level of work satisfaction, they are not considered to be motivators. The second set of factors, called Motivators, is related to the work itself and while not considered to influence the level of work satisfaction, it provides what is needed for intrinsic motivation. A recent national study (Osteen, 1994) found the rate of teachers leaving the field to be thirty-nine percent. Listed complaints included dissatisfaction with salary and benefits, lack of input into policy making, and lack of authority over the control of the classroom. Aspiring supervisors should revisit the importance of dissatisfiers to effectively address the issues of intrinsic motivators.

An earlier study (Grissmer & Kirby, 1993) suggested that salary is not only a motivator, but a major influence upon beginning level teachers. However, a similar study (Weiss & Boyd, 1989) surveyed teachers who had left the field of teaching and found more than 50 percent giving salary as the major reason for leaving the profession. The question of salary has been under investigation in many states and studies show a positive correlation between higher salaries and retention rates of beginning level teachers. Research in Indiana (Murnane, Singer, & Willet, 1988) found that a salary increase of 10 percent resulted in a 10 percent lower attrition rate. Even though Herzberg's two-factor theory places salary solely under the classification of hygiene, the educational community should accept the changing focus of teacher perceptions and understand the impact of salary upon motivation and work productivity.

Working conditions generally have received attention among those who are beginning their career as well as those who have left the field of teaching. Working conditions are described as having input into decisions, having control over the classroom

46 Chapter 2 *People and Supervision*

and subject content, as well as autonomy over the delivery of instruction. Kurtz (1983) defined working conditions to further include physical facilities, extra class assignments, sponsorships, coaching assignments as a requirement for employment, lack of direction from the district office about expectations, or any environment with an extremely high or complete lack of supervision.

Expectancy Theory of Motivation is described as the expectation held by workers that agreeable consequences, such as rewards, will follow certain behavior. Victor H. Vroom (1964) developed a model which conceptualized motivation as a product of valence, expectancy and instrumentality. Valence refers to the value that is given to the expected outcome. Values are as varied as the people involved and may be perceived by some as positive and others as negative. One person may perceive a change in job assignment from teacher to supervisor without a pay increase as a desirable increase in status. On the other hand, a colleague may perceive such as an undesirable increase in responsibilities. Expectancy is the understanding that a certain behavior will result in a predictable outcome. A supervisor who reflects a high energy level when communicating duties to teachers may anticipate greater productivity among the faculty. Instrumentality refers to the probability that certain performance will lead to a specific positive or negative outcome. Thus, high productivity, effective teaching strategies and other professional qualities will lead to positive evaluations and contract renewal.

Kaiser (1995) further interpreted expectancy theory to include the confidence which one has to attain a designated measure of performance. A teacher may have a high expectation of achieving a specified performance level, but if the performance level is perceived by the teacher to be unattainable, his or her motivation will decrease. Teachers within a school where the principal asks them to plan an innovative school open house for the following week may be reluctant to volunteer because they believe the allotted time is insufficient for successful planning and completion. A teacher, new to the school with prior experience in planning an innovative school open house, may perceive the limited time frame to be less threatening and, therefore, reflect more confidence in its organization. One's confidence in his or her own ability is a major influence upon the amount of vigor with which they perform.

Equity Theory is concerned with worker comparisons and perceived fairness between their contribution to the organization and the benefits they receive. The strategies employed during collective bargaining practices within the field of education are greatly influenced by perceptions relating to equity theory. Examples which support equity theory (House & Wigdor, 1968; Walster, Walster & Berschied, 1968) are found in the Marlow and Hierlmeier (1987) study of west central Florida teachers. Marlow and Hierlmeier (1987) concluded that :

> *[the] likely leaver,*[sic] *had become embittered with working conditions, suffered from culture shock, and had lost the support of family*

and friends. Consequently, the likely leaver,[sic] finally looks to business for prestige and success.

The worker who perceives that inequity exists due to one of the described hygiene or motivational factors will attempt to discount the perceived inequity by either a change in teaching assignment or by leaving the profession entirely.

Kaiser (p. 15, 1995) formulated equity as follows.

Inequity	*Inequity*	*Equity*
$\dfrac{PR}{PW} < \dfrac{PRRP}{PWRP}$	$\dfrac{PR}{PW} > \dfrac{PRRP}{PWRP}$	$\dfrac{PR}{PW} = \dfrac{PRRP}{PRWP}$

In this formula PR is that which the teacher perceives to be his or her individual reward and PW is that which the teacher perceives to be his or her individual work effort. For an initial good feeling the work effort must be in proportion to the realized individual's reward. Furthermore, PRRP is the individual teacher's perception of the other or *reference person*'s rewards and PWRP is the teacher's perceptions of the other or reference person's work effort. For a feeling of equity people must perceive their own rewards to be in direct proportion to their work effort and in fair comparison to the work effort and reward of their colleagues. An example might be a group of teachers who traditionally volunteer without compensation to sponsor before- and after-school activities such as tutoring and special interest clubs for low achieving students. That year, during collective bargaining talks, the district spokesperson indicates that no money is available for before- and after-school extra duty. In this case the volunteer teachers are likely to revisit the equity formula concerning their work effort and reward.

It is important for supervisors to recognize the impact which motivational factors have upon the issue of *planned change*. If teachers have a high need for security, they are likely to perceive with aversion a plan to change a school's organizational structure. Besides motivational determinants, resistance to change results from a variety of other factors including personal attitudes, lack of adequate information, satisfaction of status quo, adversarial relationships between management and the work force, and a perceived threat to job control and expertise. Reddin (1970) delineated teacher viewpoints concerning change into three categories. Those include: (a) how the change will affect "me" as an individual, (b) how the change will affect my work, and (c) how the change will influence my relationships with others within the organization. A teacher who is offered a twelve month supervisory position might ask the following questions. Will I get an increase in salary? Will I still be tenured? What will my additional days and hours entail? How will my relationships with present colleagues change? What effect will my new job, longer hours, and extended year have upon my family? The effective supervisor will provide the information necessary to answer such questions to reduce feelings of resistance and, therefore, to facilitate change and

48 Chapter 2 *People and Supervision*

professional growth. Workers of all types require the supervisor to render appropriate resources for job performance. Although there is voluminous research concerning the needs of teachers, a recent study (Osteen, 1994) found and ranked the following teacher needs: (a) the need for clear expectations and support of the administration, (b) the need for more control over and autonomy within the school and classroom environment, and (c) the need for collegial and community interaction and support.

Leadership

Although there exist myriad definitions of leadership, one that is generally accepted is *the behavior of an individual when directing the activities of a group toward a common goal* (Hemphill & Coons, 1957, p. 7). One way for determining leader effectiveness has been *outcome based measurement*. The leader's performance is measured by the extent the group is able to effectively achieve its goals. A more progressive view of effective leadership includes using worker perceptions concerning the leader. Early leadership research that focused on the identification of traits required for effective leadership found that no single trait or combination of such could be applied to the general practice of successful leadership. Ralph Stogdill (1948) conducted an extensive study to determine leadership traits. His survey suggested a low relationship between successful leadership and physical stature and a negligible relationship with appearance. Stogdill noted, however, a strong relationship between successful leadership and intelligence, specialized knowledge, communication skills, judgment, ambition, self-confidence, cooperation, and social skills. These traits were highly situational and therefore contingent upon the needs of the individual and the situation at hand. Stogdill concluded that leadership traits were *likely to vary with the leadership requirements in different situations* (p. 64). Further, *A person does not become a leader by virtue of the combination of traits. . . . The characteristics of the leader must bear some relevant relationship to the characteristics, activities, and goals of the followers* (p. 64).

Bray, Campbell, and Grant (1974) identified the following traits as predictors for leadership success: Oral communication skills, interpersonal skills, need for advancement, resistance to stress, organizational and planning skills, high energy level, creativity, range of interest, flexibility, standards, decision making, need for security, ability to delay gratification, goal flexibility, and primacy of work. The state of Florida mandated the implementation of district-level beginning principal programs which operate under a similar model for training school principals, Figure 2-6. Some school districts utilize these *principal competencies* as the foundation for administrative evaluations. Facilitative leadership focuses on a vision which is concerned with quality, multidirectional communication, and teaming. Collegiality and achievement are considered. The facilitative supervisor motivates faculty using intrinsic rewards that reinforce professional integrity. The work environment is community-embraced and emphasizes group processes such as shared decisions and quality circles. Figure 2-7 and Figure 2-8 list characteristics of both facilitative and traditional leadership styles. Circle the numbers which the people with whom you work would most likely select. To determine your style tendencies, the even numbered items tend to represent facilitative leadership while the odd numbered items tend to represent other traditional styles.

FLORIDA PRINCIPAL COMPETENCIES		
Competency	**Definition**	**Subgroup**
Proactive Orientation	Initiates action and readily takes responsibility for all situations (even beyond ordinary boundaries) for success and failure in task accomplishment	Accepts authority and assumes responsibility; takes charge; exhibits a sense of efficacy; analyzes negative and positive forces affecting the school; takes immediate steps when problems arise; projects an orientation for action; focuses resources on goals; initiates problem solving; exhibits enthusiasm; finds extra resources
Decisiveness	A readiness to make decisions, render judgments, take actions and commit oneself	Makes up one's mind promptly; expresses a disposition to settle on a purpose; exhibits self-confidence
Commitment to School Mission	Holds a set of values about the school, welfare of students, and fairness to staff. Demonstrates behavior consistent therewith	Promotes the welfare of students, faculty and staff; cares about how well people understand; interprets action by referring to school purpose; relates expectations to goals; models behavior congruent with purpose; reinforces behavior congruent with purpose; sets standards of achievement
Interpersonal Search	Is not only sensitive to the ideas and opinions of others but behaves to ensure and understanding of the feelings and verbalizations of others	Encourages others to describe their perspectives; accurately describes others' perspectives; listens to others; summarizes and paraphrases; maintains social distance to promote objectivity; encourages individual expression; demonstrates sensitivity; recognizes own affiliation needs
Information Search	Searches for and gathers many different kinds of information before arriving at an understanding of an event or a problem	Gathers information about the school; withholds making decisions until data are analyzed; keeps up to date; collects information by oral questioning; accesses computer and management information systems
Concept Formation	Forms concepts, hypotheses and ideas on the basis of information	Develops concepts to interpret diverse information; recognizes themes or patterns; recognizes causal sequences; studies problems and issues

50 Chapter 2 *People and Supervision*

Conceptual Flexibility	Uses alternative perspectives and considers information from different points of view	Describes the situation being faced; reconsiders school mission; views events from multiple perspectives; values divergent thinking; develops options; compares consequences of options; makes decisions based on analysis
Managing Interaction	Demonstrates good group process and facilitator skills	Identifies self as a team leader; forms task or work groups; motivates others to identify with mission; moderates group discussions; intervenes, negotiates, resolves conflict; facilitates communication; creates noncritical atmosphere
Persuasiveness	Influence others through a number of possible means	Ties needs to superordinate goals; convinces others to support goals; persists until ideas are clear; articulates expected outcomes; develops trust by modeling desired behavior
Concern for Image	Shows concern for the image of the school	Ties image building to mission; sets high expectations; controls negative information flow
Tactical Adaptability	Tailors style of interaction to fit the situation	Understands how own behavior affects others; estimates readiness of others; fits one's style to the group; adjusts strategies when ineffective; changes strategies to meet changing conditions; exhibits multiple interaction skills
Achievement Motivation	States high work standards	Promotes excellence by evaluating goals; sets standards for goal accomplishment; attends to organizational feedback; attends to personal feedback; assesses own strengths and limitations; shows restlessness to get things done
Management Control	Devises opportunities to receive adequate and timely feedback and follow-up on delegated activities	Schedules surveillance of activities; supervises and monitors the performance of people; monitors the performance of organization; uses technical means for keeping track; collects and records performance data; judges performance using criteria; reinforces desirable behavior; corrects undesirable behavior
Developmental Orientation	Views developing others as a property of the principal's job and works with others as a coach	Builds organizational culture to support learning; interprets performance data to stimulate improvement; coaches to improve performance; provides timely and specific feedback; reinforces growth & development; exhibits effective conferencing skills

Organizational Ability	Focuses on time, deadlines, flow of activities or resources; focuses on ways to get the job done	Establishes and clarifies goals; plans for goal accomplishment; establishes priorities; budgets and allocates resources; schedules time; assigns tasks and activities; plans for contingencies; systematizes own attention to avoid undue stress
Delegation	Delegates authority and responsibility clearly and appropriately in accomplishing organizational goals	Determines jobs to be done; assesses expertise of self and others; determines tasks to be assigned; determines tasks needing outside assistance; identifies persons who can accomplish tasks; assigns tasks; gains understanding and acceptance of tasks assigned; specifies responsibility and authority; establishes performance standards; plans time frames; provides guidance
Self Preservation	Cclearly presents one's own and others' ideas, and information in an open and genuine way	Communicates confidence and positive regard; communicates ideas clearly; communicates using analogy, metaphor and anecdotal materials; adopts group roles as needed
Written Communication	Is able to write in a clear, concise and properly structured manner	Expresses written ideas clearly; adjusts writing style to the audience
Organizational Sensitivity	The awareness of the effects of one's own behavior and decisions on other people	Understands how own behavior impacts the organization; realizes how own behavior impacts outside people and groups; informs people who need to be informed; communicates with individuals tactfully

Figure 2-6

Power and Authority

Power is generally defined in the literature as the ability to influence the behavior and attitudes of a person or groups of people toward the achievement of goals and other specified purposes. Early ideas of power focused upon behavior highly autocratic and intimidating in nature. A more contemporary view acknowledges and legitimizes the use of power so long as it does not infringe upon the rights of others. Unethical abuse of power oversteps the boundaries of authority. A supervisor observing a teacher giving a lesson is given the power by the school to observe teaching strategies and perhaps provide input and suggestions based upon effective teaching literature and personal teaching experience. The supervisor does not, however, have the right or authority to force his or her own educational philosophy, teaching styles, and lesson design upon the observed person. When exercised appropriately, power can prove effective in facilitating behavior necessary to achieve goals and improve educational outcomes. Effective use of power originates from the position which

52 Chapter 2 *People and Supervision*

the individual holds as well as from personal qualities enabling him or her to influence others.

Facilitative Leader Traits
☞ Reflects a vision toward quality
☞ Encourages an open-door policy;   Provides direction, and feedback
☞ Invites shared decision making;   Supports group recommendations
☞ Encourages multidirectional communications
☞ Shows consideration towards workforce;   Encourages creativity and risk taking
☞ Encourages professional development;   Recognizes team members as experts and change agents

Figure 2-7

French and Raven (1959) further delineated Position Power to *include reward power, coercive power* and *legitimate power*. Reward power is power derived from a person's position which enables control over the distribution of rewards whereas coercive power is concerned with the delivery of punishment. Legitimate power is described as the authority to request something because of the nature of the position. An example is the power of the position of classroom teacher when making a request to students or the power of the position of school principal when making a request to school personnel.

Personal power is concerned with both expert power, the measure of knowledge of the person, and referent power which is described as the charisma, admiration, and respect for the leader which results in worker loyalty and desire for approval. Figure 2-9 draws from Yukl's research (1981) and characterizes the influence of specific power sources and behavioral outcomes.

Chapter 2 *People and Supervision* **53**

Management Style Indicator Test
Answer each of the following questions with YES or NO

1. Do you concentrate your efforts on the completion of the task? ...... YES   NO

2. Do you prefer to engage in group discussions? .... YES   NO

3. Do you prefer a chain of command structure? .... YES   NO

4. Do you project an expectation of quality performance? .... YES   NO

5. Do you invite multidirectional communication? .... YES   NO

6. Do you prefer one person to be in charge? .... YES   NO

7. Do you prefer using a monetary reward system? .... YES   NO

8. Do you prefer to engage the workforce as experts
   concerning decisions and change? .... YES   NO

9. Do you prefer to give direct assignments to personnel for
   task completion? .... YES   NO

10. Do you prefer to control information? .... YES   NO

11. Do you prefer flexibility with job assignments? .... YES   NO

12. Do you prefer to have control over the final decision? .... YES   NO

13. Do you prefer to reach consensus rather than majority rule? .... YES   NO

14. Do you encourage professional development? .... YES   NO

15. Do you prefer to work one-on-one with individual workers? .... YES   NO

16. Do you support group recommendations? .... YES   NO

17. Do you recognize group members as experts and change agents?. YES   NO

18. Do you usually initiate change within your organization? .... YES   NO

19. Do you encourage risk taking? .... YES   NO

20. Do you prefer to work within a highly structured organization? ... YES   NO

Positive answers to questions 1,3,6,7,9,10,12,15,18,20 tend to indicate a preference to participate in a more "traditional" setting or management style.

Positive answers to questions 2,4,5,8,11,13,14,16,17,19, tend to indicate a preference to participate in a more "facilitative management" setting or style.

Figure 2-8

54 Chapter 2 *People and Supervision*

Power Type and Anticipated Workforce Response			
Power Type	**Anticipated Response**		
	Cooperation ◄──────────► *Resistance*		
Position Authority *(Authority - Legitimate)*	If request is perceived appropriate	If request is perceived necessary	If leader issues an order
Reward	If reward is not perceived as a bribe	If reward is administered consistently	If reward is perceived as a bribe
Personal Power *(Expert)*	If leader is respected	If request is perceived to be necessary	If leader is perceived to be arrogant
Charismatic	If the request is perceived to be important to leader	If request is perceived to be important at all	If the request is perceived to be harmful to group or leader
Coercive		If request is received in a positive manner	If requests are made regularly in a manipulatory manner

Adapted from Yukl, G. A. (1981) *Leadership in Organizations*. Englewood Cliffs, NJ: Prentice Hall. Table 3-1 *Major Sources of Leader Influences Over Subordinates and Likely Outcomes* (p. 45)

Figure 2-9

Leading in a Diverse Environment

Contemporary leaders recognize that the diversity of the modern workforce requires the practical leader to operate under a model of contingency, or situational, leadership rather than a single model of autocratic or democratic style. The effective leader should first diagnose the behavior of the involved people, the situation and environment to identify the most appropriate leadership style. Douglas McGregor (1960) developed a Theory X based upon the assumptions that: 1) The individual typically dislikes work and will avoid it when possible; 2) He or she will avoid responsibility and requires a direct style of supervision which may include coercive or punitive measures; and 3) Workers are mostly concerned with job security rather than more intrinsic job-related factors. These assumptions reflect a limited, highly autocratic view of supervisory behavior. McGregor's Theory Y, on the other hand, assumes that people are intrinsically motivated, view work as satisfying and, therefore, are self directing and highly responsible.

Tannenbaum and Schmidt (1958) postulated that leadership style includes a continuum of behaviors beyond those of merely autocratic and democratic styles. Hersey and Blanchard (1988) added to the body of knowledge concerning situational leadership the notion that the level of maturity of the worker should dictate the appropriate leadership style. The more mature or self directing the worker, the less directing and authoritarian the leadership style and vice versa.

A program for Clinical Educator Training created by the Florida Department of Education (1993) is supportive of the Hersey and Blanchard model and defines the *developing teacher* as those teachers at varying professional levels who are engaged in a formative process for the purpose of professional growth. The professional levels are classified as: a) preservice teachers; b) entry level beginning teachers; c) teachers who are performing at various levels and elect to enter into the process for professional growth; and d) teachers identified to be at risk concerning instructional performance and employment status.

The above professional categories are further delineated to include three levels of teacher orientation and are described as *survival, mastery* and *impact*. A teacher performing at the survival level is one who is primarily concerned with getting through the current lesson, the next class or day, and reflects a feeling of being overwhelmed, frustrated, and over time may become disappointed and disgruntled with teaching as a career. Those teacher feelings may be attributed to the lack of knowledge and inability to apply the appropriate skills toward the practical setting or an unrealistic job assignment for a teacher new to the field or inexperienced with a given situation. A teacher who is a recent graduate of a teacher preparation program is likely to experience some professional culture shock during the first weeks or months of teaching. Similarly, a teacher with fifteen years of highly successful experience within a small rural setting with an average of twenty Caucasian English speaking middle class students who transfers to an inner city school in Chicago, New York or Miami is likely to regress to some level of survival during the first few weeks on the job. The *survival* level teacher needs a great amount of support from supervisors which involves a more direct style of supervision especially when the teacher is not self directing.

56 Chapter 2 *People and Supervision*

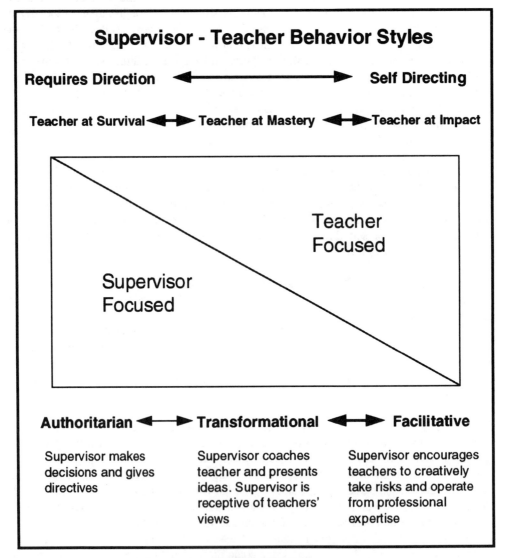

Figure 2-10

The teacher performing at the *mastery* level is most concerned with the technical part of teaching and focuses upon the mechanics of improving instructional delivery. The teacher will engage in behavior which focuses on long range planning and strategies for instructional delivery.

The *impact* teacher has progressed to a level of expertise in which technique is a natural occurrence. The teacher in this case is concerned with student learning and will adapt his or her technique and content to maximize potential. The impact teacher views the technical and skill aspects of teaching only as a worthwhile means to the end where learning occurs. Because the experience, expertise, and professional levels of the impact teacher are high, this teacher typically is more self-directing and, therefore, requires little direct supervision. The diagram shown in Figure 2-10 is drawn from various leadership theories and describes the relationship of the supervisor to the orientation and behavior of the teacher.

An emerging view of leadership focuses on transformational leadership described as being concerned with the search for an organizational community effort to achieve goals. The transformational leader is one who exerts charismatic power to elevate worker performance from self-serving to a consolidated purpose.

These theories of leadership are not exhaustive. However, they provide an overview for practical application. When selecting an appropriate leadership style, the effective supervisor should consider the individual worker's personality and maturity level, the immediate environmental characteristics, and the situation. A supervisor introducing a new reading curriculum should analyze the career stages and maturity level of the teachers, the characteristics of the respective classrooms, and other situational factors such as time of year. Figure 2-11 illustrates elements to be considered in selecting preferred styles of leadership.

Group processes such as effective communication and decision making practices are receiving more attention as a result of the movement toward school-site-based management. Group decision making can prove worthwhile when the problem is highly complex and requires a multiplicity of experience and expertise. While the literature is clear that teacher input into the decision making process is valuable, its practice can at times be inappropriate and greatly time consuming. Events requiring crisis intervention and immediate action such as fires or tornados do not lend themselves to the time consuming process of group decision making. The design of an innovative social studies curriculum, however, invites the use of creativity and brainstorming free of time constraints.

Rensis Likert (1961) delineated characteristics of the effective group to include skilled and knowledgeable membership, loyalty, understanding of roles and purpose, motivation, support of group values, positive attitude, and effective two-way communication. Group roles are generally arranged into: (a) *group tasks* which include individual functions such as the *orientor, information seeker,* and *information* and *opinion giver*; (b) *group maintenance* functions which include *gatekeeping, group observation, setting standards, harmonizing* and *encouraging*; and (c) *individual roles* which function as a *blocker, recognition seeker, dominator, avoider,* and *special interest seeker* (Benne and Sheats, 1948).

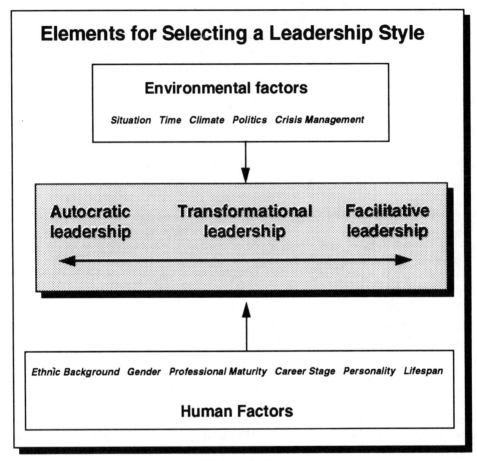

Figure 2-11

For a supervisor to successfully lead group activities, it is important to understand and identify the respective roles of group members. The supervisor must focus on providing direction for achieving goals rather than personality conflict. If a group member is known to possess a high need for power, that person may be expected to act as a blocker towards activity which directs power to other group members. Blocker behavior which reduces the group's effectiveness is eroded when the leader is straight forward in focusing the group toward an established agenda and goals. Effective communication includes focusing on positive and honest statements, a straight forward and relaxed posture, thoughtful listening behavior, and observing the nonverbal behavior of others. Figure 2-12 describes effective supervisory communication techniques.

Chapter 2 *People and Supervision* **59**

Communication Practices				
General	**Group**	**Individual**	**Open Statements**	**Closed Statements**
Words mean many different thing to different people	Establish an environment which encourages open and honest discussion	Effectiveness is a function of the experience held by the involved persons	Will you ... It works well when ...	Would you mind ... This is the worst ...
Effectiveness of a person within an "official" position is a function of the power and authority of the position	Communicated reinforcement enhances positive feelings toward change	Effectiveness will be improved if the sender selects a style which is compatible with the personality of the receiver	We will ...	Why don't you ...
Two-way communication is more effective than one-way communication	Effectiveness is improved if group guidelines and goals are first established to develop harmony	The sender will be more positively received if the viewpoints of the sender and receiver are similar	Can you tell me about ...	It's not our policy ...
The selected channel of communication should be related to the nature of the content	Effectiveness is improved if individual roles within the group are defined	Communication will be more accurately received if the sender considers the education, experience, ethnic background, and personality of the receiver(s).	How can I help ...	I can't ...
Communication that is top-down is received more accurately than that which is bottom-up			What would you like to see happen ...	I will try to ...
Use of multiple channels of communication will reduce resistance to change			What can I do for you ...	It is required ...
Be a good listener and prepare for displays of defensive and emotional behavior for such is human nature learned from prior experience				
Adapted from Alfonso, Firth, and Neville (1991). pp. 138-196				

Figure 2-12

60 Chapter 2 *People and Supervision*

The Diverse Workforce

Diversity in education was recognized early to be gender and race related. Although historically, women have held the majority of classroom teaching positions, reports indicate that women are disproportionately underrepresented within administration. Trends reflected in a study (Jones and Montenegro, 1990) suggest that administrative appointments of African-Americans, Hispanics, Native Americans and Asian/Pacific Islanders are also not keeping pace with population growth. The proportion of various ethnic groups within the field of education is indicated in Figure 2-13. Wesson (in Kaiser, 1995) points to the need for role models within higher positions in education to improve upon the socialization process of minority students. The mobility of a global society, inflow of foreign workers into the United States, and the increase in numbers of women in management positions necessitates greater understanding of cultural differences by supervisors.

Shakeshaft (1987) found women administrators to be more people-oriented, concerned with individual differences, and more knowledgeable about teaching strategies. Furthermore, personnel in buildings administered by women reflected greater job satisfaction as well as student achievement and parental approval. The female who typically has a high need for affiliation, however, can experience difficulty in organizations which are competitive by nature.

Ethnic characteristics vary greatly. Lack of appreciation of diversity can lead to embarrassment and uninvited conflict. The typical American worker does not readily accept an unequal distribution of power and is somewhat direct when interacting with others. However, in general Japanese value an indirect approach. The American work pace is deadline driven. The Japanese work pace withstands deadline pressures and is more methodical. The Hispanic worker often reflects an unhurried nature and respects the influence of fate. Unlike the Japanese worker who is concerned with group recognition and loyalty to the organization and the Hispanic worker who bases personal pride on family relationships and acquiesces to authority, the American worker is concerned with personal status, pride, and control. The need for diversity awareness in education is further emphasized inasmuch as school districts across the country currently serve populations which represent scores of languages, customs, and ever-increasing enrollments.

Supervision of Certified and Noncertified Personnel

The body of knowledge from which supervisory behavior is derived includes organizational, leadership, motivational, and other social science theories. Such research, commonly drawn from the field of business, has also proven successful within the field of education. While the above knowledge is applicable when supervising both professional and nonprofessional workers, literature pertaining to supervisory practices in education is generally concerned with the professional or certified educator. Typically, a custodian or secretary must be given guidelines in the form of a detailed job description listing specific job related tasks, responsibilities, and expectations.

Chapter 2 *People and Supervision* **61**

Race/Ethnic Stratification				
Level	**Leader**	**Faculty**	**Students**	**Board Members**
Postsecondary	8% Minority 92% Nonminority	0.3% Native-American 4.7% Asian American 4.5% African-American 2% Hispanic-American 88.5% White-American		
Secondary	Superintendency 0.8% Native-American 0.3% Asian-American 2.5% African American 0.6% Hispanic-American 95.8% White American			
Middle	9.3% African-American 2.1% Hispanic-American 88.7% White-American	8.2% African-American 2.9% Hispanic-American 88.8% White-American	0.9% Native-American 2.8% Asian-American 16.1% African-American 9.9% Hispanic-American 70.4% White-American	0.3% Native-American 0.1% Asian-American 2.2% African-American 0.8% Hispanic-American 96.5% White-American
Elementary	1.0% Native-American 1.5% Asian-American 7.8% African-American 1.5% Hispanic-American 87.9% White-American			

Source: Bell & Chase, *The Underrepresentation of Women in School Leadership*, in Catherine Marshall (Ed.), *The New Politics of Race and Gender*, 1993

Figure 2-13

62 Chapter 2 *People and Supervision*

Sergiovanni and Starratt (1993) suggested that professionalism consists of more than expertise and includes using one's expertise with good intentions and earned trust. Furthermore, they stated that professional virtue is related to: 1) a commitment to practice in an exemplary way; 2) a commitment to practice toward valued social ends; 3) a commitment not only to one's own practice but to the practice itself; and, 4) a commitment to the ethic of caring.

The goal of every supervisor is to facilitate growth among all personnel so that they perform at the best level for attaining organizational goals. A clear understanding of the theories described in this chapter will better prepare the successful supervisor to motivate teachers, secretaries, custodial, and maintenance workers to become self-directing.

Principals and Practices for Success

Following are some suggested practices to better prepare aspiring supervisors for their new role in education.

- Develop a philosophy of supervision which encompasses a balance of task orientation, conceptual skills, and human relations.

- Understand the implications of social science theory in the practice of supervision.

- Recognize that people are not alike and should be supervised with strategies drawn from leadership, organizational, motivation, lifespan, and learning theories.

- Recognize the steps within a supervisory behavior action plan.

- Understand the characteristics of the various career stages and the application of such knowledge to personnel needs.

- Recognize the value of perceptions, platforms, and associated ethical supervisory behavior concerned with power and authority.

- Understand the implications of motivational needs and equity theory as they respectively relate to the supervision of professional and noncertified personnel.

- Recognize the value of a diverse workforce and characteristics of the respective ethnic groups and members.

Summary

This chapter provided an overview of human behavior as it relates to supervision, perceptions, platforms, and prejudiced behavior.

People in organizations engage in behavior based upon how they view and understand a given situation. Such perceptions are influenced by experience, technical knowledge, educational platform, and other bias concerns. Generally, no two people will observe and describe a given event in the same way. This can be referred to as the perception field. A supervisor, certified as a science teacher, who is observing another science teacher is more likely to look for specific subject content in addition to effective teaching practices than one who is certified in history. In addition, the individual's status or position within the organization can act as an influence. A supervisor in charge of an entire elementary grade level will perceive the distribution of resources differently than will the individual teacher.

The role of the supervisor was described from a behavioral perspective which includes the practical application of theory concerned with adult lifespan, learning, career stage development, leadership, and motivation. A pragmatic model which included certified and noncertified personnel, parents, students, and other school community members was introduced. While research clearly supports no single trait of leadership as being most effective, a situational model of supervision was emphasized. The chapter concluded with information related to the importance of recognizing the value of a diverse workforce of both certified and noncertified personnel.

Case Problem: *Mrs. Baker*

You are the new principal in a middle school of approximately 1,500 students. Your staff includes a principal's administrative assistant, Mrs. Baker. She is 68 years old and has been in her current position for 35 years. She has served under no fewer than six principals. The principals' leadership styles have included autocratic, democratic and laissez faire. You are aware that Mrs. Baker was somewhat responsible for the demise of a former principal as a result of philosophical differences relating to Mrs. Baker's role. Mrs. Baker is considered very knowledgeable about both the internal operations of the school and the district. She is considered an institution in her own right. She can be strong willed and difficult at times. But, for the most part, she recognizes the "chain of command" and authority. She has accepted the responsibility of being everyone's mother. You have staff members who would competently perform Mrs. Baker's job. You also have a competent secretary from your previous building assignment. Ideally, you would like Mrs. Baker to retire.

1. Giving consideration to the various historical periods within the last 35-70 years, what are the major issues concerning Mrs. Baker's employment status?

64 Chapter 2 *People and Supervision*

2. What strategies would you implement for addressing each of the above issues?

References

Alfonso, R. J., Firth, G. R., & Neville, R. F. (1981). *Instructional supervision: A behavior system* (2nd ed.). Boston, MA: Allyn and Bacon.

Baltes, P. B., Reese, H. W., & Lipsitt, L. P. (1980). Life-span developmental psychology. *Annual Review of Psychology, 31,* 65-110.

Bandura, A. (1977). *Social learning theory.* Englewood Cliffs, NJ: Prentice Hall.

Benne, K. D., & Sheats, P. (1948). Functioning roles of group members. *Journal of Social Issues, 2,* 42-47.

Bray, D. W., Campbell, R. J., & Grant, D. L. (1974). *Formative years in business: A long term AT&T study of managerial lives.* New York: John Wiley & Sons, Inc.

Bell & Chase. (1974). The Underrepresentation of Women in School Leadership, in Catherine Marshall (Ed.), *The New Politics of Race and Gender*, 1993

Cohen, M. W. (1982). *Teacher career development: A comparison of college-aged and older-adult preservice* teachers. Paper presented at the annual meeting of the American Educational Research Association, New York. (ERIC Document Reproduction Service No. ED 255 520)

Cohen, M. W. (1983). Teacher concerns: Developmental changes in preservice teachers. Paper presented at the annual meeting of the American Educational Research Association, New York. (ERIC Document Reproduction Service No. ED 255 519)

Erikson, E. H. (1959). *Identity and the life cycle: Selected papers.* New York: International University Press, Inc.

Erikson, E. (1963). *Childhood and society* (2nd ed.). New York: Norton.

Erikson, E. H. (1968). The human life cycle. In S. Schlein (Ed.), *A way of looking at things: Selected papers from 1930 to 1980* (pp. 595-610). New York: W. W. Norton & Co.

Florida Department of Education. (1993). *Clinical educator training.* Tallahassee, FL: Division of Human Resource Development, Bureau of Teacher Education.

French, J.R.P., & Raven, B. (1959). The bases of social power. In D. Cartwiget (Ed.), *Studies in social power*. Ann Arbor, MI: Institute for Social Research.

Fuller, F. F. (1969). Concerns of teachers: A developmental conceptualization. *American Educational Research Journal, 6*, 207-226.

Gibson, J. W. (1990). *The supervisory challenge: Principles and practices*. New York: Merrill.

Grissmer, D. W., & Kirby, S. N. (1993) . *Teacher attrition: Theory, evidence and suggested policy options*. Santa Monica, CA: The Rand Corporation.

Havighurst, R. J. (1972). *Developmental tasks and education*. New York: David McKay Co., Inc.

Havighurst, R. J. (1974). *Developmental tasks and education*. New York: David McKay Co., Inc.

Hemphill, J. K., & Coons, A. E. (1957). *Leader behavior: Its description and measurement*. Columbus: Ohio State University, Bureau of Business Research.

Hersey, P. & Blanchard, K. (1988). *Management of organizational behavior* (5th ed.). Englewood Cliffs, NJ: Prentice Hall.

Herzberg, F., Mausner, B., & Snyderman, B. B. (1959). *The motivation to work.* New York: Wiley.

House, R., Wigdor, L. (1968). Herzberg's dual factor theory of job satisfaction and motivation: A review of the evidence and criticism. *Personal Psychology. 20,* 369-389.

Jones, E. H., & Montenegro, X. P. (1990). *Women and minorities in school administration.* Arlington, VA: American Association of School Administrators.

Jung, C. G. (1924). *Psychological types: A revision by R.F.C. Hill of the translation by H.G. Baynes.* Princeton, NJ: Princeton University Press.

Kaiser, J. (Ed.). (1995). *The 21st century principal.* Mequon, WI: Stylex Publishing Co., Inc.

Kiersey, D., & Bates, M. (1984). *Please understand me: Character and temperament types* (4th ed.). Del Mar, CA: Prometheus Nemesis Book Company.

Kurtz, W. H. (1983). How the principal can help beginning teachers. *NASSP Bulletin, 67,* 42-45.

66 Chapter 2 *People and Supervision*

Lerner, R. M., & Ryff, C. D. (1978). Implementing of the lifespan view of human development: The sample case of attachment. In P. B. Baltes (Ed.), *Life-span development and behavior: Vol. 1* (pp. 1-44). New York: Academic Press.

Likert, R. (1961). *New pattern of management.* New York: McGraw Hill.

Macdaid, G. (1988). *Ten most chosen careers.* Gainsville, FL: Center for Applications of Psychological Type, Inc.

Marlow, L., & Hierlmeier, R. M. (1987). *The teaching profession: Who stays and who leaves?* (ERIC Document Reproduction Services No. 315 380)

Maslow, A. (1954) . *Motivation and personality.* New York: Harper and Row.

Maslow, A. H. (1987). *Motivation and personality* (3rd ed.). New York: Harper and Row.

McClelland, D. (1961). *The achieving society.* Princeton, NJ: D. Van Nostrand.

McClelland, D. (1984). *Motives, personality and society: Selected papers.* New York: Prager.

McGregor, D. (1960). *The human side of enterprise.* New York: McGraw-Hill Book Company.

Murnane, R. J., Singer, J. D., & Willet, J. B. (1988). The career paths of teachers. *Educational Researcher, 17,* 22-30

Myers, I. B. (1962). *Myers-Briggs type indicator manual.* Palo Alto, CA: Consulting Psychologists Press, Inc.

Osteen, M. C. (1994). *Attrition and lifespan-related factors for non-traditional-aged-beginning teachers.* Unpublished doctoral dissertation, University of Central Florida, Orlando.

Reddin, W. J. (1970). *Managerial effectiveness.* New York: McGraw-Hill.

Rushton, J. P. (1980). *Altruism, socialization and society.* Englewood Cliffs, NJ: Prentice Hall.

Schein, E. H. (1978). *Career dynamics: Matching individual and organizational needs.* Reading, MA: Addison-Wesley Publishing Company, Inc.

Sergiovanni, T. J., & Starratt, R. (1993). *Supervision: A redefinition* (5th ed.). New York: McGraw-Hill, Inc.

Shakeshaft, C. (1987). *Women in educational administration.* Newbury Park, CA: Sage Publication Inc.

Stogdill, R. M. (1948). Personal factors associated with leadership: A survey of the literature. *Journal of Psychology, 25,* 35-71.

Tannenbaum, R. & Schmidt, W. (1958). How to choose a leadership pattern. *Harvard Business Review,* 36, 95-101.

Vroom, V. H. (1964). *Work and motivation.* New York: John Wiley & Sons, Inc.

Walster, E., Walster., W., & Berscheid, E. (1978). *Equity: Theory and research.* Boston: Allyn and Bacon.

Weiss, I. R., & Boyd, S. D. (1989). *Where are they now: A follow-up study of the 85-86 science and math teaching force.* Horizon Research Inc.

Wesson, L. H. (1995). Women and minorities in educational administration. In Kaiser, J. (Ed.). *The 21st century principal.* (1995). Mequon, WI: Stylex Publishing Co., Inc..

Yukl, G. A. (1981). *Leadership in organizations.* Englewood Cliffs, NJ: Prentice Hall.

Part II
Improving Instruction

Supervision
Georgia J. Kosmoski

Chapter 3

SUPERVISION AND TEACHER PLANNING
Georgia J. Kosmoski

Encouraging Teachers to Plan

Teacher education institutions emphasize and strive to provide neophyte teachers with the skills needed for good planning. They recognize that effective teaching and learning require systematic and thorough preparation. However, university time constraints limit the amount of instruction, demonstration, and practice the student teacher receives. Educational institutions, therefore, provide only the foundation and framework. Teachers are expected to continue to grow and develop on the job. The acqusition of planning skills is no exception. Teachers must continue to learn and implement new effective methods for planning.

Questions to answer after studying this chapter

✔ Why are planning skills essential to the instructional process?
✔ What procedures should the supervisor follow when helping the teacher with planning weaknesses?
✔ What are the characteristics of effective teachers?
✔ How does teacher effectiveness relate to planning skills?
✔ What are micro and macro planning? How does the role of the supervisor vary in these processes?
✔ How does planning fit within the instructional process?
✔ What is a generally accepted model for instructional design, i.e., planning?
✔ What are several planning considerations the supervisor should address?
✔ Which steps should be included when writing instructional plans?
✔ What regular supervisory practices encourage quality planning?

Supervisors' functions include assisting teachers in becoming familiar with new effective approaches in instruction. Supervisors serve as resources to facilitate teacher development and improvement of instructional skills. Planning must be included in this process. Oliva (1993) described a simplified model of instruction as a continuum with planning followed by implementation, and then evaluation.

Planning, Implementation, and Evaluation

Most specialists would agree that planning is an essential and integral part of successful instruction. The supervisor, regardless of grade level or content area, will encounter teachers with varying degrees of proficiency in planning. Some teachers will write

72 Chapter 3 *Supervision and Teacher Planning*

no instructional plans. Common excuses given by these teachers include lack of time, a desire to allow students to determine the direction of instruction during the lesson, and the claim that the teacher is so expert and familiar with the content that plans are unnecessary. Other teachers jot down key words, phrases, or a text page number. They often genuinely believe that this is more than satisfactory since the essential variables are stored in their mind and these written cues are only designed to trigger their memory of the desired instruction. Finally, the supervisor will find conscientious teachers who demonstrate high proficiency in all areas of planning.

The effective supervisor helps all teachers to develop or hone their planning skills. For the proficient teacher, the supervisor encourages continuing high-quality performance and provides staff development opportunities for staying abreast of various new planning approaches. For those teachers with deficits in planning, the supervisor:

1. Defuses resistance by sharing with the teacher the research findings which demonstrate the intrinsic value of planning.

2. Demonstrates that planning is both a complicated and essential phase of instruction.

3. Works with needy teachers, either individually or in small groups, to correct or remediate their lack of planning skills. The supervisor helps the teachers identify and develop necessary competencies.

Teacher Effectiveness

In 1973, Barak Rosenshine and Norma Furst synthesized the research conducted on teacher effectiveness in the classroom. They delineated nine teacher characteristics directly associated with gains in student academic achievement. Findings demonstrate that students whose teachers had these characteristics made greater academic gains than students of other teachers. These characteristics are:

1. Use of a variety of materials and methodologies
2. Clarity of presentation
3. Enthusiasm
4. A businesslike approach to instruction, task oriented
5. An indirect teaching style
6. An absence of harsh criticism
7. Use of structured statements that provide an overview
8. An emphasis on content covered on adopted achievement tests
9. Use of questions at various cognitive levels

Research findings since the work of Rosenshine and Furst (1973) support their contention that these nine teacher characteristics promote student learning. Of the nine characteristics listed above, all but enthusiasm may be generated or strengthened by the teacher through competent and thorough planning practices. This graphically points out the value of and necessity for strong planning skills.

Nine years after the Rosenshine and Furst report (1973), Brophy (1982) summarized the next decade of research studies that indicate teachers indeed significantly affect the learning rates of pupils in urban schools. He identified eight commonly shared characteristics and behaviors of effective teachers.

1. High expectations for student success
2. Maximize opportunities for students to engage in learning experiences (time on task)
3. Pace curriculum to maximize student success
4. Engage in active teaching with all students
5. Manage their own personal time and organize the classroom efficiently
6. Work toward mastery learning by systematically monitoring and providing feedback
7. Sensitive to individual student differences
8. Provide learning environments characterized by emphasis on cognitive objectives within climates of warmth and personal support

Ryan and Cooper (1984), admitting that their list was probably incomplete, offered their summary of the research regarding effective teacher characteristics. They, too, noted nine teacher skills that promote student learning. These skills are the ability to

1. Ask different kinds and levels of questions
2. Diagnose student needs and learning difficulties
3. Vary the learning situation to keep students involved
4. Recognize when students are paying attention and then using that information to guide student behavior and lesson direction
5. Utilize technological equipment
6. Judge the appropriateness of instructional materials
7. Define objectives in terms of student behaviors
8. Reinforce desired student behaviors
9. Relate learning to the student's experiences

Although worded somewhat differently, similarities exist among these three lists and the numerous characteristics that are initiated or strengthened through quality planning.

74 Chapter 3 *Supervision and Teacher Planning*

The wise and farsighted supervisor must feel compelled to assist teachers to develop and implement effective planning skills. A comparison of the three cited works is outlined in Figure 3-1.

A Summary of Research Findings for Effective Teacher Characteristics		
1973 **Rosenshine and Furst**	**1982** **Jere Brophy**	**1984** **Ryan and Cooper**
• variety of materials and methods • clarity • enthusiasm • task orientation • indirect style • absence of harsh criticism • overview structured statements • content covered appears on tests • questions at various cognitive levels	• high expectations • maximize learning opportunities • pace for success • active teaching with all students • time and space managed efficiently • mastery learning through monitoring and feedback • sensitivity to differences • positive learning environment	• questions at various cognitive levels • diagnoses need and difficulties • varies learning situations • recognizes student attention and has ability to modify • uses technology • judges appropriateness of materials • defines behavioral objectives • reinforces behaviors • relates learning to past experiences

Figure 3-1

Chapter 3 *Supervision and Teacher Planning* **75**

Macro And Micro Planning

Educational planning is required at all levels of instruction. These levels include the curriculum, course, unit and lesson. Macro planning refers to planning the total curriculum of the school system or the entire sequence of courses in a given content area such as mathematics. Micro planning encompasses a section of the macro curriculum such as one course or unit or lesson (Blood, 1993). System or school-wide curriculum committees are most often entrusted with planning at the curriculum and course level. Teaching and learning activities for the curriculum generally extend over a number of school years. Course planning considers instruction that extends for one semester or one school year.

Classroom teachers, working independently or in small teams, are most often responsible for planning the lesson and the unit. These are smaller chunks of instruction. The lesson is a specific individual increment of instruction lasting a few minutes or a few hours. Units are composed of a number of lessons all of which have interrelated goals. Units of instruction may last from several days to several weeks. The unit serves as the foundation or basis for all daily planning because all subsequent lessons are derived from the unit and its goals and objectives. If the goals and objectives for a given high school course unit are planned for four weeks and the class meets daily, the number of lessons required would be twenty (4 weeks x 5 days in session). For a visual representation of macro and micro planning refer to Figure 3-2.

Macro and Micro Instructional Planning				
Type	**Level**	**Usual Planners**	**Scope**	**Usual Timeframe**
Macro	Curriculum	• System or schoolwide committee	• All planned instruction • A sequence of courses	• Multiple school years
Micro	Course	• System or school-wide committee	• Sequence of units	• One semester to one school year
	Unit	• Classroom teacher or small teacher team	• Sequence of lessons	• One to several weeks
	Lesson	• Classroom teacher or small teacher team	• Individual instructional increment	• Several minutes to a few hours

Figure 3-2

The school supervisor has the challenge and responsibility of helping teachers improve their planning skills at all levels of the continuum. When planning occurs at the curriculum and course levels, the supervisor serves as a resource and active participant for the planning committee or team. More specific information regarding the supervisor's role at these levels is detailed in Chapter 10, *Supervision and Curriculum*.

When the teacher needs to improve unit or lesson planning in the classroom, the supervisor may work directly with the teacher. Another alternative is to empower the faculty by entrusting the entire responsibility to a teacher who is highly competent in the planning process. Empowerment of staff requires a true commitment by the supervisor to provide opportunities for staff development and trust in the staff's ability to make wise decisions (Kaiser, 1995).

Planning: The Initial Phase of the Instructional Process

To effectively aid the teacher in developing or strengthening planning skills the supervisor must have a clear understanding of the nature of planning and its prominent role in the overall instructional process. A comparison of the Basic Instructional Model (Oliva, 1993) accepted by most specialists with the Four-Part General Model of Instruction (Kibber, Cegala, Miles, & Baker, 1974) and the Five-Part Model of Instruction (Oliva, 1993) will illustrate the importance of planning to instruction. The reader should note that in Figures 3-3, 3-4, and 3-5 the shaded parts or areas are considered components of planning.

These figures illustrate that planning initiates instruction and is the lynchpin upon which the entire process rests. Each following step emanates from, and is shaped by, the planning phase. Quality planning should result in effective implementation and evaluation. Poor planning can only result in unsatisfactory and grossly ineffective presentation and feedback.

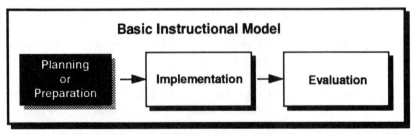

Source: P. Oliva (1993). Supervision for Today's Schools (4th ed). New York: Longman.

Figure 3-3

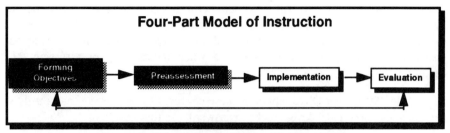

Source: D. Kibler, D. Cegala, D. Miles, & L. Baker (1974).
Objectives for instruction and evaluation. Boston: Allyn and Bacon

Figure 3-4

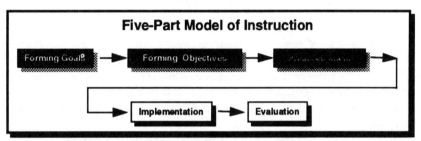

Source: P. Oliva (1993). Supervision for Today's schools (4th ed.). New York: Longman Publishing Group

Figure 3-5

Planning: The Act of Instructional Design

What exactly is meant by planning's relationship to instruction? Planning is an organized systematic approach for designing an instructional program. Planning instruction, sometime called instructional design, requires creativity and discipline from the teacher. When teachers design or build a course unit or a single lesson they are actively engaging in planning, i.e., instructional design.

Tyler (1949) suggested four basic questions that must be addressed and satisfactorily answered when developing or designing any plan for instruction. He asked:

1. *What educational purposes should the school seek to attain?*
2. *What educational experiences can be provided that are likely to attain these purposes?*
3. *How can these educational experiences be effectively organized?*
4. *How can we determine whether these purposes are being attained?*

(p. 1)

78 Chapter 3 *Supervision and Teacher Planning*

These questions are still considered crucial today. However, a fifth question added by most present instructional specialists is "What is the current condition?" Knowledge of the state of the learner, the learner's needs, skills, preferences, the material and human resources are among the items considered when determining or assessing the "current condition."

In 1993, Peter Oliva rephrases these concerns by suggesting that a truly systematic approach to instructional design seeks to answer these four questions.

1. What is it that you wish to achieve?
2. What resources do you have and need to achieve your objectives?
3. How will you go about achieving your objectives?
4. How well have you accomplished your objectives?
(p. 89)

Regardless of how these basic questions are posed, the supervisor and teacher, wishing to improve planning or instructional design, must be concerned with current conditions or status in the learning environment, meaningful goals and objectives, appropriate learning activities, methodology, and evaluation. These questions serve as the framework for a model that educators may use to plan systematically, thoroughly, and effectively.

One Model for Instructional Design

To plan well it is necessary to identify and analyze the components, phases, or steps in the process. Outlined and graphically demonstrated in Figure 3-6, this model includes seven sequential steps required in the planning process.

Step One: Assessing the Current Condition

In step one, the planner must assess the current conditions in the learning setting or environment. Included in this assessment is an in-depth examination of the learners (individually and as a group) to determine needs, readiness, past experiences, and preference in learning style. Student ethnicity, cultural affiliation, and gender are pertinent considerations (Kleinfeld & Yerian, 1995).

The planner also must become acquainted with the state of readily or potentially available teaching and learning resources. This includes items such as hard copy materials, equipment, and technology. Human resources such as teacher specialists, parents, and business leaders should be identified and contacted. A myriad of other environmental conditions, both opportunities and constraints, should be noted and where necessary treated. A few examples of environmental conditions that must be considered in the planning process are additional space requirements, movement of furniture or equipment, materials requested from home, availability of experts in the field, and flexible scheduling.

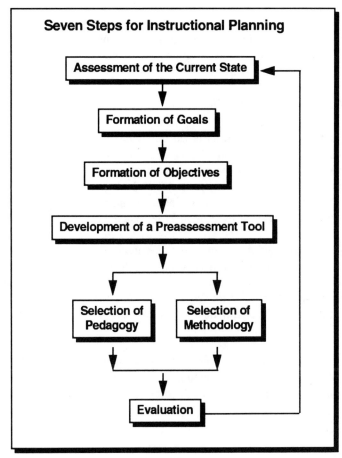

Figure 3-6

An accurate and in-depth assessment prior to any further steps should insure more appropriate and effective choices in the steps that follow. Assessment will color and in some cases alter, subsequent steps. Some ways the supervisor can help the teacher assess current conditions are to:

80 Chapter 3 *Supervision and Teacher Planning*

1. Remain open to questions.
2. Welcome, where possible, requests for resources.
3. Provide staff development training in areas such as ethnic learning preferences, different learning styles, and interpretation of test results.

Providing teachers with the resources and learning opportunities to strengthen their skills and helping them carry on their assignments only makes good sense (Joyce & Showers, 1995).

Step Two: Designing and Writing Goals

Goal statements are generally broad statements that establish the aim or purpose of the curriculum. Unruh and Unruh (1984) explained that goals play a critical part in instruction and that preparing goals require both care and deliberation. Goals must reflect policy, present conditions, available resources, and needs. They provide direction for the entire entity. The writing of goals is a crucial task requiring energy, time, and intelligence. John Dewey (in Unruh & Unruh) writing in 1938, stated:

> *The formulation of purposes and the organization of means to execute them are the work of intelligence.... The formulation of purposes is a rather complex intellectual operation involving observation of surrounding conditions, knowledge of what has happened in the past....and an evaluation of the significance of the past and present for action.*
> pp. 67-69)

Goals are usually written for larger units of instruction, namely the total curriculum, the course, and the unit. Classroom planning most often requires review and selection of established goals developed by system or building curriculum planning committees.

Step Three: Developing Objectives

Objectives are statements developed to communicate the intent of the curriculum and instruction. They express the intended outcomes of a learning experience. The outcomes are changes in the behavior of the learner (Shepherd & Ragan, 1982).

After determining goals, the teacher formulates or selects appropriate instructional objectives for the students. These objectives are most often referred to as behavioral or performance objectives since they are written to clearly express expected learner behavior or performance. When discussing these learning rubrics, Doll (1992) identified three types of educational objectives. These are cognitive, or intellectually based; affective, based in feeling or emotion; and psychomotor, related to mental activity associated with physical movement.

Instructional planners recommend that these performance objectives consider three factors:

1. The expected behavior of the learner
2. The conditions under which learning takes place
3. The acceptable level of mastery

The teacher should include each of these factors when formulating objectives. Often these objectives exist in the school curriculum and the teacher merely needs to match them with the students' needs and levels of readiness.

Regular review of teachers' plans helps supervisors assess teachers' strengths and weaknesses. The supervisor's responsibility is to aid the teacher in recognizing the importance of this planning phase and in developing the skills and techniques to formulate and select appropriate objectives. More information regarding the formulation of goals and objectives is found in Chapters 4 and 10.

Step Four: Creating the Preassessment Tool

With goals and objectives determined, the teacher designs a preassessment tool or test to determine the appropriateness of the particular goals and objectives for these specific students. The preassessment provides the teacher with valuable information regarding the pupils' readiness, prerequisite skills, and needs. The result of the preassessment guides the teacher in the final selection of goals and objectives. Analysis of the preassessment data confirms for the teacher which goals and objectives should be altered, expanded, or discarded.

Most preassessment tests are teacher-made, short, and devoted to major concepts. They are created to answer these questions:

- Do the students have the necessary prerequisite skills to successfully complete the unit or lesson?

- Do the students already possess the skills and knowledge this lesson plans to develop?

One strategy the supervisor can use when helping a teacher with this planning phase is collegial coaching. Master teachers are often willing to share their expertise with their peers and colleagues. They are willing to "teach" these specific techniques or skills to fellow teachers.

Step Five: Selecting the Pedagogy

After selecting the goals and objectives for a given unit or lesson, the teacher determines the pedagogy, or what is taught. The content for each activity must be specifically determined. Activities should be varied and consider numerous factors that influence successful learning.

Good teachers select activities that reflect various levels of expected performance. These teachers use taxonomies to ensure the incorporation of higher order skills. Time use and time-on-task are reflected in the good planning of activities. Student learning styles, ethnic and cultural learning preferences, readiness and experiences are seriously weighed when planning specific activities. The scope and sequence of activities are areas addressed and planned by highly professional teachers. Some of the myriad of considerations given to planning successful activities are illustrated in Figure 3-7.

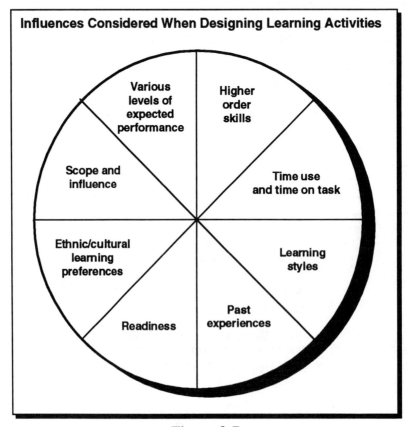

Figure 3-7

Supervisors must work directly with teachers to determine informational needs and utilization skills. Jointly, they develop a personalized development plan so that the teacher may learn these skills and strategies. Additionally, the successful supervisor provides the release time and resources necessary for the teacher to acquire these teaching tools.

Step Six: Selecting the Methodology

Like pedagogy, methodology, the way of teaching for successful learning, includes factors that must be addressed to be most effective. Beside the considerations mentioned above, methodology must address numerous influences that determine and have been proven effective in delivering instruction. First, the master teacher must determine if each information sharing session or lesson will be *direct* or *indirect*. A direct style of instruction is usually lecture, teacher directed, and critical. Indirect teaching is more discussion oriented, student directed and teacher facilitated, and accepting. Rosenshine (1979) confirms that indirect instruction is more effective.

Another consideration regarding methodology is the deliberate selection of questions (Tanner & Tanner, 1987). The type (broad and narrow) and the level (on the various taxonomies) of questioning must be preselected to achieve maximum effectiveness. Effective teachers plan and then implement a variety of questions that definitely include those that are broader and of a higher order.

Delivery formats or configurations are chosen by master teachers based upon student needs and preferences. Expert teachers select from forms such as lecture, discussion, cooperative and collaborative groups, and individualized learning center approaches. To be most effective each form requires teacher expertise and methodical planning. *Frontal teaching* is where the teacher stands in the front of the room and lectures to students seated in neatly arranged rows of desks. Overuse of this technique is considered passé by current pedagogical standards and paradigms. Methodological considerations are depicted in Figure 3-8.

Some Methodology Considerations When Planning Instruction	
Style of teacher delivery	Type of questions asked (broad or narrow)
Level of questions asked (based on taxonomy selected)	Delivery format or configuration (student grouping)

Figure 3-8

84 Chapter 3 *Supervision and Teacher Planning*

Similar to choosing appropriate pedagogy, the selection of methodology by the classroom teacher can be facilitated by a knowledgeable, involved, and concerned supervisor. The supervisor must supply, support, and provide needed direction and resources for the classroom teacher who could benefit from the available help.

Step Seven: Evaluation

The last step in planning is evaluation. The teacher must evaluate the level of student mastery and the unit or lesson success. Some pertinent questions are: Did the pupils demonstrate the acceptable mastery level? Were the desired goals and objectives met? Where is change and/or remediation required?

Each lesson should be formally or informally evaluated. Unit evaluation or assessment plans should include periodic and regular assessment throughout the unit and a final evaluation at the conclusion. These assessments may take various forms and may be either formal or informal in nature. Diagnostic, summative, and formative evaluation is recommended. Daresh (1989) explained further:

> *Students are evaluated almost continuously in most schools, and all three processes are employed. Diagnostic student evaluation might involve a simple pretest administered by the classroom teacher at the outset of a chapter or unit, to determine the level of students' awareness of central concepts to be taught; this pretest might guide the teacher in selecting appropriate instructional strategies. . . . Formative student evaluation is an ongoing practice in most schools. Teachers give "pop quizzes" precisely because they want to get some sense of how well students are learning during the course of instruction. . . . Formative evaluation need not necessarily be confined to written tests or other evaluation instruments. Good teachers use formative evaluation techniques constantly; they watch student behavior patterns. . . .A typical example of summative evaluation is the traditional final exam that concludes a marking period. . . .or the end of the instructional units.*
>
> (pp. 198-199)

Chapters 4 and 10 discuss additional ramifications of instructional evaluation and the supervisor's role as a facilitator.

Additional Planning Considerations

Some critical planning considerations are the use of time, preparation of appropriate materials and equipment, and the efficient arrangement of the teaching and learning setting. The supervisor must be aware and sensitive to these considerations and encourage teachers to address these areas.

Borg (1980) reviewed effective teaching research and found that the more time a teacher allocates to a particular content or topic, the more students learn about that area. Berliner (1987) reported that some elementary teachers spend as little as 16 minutes daily on math instruction, while others allocated as much as 50 minutes per day to mathematics instruction. At the secondary level, the time allocation of particular topics in like content areas can vary greatly between teachers. Time allocation is then a serious focus and consideration for supervision. The supervisor and the teacher working together must review the amount of time allocated to given content areas at the elementary level or topic, lesson, or unit time allocations at the secondary school.

Student "on-task" or "engaged" time is a second time consideration for the teacher and supervisor. Engaged or on-task time is the percentage or amount of time the student is attentive and actively engaged in learning during the allocated time. Classes with a high percentage of on-task time have better academic test scores than classes with lower on-task time (Borg, 1980).

Two methods the supervisor and teacher might use to increase engaged time is homework and an increase of substantive interaction in the classroom. Homework increases the amount of time students can be engaged in a lesson and extends the learning period through independent engagement. Cooper (1989) reviewed the research and concluded that for older students, homework has a positive and significant effect on academic achievement. Using the supervision process, the supervisor and teacher may examine the teacher's current homework policy and determine the type and amount of homework that would be most beneficial for the students.

Substantive interaction in the classroom increases students' on-task behavior (Fisher et al., 1980). Substantive interaction involves students in the lesson by asking questions, explaining purpose and content to the students, providing assisted and unassisted practice, and giving relevant and timely feedback. Clinical supervision (see Chapter 6) is an ideal model for teacher and supervisors if they wish to increase substantive interaction and keep students on task. Goldhammer, Anderson, and Krajewski (1993) advocated this model when the teacher wishes to improve these skills.

Along with time, another critical consideration at the planning stage is determining needed materials, equipment, and resources for a given unit or lesson. The teacher should compile a resource list that includes specific items needed to successfully complete the unit or lesson objectives. To facilitate smooth implementation, the supervisor should check that this vital component is included in the teacher's plan. If this is omitted the supervisor should work with the teacher to include it.

A third planning consideration is arrangement. If special arrangements for student, furniture, visuals, or equipment are necessary for a particular lesson, the teacher should note

86 Chapter 3 *Supervision and Teacher Planning*

that in the lesson plan. This practice will make preparation and implementation more efficient. An appropriate question that a supervisor might ask is: "Does the teacher list or note needed spatial or physical arrangements?" If the answer is no, the supervisor may wish to help the teacher understand, value, and utilize this technique when planning.

Writing and Organizing Instructional Plans

Along with understanding all the components of planning, the teacher must organize these components into a clear, concise, yet thorough plan. Written unit and lesson plans may take a number of forms but must include the essential components previously discussed. The essential parts for units and lessons are found in Figure 3-9.

Essential Components of Written Plans	
Unit	**Lesson**
• goals • objectives • preassessment • instructional procedures • resources • evaluation	• objectives for the specific lesson • instructional procedures • resources • evaluation

Figure 3-9

Source: Oliva, P.F. *Supervision for today's schools, 4th ed.* (1993). New York: Longman Press.

To illustrate what is meant by clear, concise, logical, and thorough written plans a skeletal outline for both a unit and lesson plan are presented in Figures 3-10 and 3-11, respectively.

Positive Supervisory Practices

There are several regular practices that a supervisor might adopt to facilitate and improve planning in the school. The first is the careful assignment of teacher plan time. Each teacher not only appreciates, but deserves daily plan time. If the supervisor is committed to the importance of quality planning, he or she must make every effort to schedule regular, and whenever possible, daily planning time for every teacher. With the advent of instructional strategies such as interdisciplinary units, cross level or content area peer coaching, middle school learning, and team teaching, the supervisor also must make accommodations for shared planning time. This will probably require some creative juggling of the internal schedule. However, the effort will be rewarded with an increased variety of instructional pedagogy and methodology.

Chapter 3 *Supervision and Teacher Planning* **87**

Compressed Outline for a Written Unit Plan

Title: _____

1. **Goals:** _____
   _____

2. **Objectives**
   a. Cognitive: _____
   _____
   b. Affective: _____
   _____
   _____
   c. Psychomotor: _____
   _____

3. **Preassessment:** _____
   _____

4. **Instructional Procedures**
   Pedagogy: _____
   _____
   _____
   Methodology: _____
   _____
   Time: _____
   _____

5. **Resources**
   Materials/equipment: _____
   _____
   Human: _____
   _____
   Arrangement
   Physical/Spatial: _____
   _____

6. **Evaluation**
   Formative/Periodic: _____
   _____
   Summative/Final: _____
   _____
   _____

Figure 3-10

Compressed Outline for a Written Lesson Plan

Title: _____

1. **Objectives**
   a. Cognitive: _____
   _____
   b. Affective: _____
   c. Psychomotor: _____
   _____

2. **Instructional Procedure**
   Pedagogy: _____
   _____
   Methodology: _____
   _____
   Time: _____
   _____

3. **Resources**
   Materials/equipment: _____
   _____
   Human: _____
   _____
   Arrangement-Physical/Spatial: _____
   _____

4 **Evaluation**
   Formative: _____
   _____
   Summative _____
   _____
   _____
   _____

Figure 3-11

88 Chapter 3 *Supervision and Teacher Planning*

A second method suggested to improve overall quality of planning is the supervisor's regular review or checking of written plans. Checking should not be viewed as *snoopervision*, but rather as assistance. Supervisors should advise teachers before instituting this practice of their intent and purpose for review. The explanation should reassure teachers who are unaccustomed to this procedure and reduce their feelings of mistrust and suspicion. The purpose of regular review is threefold:

1. It provides the supervisor with hard data regarding what is taught in the classroom.
2. It helps the supervisor identify teachers' areas of potential weakness or concern.
3. It serves as a source for potential individual or staff development efforts.

A third way a supervisor may upgrade planning in the school is to openly discuss, via the faculty meeting or other staff sharing sessions, research findings that emphasize the benefits of quality planning. If the staff agrees to set high planning standards and work toward that goal, quality will increase. If the supervisor is willing to embark upon this course, three generalities regarding goal theory should be noted.

1. Specific goals elicit a higher level of performance than general goals.
2. Very difficult goals may be unacceptable to the group and, thereby, void positive change.
3. Group goal-setting is more effective than goal setting by the superior (Beehr and Love, 1983; Latham and Steele, 1983).

In 1995, Kirkpatrick and Lewis further explained that telling employees to "do their best" is not as effective as having a specific goal that leads to greater motivation.

These research findings infer that the supervisor should follow certain procedures if improvement of planning is to become an organization goal.

- The goal should be specific, such as: All unit plans will include the specific components of current conditions, goals, objectives, preassessment, pedagogy, methodology, and evaluation.

- For goals to be acceptable they must be reasonably attainable by the teachers. Perhaps slowly introducing the change by content area or individual class period would be more effective than a slipshod wholesale attempt in all areas.

- The staff themselves must set the goal rather than have the goal forced upon them from above.

- To improve the staff's planning skills the supervisor must be ready and willing to supply the needed moral and physical assistance to achieve success. Regardless of what is necessary, supervisors must be committed to the effort. Positive attitude, release or altered plan time, and resources are reasonable expectations of the supervisor.

To accomplish quality planning teachers need a supervisor who is an educational leader. Lunenburg and Ornstein (1991) explained that these leaders display two essential characteristics. Leaders are viewed as trustworthy and tend to obtain the best work from their employees. Second, leaders are more people-oriented than task-oriented.

Principles and Practices for Success

- The supervisor must encourage and become actively engaged in the improvement of planning skills.

- The supervisor should become familiar with teacher effectiveness research and apply it to supervisory duties.

- The supervisor must learn to distinguish between the needs of micro and macro planning.

- The supervisor should understand that planning is the initial and most vital phase of the instructional process.

- The supervisor must be able to conceptualize that planning is the act of instructional design.

- The supervisor is able to discuss the seven steps of instructional design.

- The supervisor is able to recognize that time, preparation of materials, and arrangements are integral planning considerations.

- The supervisor understands the key components necessary when writing quality plans.

90 Chapter 3 *Supervision and Teacher Planning*

Summary

Most specialists agree that planning is an essential component of the instructional process. The role of the supervisor is to encourage and help the teacher to acquire and hone planning skills. For teachers with identified planning weaknesses, the supervisor must defuse resistance to change, encourage, and provide support and assistance.

Effective teaching research of the 1980s and 1990s identifies those teacher characteristics that are positively and directly tied to student academic achievement. Most, if not all, of these characteristics can and should be addressed in instructional planning. By encouraging teachers to improve their own planning abilities the supervisor is indirectly supporting student academic growth.

Planning occurs at the micro and macro level. Macro planning includes curriculum and course planning at the building or district level. Micro planning occurs in the classroom and encompasses planning units and lessons. The supervisor must assist the faculty in both areas.

Planning at the micro level is the initial and probably most crucial phase in the instructional process. It is composed of seven necessary steps: assessing the condition, designing goals, developing objectives, creating a preassessment, selecting the pedagogy and methodology, and evaluation. Some additional planning considerations are time, resources, and physical arrangements.

Specific components are required in the organization and writing of effective plans. Unit plans include goals, objectives, preassessment, instructional procedures, resources, and evaluation. The lesson plan includes objectives of the particular lesson, instructional procedures and resources, and evaluation (Oliva, 1993). Some supervisory behaviors that will upgrade schoolwide planning performance are creative and flexible scheduling of teacher plan time, reviewing or checking written plans, and encouraging staff to make improved planning a school goal or priority.

Case Problem: *So Fresh!*

It is 6:30 a.m. and the tenth full school day of the year. After taking another slug of his tea, Dr. Sterling Caring is ready to begin reviewing his teachers' written plans for the first time this year. Out of curiosity, Dr. Caring begins the process by opening Shirley Fresh's plan book. Ms. Fresh is an eager and vivacious first year teacher. She is presently teaching a heterogeneous fourth grade class.

Chapter 3 *Supervision and Teacher Planning* **91**

Sterling opens the plan book and freezes. He can't believe what he is seeing! Shirley's idea of lesson plans is a list of times, subjects, and text page numbers. Yesterday's "plans" begin:

8:30 Attendance and housekeeping chores.
8:45 Spelling - p. 6.
9:30 English - p. 5 exercises 3 and 4.

Dr. Caring knows that Shirley Fresh is frightened and overwhelmed by the start of school. He also realizes that she is in trouble and needs immediate help with writing effective plans. What course of action should Sterling Caring pursue? Prioritize and list each step he should take. Include a tentative time line. Be able to justify your recommendations.

Case Problem: *More of the Same*

As the science department chairperson and instructional supervisor at Central High School, you are preparing for your meeting with Mrs. Candy Same. Again you are going to try to persuade her to develop her own unit and lesson plans. Candy has taught Chemistry at Central for seventeen years and is considered a "fine" teacher by her past supervisors, her peers, and her students. However, Candy still feels that planning for lessons she knows forward and backwards is a waste of her valuable time. That the department and the school has set improved planning as a priority for this school year "cuts no ice" with Mrs. Same.

Explain what you would do to help Mrs. Same change. What approach would you use with Candy? What arguments would you use to persuade her to try writing quality plans? What information should you specifically include in your presentation?

References

Beehr, T. & Love, K. (1983). A meta-model of the effects of goal characteristics, feedback, and role characteristics in human organizations. *Human Relations, 36*, 151-166.

Berliner, D. C. (1987). Knowledge is power: A talk to teachers about a revolution in the teaching profession. In Berliner, D. C. & Rosenshine, B. V., (Eds.)., *Talks to teachers*. New York: Random House.

Blood, D. (1993). Curriculum development. in Kaiser, J. *The 21st century principal*. Mequon, WI: Stylex Publishing Co., Inc.

92 Chapter 3 *Supervision and Teacher Planning*

Borg, W. R. (1980). Time and school learning. In Denham, C. & Lieberman, A. Eds., *Time to learn*. Washington, DC: U.S. Department of Education.

Brophy, J. (1982). Successful teaching strategies for the inner-city child. *Phi Delta Kappan, 63*, 527-530.

Cooper, H. (1989). *Homework*. New York: Longman.

Daresh, J. C. (1989). *Supervision as a proactive process*. New York: Longman.

Doll, R. C. (1992). *Curriculum improvement: Decision making and process. (8th ed)*. Boston: Allyn and Bacon.

Fisher, C. W., Berliner, D. C., Filby, N. N., Marliava, R., Cahen, L. S., & Dishaw, M. M. (1980). Teaching behaviors, academic learning time, and student achievement: An overview. In Denham, C. & Lieberman, A. (Eds.). *Time to learn*. Washington, DC: U. S. Department of Education.

Goldhammer, R., Anderson, R. H., & Krajewski, R. J. (1993). *Clinical supervision: Special methods for the supervision of teachers, (3rd ed)*. New York: Harcourt Brace Jovanovich College Publishers.

Joyce, B., & Showers, B. (1995). *Student achievement through staff development: Fundamentals of school renewal (2nd ed.)*. New York: Longman Publishers.

Kaiser, J. (1995). *The 21st century principal*. Mequon, WI: Stylex Publishing Co., Inc.

Kibber, R. J., Cegala, D. J., Miles, D. T., & Baker, L. L. (1974). *Objectives for instruction and evaluation*. Boston: Allyn and Bacon.

Kirkpatrick, T. O., & Lewis, C. T. (1995). *Effective supervision: Preparing for the 21st century*. New York: The Dryden Press, Harcourt Brace College Publishers.

Kleinfeld, J. S., & Yerian, S. (1995). *Gender tales: Tensions in the schools*. New York: St. Martin Press.

Latham, G. P., & Steele, T. P. (1983). The motivational effect of participation versus goal setting on performance. *Academy of Management Journal, 26*, 406-417.

Lunenburg, F. C., & Ornstein, A. C. (1991). *Educational administration: Concepts and practices*. Belmont, CA: Wadsworth Publishing.

Oliva, P. F. (1993). *Supervision for today's schools (4th ed.)*. New York: Longman.

Rosenshine, B. (1979). Content, time, and direct instruction. In Peterson, P. L. *Direct instruction reconsidered.* Berkeley, CA: McCutchan.

Rosenshine, B., & Furst, N. (1973). The use of direct observation to study teaching. In Travers, R. M. (Ed.). *Handbook of research on teaching (2nd ed.).* Chicago: Rand McNally.

Ryan, K., & Cooper, J. M. (1984). *Those who can, teach (4th ed.).* Boston: Houghton Mifflin.

Shepherd, G. D., & Ragan, W. B. (1982). *Modern elementary curriculum* (6th ed.). New York: Holt, Rinehart, and Winston.

Tanner, T. & Tanner, L. (1987). *Supervision in education: Problems and practices.* New York: Macmillan.

Tyler, R. (1949). Basic principles of curriculum and instruction. Chicago: University of Chicago Press.

Unruh, G. & Unruh, A. (1984). Curriculum development: Problems, processes, and progresses. Berkley, CA: McCutchan.

Chapter 4

OBSERVING INSTRUCTION
Barbara A. Murray

Artistic and Scientific Approaches to Teaching

Historically, teaching has been considered a vocational trade rather than a profession. Training was limited to fewer than two years and primarily involved an apprenticeship whereby teaching strategies were learned by observing "master" teachers. The popular method for delivering instruction was explanation and demonstration. The students then imitated the teacher's behavior. The effectiveness of this method is greatly dependent upon the accuracy, breadth of knowledge, and skill level of the teacher. Furthermore, learning is highly influenced by student perceptions concerning the authority of the teacher and legitimacy of the teacher's knowledge. This view of teaching is referred to as the *artistic approach* to teaching.

Questions to answer after studying this chapter

✔ What are the differences between the artistic and scientific approaches to teaching?

✔ What general teaching behaviors are concerns for supervisors?

✔ What are the effective strategies for delivering instruction?

✔ Why do we measure and evaluate student progress?

✔ What are some of the issues related to instruction, student and teacher differences?

✔ What are the responsibilities of the supervisor during the supervision of instruction?

✔ How do collegial and professional practices influence instruction and supervision?

The artistic approach to teaching depends on the personality and charismatic power of the teacher. A major criticism of this approach is that teachers must perform both inside and outside the classroom in an exemplary fashion so that students might imitate the modeled behavior. Because teaching strategies are not scientifically tested, the delivery of instruction is based upon trial and error and a "teach like you were taught" foundation. Teachers are expected to possess a broad range of knowledge without extensive training to meet the social and career needs of every student. While the belief that teachers should serve as exemplary models is a commendable one, teaching strategies acquired merely through observation, restricted to explanation and demonstration, limit the learning process. Limitations include the failure to recognize individual differences, personalities, learning styles, and creativity. Expecting the teacher to possess an infinite amount of knowledge

96 Chapter 4 *Observing Teacher Presentation of Instruction*

during an era of "information explosion" is, at the very least unrealistic and perhaps even ridiculous.

Educational specialists have been unable to clearly describe the characteristics of a "master" teacher. They recognize that effective teaching is contingent upon student needs, student behavior, and environmental characteristics. Thus, a teacher may perform well within one educational setting and not well within another.

Early theories of teaching were concerned with the purpose of education, the learner's intelligence and behavior rather than the process of teaching. The concept of teaching as a science emerged after World War II and guided researchers to study specific teaching behaviors and their relationships to learning outcomes. The scientific approach to teaching strengthened instructional strategies by testing teaching behavior and identifying categories of effective teaching strategies. The categories generally recognized include: educational goals and objectives, teacher and pupil interactions, cognitive advancement, student and classroom management, and the influence of teacher behavior upon student behavior. The supervisor should have a clear understanding of the above categories to include them in models for assessing instructional effectiveness.

Model for Supervising Instruction

One model for effective supervision of instruction includes eight elements that are listed in Figure 4-1.

Elements For Effective Supervision of Instruction
- Supervisor-Teacher Relationship
- Supervisor and Teacher Beliefs and Platforms
- Subject Content Goals and Objectives
- Planning and Design of Instruction
- Methodology and Strategies for Delivery of Instruction
- Measurement and Evaluation of Learning and Program Outcomes
- Analysis and Interpretation of Data
- Realization of Professional Virtue

Figure 4-1

Developing the Supervisor-Teacher Relationship

The influence of supervisory behavior over worker satisfaction and productivity was discussed in Chapter Two. It is important to reiterate that workers' perceptions toward supervisors are a primary influence upon the effectiveness of the organization. Bachman, Smith and Slesinger (1968) analyzed the relationships among various types of power, worker satisfaction, and job performance. Referent power and expert power reflected a significantly higher positive correlation with job satisfaction and performance than did legitimate or reward power. Worker performance and satisfaction levels were greater when the supervisor was perceived as highly skilled, knowledgeable, and personable. Although this study was not specific to education, Hornstein (1968) studied satisfaction and power within the field of education and concluded:

> ...the effects of superior-subordinate relations in school systems are very much like those of various industrial, sales, and voluntary organizations. Teachers report greater satisfaction with their principal and school system when they perceive that they and their principals are mutually influential, especially when their principal's power to influence emanates from their perceiving him as an expert. (pp. 389)

To generate a more positive and trusting relationship among teachers, the supervisor should recognize that professional credibility depends upon developing high levels of expertise related to instruction in addition to positive interpersonal skills. Thomas Sergiovanni and Robert Starratt (1988) suggested Supervision II as a model in which teachers are considered to be superordinate to a hierarchically independent organization (Figure 4-2). The supervisor's behavior focused upon mentoring, collaboration, cooperation, and informal supervision as well as leading, managing, and evaluating.

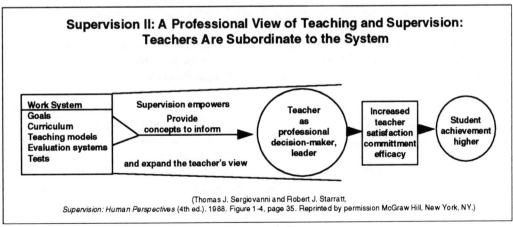

Figure 4-2

98 Chapter 4 *Observing Teacher Presentation of Instruction*

Historically, supervisory relationships were limited to formal settings and formally established meetings concerned with teacher contract renewal. Such practices led to feelings of intimidation, uncertainty, and reduced motivation. Informal supervisory practices such as casual and brief visits to the classroom, faculty lounge and hallway interactions serve as icebreakers that enhance relationships and reduce anxiety associated with more formal meetings. Sergiovanni and Starratt (1988) suggested that informal supervisory activities, accepted as part of the daily routine, communicate to teachers the importance of their role and help them to realize the significance of their work. This method of "supervision by walking around" augments empowerment and collegiality which in turn increases motivation, commitment, and teacher effectiveness.

Recognition of Educational Beliefs and Platforms

As early as the 1900s progressive educators raised the following issues: What is education? What subject matter is important? What is the nature of instructional methodology? What is the relationship between American schooling and the social process? These same issues concern today's education.

Educators operate from an internalized system of beliefs that influences how they define their role within the education process. Belief systems should not be judged to determine their correctness. Supervisors should, however, recognize that such beliefs are an integral part of an individual's personality and an influence their delivery of instruction.

Sergiovanni and Starratt (1993) describe a variety of platforms, none of which is preferred over the other, which provides the foundation for teaching. The platforms include basic competency, preparing one to function in society, preparing one for adult life, preparing one as a life long learner, preparing one for appreciation, ecological, and diversity awareness. It is important for teachers and supervisors to discuss their respective educational platforms so that each has an understanding of the foundation for lesson content. Also supervisors should communicate their beliefs concerning the fundamental role of supervision such as its purpose to coach, mentor, evaluate, develop, or terminate.

People outside the field of education also affect instruction by expressing views on the role of education. When public views enter into the political arena they evolve into societal forces that influence the direction of education. Two examples include the 1962 Educational Policies Commission's "The Central Purpose of American Education," and the 1990 National Goals For Education (U.S. Department of Education, 1991) which clearly describe the national viewpoint on education. These documents are compared in Figure 4-3.

Chapter 4 *Observing Teacher Presentation of Instruction* **99**

Governmental Forces Which Influence Education

In a report by the National Educational Policies Commission in 1962 entitled *The Central Purpose of American Education* **the following statements were made.**

1. Whenever an objective has been judged desirable for the individual or society, it has tended to be accepted as a valid concern of the school.
2. The American people have charged their schools to foster the development of the individual capacities which will enable each human being to become the best person he is capable of becoming.
3. The schools have been designed to serve society's needs.
4. The school seeks rather to equip the pupil to achieve [goals] for himself.
5. A free society has the obligation to create circumstances in which all individuals may have opportunity and encouragement to attain freedom of the mind.
6. The free man, in short, has a rational grasp of himself, his surroundings and the relationship between them.
7. The cultivated powers of the free mind have always been basic in achieving freedom. The powers involve the processes for recalling and imagining, classifying and generalizing, comparing and evaluating, analyzing and synthesizing, and deducing and inferring. These processes enable one to apply logic and the available evidence to his ideas, attitudes and actions, and to pursue better whatever goals he may have.
8. Thus the rational powers are central to all the other qualities of the human spirit. These powers flourish in a humane and morally responsible context and contribute to the entire personality.
9. Only to the extent that an individual can realize his potentials, especially the development of his ability to think, can he fully achieve for himself the dignity that goes with freedom.
10. While man is using the powers of his mind to solve old riddles, which have long intrigued him, he is creating new ones.
11. The rational powers of the human mind have always been basic in establishing and preserving freedom. In furthering personal and social effectiveness they are becoming more important than ever. They are central to dignity, human progress and national survival.
12. The purpose which runs through and strengthens all other educational purposes — the common thread of education — is the ability to think. Therefore, the development of every student's rational powers must be recognized as centrally important.

In 1990 the following goals of *America 2000 - An Educational Strategy* **were formulated and endorsed by then President George Bush.**

1. All children in America will start school ready to learn.
2. The high school graduation rate will increase to at least 90 percent.
3. American students will leave grades 4, 8, and 12 having demonstrated competency in challenging subject matter including English, mathematics, science, history, and geography; and every school in America will ensure that all students learn to use their minds well, so they may be prepared for responsible citizenship, further learning, and productive employment in our modern economy.
4. U.S. students will be the first in the world in science and mathematics achievement.
5. Every adult American will be literate and will possess the knowledge and skills necessary to compete in a global economy and exercise the rights and responsibilities of citizenship.
6. Every school in America will be free of drugs and violence and will offer a disciplined environment conducive to learning.

Figure 4-3

100 Chapter 4 *Observing Teacher Presentation of Instruction*

Other forces which influence education include special interest and pressure groups, local school boards, state and federal laws, and Department of Education regulations. Supervisors should be aware of forces likely to influence the direction of education. While such forces frequently lead to progress, some can run counter to the overall purpose of education. Pressure groups who advocate the censorship of instructional materials are such an example.

Progress may be derailed by a classroom teacher who does not believe in and, therefore, does not support a particular required program. It is not uncommon for teachers to express displeasure toward the Individuals with Disabilities Education Act (IDEA) and Section 504 of the Rehabilitation Act of 1973 that require special educational programs and services for certain students and prohibit discrimination based upon their handicapping condition. Some teachers believe that these statutes offer special privileges and rights to the very students who are often perceived as disrupting the educational atmosphere contrary to the rights of the other students.

Planning and Developing Goals and Objectives

Instructional planning is described as a process whereby teachers develop a sequence of instructional events and selected content as a guideline for delivering a lesson. The lesson or unit plan serves the teacher as the nautical chart does the sailor. An initial step during the planning process is to analyze the needs of students. In doing so, the educator must pay particular attention to age, cognitive, and other developmental levels.

Jean Piaget (1961) delineated a series of stages that describe how children at various ages process information. Understanding the relationship of these stages to learning, better enables the classroom teacher to recognize student differences and then to select appropriate strategies for delivering instruction. Supervisors should look for teaching practices that reflect the understanding and application of stage theory to lesson design and methodology. Piaget's four stages are briefly described as follows.

1) The Sensorimotor Stage spans birth to approximately two years of age and focuses primarily upon the child's ability to recognize and permanently identify objects. While language is not present during the beginning of this stage, children begin to process information and objects into symbols. An important highlight within this age is developing some sense of cause and effect.

2) The Preoperational Period ranges from age two years to approximately seven years of age and is further delineated into the Preconceptual Stage, ages two to four years, and the Intuitive Stage that includes ages four years to seven years. The Preconceptual stage is described as the

phase in which children begin to formulate and utilize concepts although they may not be as logical as in the adult world. A child at this age may know the object "duck" and upon entering a theme park become excited upon receiving a hug from a person dressed in a well-known duck suit. During the Intuitive Stage, the child's thoughts become more logical, although they are primarily based upon a child's perceptions. Children at this age have not had sufficient life experiences from which to form logic upon reason. A child who during the holiday season questions the appearance of Santa Clause standing on every corner is reflecting greater and more reasonable logic.

3) During the Concrete Operations stage, the child develops an understanding of conservation which means that an amount of something remains constant if nothing is added or taken away. The child acquires a sense that an unchanging quantity or object has an identity and if some amount is added to a quantity of a characteristic, the removal of such will return the quantity or object to its original state.

4) The Formal Operations stage focuses upon the ability of the child to think logically. This is based upon reason drawn from rules or experience. Logic can begin with hypothetical thought. During this stage, the lack of experience limits the child's definition of reality that can further cause the child to form idealistic viewpoints. It is notable that this is the age when adolescents encounter the most conflict with adults. Other circumstances for teachers and supervisors to consider include the impact of television, movies, peer pressure, and socio-economic environments upon this adolescent group.

The classroom teacher should understand that efforts to accelerate premature cognitive development have proven ineffectual. Even though some children appear to learn at higher levels, supplementary questioning usually determines their learning to be attributed to memorization rather than bona fide comprehension. Supervisors should ensure that teachers recognize circumstances which are likely to restrict cognitive development and provide for flexibility in instructional activities to stimulate growth among all students.

Benjamin Bloom (1956) developed a taxonomy of educational objectives and categorized it as the Cognitive Domain. Bloom suggests that the learning process begins with fundamental knowledge and progresses through the process of comprehension, application, analysis, synthesis, and evaluation. Bloom's Cognitive Domain is widely accepted among educators as the foundation upon which lesson objectives are developed. When reviewing lesson plans, supervisors should look for action words commonly utilized to transition students into activities related to achieving goals specific to the above domain

102 Chapter 4 *Observing Teacher Presentation of Instruction*

categories. Figure 4-4 describes the domain categories, expected student behavior and related action words. Refer to Chapter 10 for an additional representation of Bloom's taxonomy.

Bloom's Cognitive Domain		
Category	**Desired Student Behavior**	**Action Words**
Knowledge	Recall Facts	List, Select, Identify
Comprehension	Understand and redefine in own words	Define, Describe, Give examples
Application	Transfer knowledge to a new situation	Demonstrate, Apply
Analysis	Separating information and understanding the relationship of the separate parts to the information as a whole	Analyze, Compare, Contrast
Synthesis	Transferring separated information into a new situation as a whole	Design, Develop, Construct
Evaluation	Forming judgments using bits of information to determine accuracy of the information	Critique, Rank, Judge

Figure 4-4
(Adapted from Bloom, B. *Taxonomy of Educational Objectives Handbook One:
Cognitive Domain*, 1956. Reproduced by permission of
Longman Publishers, New York, NY.)

While most educators view the focus of instruction as involving the Cognitive Domain, the Affective Domain, concerning student attitudes, is important as well. David Kratwahl et al. (1967) delineated the Affective Domain beginning with the least intricate includeing the following: receiving, responding, valuing, organizing, and the value complex. Each part is described in Figure 4-5 along with words to express objectives within this area. As in the Cognitive Domain, when reviewing teacher instructional planning material and observing instruction, supervisors should look for words reflecting the Affective Domain as well as an array of activities for its development.

Kratwahl's Affective Domain		
Category	**Desired Student Behavior**	**Words**
Receiving	Develops an openness to the environment	Reflects, Tolerates, Accepts
Responding	Involuntarily or voluntarily responds to environment	Complies, Answers, Volunteers
Valuing	Identifies a list of preferences	Approves, Favors, Supports, Probes
Organizing	Orders preference into a scheme	Judges, Criticizes, Develops a platform
A Value Complex	Commits to an order of values by which one lives	(Behavior reflects beliefs)

Figure 4-5

(Adapted from Bloom, B., et al. *Taxonomy of Educational Objectives, the Classification of Educational Goals, Handbook Two: Affective Domain* . Reproduced by permission of Longman Publishers, New York, NY.)

Anita Harrow (1971) described the Psychomotor Domain as concerning the development of perceptual motor skills. While most formally planned instruction related to psychomotor development occurs within the physical education class setting, other settings should be encouraged as well. Skills such as drawing, building, writing, and walking transfer to other learning experiences such as reading, communicating, playing a musical instrument, using equipment and even driving a vehicle. The Psychomotor Domain is an important part of the educational process. Figure 4-6 describes six psychomotor categories beginning with the most rudimentary movement and advancing to the most difficult. Desired student behavior and appropriate activities are also included.

104 Chapter 4 *Observing Teacher Presentation of Instruction*

Harrow's Psychomotor Domain		
Category	Desired Student Behavior	Activity
Reflex Movement	Display of reflexes	Following movement or light with the eyes; grasp reflex
Basic Fundamental Movement	Achieving primary movement	Rolling over, crawling, walking
Perceptual Abilities	Ability to coordinate auditory/visual with physical (kinesthetic sense)	Skipping and jumping
Physical Ability	Refinement of the prior abilities to include endurance, dexterity, strength, flexibility, agility and reaction time	Long-distance running, stretching
Skilled Movement	Achieving more complex movement; performing both gross and fine-motor skills singularly or in combination in order to achieve complex movements	Kicking or catching a ball; hitting a baseball, tennis or golf
Nondiscursive Communication	Development of individual posture and expression	Mime

Figure 4-6

(Adapted from Harrow, *A Taxonomy of the Psychomotor Domain*, 1971. Reproduced by permission of author, New York, NY.)

During the planning process, the role of the instructional supervisor is to assess whether the teacher properly identifies the needs of students to determine the lesson content, materials, and activities. The supervisor should serve as a resource person to assist the teacher in this task. That does not suggest merely sending the teacher to a workshop on lesson planning, but to actively help the teacher inspect and develop each part of the planning process. To assess the overall effectiveness of the teacher planning process, the following questions should be answered.

1) Were the students interested and involved in the lesson?
2) Were the students able to recognize the significance of the lesson content and relate such to experience?
3) Were the activities selected to broaden the learning experience so that the students were able to transfer the new knowledge to real life experiences?
4) Was the classroom environment inviting so that all students were engaged and able to contribute to the lesson?

Methods of Instructional Delivery

Methodology is described as the teaching techniques utilized to facilitate the learning of subject content within the instructional environment. Some methodologies include expository teaching, inquiry, individualized instruction, and whole class instruction. The following overview of methodology provides the supervisor with information to better assist the classroom teacher to improve learning outcomes.

Expository teaching is a method whereby teachers lecture to students. This methodology is effective for communicating given facts necessary for further learning activities and where retention is the primary objective of the lesson. David Ausubel (1963) suggested that expository teaching can guide students directly to abstract concepts and higher level learning in place of more time consuming discovery methods. The teacher orients the students to major points before and during the lesson using "organizers" to augment learning. An example of expository teaching is a fifth grade teacher introducing students to the various types of cloud formations preceding a lecture on weather forecasting. This method is somewhat traditional and should be scrutinized so that the instructional focus is not upon the classroom teacher rather than the students as active learners. A teacher/student interaction analysis can be utilized to determine whether an instructional delivery method focuses too regularly upon the teacher. The manner by which a teacher engages student participation greatly influences the individual student's learning experience.

Ben Harris (1963) identified five types of questioning techniques utilized by teachers to invite student participation. The five types include:

106 Chapter 4 *Observing Teacher Presentation of Instruction*

- The solitary question
- The controlled question
- The uncontrolled question
- The spontaneous question
- The mass question

The *solitary* question occurs when the teacher identifies the student prior to the question, the student answers, and the teacher responds. When the *controlled* question is presented, the teacher calls upon the student, the student responds to the question, and the teacher responds. The *uncontrolled* question is presented following a short pause during which students raise their hands or otherwise indicate a desire to provide the answer, the teacher identifies the respondent, the student answers, and the teacher responds. The *spontaneous* question is presented following a pause until a student responds to the question, followed by another student who responds to the first student's answer, followed by another student and so on. The teacher responds at intervals to comment, acknowledge the correct answers, and to facilitate further discussion. The *mass* question is presented, the group as a whole responds simultaneously, and the teacher responds.

It is important for the teacher to select the questioning techniques most effective for the lesson. Most questions are asked using the solitary and controlled methods. It is generally accepted that uncontrolled and mass questions are ineffective as they do not check for individual student understanding. The spontaneous question is highly effective when inviting student participation and encouraging creativity so long as the teacher maintains the focus of the lesson and prevents students from straying too far from the topic. The supervisor should assess the observed teacher's questioning methods from two viewpoints. The first view concerns the selected questioning technique and the second view examines whether the questions are designed to reflect the various categories within the cognitive domain.

Inquiry and Discovery

Inquiry is a method divided into two stages: exploration and discovery. When introduced to a stimulus, a student will begin to identify, categorize, and order information so that it is more meaningful. A positive characteristic of the inquiry method is that students are actively involved in problem solving, discussion groups, creative thinking, cooperative learning, and higher level cognitive activities as well as the development of social skills and attitudes. This exploratory method encourages students to form new concepts, designs, and to develop confidence with their performance.

Discovery is described as the learning which occurs when students, rather than the teacher, are compelled to organize information and identify the relationship of concepts. It is important that teachers understand that the discovery method is effective only when students have acquired sufficient background information and experience. Students may be unable to discover the concepts of latitude and longitude without first receiving prior related information. Once learned, the students can utilize the concepts of latitude and longitude to discover specific locations of countries and cities.

A more preferred method is guided discovery, which unlike discovery includes periodic guidance by the teacher. Teacher behavior is facilitative and serves to encourage, guide, and support the learner while engaged in the testing of newly acquired knowledge. Jerome Bruner (1961) suggested that because this method leads to learning based upon codes developed by the learner, retention, motivation, and problem solving skills are increased. The following scenario highlights discovery points within a geography lesson.

A seventh grade geography teacher plans to teach a lesson on the Bahama Islands. The textbook provides general information related to the location, history, and economy of the country. The teacher selects additional materials including maps of the western Atlantic Ocean, the United States, and the northern coast of South America. The teacher then provides nautical and flight charts along with other travel materials. The students are divided into groups and asked to plan a trip to the Bahamas. Each group is assigned a specific destination based upon a unique characteristic. One group is assigned to travel to the country's capitol. The second group is assigned the location where Columbus was reported to have landed. The third group is assigned to circumnavigate the northern Bahama Islands. The fourth group is assigned to travel to the island that is the farthest from the continental United States. While planning their respective journeys, the students are asked to report the following information: distance from the United States, total distance traveled, method of travel, things they are likely to see in route, types of people found and languages spoken, how the people live and their type of work, and other important and unique findings. The lesson not only provides geographical information about the Bahamas, but may also integrate math related to speed and distance, compass navigation, culture and arts, and customs. A culminating activity is to investigate and help plan a Bahamian Junkenoo holiday festival.

A lesson delivered by the discovery method is likely to produce a great deal of classroom activity which may appear to some as chaotic. Supervisors must respect the more open structures of discovery methods and maintain their focus upon learning outcomes. It is also important to ascertain the appropriateness of the selected method and whether the provided background information was sufficient for students to engage in self-directed study.

Individualized Instruction

Individualized instruction is a classroom teaching method often used when the number of students with varying abilities is so great that traditional group instruction is less effective. Guy Lefrancois (1982) clearly described the environmental circumstances in which the use of some individualized instruction is needed.

108 Chapter 4 *Observing Teacher Presentation of Instruction*

Two students sit side by side in a seventh-grade class—Johnny, who has a low I.Q., and Frank, whose I.Q. is very high. Johnny reads at a fourth-grade level; Frank reads well as an average eleventh grader. Both are reading the same science textbook. It is a well-written seventh-grade textbook. Frank Twolips is bored; Johnny West is completely confused. Since neither of these conditions represents an optimal learning situation, any attempt to change them might be desirable. One obvious option is to have the teacher spend time with Johnny explaining this confusing text to him, spend time with Frank amplifying and enriching the content of the text, and spend a little time with all other Franks and Johnnys in the class. Then, of course, attention must be paid to the average seventh-grade students. Obviously, teachers will be able to implement this solution only on those days that have seventy-two hours, or in those classes where the pupil-teacher ratio is no more than one to ten.

A second alternative is to "track" the seventh-grade class. Tracking involves calling the bright group "bluebirds", the middle group "robins", and the low group "larks", and putting each into a separate room. The euphemistic labels are used to avoid offending parents and making life more painful for the lower groups. Interestingly, it seldom takes first-grade students more than a week to discover that "larks" are dumb and "bluebirds" are smart.

Separating a class into tracks is only the beginning of the solution. Unfortunately, it is also often the end. Bluebirds read the same material as larks; they simply do it faster. Larks write the same examinations as bluebirds; they simply do not do it as well. The misfortune is that, despite some notable exceptions, this cynical description of tracking is often warranted. (Lefrancois, 1982, pp. 158)

It is unfortunate when teachers voice concern that individualized instruction is too time consuming and, therefore, not feasible as a method for instructional delivery. These opinions are not only inaccurate but reflect a need for staff development concerning individualized instruction techniques. Time spent developing a well-designed individualized instruction program will be recovered from time no longer spent bouncing from student to student administering consequences for inappropriate behavior. Techniques for individualizing instruction include programmed instruction, computer assisted instruction, mastery learning, self-paced activity, learning activity packets, drill and practice, problem solving, manipulative learning centers, and contract learning.

1. Programmed instruction is described as information presented in small increments by an automated device without the aid of the teacher. It has proven effective for providing immediate feedback and because the information is studied at a pace established by the student. This method enjoyed some popularity during the 1960s but is not commonly utilized today. Positive characteristics concerning programmed instruction include: students are able to learn at their own pace; subject content can

be designed to meet the needs of the individual student; and time for instructional activities can be better organized, utilized more efficiently, and directed more effectively. Even though programmed instruction was viewed generally as an effective method for instructional delivery, critics advise that it fails over time to motivate students and does not allow for student interaction with others. Teachers and supervisors should, however, revisit the use of programmed instruction techniques to better serve the diverse student population in the 21st century. When delivered appropriately, programmed instruction is a valuable instructional tool that promotes learning.

2. Computer Assisted Instruction is gaining in popularity as a technique for instructional delivery. However, school based assessment plans commonly find that instructional computers are too frequently idle. Application of computer assisted instruction typically includes using the computer to compute problems, enabling students to engage in activities for drill and practice such as learning a new language, simulation such as participating in stock market games, and inquiry whereby students utilize the computer as a source of information in order to solve problems. It is important to note that computer assisted instruction is a natural vehicle for incorporating the use of programmed instruction within the diverse classroom setting. Classroom environments in which computer assisted instruction should be considered include classrooms that house a population consisting of a variety of non-English speaking students or a classroom setting including both special education and traditional students.

3. Benjamin Bloom (1976) developed a model for Mastery Learning based upon the premise that students learn at variable speeds depending on the aptitude of the learner, the quality of instruction, and the amount of time allotted to the task. Bloom's model does not specify any strategies as most effective for teaching, but suggests that learning is a result of the adaptation of the instruction to the needs of the learner. The classroom setting, in which the "mastery" method of instruction is used, will be characterized by activities including content delivery, testing for comprehension, needed remediation using a different approach to meet the learners' needs, retesting, and more content delivery. Figure 4-7 describes the steps taken in delivering the mastery method.

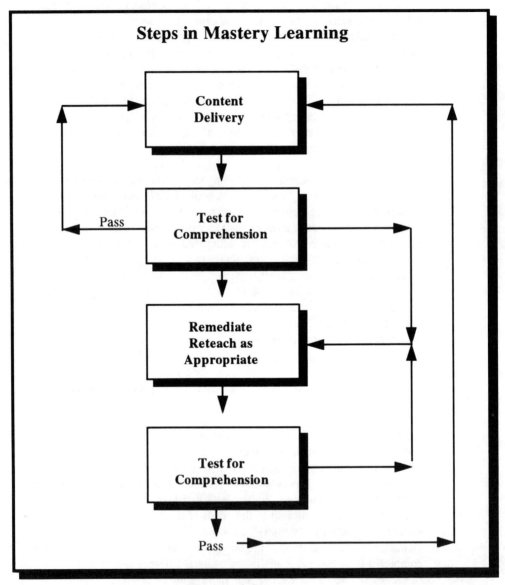

Figure 4-7

The mastery approach also maintains a record of the progress of each student assigned to the program. This record can be computer generated and incorporated into a portfolio that enables the teacher and student to monitor the student's progress. The student's file should include clearly stated objectives, suggested learning activities and assessment criteria. When remediation is necessary, the file should be revised to include remediation activities. Assessment criteria is formative and focuses upon learning progress rather than a final letter grade. The teacher should utilize criterion reference assessment to identify specific concepts and skills that the student has not yet mastered.

Classroom teachers commonly voice the concern that the mastery approach "teaches to the test." This belief is not only inaccurate but reflects a total void of understanding of effective teaching practices. The instructional supervisor should emphasize that assessment criteria for learning outcomes within all delivery systems must be based upon lesson content objectives. Otherwise assessment is arbitrary and, therefore, pointless. Curricula areas typically reflecting mastery delivery techniques include special education programs in which an individual education plan (IEP) is required for each student, and instrumental and vocal music classes, along with other performing arts.

4. Self-paced programs are designed to enable the student to work independently at a rate determined by the student. Programs of this type are available commercially or can be designed by the classroom teacher. One popular program is the reading program developed by Science Research Associates (SRA) which includes color coded, numerically ordered reading activities. The SRA instructional packets also include assessment materials for students to determine their progress. Teachers can also design packets that include objectives, individual activities and materials, and assessment criteria.

5. Contracting is utilized to gain student input into the instructional design. The student and teacher reach a consensus on lesson requirements, expected quality and quantity of work completed. Contracts can also be effectively utilized for reaching agreement concerning student behavior.

6. Learning centers are generally described as areas placed around the classroom which house information related to course content. The information can be organized for drill and practice, inquiry, problem solving, and/or manipulative activities. Learning centers also can be

utilized as resource centers for special interest activities. A third grade group of students adopts the theme "whales" for their special interest topic. The students and teacher work together to design learning centers that include information concerning types of whales, habits of whales, migratory habits of whales, and efforts to save the whales. Following the design of the learning centers, the students are permitted to utilize this information and explore each Wednesday afternoon. Such activities serve to motivate students through hands-on involvement as well as introducing new information.

The above methods for instructional delivery were provided for the supervisor of instruction to develop a general understanding of the variety of techniques available to the classroom teacher. It is important for supervisors to realize that no single delivery method is most effective and that effective teachers will employ a variety of methods to best motivate and meet the needs of their students. Supervisors should look for an assortment of methods as well as appropriateness when visiting instructional settings. Figure 4-8 describes instructional delivery methods, appropriate use, and related student behavior.

Effective Teaching Strategies

The educational supervisor is frequently placed in a supervisory setting where the subject content is not the supervisor's certified subject area. Effective teacher behavior for which the supervisor should be looking includes establishing and communicating classroom rules, procedures, and expectations related to behavior and academic performance as well as clearly delineating student responsibilities. Herman and Traymontana (1971) found that establishing specific classroom rules reduced disruptive student behavior and, therefore, allowed for more time on task. Emmer, Evertson and Anderson (1980) found that teachers perceived as good classroom managers had higher rates of instructional time on task and more positive student behavior. The visiting supervisor can determine whether the teacher has developed and communicated rules and procedures by looking to see if such are posted and clearly visible to students as well as observing the students' behavior.

It is important for students to understand the various "house-keeping" procedures such as taking attendance and submitting homework assignments. Likewise, the teacher should have the instructional materials so that time spent distributing papers is minimal. Powell and Eash (1974) found student achievement was greater when fewer instructional interruptions occurred.

Instructional Delivery Method: General Purpose and Student Learning

Delivery Type	General Purpose	More Effective	Less Effective
Expository	• To introduce facts and concepts to direct students to more abstract concepts • All subject areas when basic facts are necessary for further learning	• Older students with high levels of attention and self-discipline • For retention of facts • Student is participant	• When focus is on teacher and student is passive learner—experiences loss of motivation • Younger students and students with lower levels of attention and self-discipline

Inquiry Guided Discovery	• To encourage creativity and higher cognitive processes
	  To involve students in testing new concepts
		• All students of varying abilities	• Can be time consuming
			  Should not be used exclusively when safety is of concern, i.e., use of science lab or vocational equipment.

Computer Assisted Instruction	• To build student confidence • To increase student motivation • Allows for self-paced discovery activities	• Engages student as active learner	• Reinforcement should be timely to keep students on task • When students have a clear understanding of concepts and are able to transfer information through discussion.
Individualized Instruction	• To introduce facts and concepts at a pace which meets the needs of students	• When student range of abilities is great along with numbers of students within the classroom	• Because social interactions are limited, students can lose interest
Programmed Instruction	• To provide immediate feedback • To reinforce comprehension	• Both slower and faster learners are motivated as a result of immediate feedback	
Computer Assisted Instruction	• To provide students with a device for solving computational problems at a pace which meets the individual needs of the students • To provide students with a device for drill and practice • To provide students with a device for simulation	• To enhance memorization of facts • Will enable students to develop higher levels of cognition • Theory "hands on" activity	• If students are not "developmentally ready" for the activity
Learning Centers	• To enable students to self-pace learning experiences • To provide student method by which they can explore and discover new ideas and concepts	• All students of varying abilities • Engages student as an active learner when feed-back is provided • Especially effective when used in conjunction with cooperative learning	• When reinforcement does not occur in a timely fashion • If student becomes too isolated from others • If student does not have an appropriate understanding of background information • If content is too far above or below developmental level of student, he or she will lose interest.
Contracting	• To enable student input into their learning experiences and criteria for assessing outcomes • To enable students input into their expected behavior and criteria for assessing outcomes	• Older students concerning learning • All student concerning behavior, more effective with older students	• When involved parties are not held to accountable contract criteria • If student is too young and does not understand the concepts related to contracting
Mastery Learning	• To provide the individual student with time and a variety of methods to learn • To enable students to perform at their highest level of competence	• When teacher establishes an environment of high expectations • Teacher helps student to focus on objectives when motivated to accept responsibility • When learning of content is essential and/or performance is outcome based	• When students are not motivated and do not value the content

Figure 4-8

114 Chapter 4 *Observing Teacher Presentation of Instruction*

To assess the level of student understanding, the instructional activities for the class should begin with a review from the prior lesson with opportunities for students to ask and answer questions. While there is some literature which suggests that a single review of a previous lesson just prior to a newly introduced lesson does not increase student learning, (Wright & Nuthall, 1970), review sessions at the beginning, ending, and at various intervals throughout the lesson increase learning (Ausubel & Youssef, 1965; Good & Grouius, 1979; Rosenshine, 1983; and others). Following the review session, the teacher should present an overview of the current lesson to orient students to the upcoming topics, lesson objectives and related activities. The teacher should then review the new concepts introduced during the lesson.

Other effective teaching behavior concerns questioning strategies. Questioning strategies should reflect low order and high order questions as determined by the cognitive levels and needs of the students. The teacher will receive answers from more students by pausing briefly following each question to enable students to think while preparing their answer (Rowe, 1974). It is important to focus upon one question at a time so that students may clearly understand. Students are likely to become confused and distracted with multiple questioning techniques.

The teacher should respond to answers with the appropriate reinforcement to foster retention of accurate information. Feedback to student questions and performance is important. Although secondary students' achievement increases when they receive positive feedback, they do not need to receive it as frequently as younger children within the lower elementary grades (Pankratz, 1967; and Anderson et al., 1979). Furthermore, the method of instructional delivery influences the amount of feedback that is most effective. Students engaged in mastery or individualized instruction programs require more regular and direct feedback to progress than students within more traditional settings (Bloom, 1976).

The effective teacher will engage the students in enhancement activities and circulate among them to provide feedback and assistance as needed (Brophy & Evertson, 1976). The literature further suggests that homework improves learning and should be assigned with clearly stated directions and due dates (Goldstein, 1960; Austin, 1974). Students should begin homework during the remaining minutes of the class period to enable the teacher to assess the level of student understanding and provide assistance. Student progress evaluation should be based upon specified objectives of the lesson and criteria clearly communicated to the students.

The above teacher behavior is related directly to instruction. Other factors focus upon the teacher as an individual and includes the teacher's personality. The teacher should exhibit a friendly, caring, and businesslike nature. He or she should be knowledgeable in the subject area(s) and possess an adequate level of "general information well-roundedness." The effective teacher should be able to provide students with opportunities to transfer content related information to situations that are true to life and meaningful to the students. A third grade teacher elects to teach a unit on manatees, an endangered species. During the unit the teacher invites a marine biologist to visit the class and share pictures for the students to see. The biologist also describes career opportunities and activities related to the field of marine biology. Following the unit, the students take a field trip to a state park to view manatees in their natural environment. Later, class discussion may include a description of the manatees' natural environment, how the environment is changing, the causes of the environmental changes, and what impact the changes are likely to have upon manatees and humans. Figure 4-9 summarizes effective teaching strategies.

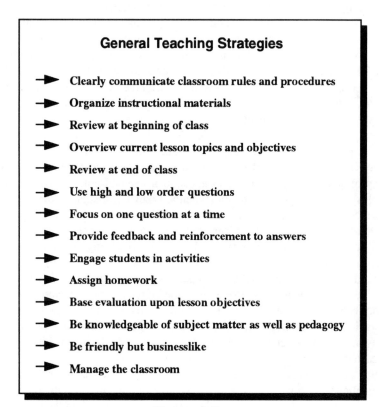

Figure 4-9

Classroom management is essential for establishing an environment conducive to learning. Marland (1975) suggested that teachers learn the names of students as well as something unique about each student as early as possible. Such teacher behavior conveys the message that the teacher is interested and willing to spend time getting to know each student. Some teachers, especially those assigned to the secondary level, voice concerns about large class sizes and the impossibility of getting to know students. Supervisors can

116 Chapter 4 *Observing Teacher Presentation of Instruction*

encourage personable teacher practices by suggesting the following. Teachers should maintain respective class listings that include a positive and brief statement about each student. On the first day of class teachers should assign students the task of submitting a one page autobiography that includes post high school education and career goals.

The importance of establishing and clearly communicating classroom rules was discussed earlier in this chapter. Once rules are established, it is necessary for teachers to enforce them with consistent and positive feedback. The supervisor concerned with classroom management and consistency of teaching strategies can review teacher discipline reports and office referrals. Students motivated and engaged in class activities are far less likely to become distracted and involved with inappropriate behavior. The effective supervisor should communicate that the first level of classroom management involves enthusiastic teacher behavior that motivates students through the excitement level of the lesson. Such teacher behavior acts as "preventive medicine" concerning student misconduct. When student behavior does not meet expectations, teachers should understand strategies that encourage student improvement.

The effective classroom teacher should consistently provide feedback and consequences for unacceptable behavior. Such management techniques should be age and situation appropriate. Younger elementary age students should not, in most cases, be held to the same rules of conduct as high school students. Likewise, a student who is late to school should not receive the same consequence as a student observed instigating a fight. It is important that teachers do not administer consequences when angry or merely to "punish." Supervisors should encourage a behavioral approach focusing upon reinforcement and motivational techniques for controlling student behavior. Kounin (1970) found that rough, angry and punitive feedback by teachers was perceived generally by students as over-zealous and, therefore, made students uncomfortable in the classroom setting. Students reported that harsh teacher behavior interfered with instruction and therefore had a negative impact upon student behavior and learning. Students, however, reported that the "rough" teacher was perceived as more capable of handling the "tougher kids." Kounin further suggested that effective teachers reflect a "with-it-ness." Teachers who are "with it." have a clear understanding of the "goings on" within the classroom and possess the skill to handle more than one situation at a time. The teacher may continue a topic discussion while walking toward and standing by a student who is otherwise not participating in the lesson.

The effective supervisor establishes a climate in which the focus of classroom management is not only to enable students to learn appropriate behavior, but to engage students in a process of higher level reasoning concerned with the selection of appropriate behavior options. Webster (1968) described discipline in terms of the three Rs: reasoning, respect and relevance. Discipline should be perceived by students as being reasonable as well as considerate and respectful. The consequences should be relative to the magnitude of the behavioral infraction. Students will respond to corrective measures more positively when the rationale is provided in a respectful manner. Furthermore, it is important that the rationale

Chapter 4 *Observing Teacher Presentation of Instruction* **117**

include examples relevant to the child's experience. A child who has grown up in an environment where food is scavenged and eaten on the street is likely to have difficulty understanding consequences for unacceptable lunch room table manners. Figure 4-10 summarizes classroom management techniques into two categories: preventive techniques and consequential techniques. For more detailed information on classroom management refer to Chapter 6.

Summary of Classroom Management Techniques	
Preventative	**Consequential**
Establish and communicate classroom rules and procedures	Consistently administer feedback and consequences
Communicate academic performance and behavior expectations	Select feedback and consequences are appropriate for the student behavior and situation
Communicate consistent feedback and consequences for student behavior and performance	Select feedback and consequences which are age-appropriate
Manage by walking around and achieving "proximity" with as many students as possible especially students who are easily distracted	Generally administer feedback and consequences so as not to interfere with the instructional momentum
Engage in activities that maintain instructional momentum. For example, take attendance while students are engaged in activity or seat work	
Learn to address more than one situation at a time. For example, begin orienting students to lesson topics while distributing materials	

Figure 4-10

Measurement and Evaluation of Student Progress

Evaluation is described as the examining and judging of processes of learning and program outcomes. Measurement differs from evaluation in that it involves a methodically structured identification of predefined outcomes or characteristics, typically expressed

118 Chapter 4 *Observing Teacher Presentation of Instruction*

quantitatively. It is important in all cases of evaluation that such not be based upon subjective information where the "mood" or personality of the evaluator has a greater influence on the outcome than the performance as it actually occurred. A written essay assignment should be evaluated for the most part on clearly defined and communicated objectives such as spelling, punctuation and grammar. Such can be expressed quantitatively and are easily understood. An essay graded solely on the basis of creativity lends itself to an evaluation that is highly subjective.

The use of portfolios as an assessment device for evaluating student and personnel performance is gaining popularity. Supervisors should be certain that the use of portfolios is not too subjective but is accompanied by clearly stated measurement and evaluation criteria.

Teachers and Student Evaluation

Teachers frequently utilize teacher-made tests which parallel the lesson content and meet the needs of the respective class members. Such tests can be in the form of multiple choice, matching, true or false, completion, and essay. Each has its advantages and disadvantages and can be administered effectively in combination with another. Teachers should recognize that students' reflect styles that are concerned with test type preferences. A student may prefer to expound upon an answer in essay form rather than be limited to a few choices.

LeFrancois (1982) suggested that there is substantial evidence which supports that students consistently do not perform better on one type of test over the other. Students who generally perform well on one type of test seemingly do well on others. Thus, teachers should, when possible, utilize a variety of test types. Figure 4-10 describes the characteristics of the respective test types along with student characteristics.

Supervisors should understand the respective test types and their use to assess evaluation practices within the classroom. It is a common practice for schools to purchase textbooks that include publisher generated test questions. While these are considered as excellent resources, classroom teachers should utilize them appropriately. When utilizing commercial test materials, the teacher should ensure that the test questions accurately measure retention of the course content and lesson objectives. Furthermore, it is critical that students are taught the subject matter represented within the test items. Supervisors should be perspicacious to practices where teachers utilize tests taken from test files five, ten or even twenty years old.

Common Test Types And Characteristics			
Type	**Advantages**	**Disadvantages**	**Best Utilized**
True - False Yes - No	• Easy to construct	• Can be ambiguous • Can reinforce incorrect information Enables guessing	• To measure recall and comprehension of facts
Multiple Choice	• Easy to score and statistically analyse • Can be constructed to measure analysis and synthesis of information	• Difficult to construct • Enables students to answer by process of elimination and unintentionally hidden clues	• To measure comprehension • To measure higher cognitive skills
Matching	• Popular with students • Can be constructed to include broad range of information	• Difficult to construct • Enables students to answer by process of elimination	• To measure comprehension by comparing and contrasting information
Short Answer Open - Ended	• Easy to construct • Adaptable to specific subject content • Minimizes guessing	• Difficult to score as more than one answer may be correct	• To measure recall of facts and specific knowledge
Fill In The Blank	• Minimizes guessing • Can be more focused and easily scored	• Difficult to score when more than one answer may be correct	• To measure recall of facts and specific knowledge
Essay	• Easy to construct • Enables students to demonstrate a broad knowledge base	• Scoring is quite time consuming • Scoring can be ambiguous • Coverage of subject content is limited • Test reliability is low	• To measure application and higher cognitive skills

Figure 4-11

Teachers and supervisors should recognize the influence of teacher behavior upon student assessment. Teachers should serve as "cheerleaders" by assuring students they are capable of performing skillfully. Gorden and Durea (1948) and Osler (1954) found that when

120 Chapter 4 *Observing Teacher Presentation of Instruction*

test examiners made remarks perceived by students as discouraging, student test performance was significantly reduced. Teachers should emphasize topics deemed to be important enough to be tested and then allow sufficient time for students to review and practice. Students should be provided with strategies for studying, such as highlighting important information, outlining and paraphrasing. Note and test taking skills significantly improve student performance (Carrier & Titus, 1981).

Supervisors should note whether the teacher establishes a classroom environment conducive to learning. It is appropriate for the classroom environment to include visual displays such as cut outs, pictures, posters, maps, and aquariums, enhancing the subject content. Visual aides to learning along with other common diversions such as hallway traffic, the smell of lunch cooking, or a visitor entering the room typically do not interfere with the performance of secondary students. However, such is not the case for elementary age students. Trentham (1975) found that when taking exams, sixth grade students were disturbed when exposed to such distractions as an alarm bell, classroom visitors, a radio playing the world series, and a blinking light. These distractions were found to negatively influence the student's test performance.

The teacher should identify and respect students who are likely to experience test anxiety. Tests should be administered in a non-threatening manner and for the purposes of assessing student comprehension and the effectiveness of instruction. Tests should not be utilized for discipline purposes. In fact, test results can be significantly influenced by a student's experience prior to an examination. A student who is late to class, injured on the playground or in the principal's office prior to a test is likely to not perform as well as he or she would otherwise.

Test anxious students generally perform worse when the "stakes are higher." Test anxiety will more greatly influence an anxious high school senior required to pass a state board examination to graduate, than the same student engaged in taking a test perceived to be not of such great importance. It is believed that elementary age girls reflect greater test anxiety than their male counterparts. However, male students became more anxious than female students following anxiety-producing test instructions, (Bauer, 1975). African-American students experience significantly greater test anxiety when engaged in standardized testing such as the Comprehensive Test of Basic Skills (CTBS) (Clawson et al., 1975).

The primary focus of creating an appropriate testing and learning environment is to enable the student to perform in a manner that accurately reflects the student's level of knowledge and ability. However, a threatening environment or one where students generally do not feel comfortable is a breeding ground for insupportable pressure which can and is likely to lead to cheating. Supervisors should closely monitor teacher and organizational behavior that is not only counter-productive to the learning of subject content, but also counter productive to the integrity of the over-all purpose of education. Studies indicate that situational factors within schools such as the teacher leaving the room, school climate, and emotional attitude within the respective classroom, have a significantly greater influence upon cheating than behavioral characteristics of the students (McQueen, 1957; Rogosen, 1951). Teaching style and the personality of the teacher were found to influence the frequency of cheating. Specifically, teachers who were disrespectful, authoritarian and openly perceived students as inferior experienced more occurrences of cheating (Shirk and Hoffman, 1961).

Teacher behavior related to measurement and evaluation of student performance is concerned with feedback. The literature suggests that feedback, in the form of specific verbal and written comments, is the most effective and should occur no sooner than 24 hours following the examination (Surber & Anderson, 1975). It is better for the teacher to return and review an exam the following day than soon after the exam is taken. Furthermore, learning is increased when teachers provide written comments specific to the incorrectly answered test item (Page, 1958). Effective teachers should recognize that students show greater understanding of material when taking in-class examinations as compared to the take-home exam (Marsh, 1980).

Supervisors should monitor the methods by which teachers grade exams and provide feedback to students. The use of electronically graded systems may appear to make life easier for the classroom teacher. However, the impact of this form of scoring upon feedback and learning is likely to be less productive over a long period of time. The effective supervisor should be knowledgeable as well as creative in assisting teachers with strategies for providing feedback to students that will enhance learning.

One effective strategy is as follows. After returning a test to students, rather than providing the answers to the test questions, assign students to cooperative learning groups to search in a "scavenger hunt" style for unanswered or incorrectly answered test questions. Following group discussions, students are given the option to retake items originally missed with a brief explanation of the new answer. To receive additional credit, students must return their new paper with a parent signature. This method is effective in several ways. First, it motivates students to take control of the learning process. Second, students are motivated while engaged in group discussion and activities. Third, the discovery method opens avenues for higher level learning and discussion. Finally, students are provided an attainable opportunity to raise their test grade and involve their parents with their school progress. Figure 4-12 provides a summary of effective teaching practices concerning measurement and evaluation of student performance.

122 Chapter 4 *Observing Teacher Presentation of Instruction*

Effective Teaching Practices for Evaluating Student Performance

➤ Establish and communicate specific goals and predefined criteria

➤ Encourage students by assuring them that they are capable of doing well

➤ Provide review, practice, and study time

➤ Create a learning environment free of distractions

➤ Provide students with note taking strategies and highlight information

  of particular importance

➤ Recognize test anxious students and provide a variety of evaluation methods

➤ Treat students with respect and establish a caring environment. Try to

  alleviate anxiety and feelings which lead to cheating

➤ Provide in a timely fashion positive feedback and specific written comments

  following an examination or graded assignment to provide for greatest

  retention

Figure 4-12

Effective teachers communicate to supervisors what they believe to be the various purposes of testing. One teacher may describe the purpose of testing to be to assess the level of student understanding regarding certain information. Another teacher may view testing as an integral part of the learning process, used in a formative way to further learning and help determine future teaching strategies. Others may see the purpose of testing only as a summative process to assign letter grades. Whatever the teacher perceives as the purpose of the testing process will have some influence upon how the teacher interprets and utilizes the test results.

Understanding Student Differences

Expectations can result in a self-fulfilling prophecy. R. Rosenthal and L. Jacobson (1968) studied the influence of teacher expectations upon students attending a lower middle class school. Teachers were informed before administering a test that lower achieving students frequently reflect signs of significantly increased achievement. The following fall, teachers were informed of the students who, during the previous year, showed bursts in

Chapter 4 *Observing Teacher Presentation of Instruction* **123**

achievement. However, the students were actually randomly selected from the general school population. The only difference between the selected group and the other students was the teacher's understanding of which students had shown bursts of achievement. Rosenthal and Jacobson found that the students whom the teachers thought were the "achievers" increased not only in general performance, but in intellectual ability as well. While the Rosenthal and Jacobson study has been criticized by some, educators recognize the potential for teacher behavior and expectations to influence the student's performance level.

Other issues concerning student differences include questions about culturally biased tests, curricula and teacher behavior inhibiting student creativity and expression. It is unfortunate when educators unknowingly exhibit bias. It is a tragedy when such is a result of attitude. One way of assessing student and teacher attitude is for supervisors to administer the Pupil Control Ideology Scale (PCI) developed by Donald Willower, Terry Eidell and Wayne Hoy (1967). The (PCI) assesses the attitudes of teachers and administrators toward students on a continuum from rigidly controlled to humanistic. Turner and Denny (1969) found that teachers who exhibit more humanistic behavior are more likely to encourage creativity in their students. Teachers should recognize the importance of promoting creativity rather than stifling students into a world of uniformity. Likewise supervisors should encourage creativity and autonomy in their teachers so as not to stifle the practices recognized to be creative and effective teaching. Guy Lefrancois (1982) described the school which "promotes ordinariness."

*Creativity is that special quality in students that **other** teachers in **other** classrooms stifle. **Other** teachers are rigid, rule-bound, and authoritarian. They reward students for sitting properly in well-aligned, straight-rowed desks, with their feet firmly on the floor and their heads some considerable distance below the clouds. They stifle creativity by insisting on excessive conformity to arbitrary regulations, by giving high grades for neat, correct, unimaginative solutions to problems, executed and reported in exactly the prescribed manner, and by refusing to admire the mistaken gropings of a child reaching toward the unknown. They stifle creativity by forbidding spontaneity and rewarding mediocrity. They crush the joyful inquisitiveness of young children by not hearing or not answering their questions. They are dry, sober, humorless keepers of the culture of their ancestors. Their generation is of another age. Those are **other** teachers in **other** classrooms. Today's teacher is very different from the teacher described above. (Lefrancois, 1982, p. 274)*

Teachers should recognize that because students have different strengths and learning styles, they should tailor instruction to accommodate these. Learning styles are described in many ways. Cornett (1983) defined them as the overall patterns that provide direction to learning and teaching. Generally, there is no correct way to learn or teach. However, there are styles proven to be more effective during certain circumstances and with certain learning personalities. Some literature delineates learning styles into three areas: cognitive, affective and physiological. It further suggests that learners reflect tendencies

124 Chapter 4 *Observing Teacher Presentation of Instruction*

toward the process by which they learn. Messick (1976) described the cognitive learning style as the way a person perceives, remembers, and solves problems and focuses upon "how I learn" rather than "what I learn." Dunn and Dunn (1978) described the affective learning approach as emotional characteristics such as learner locus of control and how the learner interacts with peers during the learning process. The Physiological approach is based upon how the learner reacts to the physical environment. That may be influenced by how the learner relates to sex differences and the importance of nutrition and physical stature, (Dunn & Dunn 1978).

Howard Gardner (1983) broadened the scope of intelligence to include a new paradigm for recognizing student learning differences and delineated seven categories. The categories include the following: logical and mathematical intelligence, verbal and linguistic intelligence, spatial intelligence, musical intelligence, bodily and kinesthetic intelligence, interpersonal intelligence, and intrapersonal intelligence. Gardner suggests that each of us possesses all of these intelligences but all are not developed in the same manner and therefore are not utilized equally effectively.

Armstrong (1994) suggested that typically, one or two intelligences are preferred, thus receiving the most attention and, therefore, becoming more fully developed. The capacity to learn at all levels, however, is possible. Educators should recognize the various stimuli likely to influence the development of the above areas of intelligence. Culture, socioeconomic status, and even student placement into special programs, such as special education, play important roles in educators' perceptions of the development of student intelligences. Armstrong (1994) stated that schools and society reinforce certain types of intelligence by the way a child is labeled as gifted, learning disabled, or at risk. Furthermore, selected criteria for determining intelligence, student placement and the instruments selected for measuring are known to be generally limited and, often times, biased.

Butler (1988) separated learners into observers and doers. He notes that the observers must refine their reflective gifts and further develop their courage to experiment. The doers must refine their experimental gifts in order to develop patience and the talent of reflection.

Whittrock (1990) delineated learning styles into the following four categories.

1) The imaginative learners utilize listening and the sharing of ideas to learn. They strive for harmony and sometimes reflect difficulty in making decisions because they are concerned for all sides. They perceive school as too structured and instruction fragmented.

2) The analytical learners develop theories by integrating what they know with what they observe. They learn by thinking through ideas and are concerned with facts and details. They find school well suited to their needs and are avid readers. But, they enjoy personal time and can appear aloof and cool at times.

3) The common sense learners integrate theory and practice and are pragmatic. They are skill oriented and prefer to seek solutions for themselves by experimenting and tinkering. They find school frustrating and reflect a need to always know how knowledge is of good use to them.

4) The dynamic learners learn by trial and error. They are enthusiastic when trying new things and highly adaptable to change. They are risk takers, pushy at times and usually emerge as the group leader. They are frequently frustrated with school because they prefer to pursue their interest in more creative ways.

Understanding Teacher Differences

Bruce Tuckman (1976) described many characteristics of the teacher in the Tuckman Teacher Feedback Form. Some of those characteristics include patience, warmth, gentleness, fairness, a tendency to experiment, imagination, outgoingness, dominance, assertiveness and adventurousness. Kiersey and Bates (1984) utilize temperament to describe various teaching styles. Figure 4-12 summarizes characteristics of teaching styles into what the teacher values, favorite teaching areas, and preferred teaching techniques.

4-13

The True Colors Reference Guide, developed by Don Lowry (1987), divides teaching styles into four groups. The groups generally represent styles which range from highly structured to spontaneous, democratic to autocratic, and traditional and textbook based instruction to exploratory and critical thinking. Figure 4-13 describes the four models of teaching styles and compares them to student learning expectations.

126 Chapter 4 *Observing Teacher Presentation of Instruction*

				Teaching in Style-Summary			
Index Log (see Fig. 2-4)	**Prime Value in Education**	**% of Teachers and Length of Service**	**Favored Teaching Areas**		**Favored Instructional Techniques**	
SPs	Growth of Spontaneity and Freedom	4% Short stay in teaching	Arts, Crafts, Sports	Drama, Music, Recreation	Projects, Contests, Games	Demon-strations, Shows
SJs	Growth of Responsibility and Utility	56% Long stay in teaching	Agriculture, Clerical, Business, Sports, Social Sciences	Political Science Homemaking, History, Geography	Recitation, Drill, Composition	Tests/ Quizzes, Demon-strations
NTs	Growth of Knowledge and Skills	8% Medium stay in teaching	Philosophy, Science, Technology	Communications, Mathematics, Linguistics	Lectures, tests, Compositions	Projects, Reports
NFs	Growth of Identity and Integrity	32% Long stay in teaching	Humanities, Social Sciences, Theater, Music	Foreign Languages, Speech, Theology	Group Projects, Interaction\ Discussion	Shows, Simu-lations, Games

Key:
SPs recognize creativity and process rather than product
SJs recognize accuracy and is product oriented
NTs Value appreciation for intelligence and capabilities rather than comments of a personal nature
NFs Value appreciation which is personal and desires constant feedback which recognizes feelings and ideas

(Kiersey, D. & Bates, M. *Please understand me: Character and temperament types* (4th ed.), 1984, page 166. Reprinted by permission Prometheus Nemesis Book Co., Amhurst, NY)

Figure 4-13

Implications for Supervision

An abundance of literature supports the premise that the success of the school is related to the manner by which it is supervised. The successes by which today's schools are measured includes student academic performance and how well the student grows to become a productive citizen in a global society. To influence the quality of instruction, recommendations should be drawn from actual teacher behavior observed by a supervisor who is knowledgeable about teaching methodology, strategies, teaching and learning styles and various models of instruction. The Florida Department of Education Office of Teacher Education developed a tool for assessing teacher performance. The Florida Performance

Chapter 4 *Observing Teacher Presentation of Instruction* **127**

Measurement System (FPMS) (1982) delineates teaching performance into six domains which include planning, management of student conduct, organization of instruction, presentation of subject matter, communication, and evaluation of achievement. Each domain is further divided into specified concepts recognized to be effective teaching practices. Figure 4-14 describes the various domains and concepts contained within the Florida performance measurement model.

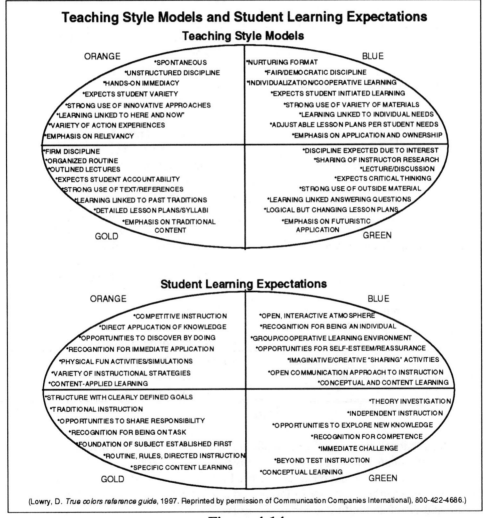

Figure 4-14

128 Chapter 4 *Observing Teacher Presentation of Instruction*

Domains and Concepts within the Florida Performance Measurement System	
Domain	**Basic Concepts**
Planning	• Content coverage • Utilization of instructional materials • Activity structure • Goal focusing • Diagnosis of learner
Management of Student Conduct	• Rule explication and monitoring • Teacher "with-it-ness" • Quality of desist • Group alert • Movement slow-down • Effective praise
Instructional Organization and Development	• Efficient use of time • Review of subject matter • Lesson development • Teacher treatment of student talk • Teacher academic feedback • Management of seat-work and home-work
Presentation of Subject Matter	• Presentation of conceptual knowledge • Presentation of law-like knowledge • Presentation of academic rules • Presentation of value knowledge
Communication	• Control of discourse • Emphasis • Teacher speech • Teacher body language
Evaluation of Achievement	• Preparing for testing • Test administration • Formative feedback

Figure 4-15

Instructional supervisors are formally trained to administer this instrument for both formative and summative purposes. The instructional supervisor conducts a formal observation and records actual observed teacher behavior on a FPMS screening instrument sheet. It is recognized that this type of formalized assessment system is highly mechanical in structure and therefore limiting in terms of supervisory freedom. The scientific nature of it, however, lends itself to concrete data that is neither arbitrary nor capricious and can be effective for establishing credible base-line data for future professional growth and clinical needs.

Supervisors should understand that:
- Their own beliefs and personalities filter their perceptions.
- Creativity is often an energy in beginning teachers that is stifled by autocratic, and inflexible supervisors. The creativity of experienced teachers may also be stifled.
- Rewarding teachers for status-quo, for not "rocking the boat," for being quiet, for insisting on arbitrary and pedagogically meaningless regulations, for mediocrity, and for not challenging the system inhibits creativity.
- Being a humorless keeper of the culture of one's teaching predecessors may crush the joyful enthusiasm of the young adult proud to be entering the field of education.

Principles and Practices for Success

- Understand the approaches and categories common to the general practice of effective teaching.
- Recognize the eight elements for supervising instruction.
- Understand the influence of platforms upon instruction and supervision.
- Recognize the various performance components within the model of teaching.
- Understand the methodology and strategies common to the general practice of effective teaching.
- Identify the various uses of measurement and evaluation.
- Understand the relationship of the various models of intellegence to the practice of teaching.
- Understand the relationship of the models of teaching styles to student performance.
- Identify supervisory practices that best meet the needs of the respective teaching styles.
- Identify and develop a style of supervision that is most effective for improving the quality of instruction.

Summary

This chapter presented the characteristics of teacher presentation of instruction. The artistic and scientific approaches to teaching were discussed along with a model for supervising instruction. The various components of the teaching model were described as planning, developing goals and objectives, methodology and delivery systems, effective strategies and assessment practices. The chapter emphasized the need for effective supervision to be based upon a scientific knowledge base supportive of effective teaching

130 Chapter 4 *Observing Teacher Presentation of Instruction*

practices. An overview of teacher and student personality types was provided along with characteristics of teaching and learning styles to provide essential information for improving the quality of instruction. The need for both highly structured and open models of supervision was suggested. The chapter concluded with words of caution and suggestions for selecting a style for supervising instruction that establishes a learning environment that meets the individual needs of students as well as the individual needs and professional growth of teachers.

Case Problem: *Judy Timmons*

Judy Timmons is a high school business education teacher in a metropolitan school district. John Adams High School has an enrollment of 2200 students with 42% minorities. Judy has successfully taught for 22 years, beginning as a junior high school special education teacher. She has taught high school typing, notehand, and business math for the last seven years. Many of Judy's students are planning to enter vocational training and careers immediately following graduation. Judy has arranged for you to visit and conduct one of two required annual observations during the second period Typing 1 class. At the beginning of class Judy presents an overview of the day's activities with detailed instructions. Next, she provides students with practice time and circulates around the front half of the classroom adjacent to her desk to answer questions. Three male special education students are seated across the back of the room. During the lecture part of the lesson, two of the students are at times off task and one is disassembling the typewriter. On four occasions two of the young men raise their hands to participate in class discussion and go without notice. The bell to end the class rings and the students leave for their next class. Judy notices the typewriter in several pieces and expresses her displeasure toward having so many exceptional education students in one class period. She complains that her typing classes are used by the guidance department as dumping grounds.

1. What are the issues concerning the classroom learning environment?

2. What suggestions can you provide to Mrs. Timmons about her selected instructional delivery methods and teaching strategies?

3. What is Judy's teaching style and how does it relate to the student learning styles within the class?

4. What information would you share with Judy to improve the overall quality of instruction within her 2nd period class and how would you communicate your expectations related to such?

References

Anderson, L., Evertson, C., & Brophy, J. (1979). An experimental study in first grade reading groups. *Elementary School Journal, 79,* 193-223.

Armstrong, T. (1994). *Multiple intelligences in the classroom.* Alexandria, VA: Association for Supervision and Curriculum Development.

Austin, J. D. (1974). *Homework research in mathematics, 1900-1974.* Paper presented at the 1974 annual Georgia Mathematics Education Conference, Rock Eagle, GA.

Ausubel, D. P. (1963). *The psychology of meaningful verbal learning.* New York: Grune & Stratton.

Ausubel, D. P., & Youssef, M. (1965). The effect of spaced repetition on meaningful retention. *Journal of General Psychology, 73,* 147-150.

Bachman, J. D., Smith, C. G., & Slesinger, J. A. (1968). Control, performance and satisfaction: An analysis of structural and individual effects. *Journal of Personality and Social Psychology, 4,* 127-136.

Bauer, D. (1975). The effects of instructions, anxiety and locus of control on intelligence test scores. *Measurement and Evaluation in Guidance, 8,* 12-19.

Bloom, B. S. (1956). *Taxonomy of educational objectives - Handbook 1: Cognitive domain.* New York: David McKay Company.

Bloom, B. S. (1976). *Human characteristics and school learning.* New York: McGraw Hill.

Bloom, B., Englehart, M., Hill, W., Furst, G., & Krathwohl, D. (1968). *Taxonomy of educational objectives, the classification of educational goals - Handbook I: Affective domain.* New York: David McKay Company.

Brophy, F., & Evertson, C. (1976). *Learning from teaching: A developmental perspective.* Boston, MA: Allyn and Bacon.

Bruner, J. S. (1961). The act of discovery. *Harvard Education Review,* pp. 21-32.

Butler, K. A. (1988). Learning styles are the blueprints for building student strengths. *Learning,* pp. 30-38.

132 Chapter 4 *Observing Teacher Presentation of Instruction*

Carrier, C. A., & Titus, A. (1981). Effects of note taking and test made expectations on learning from lectures. *American Educational Research Journal, 18*, 385-397.

Clawson, T. W., Firment, C. K., & Trower, T. L. (1981). Test anxiety: Another origin for racial bias in standardized testing. *Measurement and Evaluation in Guidance, 13*, 210-215.

Cornett, C. (1983). *What you should know about teaching and learning styles.* Bloomington, IN: Phi Delta Kappan Educational Foundation.

Dunn, R., & Dunn, K. (1978). *Teaching students through their individual learning styles: a practical approach.* Reston, VA: Reston Publishing Company, Inc.

Emmer, E. T., Evertson, C. M., Anderson, L. M. (1980). Effective classroom management at the beginning of the school year. *Elementary School Journal, 80*, 219-231.

Gardner, H. (1983). *Frames of mind: The theories of multiple intelligences.* New York: Basic Books.

Goldstein, A. (1960). Does homework help? A review of research. *Elementary School Journal, 1*, 212-224.

Good, T., & Grouius, D. A. (1979). The Missouri mathematics effectiveness project: An experimental study in fourth-grade classrooms. *Journal of Educational Psychology, 74*, 355-362.

Gorden, L. V., & Durea, M. A. (1948). The effect of discouragement on the revised Stanford-Binet Scale. *Journal of Genetic Psychology, 73*, 201-207.

Harris, B. (1963). *Supervisory behavior in education.* Englewood Cliffs, NJ: Prentice Hall.

Harrow, A. J. (1971). *A taxonomy of the psychomotor domain.* New York: David McKay.

Herman, S. F., & Traymontana, J. (1971). Instructions and group versus individual reinforcement in modifying disruptive group behavior. *Journal of Applied Behavior Analysis, 4*, 113-119.

Hornstein, H. A. (1968). Influence and satisfaction in organizations: A replication. *Sociology of Education, 41*(4), 389.

Kiersey, D., & Bates, M. (1984). *Please understand me: Character and temperament types* (4th ed.). Del Mar, CA: Prometheus Nemesis Book Company.

Kounin, J. S. (1970). *Discipline and group management in classrooms.* New York: Holt, Rinehart and Winston.

Krathwahl, D., Bloom, B., & Masia, B. (1967). *Taxonomy of educational objectives, the classification of educational goals - Handbook II: Affective domain.* New York: David McKay.

Lefrancois, G. R. (1982). *Psychology for teaching.* Belmont, CA: Wadsworth Publishing Company.

Lowry, D. (1987). *True colors reference guide.* Laguna Beach, CA: Communication Companies International.

Marland, M. (1975). *The craft of the classroom: A survival guide to classroom management in the secondary school.* London: Heinemann Educational Books.

Marsh, R. (1980). Should we discontinue classroom tests? An experimental study. *High School Journal, 63,* 288-292.

McQueen, R. (1957). Examination deception as a function of residual background and immediate stimulus factors. *Journal of Personality, 25,* 643-650.

Messick, S. (1976). *Individuality in learning.* San Francisco: Jossey-Bass.

Office of Teacher Education, Certification and Inservice Staff Development. (1982). *Domains: Concepts and Indicators of Effective Teaching: Florida Performance Measurement System.* Florida Department of Education, Tallahassee, Florida.

Osler, S. F. (1954). Intellectual performance as a function of two types of psychological stress. *Journal of Experimental Psychology, 47,* 115-121.

Page, E. B. (1958). Teacher comments and student performance: A seventy-four classroom experiment in school motivation. *Journal of Educational Psychology, 49,* 173-181

Pankratz, R. S. (1967). Verbal interaction patterns in the classrooms of selected physics teachers. In E. J. Amidon & J. B. Hough (Eds.), *Interaction analysis: Theory, research and application.* Reading, PA: Addison Wesley.

Piaget, J. (1961, March). The stages of the intellectual development of the child. *Bulletin of the Nennunger School of Psychiatry.*

134 Chapter 4 *Observing Teacher Presentation of Instruction*

Powell, D., & Eash, M. (1974). Secondary school cases. In H. Walberg (Ed.), *Evaluating educational performance* (pp. 277-293). Berkeley, CA: McCutchan.

Rogosen, H. (1951). What about "cheating" on examinations and honesty? *School and Society, 74*, 402-403.

Rosenshine, B. (1983). Teaching functions in instructional programs. *The Elementary School Journal, 38*(4), 335-353.

Rosenthal, R. & Jacobson, L. (1968). *Pygmalian in the classroom: teacher expectations and pupils' intellectual development.* New York: Holt, Rinehart & Winston.

Rowe, M. B. (1974). Wait time and rewards as instructional variables, their influence on language, logic and fate control: Part one - Wait time. *Journal of Research in Science Teaching, 11*, 81-94.

Sergiovanni, T. J., & Starratt, R. J. (1988). *Supervision: Human perspectives (4th ed.).* New York: McGraw Hill.

Sergiovanni, T. J., & Starratt, R. J. (1993). *Supervision: A redefinition (5th ed.).* New York: McGraw Hill.

Shirk, E., & Hoffman, R. W. (1961). The academic setting of the dishonest student. *Improving College and University Teaching, 9*, 130-134.

Surber, J. R., & Anderson, R. C. (1975). Delay-retention effect in natural classroom settings. *Journal of Educational Psychology, 67*, 170-173.

Trentham, L. L. (1975). The effect of distractions on sixth-grade students in a testing situation. *Journal of Education Measurement, 12*, 13-18.

Tuckman, B. W. (1976, January). Feedback and the change process. *Kappan*, pp. 341-344.

Turner, R. L. & Denny, D. A. (1969). Teacher characteristics, teacher behavior, and changes in pupil creativity. *The Elementary School Journal*, February, 265-270.

U.S. Department of Education. (1991). *America 2000: An education strategy.* Washington, D.C.: Author.

Webster, S. W. (1968). *Discipline in the classroom: Basic principles and problems.* New York: Chandler.

Whittrock, M. C. (1990). Teaching for the two-sided mind. *Learning and Instruction*, pp. 102-119.

Willower, D. J., Eidell, T. I., & Hoy, W. K. (1967). *The school and pupil control ideology. Pennsylvania State University Studies No. 24.* State College: Pennsylvania State University.

Wright, C. J., & Nuthall, G. (1970). Relationships between teacher behavior and pupil achievement in three experimental elementary science classes. *American Educational Research Journal, 7,* 477-492.

Chapter 5

HELPING TEACHERS WITH STUDENT EVALUATION
Georgia J. Kosmoski

The Need for Student Assessment

Schools entering the 21st century find they exist in a social and political climate which demands positive and ever-improving student performance. Accountability is a major component of today's education. Public concern for retention and dropout rates, achievement scores, and employability serves as a driving force for school improvement and strategic planning. Emphasis on improvement fosters a greater need for quality and measurable student assessment. Educators, particularly instructional supervisors, must become familiar with the proven forms of assessment and possible future initiatives.

Reynolds (1992) reviewed the literature and concluded that teachers are expected to possess the knowledge of how to assess student learning using various instruments and have the ability to adapt instruction to accommodate the assessment results. She further suggests that the ability to use various assessment strategies measures not only student performance but also professional standards and classroom instruction.

Questions answer after studying this chapter

✔ Why do schools need quality assessment?
✔ What are some of the emerging trends in national assessment?
✔ What three criteria are used to judge test quality?
✔ What three standard methods are used to determine test reliability?
✔ What factors are used to determine test validity?
✔ What characteristics identify test usability?
✔ How do standardized and nonstandardized tests differ?
✔ What are the most commonly used types of norm-reference and criterion-reference tests?
✔ What are the characteristics of norm-reference and criterion-reference tests?
✔ How are scores on norm-reference tests reported?
✔ What are the five major differences between norm-reference and criterion-reference tests?
✔ Which five factors are considered when selecting essay or short-answer tests?
✔ What is performance assessment?
✔ What supervision practices improve test administration?
✔ When returning tests, what teaching strategies increase student test performance?
✔ What pertinent information on test anxiety should supervisors possess?
✔ What supervision practices improve test conditions?
✔ How should a supervisor use technology to facilitate record keeping and use of information?
✔ How does quality testing improve special services?

-137-

138 Chapter 5 *Helping Teachers with Student Evaluation*

Judith Little (1993) sums up the urgency for supervisors and teachers to become proficient in quality assessment practices when she argues that educators face major reforms in the types and use of student assessment. Expanded and more open-ended standardized, alternative, and performance-based testing require a new understanding of testing purposes, the examinations, and additional clinical skills.

National Assessment Initiatives

National assessment initiatives worthy of consideration by supervisors and teachers include newly created open-ended national standardized tests, locally designed criterion-referenced classroom tests, and *performance testing* where students demonstrate competence through projects and portfolios.

Several efforts have been launched to transform the way pupil learning is assessed by moving from the standardized test to the performance-based assessment predicated upon materials produced for projects and portfolios. One effort is the New Standards Project (NPS) funded by the Pew Memorial Trust and the Mac Arthur Foundation in Rochester, Philadelphia, and Chicago. NPS is charged with developing a national consensus for educational assessments. Students throughout the country would be assessed using the same instruments in five core subject areas. These proposed examinations would carry great importance or *high stakes* and would be compatible with nationally accepted curriculum standards (Odden, 1995).

A second national testing initiative is the National Assessment of Educational Progress (NAEP). Since the 1970s, NAEP has conducted national student achievement assessments in core subject areas (National Center for Educational Statistics, 1993a and 1993b; Mullis, Owen, & Phillips, 1990). NAEP is overseen and funded by the U.S. Department of Education. Using national samples and three year updates, NAEP has identified changes in student achievement in subjects like foreign language and science. Key members of professional curriculum associations worked to develop the NAEP tests. In 1990, NAEP provided state-by-state comparisons of mathematics achievement for eighth grade students. In 1992, achievement comparisons were provided for eighth grade reading and mathematics and fourth grade mathematics. In 1994, science was added and three grade levels were assessed in reading, mathematics, and science (Odden, 1995). Increasing state-comparison data will greatly influence the direction of state and national curriculum and assessment practices.

Supervisors must work diligently to remain informed of these national initiatives. Current trends will undoubtedly affect the course of assessment in the local district and within the school building. Teachers will look for guidance and support from their instructional leader and supervisor. Questions which supervisors must consider are:

- How does one determine the quality of any test?
- What types of tests are useful for our teachers and students?
- What are the purposes of current and future tests?
- How does one interpret and use test data?

Test Criteria: Reliability, Validity, and Usability

The quality of a test is judged by three major criteria: *reliability, validity,* and *usability.* A test is considered reliable if it can provide consistent results. When a reliable test is repeated by the same students over a short time or when two forms of a reliable test are administered to the same students, the results obtained will be similar. Reliable tests are predictable, consistent, stable, and dependable. Validity refers to the truth or accuracy of the test or measurement. Validity is the accuracy of the test, the test measures what it is supposed to measure, and the results are true. Conversely, an invalid test does not measure what it should. Usability refers to appropriateness and ease of use.

Reliability

Test reliability can be computed and expressed numerically. A reliability coefficient of .80 or higher indicates high reliability, .40 to .79 fair reliability, and less than .40 low reliability (Kerlinger, 1986). Standardized tests generally report an overall reliability coefficient for each content test and coefficients for each subtest within the content area. For third grade students the Stanford Achievement Tests for Reading might report an overall reliability coefficient of .96 with a reading comprehension subtest coefficient of .95 and a reading vocabulary subtest coefficient of .97.

There are three standard methods for determining test reliability: *test-retest, parallel forms,* and the *split-half* reliability method. Anne Anastasi (1991) explained that in the test-retest method, a test is administered to the same students twice, usually within a short time (between 10 and 30 days). The higher the correlation between the two test results the higher the reliability. In the *parallel forms method,* two forms of the same test are given to the same students. The correlation between test results provides the measure of reliability (Nunnally, 1982). The third method of determining reliability is the split-half method. A test is split into equal or nearly equal halves (often odd/even items), and each half or subtest is used as a separate test when statistically determining the reliability of individual items (Smith, 1985; Ornstein, 1995).

140 Chapter 5 *Helping Teachers with Student Evaluation*

Validity

There are several different types of validity. The four most commonly used types of validity applicable to the public schools are content, construct, criterion, and predictive.

Content Validity. Content validity is probably the most important form of validity. It indicates to what extent the test items adequately reflect the specific content of the subject being tested. Simply stated, the test reflects what is taught. The Reading Subtests for the Iowa Test of Basic Skills tests reading vocabulary and comprehension.

Construct Validity. Construct validity indicates the extent to which the test measures the *construct* or qualities it is intended to measure. Examples of construct validity would include a reading aptitude test that measures reading ability, an IQ test that measures general intelligence, and a general science examination that measures scientific aptitude.

Criterion Validity. Criterion validity measures the extent to which a particular test correlates with a test already proven valid. If results of the two tests correlate highly, the previously unproven test is considered to have criterion validity. *What I Think About Myself,* a new and previously unproven self-esteem assessment for young children, has a strong correlation with the highly valid *Piers-Harris Children's Self-concept Scale.* What I Think About Myself is, therefore, considered to have criterion validity (Kosmoski, Pollack, & Estep, 1994).

Predictive Validity. Predictive validity is the extent to which a given test can predict future performance. The Graduate Record Examination (GRE) is an aptitude test with high predictive validity in measuring success in graduate school (Vockell, 1983; Kerlinger, 1986; Ornstein, 1995).

Usability

Tests are considered usable if they are easy for the student to understand, easily administered and scored, cost acceptable, and appropriate for conditions and degree of difficulty. These criteria should be examined before a district, school, or classroom teacher selects any given test (Kirkpatrick & Lewis, 1995; Ornstein, 1995).

Supervisors have a responsibility to monitor the selection and use of tests to ensure their quality. They must share the importance of these criteria with the faculty and champion careful selection and use. An overview of the criteria for selecting tests and the characteristics of these criteria are in Figure 5-1.

Characteristics of Test Selection Criteria		
Reliability	**Validity**	**Usability**
• Determine reliability using test-retest, parallel forms, and split-half methods • Insures the test is predictable, consistent, stable, and dependable • Using statistical analysis may be computed and expressed numerically	• Identified forms include content, construct, criterion, and predicton • Insures the test measures what it was intended to measure • Relies on level of reliability	• Easy for students to understand • Easily administered and scored • Cost acceptable • Appropriate to conditions and situation • Appropriate level of difficulty

Figure 5-1

Types of Tests

For purposes of accountability, today's students are given a variety of tests and test batteries. These tests are used for diagnostic, formative, and summative purposes. Supervisors often act as human resources for their staff when it comes to interpreting and understanding test results. Astute supervisors can increase the value of testing by helping teachers to understand and interpret results both for individual students and class groups. Supervisors may use test results to identify school and district trends, strengths, and weaknesses. To accomplish these goals, supervisors must be well informed about the various types, intent, and interpretation of tests.

Standardized and Nonstandardized Tests

All tests can be categorized as either *standardized* or *nonstandardized*. A standardized test is a measurement, tool, or instrument, that includes a set of items that are administered and measured with uniform standards. These tests are piloted with representative populations to gain normative data. Normative data is useful in interpreting individual scores and in ranking individual test scores within a comparative population. Scores are reported in a multitude of forms such as stanines, percentiles, bands, normal curve equivalencies, and anticipated normal curve equivalencies. Most standardized tests are produced by testing corporations, universities, and text book companies (Oliva, 1993; Ornstein, 1995).

142 Chapter 5 *Helping Teachers with Student Evaluation*

Standardized Tests. For "regular education" students, the three most commonly used standardized tests are the achievement test, intelligence test, and the aptitude test. Often added for special education placement is a fourth type of standardized test, the personality test.

Achievement Tests. Achievement tests are standardized tests that measure achievement or level of understanding in specific content or performance areas. Some of the most commonly used achievement tests are:

1. *General or Survey Achievement Tests.* General or survey achievement tests are designed to measure skill and knowledge in subject areas. Commonly used batteries include the *Comprehensive Test of Basic Skills (CTBS)*, the *Iowa Test of Basic Skills*, and the *Stanford Achievement Tests*.

2. *Competency Tests.* Competency tests are designed to test if students are competent in basic skill areas. If students "pass" they are allowed to continue their course of study. Students who "fail" to reach the required level of competency are usually provided remediation and retested. Many school districts across the nation administer competency tests to students every few years during the twelve year public school experience. These testing points are often referred to as "gates" or "gateway tests" and most often occur every three years at 3rd, 6th, 9th, and 12th grades. Student passage from one school level (primary, intermediate, middle, and secondary) to the next requires satisfactorily passing a competency examination.

Intelligence Tests. Intelligence tests are designed to measure cognitive ability or what is commonly referred to as intelligence quotient (IQ). Responding to current criticism, test companies are reporting results in spreads, bans, or bands. Common instruments at the public school level are the *Cognitive Ability Test (CAT)* and the *Stanford-Binet (SB)*.

Aptitude Tests. Aptitude tests attempt to predict future achievement. Unlike the achievement test that provides information about what is or should be taught in schools, the aptitude tests may not stress what has been previously taught. Aptitude tests measure the capacity to apply abilities, skills, and interests to the successful performance of tasks. Some aptitude tests used today are the *Scholastic Aptitude Test* (SAT), the *American College Testing program (ACT), Miller Analogies Test (MAT)*, and the *Graduate Record Examination (GRE)* (Ornstein, 1995).

Nonstandardized Tests. Nonstandardized tests are most often referred to as classroom or teacher-made tests. As the names imply these are tests made by teachers. Teacher-made tests are the tests most used in the schools. While standardized tests are administered

Chapter 5 *Helping Teachers with Student Evaluation* **143**

once or twice a year, the teacher-made test is regularly given before, during, and at the conclusion of instruction units. Teachers use these instruments to monitor and assess student knowledge of the content taught. Results aid the teacher in assessing needs, determining strengths and weaknesses, and making future instructional plans. Traditionally, these tests provide scores that are translated into report card grades.

Norm-referenced and Criteria-referenced Tests

Norm-reference tests. Gage and Berliner (1992) explained that *norm-referenced tests* are standardized tests that allow comparison of one individual with others. Norm-reference tests provide norms based upon very large (nation-wide) population samples. Therefore, norm-reference tests usually have excellent reliability and validity, and they allow the comparison of the scores of an individual student with scores of other students in the school, community, state, and nation. One may also compare an individual student with other students of like characteristics and demographics. One could determine how a Hispanic female inner-city student in a given building ranks nationally within that specific group. Recent forms of the norm-reference tests have included items specifically designed to measure higher-order or abstract thinking skills.

Test scores on norm-reference instruments are reported in various forms. Supervisors must be knowledgeable about the various reporting systems to accurately interpret results. Some common forms of reporting and their meanings are:

- *Percentiles.* Percentiles range from 1 to 99 and represent the percentage of scores that were lower than the individual score reported. Therefore, it is possible for a pupil to correctly answer all items on a norm-reference test and rank in the 98th percentile. The 98th percentile indicates that 98% of the students taking the test scored lower than this particular student while 2% of the students scored the same.

- *Stanines.* Stanines are arbitrary scores reported on a scale of 1 through 9 with 1 the lowest and 9 the highest. A student scoring in the 4th and 5th stanine would be doing average work. The 8th stanine would indicate well above average, and so forth.

- *Grade Equivalence.* A third commonly used method for reporting test scores is the grade equivalence. In this case, the score is reported by expected performance on a school-time continuum. For example, a fifth grade boy might score 6th grade 5th month on a reading comprehension test. If the test was given in April (5th grade 8th month), the student performed 6 months above the expected for reading comprehension.

144 Chapter 5 *Helping Teachers with Student Evaluation*

- *Bans or Bands.* Frequently today, intelligence tests such as the Cognitive Ability Test (CAT) report results as a numeric value within spreads or bands to account for margin of error. A typical student IQ score would be reported as 112 within a band of 108 to 116.

- *Normal Curve Equivalence (NC)* and *Anticipated Normal Curve Equivalence* (ANCE). Normal curve equivalence scores are mathematically adjusted percentages which can be statistically compared and correlated. Anticipated normal curve equivalence scores are expected scores for students of like characteristics. Characteristics would include such qualifiers as geographic location, grade, IQ, socio-economic status of the school population, student ethnicity, and gender. McGraw-Hill reports scores on the Comprehensive Test of Basic Skills in NCEs and then compares an individual's achievement with students of like characteristics, the ANCE. An African-American fourth grade inner-city student could score a 58 NCE in Mathematical Computation and a 51 ANCE for the same subtest. This would indicate that the student's actual performance was higher than the expected performance for students with like characteristics and IQ scores.

Tanner and Tanner (1987) pointed out that schools do not exist in isolation but rather as part of a national and global community. Parent and civic groups believe that both the school and the individual classroom teacher are responsible and accountable for student academic growth, hence, the need for reliable normative data to measure and compare student progress.

Criterion-reference tests. Criterion-reference tests are designed to measure the students' ability in regard to a previously set criterion or specific body of knowledge or skill. Criterion-reference tests are used to determine the students' level of achievement in a given domain of learning rather than how they compare to other students. These tests are usually made at the building or district level and are not tested on large populations as is the norm-reference test. Criterion-reference tests, therefore, do not have the same high level of general validity and reliability as the norm-reference test.

However, the criterion-reference test allows teachers to evaluate students on the specific content or curriculum presented in the classroom. The characteristics of the criterion-reference test are that they:

- Provide feedback on student proficiency for a specific body of learning.
- Measure changes in learning over time.
- Measure growth for predetermined goals and objectives.

Gronlund and Linn (1990) suggest five differences between the norm-reference test and the criterion-reference test.

1. Norm-reference tests measure a large and general domain of learning tasks using only a few items to measure each task. Criterion-reference tests measures a specific and limited domain with a large number of items to measure each task.
2. Norm-reference tests discriminate among students in terms of achievement. Criterion-reference tests focus on which learning tasks the students can or cannot perform. No comparisons are made between scores.
3. Norm-reference tests omit easy and difficult items in favor of average difficulty items. Criterion-reference tests use all levels of item difficulty when matching appropriate items with the learning task.
4. Norm-reference tests are used for general or survey testing. Criterion-reference tests are used to measure mastery.
5. Norm-reference test interpretations are based upon a defined group, and students are evaluated based upon their standing within the group. Criterion-reference test interpretations are based upon the learning domain, and the student is evaluated for mastery as determined by the number of items answered correctly.

| A Comparison of Norm-referenced and Criterion-referenced Tests ||
Norm-reference	Criterion-reference
• High reliability because of typically large samples • High general validity • Allows ranking and comparison of scores • Draws from national populations • Used occasionally • Provides student comparative data • Used for general or survey testing • Measures a large and general learning domain • Uses average difficulty items	• Often low reliability because of typically small sample • Questionable general validity but high curricular validity • Measures ability in regard to a set criteria • Constructed at the district or building level • Used regularly • Provides instructional feedback • Used to measure mastery • Measures specific and limited learning domain • Uses various difficulty levels for items depending on appropriate match of item to task

Figure 5-2

146 Chapter 5 *Helping Teachers with Student Evaluation*

Supervisors who understand the characteristics and differences of these two types of tests are better able to determine appropriate use. They are better equipped with the skills necessary to facilitate general building and district practices and to advise individual classroom teachers (see Figure 5-2).

Teacher-made Tests

Most tests administered in schools are criterion-referenced classroom or teacher-made tests. Teachers are often expected to construct their own assessment instruments. The major limitations of these tests are the unknown (because most teachers do not know how to check for reliability or how to ensure appropriate content weighing) and questionable validity due to lack of reliability (Stiggens, 1991). Regardless of these limitations, D. W. Dorr-Bremme (1982) emphasizes the usefulness of these tests and cites six ways classroom tests provide valuable information. They help the teacher:

1. to initially place and group students
2. vary pedagogy and methodology to meet student ability and achievement levels
3. monitor continuing progress
4. change student placement or grouping
5. select teaching approaches
6. evaluate student performance

No one type of teacher-made test serves all purposes. Teachers must determine which type of test is most appropriate for differing contents, situations, and students.

Ornstein (1995) explains that most teacher-made tests fall into two categories: the essay (also referred to as the discussion or free-response) test and the short-answer test. Types of short-answer tests are the true-false or yes-no tests, the multiple choice, matching, short answer open-ended, and the fill-in-the-blank-tests. Essay tests usually consist of a few questions requiring lengthy answers. The short-answer tests consist of many questions, each requiring little time to answer. Students must provide a specific and brief answer in these types of tests.

Both the essay and short-answer tests have advantages. Essay tests allow students to demonstrate higher-order thinking skills. They measure application and higher levels of cognitive skills. The content sampling and reliability of the short-answer test is usually higher than that of the essay. Figure 5-3 lists the advantages, disadvantages, and best utilization for these various types of classroom tests.

Chapter 5 *Helping Teachers with Student Evaluation* **147**

Common Teacher-Made Tests: Types and Characteristics			
Type	**Advantages**	**Disadvantages**	**Best Utilized**
True - False Yes - No	• Easy to construct	• Can be ambiguous • Can reinforce incorrect information • Facilitates guessing	• To measure recall and comprehension of facts
Multiple Choice	• Easy to score and statistically analyze • Can be constructed to measure analysis and synthesis of information	• Difficult to construct • Enables students to answer by process of elimination and unintentionally hidden clues	• To measure comprehension • To measure higher cognitive skills
Matching	• Popular with students • Can be constructed to include broad range of information	• Difficult to construct • Enables students to answer by process of elimination	• To measure comprehension by comparing and contrasting information
Short Answer Open Ended	• Easy to construct • Adaptable to specific subject content • Minimizes guessing	• Difficult to score as more than one answer may be correct	• To measure recall of facts and specific knowledge
Fill In The Blank	• Minimizes guessing • Can be more focused and easily scored	• Difficult to score when more than one answer may be correct	• To measure recall of facts and specific knowledge
Essay	• Easy to construct • Enables students to demonstrate a broad knowledge base	• Scoring is quite time consuming • Scoring can be ambiguous • Coverage of subject content is limited • Test reliability is low	• To measure application and higher cognitive skills

Source: Adapted from B. Murray (1995). *Common test types and characteristics.*
Unpublished figure. Orlando, FL: University of Central Florida.

Figure 5-3

Essay vs. Short Answer. Mehrens and Lehmann (1991) identifies five factors teachers and supervisors should consider when choosing between the essay and short-answer test.

148 Chapter 5 *Helping Teachers with Student Evaluation*

1. *Test purpose.* If the purpose of the test is to measure critical thinking or written expression, the teacher should select the essay test. However, if the purpose of the test is to measure knowledge of the subject or results of learning, the teacher should choose short-answer.

2. *Time.* Each type of test requires teacher time. Essay tests take little time to prepare but much time to score. The reverse is true for short-answer tests which take considerable time to construct but little time to score. Time constraints should be a genuine consideration when selecting a test type.

3. *Number of students tested.* For practical reasons, the essay test is most often used when fewer students are tested. Short-answer tests are more practical when the teacher needs to test large groups.

4. *Facilities.* Short-answer tests require typing and reproducing copies. If these options are limited the teacher may prefer to select the essay test.

5. *Teacher's skill.* Test writing is a skill and short-answer tests require constructing numerous items. Each type of short-answer test requires different skills in writing. The teacher needs to practice and become proficient in these test writing skills. The essay test requires teacher skills not only in writing, but also in interpretation and scoring.

See Figure 5-4 for a helpful display of decision points for choosing essay tests or short answer tests.

Factors Considered When Selecting A Teacher-Made Test	
Choose Essay if....	**Choose Short-Answer if....**
• Must assess critical thinking or written expression • There is little time to construct and ample time to score • Testing few students • Typing and reproduction of copies are a problem • Proficient at writing questions at various cognitive levels • Proficient at interpreting student responses	• Must assess knowledge of a subject or learning results • There is ample time to construct and little time to score • Testing a large group • Typing and reproduction of copies are no problem • Proficient at writing numerous forms of test items

Figure 5-4

<u>Constructing Teacher-made Tests.</u> When writing short-answer tests the teacher seeks to find the most appropriate manner to pose questions or problems to the student. Test items most often involve recall to emphasize knowledge of facts, names, and terms.

Chapter 5 *Helping Teachers with Student Evaluation* **149**

Questions may be designed to require higher-order thinking abilities. The multiple-choice test is the easiest short-answer form to use when measuring some higher cognitive skills. To successfully use short answer tests, teachers must possess these skills: knowledge of the content, the ability to translate predetermined course or unit objectives into specific recall and higher-order test items, and the ability to construct items that distinguish between students who do and do not know the tested material.

To measure imaginative, subjective, and divergent thinking, teachers need more than the short-answer test. They must become proficient in the construction of the essay examination. Tuckman (1991) claims that the essay test is the best form of classroom test to measure higher mental processes for middle school through college.

Ornstein (1995) discusses the advantages and disadvantages of essay test questions as follows:

> *Essay questions can be effective for determining how well a student can analyze, synthesize, evaluate, think logically, solve problems, and hypothesize. They can also show how well he or she can organize thoughts, support a point, and create ideas, methods, and solutions. The complexity of the questions, and the complexity of thinking expected of the student, can be adjusted to correspond to the students' age, abilities, and experience. Another advantage is the ease and short time involved in constructing an essay question. The major disadvantages of essay questions are the considerable time to read and evaluate answers and the subjective scoring. (The length and complexity of the answer, as well as the standards for responding, can lead to reliability problems in scoring).* pp. 387-388.

Three types of essay questions are based upon item specificity and structure.

Type 1. These questions require students to demonstrate essential knowledge and concepts, integrate the subject matter, analyze information, make inferences, and show cause and effect relationships. Type 1 questions may lead to extended responses. They use the words, "how," "why," and "what consequences."

Type 2. The object of these questions is to determine how well the student can organize, select, and reject information from several sources. Although more structured and restrictive than Type 1 essay questions, these questions may lead to tangential and extended responses. Examples of directive words used at this level are "examine," "explain," "discuss," and "infer."

Type 3. These questions require that the student select and organize specific data. These essay questions demand a "focused response" which leads to simple recall of facts and the accompanying details. Type 3 questions achieve the most structure through the use of the words "compare," "contrast," and "identify" (Ornstein, 1988; Rosenshine and Meister, 1992).

Performance Assessment

Performance assessment is also referred to as authentic or alternative assessment. This criterion-reference measurement allows the student the opportunity to present an actual demonstration involving a given range of learning. This demonstration should be in a performance context, deal with process, and be an intended student outcome. The essay test, a video tape of a student writing and then orally reading a letter in Spanish, and a student observed performing a chemistry experiment are illustrations of performance assessments. Portfolios and computerized portfolios of the students' "best work" in a given content area are used widely as performance assessment.

The advantages of this form of assessment include the ability to test higher-level cognitive abilities, focus upon capabilities and competencies expected by all students, and measure academic growth and degree of mastery. Major difficulties or problems associated with performance assessment are the class time necessary to have each student demonstrate or perform a one-on-one selected task or assignment, consistent criteria for measuring and comparing, and teacher subjectivity. To counter some of the disadvantages of performance assessment, the teacher should use several similar tasks to measure one concept or skill.

Performance Characteristics

Since the trend toward performance assessment is growing, both supervisors and teachers must become knowledgeable in this area of testing. The use of this type of testing will require educators and students to adjust their normal classroom routines. Methodology, scheduling, long-range goals, and a shift to more cooperative learning patterns are predicted changes (See Figure 5-5).

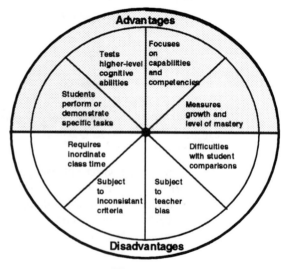

Figure 5-5

Test Administration Practices

Good supervisors realize that student test scores may be positively or negatively influenced by the quality of the test administration and feedback. Supervisors should work with teachers to improve their practices and procedures when giving and returning tests.

Teacher practices and procedures recommended for test administration occur before and during the actual testing. Long before the actual testing, teachers should plan for testing. Areas for consideration include content to be assessed, the purpose for testing, the choice of assessment instrument, length and time frame for testing, and scheduling. When scheduling tests, teachers should keep in mind the desired frequency of testing, when to administer in relation to the actual unit of instruction (before teaching, during learning, or after learning), and date selected. It would be detrimental to schedule a test when many students are engaged in an all day field trip, the day before the big game or a vacation, or party day.

Before any testing, teachers should establish test mechanics or procedures. These include routines for passing out needed materials before the test and collecting tests and materials upon completion. Students should be instructed how to ask for assistance while the test is in progress and what to do when they have completed the test. Seating arrangements while testing should be determined and discussed with the students. Methods for time keeping or posting during the test administration should be established. Several days before testing, teachers should closely examine the test itself for direction and question clarity, errors, and misprints.

Immediately before testing, teachers should adopt certain practices. They should encourage students to do their best work and use words of reassurance to reduce test anxiety. The classroom door should be shut and marked with a "Do not disturb. Testing." sign. This, along with notifying the office just prior to testing, will reduce unnecessary outside interruptions. Teachers should check that students have the supplies needed for taking the test and provide, where needed, the missing items. Teachers should be sure they have an adequate number of tests and support materials. Having extra copies of the test is a good safeguard.

As the test begins, teachers should check that all students have the necessary supplies and materials. Teachers should give clear instructions so that students understand both the directions and the questions. Students should be reminded of the previously established testing procedures.

During the test, teachers should remain vigilant, alert, and quiet. Close observation and supervision will reduce attempts at cheating (Canner, 1992). Walking periodically around the class is a wise practice. Teachers should promptly and quietly answer students' questions regarding mechanics, but should not provide help with the questions and content.

152 Chapter 5 *Helping Teachers with Student Evaluation*

Finally, the teacher should monitor time by periodically reporting or posting the remaining time. This is particularly important during the last fifteen minutes of the session. Upon conclusion of the test, teachers should collect all test materials efficiently and orderly (Ornstein, 1995).

Establishment by the teacher of these common sense practices will improve student performance. Supervisors need to encourage teachers to faithfully execute these procedures. An outline of these practices is found in Figure 5-6.

Positive Testing Practices For Teachers		
Prior to Testing	**During Testing**	**Immediately Following Testing**
• Plan for testing • Establish test procedures • Examine test copy for clarity and accuracy • Use language to encourage students' best work and reduce anxiety • Reduce outside interruptions • Supply test materials • Give clear instructions	• Check that all students have needed materials • Remain vigilant, alert, and quiet • Circulate throughout the room • Answer (promptly and quietly) students' mechanics questions • Monitor and post time remaining	• Collect all tests, support materials, and supplies

Figure 5-6

Giving Students Feedback

Tests should be returned to students as soon as possible. The instructional value of test feedback decreases as time passes. Teachers should make every effort to return scored tests within two or three days of administration (Ornstein, 1995).

When tests are returned, teachers should provide the students with meaningful feedback. Positive and specific comments about correct and insightful responses reinforce the students' desire to continue "best work" and enhances students' self-esteem. If a number of students miss the same question, the teacher should explain the confusion or misconception for the entire class.

To use tests as vehicles for learning, teachers should insist that students correct wrong answers. One activity which illustrates this strategy would be to have students work in teams to find the correct answers and then document their source of information. The teams would report their findings to the class. This activity provides verbal and visual remediation, relearning, and reinforcement (See Figure 5-7).

Positive Test Return Practices For Teachers

- Return as soon as possible
- Provide positive and specific comments for correct responses
- Remedy class confusion or misconceptions
- Use returned tests as vehicles for learning
- Provide post-test activities for remediation, relearning, and reinforcement

Figure 5-7

Test Anxiety

Test anxiety is a real, common, and potentially debilitating condition experienced by many students throughout their educational careers. Students of all ages report suffering from this malady. Test anxiety is the state of excessive worry and negative emotions that occur before and/or during testing. Most students have experienced some measure of test anxiety. Low test anxiety is controllable and does not interfere with student performance during testing. When not adequately controlled, this condition is referred to as high test anxiety and may seriously affect student test performance and make the test itself suspect.

High test anxiety has a strong correlation with feelings of helplessness, academic inadequacy, and the anticipation of failure. After reviewing more than 500 studies related to test anxiety, Ray Hembree (1988) reports that after grade 4, students who experience high test anxiety consistently perform poorly on tests. Anxiety is high during "big," "important," and "high stakes" tests. Students experience the highest anxiety during standardized tests (Hass, 1989).

Students with high test anxiety exhibit numerous, recurring, often escalating, and serious symptoms. Secondary students' symptoms (in descending order) include truancy,

154 Chapter 5 *Helping Teachers with Student Evaluation*

aggression, irritability, unreasonable time concerns, complaints of feeling very cold in the classroom, and headaches. Although in a somewhat different order, younger students experience many of the same symptoms as their high school counterparts. Teachers of elementary children express (in descending order) these anxiety-related symptoms: unreasonable time concerns, feelings of freezing temperatures during tests, headaches, irritability, aggression, and stomach aches (Nolan, Haladyna, & Hass, 1992).

Supervisors and teachers must respond to students who experience high test anxiety. Research identifies two practices that educators can use to reduce the level of test anxiety. Teachers must teach students study skills and test-taking skills (Hembree, 1988). Recognizing the importance of these skills, supervisors must encourage the faculty to develop and implement a curriculum that contains these components. Chapter 4 provides additional information regarding test anxiety. For an outline of this information refer to Figure 5-8, Student Test Anxiety.

Supervision Practices to Improve Testing Climate

Many supervision practices improve testing conditions. Supervisors should provide staff development opportunities for teachers in the areas of test anxiety, selecting and constructing appropriate tests, and teaching study and test-taking skills. Teachers must be provided with needed testing materials which include sufficient test copies (with spares) and the administration manual. It is important that supervisors provide all materials in sufficient time to allow teachers to become familiar with the mechanics of the particular test.

During building-wide testing, supervisors should strive to minimize classroom interruptions. A policy of issuing no visitor passes and allowing only dire emergency intercom communication during actual testing will greatly reduce outside distractions. When scheduling school-wide events, supervisors must consult and give priority to the building testing schedule.

Supervisors should expect and schedule for total staff involvement during standardized testing. Every professional and paraprofessional on staff has responsibility for test administration. Counselors, school psychologists, library aides, etc., should be assigned to help classroom teachers with the mechanics and logistics of administering standardized tests (Kaiser, 1995).

In the role of instructional leader, supervisors must personally encourage students and teachers to do their "best work." When supervisors emphasize high expectations for students and teachers, the learning climate and the testing climate improve (Rutter et al.,

Chapter 5 *Helping Teachers with Student Evaluation* **155**

1979). Small, appropriate, and periodic student rewards during a long testing session are encouraged.

During "test week," parent cooperation and support should be elicited. The long held practices of encouraging test preparation at home still hold true. When parents insist that their children attend school, arrive on time, get a full night's sleep and a nourishing breakfast, student test performance is enhanced. Supervisors should use a variety of communication channels to address this school and parent challenge. Newsletters, telephone hot lines, and PTA or PTO meetings are appropriate forums for sending out the call for help. Figure 5-9 lists these suggested activities and attitudes.

Technology to Facilitate Accessible Information

Technology has revolutionized schools' student record keeping and retrieval capabilities. Computers have made a major impact on record gathering, storage, access, and retrieval. One minicomputer can easily handle a K-12 data base and keep the data on-line at the display terminal on the desks of supervisors, principals, and service personnel professionals.

Instant accessibility to current student information by school professionals has dramatically enhanced academic monitoring, counseling, individual, and group services. Some advantages of computerized record keeping include automatic "red flagging" if students' grade-point averages (GPA) or attendances drop below a predetermined figure, immediate retrieval of emergency contact numbers in case of crisis, and access to records on student extra-curricular activities when writing recommendations. Today's supervisors may examine and manipulate individual and group test results along with other pertinent student information to better serve the school and students.

156 Chapter 5 *Helping Teachers with Student Evaluation*

Student Test Anxiety				
Types	**Characteristics**	**Secondary Students' Symptoms (in descending order)**	**Elementary Students' Symptoms (in descending order)**	**Remedies**

• Low test anxiety
 	
  – Controllable
 	
  – Not debilitating
 	
• High test anxiety
 	
  – Uncontrollable
 	
  – Debilitating
	• Appears at all levels
	
	• To some degree, common among most students
	
	• Potentially debilitating
	
	• Affects student test performance
	
	• Affects student conduct
	
	• May invalidate test
	
	• Increases as test importance increases
		• Truancy
		
		• Aggression
		
		• Irritability
		
		• Unreasonable time concerns
		
		• Feelings of cold
		
		• Headaches
			• Unreasonable time concerns
			
			• Feelings of cold
			
			• Headaches
			
			• Irritability
			
			• Aggression
			
			• Stomach aches
				• Provide a curriculum with study skills
				
				• Provide a curriculum with test-taking skills

Figure 5-8

Ten Supervision Practices
to Improve the Testing Climate

1. Provide staff development on testing and related topics.

2. Supply adequate test materials.

3. Provide materials in a timely fashion.

4. Minimize interruption during testing.

5. Give priority to test scheduling.

6. Involve all staff in test administration.

7. Encourage all students to do their "best work."

8. Maintain high expectations and standards.

9. Reward effort.

10. Communicate and acquire home support.

Figure 5-9

Student data most often gathered and stored as a computerized permanent record include standardized test results, grades, GPAs, attendance, participation activities, identification or directory information (parent name, address, phone, emergency contacts, etc.), and health files. Access to this information makes the supervisor and student service personnel more effective and efficient. It greatly increases their ability to aid the students in a timely and accurate manner. However, caution must be maintained concerning accessibility. With instant availability of personal student information the principal and supervisor must institute strong specific safeguards to ensure compliance with the Family Educational Rights and Privacy Act. Practices such as terminal access should be based upon the need to know. The right to know should be guarded by passwords and a programmed security system. Confidentiality must not be breached.

Testing and Special Education

One final reason supervisors must demand a quality assessment program is the vital role testing plays in the determination of a student's eligibility for special education services. A variety of information must be gathered and analyzed when a disability is suspected. To protect student rights, Congress and state legislatures adopted requirements that shape the

158 Chapter 5 *Helping Teachers with Student Evaluation*

process and practices of assessing and placing students with disabilities. Compliance with these requirements is aided by proven quality assessment practices.

Kaiser and Prasse (1995) point out that:

No single procedure may be used as the sole criterion for determining eligibility. The evaluation must be conducted by a multidisciplinary team, and the child must be assessed in all areas related to the suspected disability. Professionals considering a child's placement in a special education program must draw upon information from a variety of sources, including aptitude and achievement tests, teacher recommendations, physical condition, social or cultural background and adaptive behavior. (p. 275)

Principles and Practices for Success

- Recognize and champion the selection and use of quality and meaningful assessment.
- Stay abreast of national assessment initiatives.
- Use the recognized criteria for judging the quality of tests.
- Understand the various methods for determining test reliability.
- Examine potential tests for reliability, validity, and usability.
- Understand the uses and purposes of various standardized and nonstandardized tests.
- Accurately interpret and explain various norm-reference test reporting systems.
- Recognize the value and appropriate use of criterion-reference tests.
- Distinguish the differences between norm-reference and criterion-reference tests.
- Identify the types of teacher-made tests, and the factors that determine appropriateness.
- Provide collegial expertise in the construction of essay and short-answer tests.
- Disseminate to faculty information regarding the benefits of performance assessment.
- Encourage teachers to use positive test administration and feedback practices.
- Champion adoption of curriculum that includes study and test-taking skills, thereby decreasing test anxiety.
- Use available technology when gathering, accessing, and storing student test results and general information.

Chapter 5 *Helping Teachers with Student Evaluation* **159**

Summary

Public demand for accountability has made the need for quality student assessment an educational priority. National assessment initiatives have focused attention on the possibility and feasibility of a national curriculum and assessment program. Supervisors must strive to understand these new developments and apply them in their buildings.

Supervisors and teachers must be able to evaluate the quality of student assessments. To accomplish this task, they must understand the three criteria of reliability, validity, and usability for measuring the value of tests. Test reliability is expressed with a numerical coefficient (.80 high, .79-.40 fair, and less than .39 poor). Standard methods for determining reliability are test-retest, parallel forms, and split-half. Validity refers to the truth or accuracy of the test. The types of validity are content, construct, criterion, and predictive. Usability refers to the test being easy for the student to understand, easy to administer and score, cost acceptable, and appropriate.

All tests may be categorized as standardized or nonstandardized. Standardized tests include a set of items that are administered and measured with uniform standards. These tests provide normative data that are useful in interpreting individual scores and in ranking scores within a comparative population. Three standardized tests commonly used in schools are achievement, intelligence, and aptitude tests. Nonstandardized tests are teacher-made tests. Most frequently used in classrooms, these tests do not provide normative data but rather measure content mastery.

Tests may also be categorized as either norm-referenced or criterion-referenced. Norm-reference tests have excellent reliability and validity, and they provide comparisons of scores. Norm-referenced tests report scores in various forms: percentiles, stanines, grade equivalence, bands, NCE, and ANCE. Criterion-referenced tests are designed at the building or district level to measure students' abilities regarding a previously set criterion rather than to compare students.

One form of criterion-reference tests is the classroom or teacher-made test. Teacher-made tests fall into two categories: essay or short-answer tests. Each type has advantages and disadvantages. Selection should be made using five factors: Purpose, time, number of students tested, facilities, and teacher skills. A second criterion-reference measurement is performance assessment. Also called authentic or alternative, this assessment allows students to physically demonstrate their knowledge, skill, or ability. A nation-wide trend toward use of this assessment is growing because it tests higher-level cognitive abilities, focuses on competencies, and measures growth and mastery.

Test administration and return practices positively or negatively affect test scores. Supervisors must encourage teachers to adopt identified positive practices when

160 Chapter 5 *Helping Teachers with Student Evaluation*

administering and returning tests. Supervisors and teachers alike must be cognizant and proactive when dealing with test anxiety. Study and test-taking skills are identified as curriculum that diminishes high test anxiety. Other supervision practices that facilitate a positive testing climate are supplying ample materials sufficiently in advance of administration, minimizing outside interruptions, involving the entire staff in administration, encouraging and rewarding students for "best work," and involving parents.

Technology is a great help to supervisors when reviewing students' test and general information records. Technology in the school is now an essential tool of the supervisor and student service professionals. Confidentiality safeguards must be instituted.

Finally, the supervisor must demand a quality assessment program to ensure compliance with federal and state requirements for special education placement. Quality assessment enhances programs and services provided for all students.

Case Problem: *Finding Waldo*

Ms. Mary Trusting enters the office of Dr. Noah All, the scholarly principal of Central Middle School. Ms. Trusting is a seventh grade mathematics teacher worried about one of her second period students. She believes Noah All genuinely cares about the needs of each student and she respects his expertise as an instructional leader. She has come to ask Noah All to help her find an answer for her concerns about Waldo's academic performance and erratic behavior.

Ms. Trusting explains that both her observations and his intelligence test score suggest that Waldo is very bright. However, his achievement tests, including math, indicate barely average performance. Further, Ms. Trusting explains that Waldo's behavior is usually good. She describes him as kind and sensitive "most of the time." However, she noticed that Waldo becomes very irritable and occasionally aggressive for a day or two around test time. She had learned that he was "off the wall" during last year's achievement test administration. She is troubled with "finding Waldo."

If you were Dr. Noah All what inferences and course of action would you suggest? What things would you do and who else would you involve? What information and attitudes would be beneficial while helping find Waldo?

Chapter 5 *Helping Teachers with Student Evaluation* **161**

Case Problem: *New Broom Sweeps In*

Superintendent Catherine Newbroom motions you into her office and asks you to sit down. Even though she had assumed the position of superintendent only last month, you can tell she has something serious on her mind. As Assistant Superintendent of Curriculum and Instruction, you are eager to help.

Superintendent Newbroom explains that one of the major reasons the school board hired her was that she had promised to improve test scores, and that was now a priority. She tells you she has been reviewing the district's past practices over the last five years and sees no coordinated effort. The testing and reporting system is antiquated. She feels that the entire process needs to be reviewed and revamped. Superintendent Newbroom admits that instruction, and therefore testing, is not her forte. Therefore, she is relying upon you to develop a district-wide plan for testing and raising test scores.

As you return to your office, you are mentally beginning a list of all the various components you will have to juggle and determine. What major areas will you address? Who will be involved? What are the real goals and objectives? How will you structure this new process? How will you choose specific materials? What does the research say about test improvement? Answer these and any other relevant questions while you lay out your plan for the district testing program.

References

Anastasi, A. (1991). Psychological testing, 6th ed. In Mehrens, W. A., & Lehmann, I. J., *Measurement and evaluation in education and psychology* (4th ed.). Fort Worth, TX: Holt and Rinehart.

Canner, J. (1992). Regarding the public trust: A review of school testing programs, practices. *NASSP Bulletin, 76* (545), 6-15.

Dorr-Bremme, D. W. (1982, March). *Assessing students: Teacher's routine practice and reasoning.* Paper presented at the annual meeting of the American Educational Research Association. New York: American Educational Research Association.

Gage, N. L., & Berliner, D. C. (1992). *Educational psychology* (5th ed.). Boston: Houghton Mifflin.

Gronlund, N. E., & Linn, R. L. (1990). *Measurement and evaluation in teaching*, 6th ed. New York: Macmillan.

162 Chapter 5 *Helping Teachers with Student Evaluation*

Hass, N. (1989). Standardized testing in Arizona. *Technical report, 89,* 3. Phoenix: Arizona State University.

Hembree, R. (1988). Correlates, causes, effects, and treatment of test anxiety. *Review of Educational Research, 30,* 47-77.

Kaiser, J. S. (1995). *The 21st century principal.* Mequon, WI: Stylex Publishing Company.

Kaiser, J. S., & Prasse, D. (1995). Administering special education. In Kaiser, J. S., *The 21st century principal.* Mequon, WI: Stylex Publishing Company.

Kerlinger, F. N. (1986). *Foundations of behavioral research* (3rd ed.). New York: Holt, Rinehart, and Winston.

Kirkpatrick, T. O., & Lewis, C. T. (1995). *Effective supervision: Preparing for the 21st century.* Fort Worth, TX: Dryden Press, Harcourt Brace College Publishers.

Kosmoski, G. J., Pollack, D., & Estep, S. (1994). Reliability of children's self-esteem assessment: What I think about myself. *Psychological reports, 75,* 83-88.

Little, J. W. (1993). Teachers' professional development in a climate of educational reform. *Educational Analysis and Policy Analysis, 15* (2), 129-152.

Mehrens, W. A., & Lehmann, I. J. (1991). *Measurement and evaluation in education and psychology,* (4th ed.). Fort Worth, TX: Holt and Rinehart.

Mullis, I., Owen, E. H., & Phillips, G. (1990). *Accelerating academic achievement.* Princeton, NJ: Educational Testing Service.

Murray, B. (1995). *Common test types and characteristics.* Unpublished figure. Orlando, FL: University of Central Florida.

National Center for Educational Statistics. (1993a). *NAEP 1992 reading report card for the nation and the states.* Washington, DC: Department of Education.

National Center for Educational Statistics. (1993b). *NAEP 1992 mathematics report card for the nation and the states.* Washington, DC: Department of Education.

Nolan, S. B., Haladyna, T., & Hass, N. S. (1992). Uses and abuses of achievement tests. Educational measurement, 11, 9-15.

Nunnally, J. C. (1982). Reliability in measurement. In Wittrock, M. C., *Encyclopedia of educational research*)5th ed.). New York: Macmillan.

Odden, A. R. (1995). *Educational leadership for America's school.* New York: McGraw-Hill, Inc.

Oliva, P. F. (1993). *Supervision for today's schools* (4th ed.). New York: Longman.

Ornstein, A. C. (1995). *Strategies for effective teaching* (2nd ed.) Chicago: Brown and Benchmark.

Ornstein, A. C. (1988). Questioning: The essence of good teaching. *NASSP Bulletin, 72,* 72-80.

Reynolds, A. (1992). What is competent beginning teaching: A review of the literature. *Review of Educational Research, 62,* 1-36.

Rosenshine, B. V., & Meister, C. (1992). The use of scaffolds for teaching higher-level cognitive strategies. *Educational leadership, 49(7),* 26-33.

Rutter, M., Maughan, B., Mortimore, P., Ousten, J., 7 Smith, A. (1979). *Fifteen thousand hours: Secondary schools and their effects on children.* Cambridge: Harvard University Press.

Smith, G. (1985). *Statistical reasoning.* Boston: Allyn and Bacon.

Stiggins, R. J. (1991). Relevant classroom assessment training for teachers. *Educational measurement, 10,* 7-12.

Tanner, D., & Tanner, L. (1987). *Supervision in education: Problems and practices.* New York: Macmillan.

Tuckman, B. W. (1991). Evaluating the alternative to multiple-choice testing for teachers. *Contemporary Education, 62,* 299-300.

Vockell, E. L. (1983). *Educational research.* New York: Macmillan.

Chapter 6

HELPING TEACHERS TO MANAGE CLASSROOMS
George E. Pawlas

Are Discipline Problems All That Serious?

Each year since 1969, Phi Delta Kappa, international society in education, in conjunction with George Gallup, has surveyed the public's attitudes toward the public schools. In the annual polls, which are published in the journal *Phi Delta Kappan*, lack of discipline has consistently appeared at, or near, the top of the public's list of problems in the public schools.

While it can be said that public opinion can be influenced by the sensational, such as physical attacks on teachers and vandalism in schools, the topic of discipline is of interest and concern to the taxpaying public. Most teachers maintain that student misbehavior interferes significantly with their teaching (Elam, 1989).

Questions to answer after studying this chapter

✔ Is there a process for developing an effective classroom management plan?
✔ What are the five keys to good room arrangement?
✔ What are the four elements of effective teaching?
✔ What are the steps in building good discipline through modeling?
✔ What does the term *withitness* have to do with classroom management?
✔ What do the concepts of behavior have to do with classroom management?
✔ What are the four goals of student misbehavior?
✔ Are there any discipline programs that teach children respect and responsibility?

The results of the *26th Annual Phi Delta Kappa/Gallup Poll of the public's attitudes toward the public schools*, released in September 1994, revealed that for the first time ever the category of "fighting, violence, and gangs" shares the number one position with "lack of discipline" as the biggest problem confronting local public schools. Eighteen percent of the 1,326 adults questioned in the poll identified these two categories as their number one concern (Elam, 1994).

At the 1989 Education Summit in Charlottesville, Virginia, the nation's governors and the President reached agreement and adopted six National Education Goals that set high expectations for educational performance at every stage of a learner's life, from the preschool years through adulthood. In 1994, Congress adopted the six goals and expanded the number to eight. Goal 7 is, "Every school in the United States will be free of drugs, violence, and the unauthorized presence of firearms and alcohol and will offer a disciplined environment conducive to learning" (*The National Education Goals Report*, 1994, pp. 13, 14).

166 Chapter 6 *Helping Teachers to Manage Classrooms*

Good classroom management is taken for granted and people do not notice it unless it is missing. New and experienced teachers recognize quality classroom management as one of the most important foundations of effective instruction. Good classroom management, however, does not just happen. Smoothly running classrooms where students are actively involved exist because effective teachers have a clear idea of the classroom conditions and student behaviors that are necessary for a productive, healthy learning environment. These teachers have a vision of what they want their classroom to be. They work very hard to create and maintain those conditions. Their plan can be outlined as follows in Figure 6-1.

The Process of Developing an Effective Classroom Management Plan

- Before the school year begins, planning is done in several key areas.
- At the beginning of the school year, the plan is implemented and effective management procedures are established.
- Effective management procedures are maintained throughout the school year.

Figure 6-1

Organizing the Classroom

Time spent by a teacher, before the school year begins, in arranging the classroom for teaching is the first step in developing an effective management plan. While the plans may vary depending on the classroom level, certain key conditions must exist. According to Emmer, Evertson, Clements, and Worsham (1994), five keys that can serve as guidelines to good room arrangement are: keep high traffic areas free of congestion, use a room arrangement consistent with instructional goals and activities, be sure all students are easily seen by the teacher, keep frequently used teaching materials and student supplies readily accessible, and be certain students can easily see instructional presentations and displays.

Classroom Climate

Climate refers to 1) the *affective* aspects of the classroom, which include the feelings generated by and about the teacher, the students, and the subject matter and 2) the *physical* aspects of the classroom that contribute positively or negatively to the learning atmosphere.

Teachers should strive to establish a supportive yet businesslike climate in their classrooms because these will facilitate learning while limiting problems. Teachers can work purposefully at effecting a productive learning climate by attending to the implications of four elements of effective teaching as identified in the research of Kindsvatter, Wilen, and Ishler (1988). These are *academic climate, high standards, orderly environment,* and *expectations for success.*

Academic Climate

The first element for building a productive learning climate comes from the effective school model (Lezotte, 1984), which emphasizes *academics.* With the focus on decision making about curriculum and instruction, the teacher focuses classroom activities on the completion of academic objectives.

Eight practices teachers can use to generate an academic climate in the classroom (Kindsvatter et al., 1988) are found in Figure 6-2.

Practices That Generate An Academic Climate

- Be task oriented.
- Keep students on task.
- Encourage students to do homework.
- Encourage students to master materials.
- Give daily feedback.
- Convey to students confidence in their ability to succeed.
- Provide learning activities that offer academic challenges.
- Be supportive of students' efforts.

(Kindsvatter, Wilen, & Ishler, 1988)

Figure 6-2

High Standards

The second element of effective teaching, *high standards,* was mentioned in the National Commission on Excellence in Education's report, *A Nation at Risk* (1983). The report called for the upgrading of national education standards by increasing basic academic requirements for graduation. Several research studies conducted before the report supported the call for higher standards. Each of these studies (Rutter, Maugham, Mortimore, & Ouster, 1979; Wellisch, MacQueen, Carriere, & Duck, 1978; and Levin & Long, 1981) pointed to the creation of a climate in the classroom that conveys that the business in the classroom is to learn, a student is expected to achieve, the teachers have high standards for themselves and their students, and that the school is concerned with achievement.

168 Chapter 6 *Helping Teachers to Manage Classrooms*

Eight teacher practices that can convey to students that high standards are important in the classroom (Kindsvatter et al., 1988) are listed in Figure 6-3.

High Standards In The Classroom

- Setting an academic performance level that all students must meet
- Establishing an organizational system for remediation
- Maintaining a standard of performance
- Rewarding excellent work and effort
- Maintaining a professional image in the classroom
- Encouraging students to discover the excitement of learning
- Requiring a level of work that challenges but does not frustrate
- Emphasizing higher-level thinking as well as memory-level and comprehension-level cognitive functioning

(Kindsvatter, Wilson, & Ishler, 1988)

Figure 6-3

Orderly Environment

The third important climate condition is the existence of an *orderly environment*. This relates to the classroom as a social group and focuses on the maintenance of a climate that encourages cooperation and productivity within the group.

Many research studies have focused on the characteristics of an orderly classroom. Classroom order is best initiated very early in the school year by establishing class procedures, routines, and rules. Anderson and Evertson (1978) studied teachers during the first three weeks of school. They found effective teachers who managed with high student engagement rates spent the first few days of school emphasizing management and organizational planning. They taught students procedures for the use of the room and management routines. They gave students guided practice in class procedures such as timing student movement into various instructional activities and gave the students feedback on the results. These teachers taught management of the classroom as they would any other unit of study. Classroom rules were included in lesson plans, and practice and feedback were given to students on their progress in learning and following rules.

Chapter 6 *Helping Teachers to Manage Classooms* **169**

Teachers make important decisions that influence order in the classroom. These decisions focus on the factors of establishing rules and procedures, handling deviant student behavior, organizing groups, and timing activities.

Other teachers who have been identified as effective classroom managers have revealed that they review classroom rules and procedures on a regular basis. They indicated this is especially true following a vacation period or extended weekends, or when new students were assigned to the classroom.

These teachers said they involved the students in the development of the classroom rules. Figure 6-4 lists teacher expectations necessary to maintain an orderly environment.

Maintaining an Orderly Environment
- Develop, discuss, and review class rules, routines, and procedures
- Inform students about what they are expected to accomplish and how they are progressing
- Be prepared to teach all lessons
- Use instructional times effectively
- Keep students on task
- Make transition times short and focused
- Deal with disruptions and interruptions promptly

(Kindsvatter, Wilen, & Ishler, 1988)

Figure 6-4

An orderly classroom is a structured classroom in which students know the expectations the teacher has for them. An orderly classroom provides a framework in which the class functions smoothly. Students should be encouraged to share ideas, and as a result, some lesson plans may need to be changed or discarded. The needs of individual students may be addressed, and group processes should be considered in the teacher's decision making.

Expectations for Success

The fourth element in effective teaching, *expectations for success*, centers on the influence the teacher's attitude has on students' performance. The classic but controversial study, "Pygmalion in the Classroom," by Rosenthal and Jacobson (1968) revealed how teachers' attitudes do influence the academic performance of students. Many research studies of the late 1970s and early 1980s, such as Rutter et al. (1979) and Edmonds (1980), identified the impact of teachers' beliefs on student achievement. Teacher expectations do have an impact on the learning rates of

170 Chapter 6 *Helping Teachers to Manage Classrooms*

students. Indeed, Rosenthal (1991) discussed the results of 448 studies of interpersonal expectancy effects in classroom settings.

Research done by Bandura (1985), as cited in Ornstein (1990), revealed that building good discipline through *modeling* includes the following:

- **Demonstration**—Students know exactly what is expected. Besides having expected behavior explained to them, they see and hear it.
- **Attention**—Students focus their attention on what is being depicted or explained.
- **Practice**—Students are given opportunity to practice the appropriate behavior.
- **Corrective feedback**—Students receive frequent, specific, and immediate feedback.
- **Application**—Students are able to apply their learning in classroom activities (role playing, modeling activities) and other real-life situations.

Figure 6-5 lists behaviors that relate to a climate for success in the classroom.

High Expectations For Student Success
- Develop positive attitudes concerning student abilities.
- Develop positive attitudes in students toward their success in each subject.
- Help students understand that success can be reached through their efforts.
- Demonstrate that the teacher and the school support student success.
- Adapt learning activities and materials to fit student abilities for success.
- Provide all students with opportunities to be successful.
- Give effective feedback.
- Show interest in all students.
- Check for each student's understanding.

(Kindsvatter, Wilen, & Ishler, 1988)

Figure 6-5

Kounin's Techniques

Withitness

Kounin (1977) coined the term *withitness* to describe teachers knowing what is going on in all areas of the classroom at all times. This is similar to the familiar "eyes in the back of the head." Kounin determined that this trait is communicated more effectively by teachers' behaviors than by their words. It is effective only if students are convinced that the teacher really knows what is happening. If students are not working, the teacher's behavior or words must clearly communicate expectations to the uninvolved students. Withitness is one of five techniques Kounin has promoted and which help to prevent discipline problems.

Kounin found that if students perceive that teachers are "with it"—that is, the teacher treats the right culprit with respect and corrects the misbehavior, the students are less likely to misbehave. Handling the correct deviant on time, and with respect, is more important to classroom control than is firmness.

Perhaps the withitness of teachers can be reduced to five questions effective teachers ask themselves and their students (see Figure 6-6). These questions reinforce established classroom rules (Meyers & Pawlas, 1989).

Five Simple Questions for Students and Teachers
- Are you respecting others' rights to learn?
- Are you respecting others' rights to not be hurt physically or by verbally?
- Are you respecting others' rights to their personal property?
- Are you helping others?
- Are you making others feel good by giving compliments or by inviting them to join you in some activity?

(Meyers & Pawlas, 1989)

Figure 6-6

Overlapping

Kounin's second technique for preventing discipline problems is *overlapping* (Christopher, 1992). A teacher uses this technique when two events are attended to at the same time. For instance, if a teacher is working with a group of students and another student signals that a trip to the lavatory is necessary, the teacher acknowledges the student's request and goes right on with the instruction to the small group of students.

172 Chapter 6 *Helping Teachers to Manage Classrooms*

Smoothness

When a teacher uses Kounin's third technique, *smoothness* (Christopher, 1992), the focus of the lesson is maintained on objectives.

Momentum

Maintaining the *momentum* of the lesson is the fourth technique identified by Kounin (Christopher, 1992). This occurs when a teacher keeps a lesson moving at a pace that allows students to learn and understand.

Group Alerting

Group alerting occurs when the teacher keeps students on their toes or in suspense as to when they will be called upon to answer a question. If some students are working at the chalkboard, students at their seats are expected to complete the same assignments (Christopher, 1992).

Rules should be jointly formulated by teachers and students, be reasonable, be related to efficient learning, and **always** enforced. Classroom rules should support a learning environment that facilitates individual and group achievement. Agreed-on rules should be constantly reevaluated for their purpose and can lead to class and individual group success.

Rules should be adapted to the age and ability of the students. Some examples of appropriate rules at various grade levels follow as Figure 6-7.

According to Albert (1989), there are three basic concepts of behavior:

1. Students choose their behavior.
2. The ultimate goal of student behavior is to fulfill the need to belong.
3. Students misbehave to achieve one of four immediate goals: attention, power, revenge, and avoidance-of-failure.

Age-Appropriate Classroom Rules

Primary Level
- Take turns.
- Walk in the classroom.
- Help others.
- Raise your hand to talk.

Intermediate-Elementary/Middle School Level
- Be kind and courteous to others.
- Follow directions.
- Autograph your work with excellence.
- One person may talk at a time.

Secondary Level
- Be considerate and respectful of other people.
- Be prepared; come to class with assignments and materials.
- Be prompt and on time.
- Return materials and supplies you use.

Figure 6-7

Chapter 6 *Helping Teachers to Manage Classrooms* **173**

There are many explanations of behavior. Understanding that behavior is based on choice can provide us with the leverage to cope with inappropriate behavior and to encourage positive, or appropriate, behavior of students. Before significant progress can be seen in correcting the behavior of students, a teacher must learn how to interact with students so that they will want to choose appropriate behavior and follow established rules.

Concepts of Behavior

Understanding the second basic concept of behavior, fulfilling the need to belong, or to feel significant and important, is necessary to understand students' actions. Albert (1989) suggests that young people choose different behaviors to feel significant and important in different groups—the family, the drama club, the class, and the ball team. Teachers' recognition of this need to belong helps students choose appropriate behavior.

If students cannot achieve their need to belong through appropriate behavior, they may resort to misbehavior in an attempt to obtain immediate gratification. What they want usually corresponds to one of four goals:

1. Attention
2. Power
3. Revenge
4. Avoidance-of-failure

Attention

By choosing to misbehave, some students feel they can get extra attention. They want to distract the teacher and students to gain attention.

Power

In a search for power, some students choose to misbehave. By refusing to follow their teacher's requests or directions, refusing to follow classroom rules, and disrupting classroom order, students demonstrate a need for power.

Revenge

Some students choose revenge against others as their method of getting attention by misbehaving. They may strike out at other students, the teacher, or both in their quest for repaying a real or imagined hurt.

174 Chapter 6 *Helping Teachers to Manage Classrooms*

Avoidance of Failure

Some students want to avoid repeated failure. Because they cannot live up to their own expectations and those of others—their parents and their teachers—they might choose withdrawal behaviors. By appearing to be inadequate, they hope everyone will back off and leave them alone.

By identifying a student's goal in misbehaving (attention, power, revenge, or avoidance of failure), teachers can promptly intervene to prevent future problems. By using encouragement techniques that build self-esteem, students will, over time, learn appropriate ways to feel capable, to connect, and to contribute. While teachers cannot change a student's behavior, they can influence behavior to become more positive and appropriate.

Discipline Profiles

Through the years, educators have used various approaches to maintain order in their classrooms. In recent years, four discipline programs have been identified that share a common goal: to teach children respect and responsibility rather than blind obedience to authority. Each program is positive in its approach, has been proven to work in the classroom, and uses practical strategies. Each program is based on the belief that student misbehavior can be avoided when students' basic needs are being met. Brief descriptions of the four discipline programs follow (Teaching Kids Responsibility, 1994).

Cooperative Discipline

Linda Albert has based her program on the works of Alfred Adler, Rudolph Dreikurs, William Glasser, Albert Ellis, and Eric Berne. Supporters of this approach feel students must be affirmed and given the opportunity to share in the responsibility for their own behavior. By identifying the goals of a particular misbehavior, intervening at the moment of misbehavior, building student self-esteem for future positive interactions, and involving students, colleagues, and parents in the process, teachers will be meeting the students' basic needs to belong and to know they significantly contribute to the group.

The cooperative discipline approach:

- Builds self-esteem through encouragement.
- Implements strategies for positive classroom control.
- Increases motivation that leads to higher academic achievement. (Albert, 1989)

By using this approach to classroom management, students are taught to feel capable, to connect, and to make contributions to the lessons.

Discipline with Dignity

Allen Mendler and Richard Curwin (Teaching Kids Responsibility, 1994) have used the work of William Glasser as the foundation of their program. By focusing on problem solving, prevention, and student involvement in the discipline process, Mendler and Curwin feel students are allowed to internalize the values that underlie desired behaviors. Students are also made to feel and believe they are capable and successful. The students come to realize they are capable of influencing events and people.

Kids are Worth It!

Barbara Coloroso (Teaching Kids Responsibility, 1994) has used her experiences as a parent, teacher, and university instructor as the basis for the program. Students are taught how to think, not just what to think. Coloroso believes students can develop self-discipline if treated with respect, given responsibilities and choices, and allowed to experience reasonable and realistic consequences for the choices. This program focuses on showing students what they have done wrong, giving them ownership of the problem, and showing them ways to solve problems while leaving their dignity intact.

Coloroso and supporters of *"kids are worth it!"* believe students need these six critical life messages each day:

- I believe in you.
- I trust you.
- I know you can handle it.
- You are listened to.
- You are cared for.
- You are very important to me.

Positive Classroom Discipline

The underlying beliefs of this program's major proponent, Fred Jones (Teaching Kids Responsibility, 1994), are that classroom management procedures must be positive, must set limits, and build cooperation without coercion. These procedures must be practical, simple, and designed ultimately to reduce the teacher's workload. Jones based his program on his experiences as a clinical psychologist working with special and regular student populations, and his work with outstanding teachers who helped clarify effective teaching practices.

176 Chapter 6 *Helping Teachers to Manage Classrooms*

The main focus of Jones's program is the management of group behavior to reduce classroom disruptions. Students' behavior improves because they have internalized discipline, are in a structured classroom, work within acceptable limits and incentive systems, and are learning to manage their behavior outside the classroom.

Roles and Responsibilities of Supervisors

Principals are the prime supervisors of instruction. In large school districts, principals' jobs may be supported by supervisors from the district office; however, in the vast majority of schools around the country, principals are the supervisors. Principals are instructional leaders setting standards and expectations for teacher behavior in providing quality instruction. Principals also provide leadership in establishing schoolwide rules for student behavior and standards for learning. These rules are translated into the rules for every classroom. Where effective instruction is present and student behavior is appropriate, a climate of high expectations for achievement is established. This climate is the result of the joint efforts of teachers and students for the appropriate actions of everyone in a classroom.

Principals should have a vision of the goals for student learning and the methods of age-appropriate instruction provided by teachers. With the advent of school-based management or site-based decision making in many schools across America, school principals have seen their roles and responsibilities adjusted. Their power base has not been eroded; rather, the base from which meaningful, longer-lasting decisions result has been strengthened. A principal's vision of appropriate student behavior will be mirrored in every classroom. Most principals are aware of public concern about discipline problems and are using the school's resources to remedy inappropriate student behavior. The tendency is to incorporate discipline plans that focus on teaching students respect and responsibility.

Principles and Practices for Success

- Supervisors will help teachers become successful in developing an effective classroom management plan by planning before the school year begins, implementing the plan and effective management procedures, and maintaining these strategies throughout the school year.

- Supervisors will help teachers become successful classroom managers by sharing the five keys of good room arrangement with them: keep high-traffic areas free of congestion, use a room arrangement that supports instructional goals and activities, be sure all students can be seen by the teacher, have regularly used teaching materials and student supplies readily available, and be sure all students can see the instructional presentations.

Chapter 6 *Helping Teachers to Manage Classooms* **177**

- Supervisors will encourage teachers to use the four elements of effective teaching: academic climate, high standards, orderly environment, and expectations for success.

- Supervisors will help teachers become successful at building good discipline by modeling it through: demonstrating what is expected; keeping students' attention on expectations; practicing the appropriate behavior; providing corrective feedback; and applying the new learning in classroom activities.

- Supervisors will make teachers aware that they must respectfully communicate their "withitness" or "eyes in the back of their heads" to be effective in the classroom.

- Supervisors will help teachers understand the three basic concepts of behavior:

  - Students choose their behavior.
  - The ultimate goal of student behavior is to fulfill the need to belong.
  - Students misbehave to achieve one of four immediate goals: attention, power, revenge, and avoidance of failure.

- Supervisors will help teachers understand at least four discipline programs that teach students respect and responsibility: *cooperative discipline, discipline with dignity, kids are worth it!,* and *positive classroom discipline.*

Summary

Classroom management is the orchestration of classroom life and includes planning the curriculum and instructional strategies, organizing resources and procedures, arranging the classroom setting to maximize efficiency, monitoring student progress, relating high expectations of student achievement, and anticipating potential problems. The classrooms of successful teachers often appear as magic shows because students are able to go from one activity to the next without delays. Teachers in these classrooms have mastered specific techniques for planning meaningful activities, for anticipating potential problems, and for creating a classroom environment that is enriched and inviting. Some ways of establishing effective classroom rules follow in Figure 6-8.

Effective Classroom Rules Should Be
- Established jointly by the teacher and students
- Reasonable
- Observable
- Brief and specific
- Enforceable
- Constantly evaluated
- Clearly stated
- Positively stated
- Few in number
- Enforced

Figure 6-8

178 Chapter 6 *Helping Teachers to Manage Classrooms*

Students who have been observed in these well-managed classrooms appear to know what is expected of them, are satisfied with their progress, and know what to do when they need assistance. Their teachers are able to provide meaningful options matched to the students' learning needs. Consistent application of rules and continuous administrative support of teachers' efforts are mandatory for successful classroom management.

Case Problem: *Effective Mentoring*

How would you approach an experienced teacher to serve as a mentor for a first-year teacher who will be joining the faculty? From your experiences and professional reading, you are aware that classroom management problems are one of the most important concerns of first-year teachers. To help you prepare yourself for your meeting with the experienced teacher, you have decided to make a list of possible discipline problems the new teacher may have and which the mentor may help to solve. In addition, you identified and listed some possible preventive disciplinary techniques to use. The principal thought this approach has strong merit and offered you these three classroom situations:

1. a student constantly talks or shouts out;
2. a student refuses to work;
3. a student begins to argue with the teacher or another student.

Considering your experiences, add as many other situations you think the new teacher may face and include a preventive disciplinary technique for each situation.

References

Albert, L. (1989). *A teacher's guide to cooperative discipline*. Circle Pines, MN: American Guidance Services.

Anderson, L., & Evertson, C. (1978). *Classroom organization at the beginning of school: Two case studies*. Austin, TX: University of Texas.

Christopher, C. (1992). *Nuts and bolts survival guide for teachers*. Lancaster, PA: Technomic Publishing Co.

Edmonds, R. (1980). *Schools count: New York City's school improvement project*. Cambridge, MA: Harvard Graduate School of Education Association Bulletin.

Elam, S. (1989). The second Gallup/Phi Delta Kappa poll of teacher's attitudes toward the schools. *Phi Delta Kappan 70*, 10: 785-798.

Elam, S. (1994). The 26th Annual Phi Delta Kappa/Gallup Poll of the public's attitudes toward the public schools. *Phi Delta Kappan, 76*, 4: 41-56.

Emmer, E., Evertson, C., Clements, B., & Worsham, M. (1994). *Classroom management for secondary teachers.* Boston: Allyn & Bacon.

Kindsvatter, R., Wilen, W., & Ishler, M. (1988). *Dynamics of Effective Teaching.* New York: Longman.

Kounin, J. (1977). *Discipline and group management in classrooms.* New York: Holt, Rinehart & Winston.

Lezotte, L. (Ed.). (1984). Conducting an effective school program. *The effective school report, 2, 10*, 1.

Levin, T., & Long, R. (1981). *Effective instruction.* Alexandria, VA: Association for Supervision and Curriculum Development.

Meyers, K., and Pawlas, G. (1989). *The principal and discipline. #5 The new principal series.* Bloomington, IN: Phi Delta Kappa Educational Foundation.

National Commission on Excellence in Education. (1983). *A nation at risk: The imperative for educational reform.* Washington, DC: U.S. Government Printing Office.

The National Education Goals Report. (1994). Washington, DC: U.S. Government Printing Office.

Ornstein, A. (1990). *Strategies for effective teaching.* New York: Harper & Row.

Rosenthal, R. (1991). Teacher expectancy effects: A brief update 25 years after the Pygmalion experiment. *The Journal of Research in Education. 1*, 1: 31-12.

Rosenthal, R., & Jacobson, L. (1968). *Pygmalion in the classroom: Teacher expectation and pupils' intellectual development.* New York: Holt, Rinehart & Winston.

Rutter, M., Maugham, B., Mortimore, P., & Ouster, J. (1979). *Fifteen thousand hours.* Cambridge, MA: Harvard University Press.

Teaching Kids Responsibility (Vol. I, No. 1). (1994). Bloomington, IN: National Educational Service.

Wellisch, J., MacQueen, A., Carriere, R., *and* Duck, F. (1978). School management and organization in successful schools. *Sociology of Education, 51*, 211-266.

Chapter 7

Clinical Supervision
Georgia J. Kosmoski

Introduction

Since the beginning of formalized teacher supervision in America, the most common model was *supervision equated to evaluation*. Through observation and sometimes hearsay, supervisors would monitor or inspect the behaviors of teachers. They would then report orally or in writing their judgment as to the quality of the teacher's performance and his or her compliance with established rules and guidelines. Supervisors would share these "findings" with the appropriate superordinates and the involved teacher.

This model was often viewed by teachers and administrators as a negative, suspicious, threatening, and punitive process. Many educators believed that a proven alternative form of supervision was necessary. Today one of the most widely accepted and used alternative models is *clinical supervision* which exists and is practiced in a variety of forms. This chapter will define clinical supervision, discuss major components, identify various models, address pitfalls, and provide suggestions for successful implementation.

Clinical Supervision Defined

Experts in the field of supervision have

Questions to answer after studying this chapter

✔ What is supervision equated to evaluation?
✔ What is the definition of clinical supervision?
✔ Who are some experts in clinical supervision?
✔ What are three models of clinical supervision?
✔ What are the common components of all models of clinical supervision?
✔ What are the three essential ingredients of clinical supervision?
✔ What are the five stages of the Goldhammer model?
✔ What are the eight phases of Cogan's model?
✔ How does the Acheson and Gall model differ from the others?
✔ What are the major stumbling blocks to implementing clinical supervision?
✔ What characteristics indicate that a supervisor is prepared to undertake the implementation of clinical supervision?
✔ How does a supervisor prepare a staff for implementing clinical supervision?
✔ What are some successful supervisory practices at the preobservation conference?
✔ What are some successful supervisory strategies used during an observation?
✔ What practices should a supervisor employ during the postobservation conference?

not agreed upon a definition for clinical supervision. However, each definition listed below has value and adds to the growing body of information that gives insight to this process.

-181-

182 Chapter 7 *Clinical Supervision*

The first person to define clinical supervision was Morris Cogan (1973), who described it as:

> *the practice designed to improve the teacher's classroom performance. It takes its principle data from the events of the classroom. The analysis of these data and the relationship between the teacher and supervisor form the basis of the program, procedures, and strategies designed to improve the students' learning by improving the teacher's classroom behavior.*
> (p. 9)

Lovell and Wiles (1983) expanded the original definition and emphasized the need for objectivity to achieve change and improvement of teacher performance. They stated that clinical supervision is:

> *a problem-solving approach to instructional supervision in which objective observation and analysis of teaching is the basis for the feedback as frameworks for change and improvement of performance.* (p. 69)

Sergiovanni and Starratt (1988) added the dimension that clinical supervision is designed to improve instruction, which makes it a positive form of professional growth for the teacher. They stated that clinical supervision:

> *refers to face-to-face contact with teachers with the intent of improving instruction and increasing professional growth. In many respects, a one-to-one correspondence exists between classroom instruction and increasing professional growth, and for this reason staff development and clinical supervision are inseparable concepts and activities.* (p. 304)

Keith Acheson and Meredith Gall (1992) not only defined clinical supervision, but identified necessary characteristics, emphasis, and its goal. They state that clinical supervision is:

> *a face-to-face relationship between teacher and supervisor and a focus on the teacher's actual behavior in the classroom. . . . However, the primary emphasis of clinical supervision is on professional growth, and the primary goal of this supervision is to help the teacher improve his or her instructional performance. . . . (It is) interactive rather than directive, democratic rather than authoritarian, teacher-centered rather than supervisor-centered.* (p. 9)

Drawing upon the common elements found in these definitions and relying upon a basic human relations philosophy, clinical is defined as follows:

Clinical supervision is a continuing cyclical process of supervision, the purpose of which is to improve classroom instruction through the collegial interaction between the teacher and the supervisor.

Identified Components

Three of the most often used forms of clinical supervision are the Goldhammer 5 Stage Clinical Supervision Model (Goldhammer, 1969), Cogan's 8 Phase Model of Clinical Supervision (Cogan, 1973), and Acheson and Gall's 3 Phase Model (Acheson & Gall, 1992). These models have a certain commonality. Each identifies a number of components essential to successful implementation. They all emphasize that clinical supervision is a process:

- To improve teacher instruction, and thereby, improve student achievement,

- Which is continual in nature and with never an end to the effort,

- Which is cyclical where the last step naturally leads back to the first step and the initiation of the cycle again,

- That is collegial, democratic, and trusting,

- Where the teacher and supervisor jointly assume responsibility,

- Which identifies specific phases, stages, or steps where the supervisor and teacher, together or separately, perform certain specific tasks or activities, and

- Where the focus is upon the teacher's needs rather than the needs or wishes of the supervisor (Acheson & Gall, 1992; Cogan, 1973; Goldhammer, 1969).

Oliva (1993) identified the key components somewhat differently. He explained that although various models may differ in the number of steps, stages, or phases, they all have three essential ingredients.

1) There is some kind of contact or communication with the teacher prior to an observation;
2) There is some type of classroom observation; and
3) There is some kind of follow-up to the observation. (p. 483)

184 Chapter 7 *Clinical Supervision*

Three Models of Clinical Supervision

A closer examination of the models mentioned above provides a clearer insight to the nature of clinical supervision, and provides alternatives when selecting a model for implementation. The models to be examined are Goldhammer's (1969) 5 Stages of Clinical Supervision, Cogan's (1973) 8 Phases of Supervision, and Acheson and Gall's (1992) 3 Phase Model of Clinical Supervision.

The Goldhammer Model

Robert Goldhammer (1969) developed the first model of clinical supervision in the 1960s at the Harvard School of Education. He identified five major steps or stages in the process. These stages are the preobservation conference, the observation, analysis and strategy, supervision or postobservation conference, and the postconference analysis.

1. *The Preobservation Conference.* The preobservation conference occurs before any formal observation and is considered the most important stage of the clinical supervision cycle. Responsibility for this stage rests with both the teacher and the supervisor. Its purpose is threefold.

   - To set the contract between the teacher and supervisor of what is to be observed, that is, what will be taught and learned during the observation. This includes lesson objectives, the relationship between those objectives and the curriculum to be implemented, activities, possible changes, and the items or problems for which the teacher wishes feedback.

   - To set the ground rules and mechanics for the observation. Included in this area are the time, place, and length of the actual observation.

   - To determine the plan for observing. The supervisor and teacher will agree upon which action or actions will be observed and how the data will be recorded. They will determine where the supervisor will be located during the lesson, if special preparations or materials are needed for the observation, and whether the supervisor should or should not interact with the students. An agreement on potential contingencies is essential to avoid surprises and misunderstandings (Goldhammer, Anderson, & Krajewski, 1993).

2. *The Observation.* The second stage of the Goldhammer model is the observation. It is the systematic observation by the supervisor of the teacher's performance. The focus of the observation should be what the teacher does, how the students react, and what occurs during the actual teaching. The data collected should be objective

and shared with the teacher. Data collected should only relate to the agreed upon areas determined in the preobservation conference. Every effort should be made by both the teacher and supervisor to fulfill all the terms planned and agreed upon at the preobservation conference. Responsibility for the second stage is held jointly — the teacher demonstrates performance, i.e., teaches, and the supervisor observes (Goldhammer, 1969; Krajewski, Martin, & Walden, 1983; Sergiovanni, 1987).

3. *Analysis and Strategy.* The third stage is comprised of two tasks performed by the supervisor. The supervisor first analyzes the record of teaching found in the gathered data. The supervisor hopefully identifies noteworthy or unusual incidents and patterns of teaching regarding the areas previously agreed upon at the preobservation conference. These become the topic of discussion for the forthcoming postobservation conference. He or she then organizes and translates the gathered data into meaningful information that can be easily understood by the teacher.

Next, the supervisor develops a supervisory strategy for working with the teacher to achieve change and improvement of instruction. The supervisor should keep in mind the teacher's trust level, amount of experience, ability level, personality, and any existing evaluation issues (Goldhammer, 1969; Krajewski, Martin, and Walden, 1983; Sergiovanni, 1987).

4. *The Postobservation Conference.* The postobservation conference is the fourth stage in this model of clinical supervision and is the shared responsibility of both parties. This conference provides feedback to the teacher of the supervisor's observations regarding the predetermined areas of interest. The teacher, with the help of the supervisor, analyzes the gathered data (Glenn, 1993; Krajewski, Martin, & Walden, 1983).

5. *The Postconference Analysis.* The last stage is the postconference analysis where the teacher and supervisor jointly determine a future plan of action to improve instruction. This stage is both an end and a beginning for the clinical supervision cycle. It brings closure to this cycle and sets the focus for the next cycle beginning with its own preobservation stage. It should be noted that stages four and five, Postobservation Conference and Postconference Analysis, most often occur during the same meeting with stage five immediately following stage four (Glenn, 1993; Goldhammer, 1969; Sergiovanni, 1987). See Figure 7-1.

186 Chapter 7 *Clinical Supervision*

Goldhammer's 5 Stage Clinical Supervision Model

Stage I: Preobservation Conference
(Most important stage)
- Teacher and supervisor present
- Set contract for what is taught
- Set ground rules
- Determine observation plan

Stage II: Observation Conference
- Teacher and supervisor present
- Systematic collection of data
- Adherence to the terms specified in stage I

Stage III: Analysis and Strategy
- Supervisor present
- Analyze collected data
- Formulate supervisory strategy

Stage IV: Postobservation Conference
- Teacher and supervisor present
- Teacher analyzes data with supervisor's help

Stage V: Post-Conference Analysis
- Teacher and supervisor present
- Formulate plan for improvement of performance

Figure 7-1

The Cogan Model

Also working at the Harvard School of Education, Morris Cogan followed Goldhammer and coined the title "clinical supervision" to describe this form of supervision. He introduced an expanded form of clinical supervision that included eight distinct phases or steps. Phases in Cogan's model that are identical or very similar to the Goldhammer model will only be discussed briefly. Cogan's 8 Phases of Supervision are:

1. *Establishing the Teacher-Supervisor Relationship.* The first phase of the Cogan clinical supervision model is the establishment of the teacher-supervisor relationship. Cogan, like Goldhammer (1969) before him, indicated that the first phase has particular importance. He insisted that the success or failure of the entire clinical supervision cycle rests on this phase. Phase 1 establishes a collegial relation between the teacher and the supervisor where both believe they share the responsibility for all forthcoming steps and activities in the supervision cycle. Cogan identified two distinct tasks that promote the establishment of this collegial relationship. These are:

   • Building a relationship based on mutual trust, respect, and support.

   • Inducing and guiding the teacher into the role of cosupervisor.

   Cogan insists that both tasks should be well advanced before the other phases are initiated (Cogan, 1973; Sergiovanni & Starratt, 1988).

2. *Planning for the Lesson.* The teacher and supervisor mutually plan the lesson to be observed including outcomes, activities, materials, strategies, processes, potential problems, and feedback techniques. Most often this phase occurs at a conference scheduled just before the observation.

3. *Planning the Observation Strategy.* A plan for observing behaviors in the classroom which are of interest or concern of the teacher is established. Method(s) for collecting the data are selected. This phase is usually considered the responsibility of the supervisor. However, as the teacher becomes more experienced and versed in observation techniques, he or she is encouraged to become more involved with the process (Cogan, 1973; Glenn, 1993). Most often, Phases 2 and 3 occur at the same conference before the classroom observation.

4. *Observing.* The supervisor observes the teacher teaching in the classroom and collects the predetermined data. Both the teacher and the supervisor adhere to the predetermined guidelines established during the previous phases.

188 Chapter 7 *Clinical Supervision*

5. *Analyzing the Teaching-Learning Process.* In contrast to the Goldhammer model, this phase requires that both the teacher and supervisor analyze the data that records what occurred in the classroom. If the teacher is inexperienced or new to the teacher-supervisor relationship, it is possible to analyze the data separately. Ideally, when the teacher is ready to work collegially, this phase should be done by the teacher and the supervisor together.

6. *Planning the Conference Strategy.* Usually, this phase is done by the supervisor, but may involve the teacher. Plans and strategies are developed for the forthcoming conference.

7. *The Conference.* The teacher and the supervisor meet and exchange information, their inferences, and interpretations of what occurred during the observation.

8. *Renewed Planning.* The teacher and supervisor collegially determine what changes should be made in the classroom. They then decide what will happen in the future. This initiates the supervision cycle again (Cogan, 1973; Glenn, 1993; Sergiovanni and Starratt, 1988). For a visual illustration of this model see Figure 7-2, Cogan's 8 Clinical Supervision Phases.

The Acheson and Gall Model

Acheson and Gall (1992) advocated a streamlined version of clinical supervision. They identified three phases in the process.

1. *Planning Conference.* The planning conference is the conference held between the supervisor and the teacher where the teacher is able to state goals, concerns, needs, and aspirations for his or her teaching performance. Current performance is compared to ideal instruction and any perceived discrepancies are discussed. The teacher and the supervisor mutually decide the lesson to be taught, the behavior(s) to be observed, and the purpose or goal of the observation. The method of data collection is jointly agreed upon.

2. *Classroom Observation.* During the observation the teacher conducts the lesson and the supervisor observes and gathers data. Each strictly adheres to the procedures and decisions mutually agreed upon at the planning conference.

Cogan's 8 Stage Clinical Supervision Model

Stage I: Establishing the Teacher-Supervisor Relationship
(The most important phase)
- Builds a trust and support relationship
- Induces teacher into a role of cosupervisor
- Occurs long before other phases begin

Stage II: Planning the Lesson
- Teacher and supervisor jointly plan the lesson
- All details are determined

Stage III: Planning the Observation Strategy
- Teacher decides area of interest
- Supervisor chooses appropriate observation technique(s). Teacher may participate when ready.

Stage IV: Observation
- Teacher teaches while supervisor observes and collects data

Stage V: Analyzing the Teaching-Learning Process
- Teacher and supervisor analyze the data
- May occur separately or together

Stage VI: Planning the Conference Strategy
- Supervisor develops strategy for conference
- Teacher may participate when ready

Stage VII: The Conference
- Teacher and supervisor meet
- Teacher and supervisor exchange information

Stage VIII: Renewed Planning
- Teacher and supervisor determine changes needed for instructional improvement
- New behaviors and remedies are determined and cycle begins again

Figure 7-2

3. *Feedback Conference.* The final phase is the feedback conference. Working together, the teacher and the supervisor review and analyze the observational data. The supervisor encourages the teacher to take the lead and to make inferences from the gathered data. At this point, the feedback conference becomes a planning conference. The teacher and supervisor decide together if more data should be collected or if the data is sufficient to develop a professional growth or development plan for the teacher involved. For each component of this phase the supervisor encourages and urges the teacher to take the lead (Acheson & Gall, 1992). Figure 7-3 is a visual representation of this three-phase model.

These are only three of the clinical supervision models available to today's supervisor. Many other models exist and are successfully used by American supervisors. These three models, do however, provide an opportunity to compare and contrast possibilities. For a visual representation of these forms or models of clinical supervision, refer to Figure 7-4, A Comparison of Three Clinical Supervision Models.

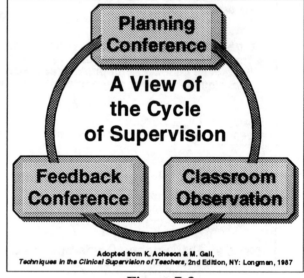

Figure 7-3

Stumbling Blocks to Successful Clinical Supervision

The major stumbling blocks to a successful clinical supervision process are lack of time, insufficient funds, established policies or contracts that require a contrary supervisory approach, and limitations within the participating individuals. Some of these may be overcome by committed supervisors.

A Comparison of Three Clinical Supervision Models		
Goldhammer	**Cogan**	**Acheson & Gall**
	1. Establishing the Teacher-supervisor Relationship (T* & S*)	
1. Preobservation Conference (T & S)	2. Planning the Lesson (T & S)	1. Planning Conference (T&S)
	3. Planning the Observation Strategy (S or T & S)	
2. Observation (T & S)	4. Observing (T & S)	2. Classroom Observation (T & S)
3. Analysis & Strategy (S)	5. Analyzing the Teaching-Learning Process (T&S) 6. Planning the Conference Strategy (S)	
4. Postobservation Conference (T&S) 5. Postconference Analysis ((T & S)	7. The Conference (T & S) 8. Renewed Planning (T & S)	3. Feedback Conference (T & S)
T = Teacher present S = Supervisor present		

Figure 7-4

Much time is required if clinical supervision is to be successful. The "supervision equated to evaluation" model requires much less time than does this alternative. Little time is needed for a supervisor to walk into the classroom with a checklist in hand, subjectively mark the Likkert scale, and return to his or her office. However, the clinical supervision cycle demands substantial time from both the supervisor and teacher. This process can only be successful if all parties willingly accept and embrace this time commitment.

Lack of funds to provide an adequate ratio of supervisors to teachers is a genuine stumbling block to the process. Ideally in high quality clinical supervision, the supervisor and teacher engage in numerous cycles during a school year. It becomes most difficult to be effective when only one supervisor is employed to work with as many as twenty teachers. If sufficient funding is not forthcoming, the only solutions open to the supervisor are to accept the conditions as they exist and conduct as many supervision cycles as are humanly possible.

If the district policy or the teachers' contract require a particular supervision model which precludes clinical supervision, the supervisor has no choice but to abide with the existing condition. The committed supervisor should work within the organization to change this situation in the future.

Participants are the final stumbling blocks to clinical supervision. Many teachers are apprehensive, suspicious, and disenchanted with all forms of supervision. Many have only experienced supervision equated to evaluation and have found that approach threatening, and at best, useless. The only way to successfully combat this problem is to provide the teacher with accurate information and develop a solid teacher-supervisor trust and support relationship.

The supervisor may also be a stumbling block to the process. To eliminate this problem the supervisor must demonstrate commitment and expertise.

Ms. Jones, here are the areas for improvement

Source: P. Whitaker (1997) Unpublished Cartoon

Implementing Clinical Supervision

The Supervisor's Readiness

To successfully implement any form of clinical supervision in the school, supervisors must be personally prepared to begin the process. Supervisors should be thoroughly familiar with all phases of the selected model, understand what activities or behaviors are associated with each step, and anticipate any pitfalls and their remedies. Supervisors must expect and be willing to devote the necessary time and energy required to complete each phase. Committed supervisors must truly believe in and practice democratic leadership and be prepared to work collegially with teachers. Since teachers respond most favorably to a nondirective style of supervision (Acheson & Gall, 1992), supervisors are

Chapter 7 *Clinical Supervision* **193**

urged to adopt this style. As Glickman (1985, 1981) explains, supervisors must determine which dominant behavior will be most effective with each teacher. Finally, successful implementation of clinical supervision demands that supervisors be accomplished in interpersonal and communications skills. See Figure 7-5.

Supervisory Characteristics for Successful Clinical Supervision

1. Be familiar with the steps of the selected model.

2. Understand stage (phase) behaviors and activities.

3. Anticipate problems and potential remedies.

4. Devote sufficient time and energy to the process.

5. Use a democratic leadership style.

6. Work collegially.

7. Use appropriate interpersonal and communications skills.

Figure 7-5

Preparing the Staff

A number of preimplementation strategies are available to supervisors. To ensure successful implementation of any clinical supervision model, all involved parties must be versed in the process, accept it as a positive alternative, and be willing to give it a genuine try. Supervisors can guide teachers in this process in many ways. There should be no surprises or misunderstandings at the time of implementation. Teachers must be intimately involved and have freedom of choice for change to occur (Hoy & Miskel, 1987; Mosher & Purpel, 1972).

The following four-stage preimplementation strategy is recommended for soliciting faculty support before implementation.

1. *Continue to build a trust relationship with each teacher.* From the very first contact between a given supervisor and teacher a relationship is established. Every subsequent encounter strengthens that relationship. New relationships are fragile and only become cemented over time. The committed supervisor must make a

194 Chapter 7 *Clinical Supervision*

conscious effort to establish and maintain a positive, trust and support relationship with each teacher. Ideally, supervisors should be a respected confidant of the teacher (Garman, 1982).

2. *Meet with the teachers to explain aspirations, intentions, purposes, and plan.* Supervisors should invite teachers to a meeting to candidly share the desire to engage in the process. Supervisors should include:

- Beliefs that: Good teaching leads to improved student achievement, instruction can be systematically improved, teachers are professionals responsible for their own improvement of instruction, the involved teachers are true professionals, and the role of supervisors is to work with each teacher to accomplish this goal.

- Belief that the chosen model of supervision is the vehicle that will facilitate the improvement of instruction and professional development for these teachers.

- A review of the literature regarding the effectiveness of this model.

- A personal desire to implement this model, if and only if, the involved teachers are willing to agree to a limited try after learning more about the process.

- An agreement from the teachers to participate in an inservice program to learn more about the process.

3. *Provide an inservice session to explain the model and the associated process.* Supervisors should personally conduct and lead this inservice session, thereby demonstrating commitment, expertise, and credibility. Supervisors should provide thorough information regarding the purpose, activities, and the expected behaviors of teachers and supervisors during each phase. He or she should allow ample time for questions and answers. Handouts, videotapes of an actual cycle, and discussion with teachers and supervisors presently engaged in this process are highly recommended. (Note: Many State Departments of Education and some professional organizations, such as the Association for Supervision and Curriculum Development, have materials and videos available.)

4. Ideally, at the conclusion of the inservice the teachers will be willing to make a commitment to participate in the process for a reasonable time. A one, preferably two-year, trial commitment is necessary to reap the potential benefits of any process. Refer to Figure 7-6 for an outline of these preimplementation strategies.

New teachers might join the staff after a new supervision model is implemented. These new teachers should be expected to participate in the process. Provisions should be made to give them the same support and information as the original staff members.

Preimplementation Supervisory Strategies

1. Build individual teacher-supervisor trust relationships.
2. Meet with involved teachers.
   - Explain aspirations, intentions, plans, and goals.
   - Secure teachers agreement for inservice training activities.
3. Provide inservice training activities on clinical supervision.
4. Secure a trial implementation commitment from involved teachers.

Figure 7-6

Practices for a Successful Preobservation Conference

Preparation and attention to detail are key to this most important phase in the clinical supervision cycle. This is a face-to-face meeting between the teacher and supervisor occuring before the observation (Oliva, 1993). Supervisors may increase the possibility of success by holding the conference at an appropriate time and place. Ample time should be provided. The conference should be scheduled at a convenient time for both individuals. The location of this conference might be crucial to its success. It should be held "on neutral ground" where the teacher feels secure and comfortable. The location must be private, insure confidentiality, and be free from constant interruptions. Supervisors' offices or the teachers' classrooms may not be the best choice for this meeting. A small conference room is ideal, but not essential.

Because each preobservation conference has multiple objectives, supervisors must keep meetings on course. Supervisors often keep short lists of the objectives of the

196 Chapter 7 *Clinical Supervision*

preobservation conference in plain sight during the meeting. A sample list of the preobservation purposes is found in Figure 7-7.

Preobservation Purposes

- Determine what will be taught during the observation.
  - lesson objectives
  - activities
  - materials, conditions, etc.
- Set ground rules.
  - time
  - place
  - length
- Determine the goal of the observation.
- Determine the behavior(s) of interest during the observation.
- Determine observational techniques.

Figure 7-7

Another consideration for this and the postobservation conference is verbal exchange. Because this process is designed to help teachers to improve instruction, teachers should be encouraged to verbalize their needs, interests, and concerns. Many teachers may initially feel reticent to share information. Supervisors must be supportive, sensitive to teachers' needs, nonjudgmental, and patient (Acheson & Gall, 1992).

Document the decisions mutually made by the teacher and supervisor. A written record of what was decided gives the teacher another security device. This written record need not be lengthy or complicated. Rather, it should be brief and easy to understand. A copy should be made for both parties. Figures 7-8 and 7-9 are examples of possible documentation forms.

Chapter 7 *Clinical Supervision* **197**

Observation Lesson

Teacher:_____

Time/Length: _____

Place: _____

Subject Area:_____

Objective(s): _____
_____

Activities: _____
_____

Anticipated Problems: _____
_____

Other Concerns: _____
_____
_____
_____

Figure 7-8

Observation Plan

Teacher:_____

Supervisor: _____

Time: _____

Place: _____

Length: _____

Goal(s) of the Observation:_____
_____
_____

Behavior(s) to Observe: _____
_____
_____
_____

Observational Technique(s) Used: _____
_____
_____
_____

Figure 7-9

198 Chapter 7 *Clinical Supervision*

Practices for a Successful Observation

Two areas of special interest to supervisors are: 1) the types of observation techniques available and, 2) methods of identifying effective teaching. Teachers often rely upon supervisors to determine which observation technique should be used to accurately examine a given behavior.

Observation Techniques. Many observation techniques and corresponding tools are available to supervisors. Many require practice to be accurate. Supervisors are urged to regularly experiment with various techniques, practice frequently, and remain abreast.

Numerous books, workshops, and training sessions are available to help supervisors learn and master specific observation techniques.

An overview of the most widely accepted and used observational techniques are:

- *Wide lens.* Wide lens or note taking is probably the most widely used technique. During the observation supervisors make anecdotal records or brief notes on general classroom events. Shortly following the observation the teacher and the supervisor review the written record to identify patterns and possible areas to examine in the future. This technique is particularly useful for the beginning teacher who needs feedback regarding overall performance and for the insecure teacher who has yet to identify a specific area for improvement.

- *Selective verbatim.* Selective verbatim is exactly what its name implies. It is the verbatim transcript of some verbal event in the classroom. Some verbal events that lend themselves to scrutiny by selective verbatim are the teacher's feedback statements, teacher questions, directions, and classroom management statements. Using this technique, supervisors record verbatim the chosen verbal event. When a teacher is concerned about feedback statements and chooses that as an area to examine, the supervisor would record *word-for-word* every praise or criticism statement the teacher uses. Later the teacher and supervisor would examine the statements looking for patterns. Note: Video or audio tape may supplement the written record, but should not replace a hard copy as documentation.

- *Seating chart observational records.* Seating chart observational records or *charting* are useful when the teacher and administrator have agreed to examine verbal flow between the teacher and the students, traffic or movement patterns, or student at-task behavior. On seating charts supervisors use symbols, usually arrows, to indicate what is happening during the observation. This seating chart is then analyzed to determine patterns. Nonthreatening objective information may be gleaned from this technique.

- *Checklists and timeline coding.* Checklists and timeline coding, often referred to simply as instruments, are more structured and are an attempt to objectify observation techniques. Checklists are designed to identify the type and quantity of selected teacher or classroom behaviors. These are often designed and produced for purchase. Two examples of these types of instruments are *Flanders' Interaction Analysis Category System* (FIAC) (Flanders, 1970) and Jacob Kounin's (1970) *Discipline and Group Management in Classrooms.* Timelines combine checklists with time. Specific behaviors are identified and recorded as they occur periodically, usually every minute. This is designed to provide the teacher and supervisor with information concerning both the quality and quantity of specific behaviors (Acheson & Gall, 1992; Glenn, 1993; Goldhammer, Anderson, & Krajewski, 1993; Oliva, 1993; Sergiovanni & Starratt, 1988).

Identifying Effective Teaching.

Supervisors must understand effective teaching to identify its presence or absence. Effective teaching is discussed in great detail in Chapter 4, *Observing Teaching.* If the goal of clinical supervision is to improve instruction, supervisors must be knowledgeable about *effective school research* and be able to apply that knowledge to the present situation. A review of the information provided in Chapter 4 is strongly advised.

One strategy supervisors may employ when working with teachers and effective teaching practices is to mutually identify the characteristics of good teaching. This may be accomplished by group brainstorming at an inservice workshop or similar opportunity. Acheson and Gall (1992) conducted such a workshop where the following list was generated.

Characteristics of a Good Teacher

- *Has positive relations with students*
- *Deals with students' emotions*
- *Maintains discipline and control*
- *Creates a favorable environment for learning*
- *Recognizes and provides for individual differences*
- *Enjoys working with students*
- *Obtains students' involvement in learning*
- *Is creative and innovative*
- *Emphasizes teaching of reading skills*
- *Gives students a good self-image*
- *Engages in professional growth activities*
- *Knows subject matter in depth*
- *Is flexible*
- *Is consistent*
- *Displays fairness*

(p. 23)

200 Chapter 7 *Clinical Supervision*

Oliva (1993) reviewed the effective school research and identifies eight characteristics of teachers who develop students that tend to have high achievement scores. These characteristics include:
- Has high expectations of students
- Sets clear classroom goals
- Focuses on academics
- Maintains order
- Uses appropriate instructional materials
- Provides feedback to students about performance
- Monitor student performance
- Uses positive reinforcement

Supervisors are urged to do likewise by establishing a list, and thereby, criteria for judging future decisions regarding effective teaching. When supervisors and teachers know the criteria for good teaching, observations are more understandable and valuable to the teacher who wishes to improve instruction.

Practices for a Successful Postobservation Conference

Successful supervisory practices for the postobservation or supervision conference are very similar to those for successful preobservation conferences. Postobservation conferences should be private, confidential, and candid. They should be held soon after the observation, at convenient times, and at acceptable locations. Teachers should be encouraged to speak openly as professionals.

Together we make a positive difference.
Source: P. Whitaker (1997) Unpublished cartoon

It is often difficult for teachers to share inferences regarding the observation with their supervisors. Some teachers feel that to admit to imperfection demeans them in the mind of their supervisor. Some ways to combat this misconception are to remain supportive, praise the teacher's efforts to infer, and remain nonjudgmental.

Supervisors must remember that teachers lead the way in identifying areas for improvement. Teachers may not interpret the data in the same way as supervisors. This may be very disconcerting to supervisors, but must be expected. Supervisors must remain patient and allow teachers to determine the course of action. Only those areas of weak behavior that teachers are willing to address will be successfully changed. It is to be hoped that, over time, teachers will identify their individual areas for improvement and choose to address these illusive areas.

Supervisory Practices During a Clinical Supervision Cycle

- Before the cycle
  - Prepare self
  - Prepare teacher(s)
  - Solidify teacher-supervisor relationship

- At the preobservation conference
  - Provide proper conditions and setting
  - Fulfill conference purposes
  - Encourage teacher participation

- At the observation
  - Skillfully use appropriate observational technique(s)
  - Employ knowledge of effective teaching

- At the post observation conference
  - Provide proper conditions and setting
  - Enourage teacher to openly analyze and infer
  - Remain nonjudgmental
  - Ensure appropriate corrective followup

Figure 7-10

Finally, supervisors must insure that agreed upon plans for improvement are appropriate and possible. Supervisors must help teachers set reachable goals. They must provide teachers with human and material resources to accomplish change and achieve goals.

202 Chapter 7 *Clinical Supervision*

Figure 7-10 provides an overview of the suggested supervisory strategies for a successful supervision cycle.

Principles and Practices for Success

- Understand the differences between supervision equated to evaluation and clinical supervision.

- Define clinical supervision.

- Identify at least three different models of clinical supervision.

- Be able to compare and contrast the components of several models of clinical supervision.

- Understand the stages of the Goldhammer, Cogan, and Acheson and Gall models.

- Recognize the major stumbling blocks to implementing clinical supervision.

- Be able to prepare teachers and self for implementation of clinical supervision.

- Understand and exercise successful supervisory strategies or practices during the preobservation conference, the observation, and the postobservation conference.

Summary

This chapter explained that historically the most common type of supervision used in America was supervision equated to evaluation. The desire for an alternative form was discussed and *clinical supervision* was offered as that alternative. Clinical supervision was defined as:

a continuing cyclical process of supervision, the purpose of which is to improve classroom instruction through the collegial interaction between the teacher and the supervisor.

Chapter 7 *Clinical Supervision* **203**

Major components found in clinical supervision models were discussed. They included: improvement of instruction, continuity, cyclical structure, collegiality, trust relationships, teacher-focused, and comprised of distinct steps.

Three widely acknowledged and accepted models of clinical supervision were examined closely. These were: Goldhammer's (1969) 5 Stage Model of Clinical Supervision, Cogan's (1973) 8 Phase Model of Clinical Supervision, and Acheson and Gall's (1992) 3 Phase Model. These models were scrutinized, compared, and contrasted.

Stumbling blocks to the implementation of clinical supervision in school settings were addressed. The effects of time expenditure, lack of funding, teacher reticence, and unprepared and uncommitted supervisors were highlighted.

Suggestions were made for the implementation of a clinical supervision model in schools. Supervisor readiness was discussed along with specific suggestions for preparing the teachers before implementation. Steps to prepare teachers include continued trust building, a candid forum of discussion, inservice training, and teachers' formal commitment.

Successful supervisory practices and strategies at preobservation conferences, classroom observations, and the postobservation conference were addressed. At the preobservation conference, preparation, attention to detail, ample time allotment, comfortable surroundings, and at-task behaviors were emphasized.

Strategies for successful supervision during the observation stage included knowledge and ability to apply a number of observation techniques and knowledge of effective teaching research. Observational techniques of wide lens, selective verbatim, seating chart records, checklists, and time coding were briefly explored. Supervisors were urged to become thoroughly versed in various observational techniques before implementation. Teaching behaviors which promote improved student performance were offered. Readers were encouraged to review Chapter 4 for a greater understanding of effective teaching behaviors.

Practices to increase the chances of successful postobservation conferences were discussed. Many suggestions were identical to good practices advocated at the preobservational conference. Special attention was given to the teacher's prominent role at this conference and the importance of the follow-up corrective measures mutually agreed upon by the supervisor and the teacher. The chapter concluded with a list of principles and practices for successful supervision.

204 Chapter 7 *Clinical Supervision*

Case Problem: *Newfangled Ideas*

Mrs. Peg Whichaker, a veteran of 23 years of teaching, is preparing for her first preobservation conference with the new assistant principal at her high school. She knows this assistant is young, eager, and full of newfangled ideas. She is somewhat apprehensive and even more annoyed at the prospect of this meeting. How can this youngster be her new supervisor? She wonders just what this person can tell her about teaching. She has received a superior rating on every evaluation for the last sixteen years. Help her improve? Ridiculous! She is convinced that this new district-approved clinical supervision process is complicated, confusing, time consuming, and probably, only a temporary measure.

If you were the new assistant principal, how would you deal with Mrs. Whichaker? What information and feelings would you share with her? How would you erase her misconceptions? What style and approach would you employ as you worked together? What other areas would you consider? What specific problems would you anticipate during the forthcoming clinical supervision cycle? How would you remedy them? Support your answers with information learned in this chapter.

Case Problem: *Out of Step*

Ms. Sandi Step is the new principal of Hometown Elementary School. Her new district and school, which seemed so progressive, still uses a form of supervision by evaluation. Sandi Step is a strong advocate and supporter of clinical supervision. Ms. Step feels out of step! She makes herself a promise to change the supervision system in her new school and district.

What suggestions and information would you share with Ms. Step to help her successfully accomplish her goal? What pitfalls do you envision she will face? How might she overcome them?

Case Problem: *Perplexed Professor*

Dr. Loren Moore, a professor of Educational Administration, is preparing for her *Foundations in School Administration* class. The topic for the three hour class is supervision and evaluation. Since this is the first time Dr. Moore has taught this course, she is considering what should be included for her students. The professor is perplexed.

Pretend you are Professor Moore. Keep in mind that this is a survey course designed to provide the students with a brief overview. What theories, concepts, models, paradigms, and practices should be included? What would you include about evaluation and supervision in general? What specifically would you include about clinical supervision — history, models, characteristics, and practices?

References

Acheson, K. A., & Gall, M. D. (1992). *Techniques in the clinical supervision of teachers* (3rd ed.). New York: Longman.

Cogan, M. (1973). *Clinical supervision.* Boston: Houghton Mifflin.

Flanders, N. (1970). *Analyzing Teacher Behavior.* Reading, MA: Addison-Wesley.

Garman, N. (1982). The clinical approach to supervision. T. Sergiovanni, (Ed.). *Supervision of teaching*, 1982 yearbook. Alexandria, VA: Association for Supervision and Curriculum Development.

Glenn, S. A. (1993). Supervision and evaluation of teachers. In J. Kaiser (Ed.), *Educational administration* (2nd ed.). Mequon, WI: Stylex Publishing Company.

Glickman, C. D. (1981). *Developmental supervision: Alternative practices for helping teachers improve instruction.* Alexandria, VA: Association for Supervision and Curriculum Development.

Glickman, C. D. (1985). *Supervision of instruction: A developmental approach.* Boston: Allyn and Bacon.

Goldhammer, R. (1969). *Clinical supervision.* New York: Holt, Rinehart, and Winston.

Goldhammer, R., Anderson, R., & Krajewski, R. (1993). *Clinical supervision: Special methods for the supervision of teachers* (3rd. ed.). New York: Harcourt Brace Jovanovich.

Hoy, W. K., & Miskel, C. G. (1987). *Educational administration: Theory, research, and practice.* New York: Random House.

Kaiser, J. (1993). *Educational administration* (2nd ed.). Mequon, WI: Stylex Publishing Company.

Kounin, J. (1970). *Discipline and group management in classrooms.* New York: Holt, Rinehart, and Winston.

Krajewski, R., Martin, J., & Walden, J. (1983). *The elementary school principalship: Leadership for the 1980s*. New York: Holt, Rinehart and Winston.

Lovell, J., & Wiles, K. (1983). *Supervision for better schools* (5th ed.). Englewood Cliffs, NJ: Prentice-Hall.

Mosher, R., & Purpel, D. (1972). *Supervision: The reluctant profession*. Boston: Houghton Mifflin.

Oliva, P. F. (1993). *Supervision for today's schools* (4th ed.). New York: Longman.

Sergiovanni, T. (1987). *The principalship: A reflective practice perspective*. Boston: Allyn and Bacon, Inc.

Sergiovanni, T., & Starratt, R. J. (1988). *Supervision: Human perspectives* (4th ed.). New York: McGraw-Hill.

Whitaker, P. (1997). *Miss Jones, here are the areas for improvement*. Unpublished cartoon.

Whitaker, P. (1997). *Together, we make a positive difference*. Unpublished cartoon.

Part III
Evaluation, Curriculum
and
Staff Development

Supervision
Georgia J. Kosmoski

Chapter 8

SUPERVISION, EVALUATION, AND THE LAW
Barbara A. Murray

Understanding Evaluation

Evaluation in education is defined as the assessment of programs, learning processes and outcomes, personnel performance, budgetary accountability, and cost benefit. This chapter is concerned with supervision of teacher performance and teacher evaluation. There are two purposes for evaluating teachers.

The *formative evaluation* is individual oriented and nonjudgmental. It serves as an continuous process that fosters skill improvement, professional growth, and overall improvement of instruction. The teacher and supervisor generally pursue the following steps during the formative process.

Questions to answer after studying this chapter

✔ What is the definition of evaluation?
✔ How is evaluation different from supervision?
✔ What are the characteristics of summative evaluation?
✔ What conflicts do principals face within the respective roles as supervisors and evaluators?
✔ How does the collective bargaining process influence supervision and evaluation?
✔ What limitations do teacher contracts impose upon the evaluation process?
✔ What are some methods that will reduce friction during the supervision and evaluation process?
✔ What are effective models for teacher evaluation?

---

1. The teacher and supervisor identify strengths and weakness exhibited by the teacher.
2. They both design an improvement plan that includes strategies and timelines for the teacher to improve designated weakness.
3. They implement the plan and determine whether an acceptable amount of improvement has occurred.
4. If acceptable improvement has occurred, they may elect to establish new objectives for further professional growth.
5. If an unacceptable amount of improvement has occurred, the teacher may develop new strategies for improvement or after a specified amount of time the teacher may be directed to exit the supervisory process and enter the *summative evaluation* process for dismissal. Refer to Figure 8-1.

-209-

Chapter 8 Supervision, Evaluation, and the Law

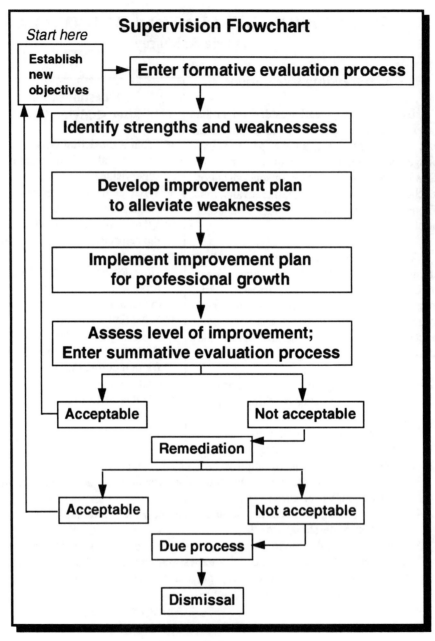

Figure 8-1

Chapter 8 *Supervision, Evaluation, and the Law* **211**

The literature describes supervisors engaged in the formative process as coaches, developers of talent, trusted mentors, counselors, teacher-sponsors, and colleagues. Gorton (1983) contrasts supervision with evaluation. He states that supervision is a process that recognizes performance strengths and provides feedback to support change that will improve upon weaknesses. Evaluation is used to form conclusions about the drawbacks of an individual's performance. Oliva (1989) describes nonevaluative supervision as focusing upon improvement of instruction through feedback which is consultative by nature. Oliva explained that evaluative supervision focuses upon personnel decisions which are related to contract renewal and career ladder promotions.

The summative or *judgmental* evaluation process is concerned with the purpose of the organization rather than the individual. Included are: 1) standardized performance criteria used to define that which is acceptable performance, and 2) feedback which is required within the various steps of due process and dismissal. McGreal (1988) suggests the following purposes for teacher evaluation: improvement of skills and knowledge, improvement of instructional practices, assisting marginal teachers, providing information for administrative decisions concerning career ladders and compensation programs, and acquiring information for decisions about renewal, transfer, or dismissal of personnel.

Wise and fellow authors (1984) suggested that the following conditions are important for a school district to maintain an effective teacher evaluation program.

- The program must parallel the educational philosophy and goals of the school district, district personnel and community, as well as the existing management style.
- The school district must define the purpose of supervision and develop a process that reflects the purpose. If the school district determines the purpose of supervision to be to improve instruction and encourage professional growth, the district practices should include resources and support for clinical supervision and staff development activities.
- The district must make a commitment to providing resources and assure that the process is viewed as serving the needs of personnel.
- The school district should encourage the involvement and responsibility of teachers to improve upon the evaluation process.

Even though school districts maintain the ultimate responsibility for the hiring, retention and dismissal of teachers, principals are faced with administering supervision and evaluation processes. Sergiovanni and Starrat (1988) address the dilemma of principals serving in both supervisory and evaluative capacities.

Evaluation is an integral part of supervision, and this reality cannot be ignored by supervisors and teachers. Indeed, attempts to mask evaluation aspects of supervision by not using the term or by denying that evaluation occurs or by declaring that evaluation is reserved only for the annual administrative review of one's teaching will not be convincing. Despite the rhetoric, everyone involved knows that evaluation is part of the process of supervision. (pp. 350-351)

Figure 8-2 represents a continuum of the principal's role during the supervision and evaluation process.

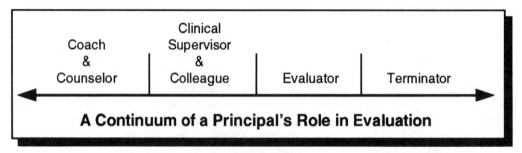

Figure 8-2

Resolving Conflict Between Supervision and Evaluation

Schmidt (1990) states "that teachers who know that their evaluators could eventually recommend their discharge will be less likely to discuss the difficulties they are encountering." The principal should understand that the role conflict between serving as a supervisor, counselor and coach, and as an administrator, evaluator, and terminator need not occur.

Typically, aspiring principals focus on training how to terminate (fire) teachers when in reality they can not get rid of many people. Principals should instead focus on changing teacher behavior to improve instruction and teacher performance. Behavior changes more readily following positive reinforcement. People who discover that they are in trouble will confide in someone whom they can trust and whom they perceive as possessing the knowledge and wisdom to help.

Figure 8-3 suggests fundamental procedures that encourage a professional climate conducive to good supervisory and evaluative practices. The first procedure is to communicate the school district's purpose and principal's philosophy concerning teacher evaluation with consideration towards personnel and the students. The second procedure is to assure the teacher that the evaluation will be administered ethically, legally, and within the guidelines of the teacher contract. Supervisors should openly communicate the criteria

Chapter 8 *Supervision, Evaluation, and the Law*   **213**

and procedures used during the evaluation process along with expectations of performance. They should assure the teacher by providing examples that validate and reinforce directives communicated to change teacher behavior and improve performance.

Fundamental Procedures for the Principal's Role in Evaluation

☞ **Communicate school district purpose and principal's philosophy considering personnel and students**

☞ **Evaluate ethically, legally, and within the guidelines of the master contract**

☞ **Openly communicate evaluation criteria and performance expectations**

☞ **Provide examples to validate information**

☞ **Utilize evaluation as a basis for directing performance improvement**

Figure 8-3

The Influence of Collective Bargaining

Executive Order 10988, January 1962, mandated that federal government employees be given the right to form and join any employee organization without fear of penalty. The mandate also granted each governmental agency the authority to recognize a

214 Chapter 8 *Supervision, Evaluation, and the Law*

single employee organization as the exclusive representative body of the employee unit. Executive Order 11491, October 1969, expanded the prior Order to include implementation of collective bargaining and the right to negotiate within the public sector.

No federal statutes specifically address collective bargaining practices between teacher groups and school boards. Such is left to the discretion of the respective states. Because collective bargaining laws and court decisions differ among the fifty states, persons who supervise personnel should familiarize themselves with their respective state and school district laws and policies. When state statutes do not specifically provide for collective bargaining practices, authority is delegated to the respective school boards as to whether they wish to recognize or not recognize them.

Florida typifies the current condition of most states. Collective bargaining within the public schools of Florida is regulated by Florida Statute §447, Public Employees Collective Bargaining Act, which was enacted pursuant to Article I, Section 6 of the Florida Constitution. This law, enacted in 1975, specifies the process by which representatives of each local school board and those of each public employee collective bargaining unit negotiate an agreement concerning wages, hours, and conditions of employment for the employees included within the specific bargaining unit. In this case *bargaining unit* is defined as a group of employees having a particular community of interest that is deemed appropriate by the Florida Public Employees Relations Commission.

As of the beginning of this decade 41 states had enacted similar laws. However, 23 of the 41 states were operating under collective bargaining laws without employment relation agencies to resolve labor disputes. Currently, there are approximately two and a half million members within the National Education Association and American Federation of Teachers.

Generally, employees may not opt out of the bargaining unit if their job is one which is included. The *bargaining unit* should not be confused with the *employee organization*, which is a labor organization or union which represents or seeks to represent the bargaining unit. As a matter of law, the *collective bargaining agreement*, or *master contract*, is incorporated into the personal employment contract of each belonging to respective bargaining unit.

Educational groups formed to bargain collectively include teachers, secretarial and maintenance staff, food service, and school bus drivers. There is currently a trend in some areas to include teachers and paraprofessionals within a single bargaining unit. However, other classified employees often do not belong to the same bargaining unit as the teachers.

In some parts of the country administrators have attempted to organize. However, it is more typical that supervisory employees, including principals, assistant principals, or any other person with the authority to hire, transfer, suspend, layoff, recall, promote, discharge,

Chapter 8 *Supervision, Evaluation, and the Law* **215**

assign, reward, or discipline other employees may not bargain collectively and therefore can not belong to a bargaining unit.

Employee organizations in many states may request recognition by the school board by showing that a majority of the employees in the unit favor the employee organization to represent them. Upon recognition, the employee organization may be required by law to petition the state employee relations agency for official certification as the exclusive representative for all employees within the bargaining unit. Following a review and determination that the petition process and papers are in order by the designated state agency, the proposed unit will be certified. In the case that a school board refuses to recognize the employee organization, the process may allow for the employee organization to petition directly to a designated state agency.

The Bargaining Process

The bargaining process differs among states and school districts. Murray and Murray (1994) describe collective bargaining procedures common to school districts. A bargaining agent with an existing collective bargaining agreement usually begins bargaining with the school board a few months before the expiration date of the existing agreement. The bargaining agent and the school board are most often represented at the bargaining table by teams of three to ten persons. The teams each consist of a chief negotiator, who actually does the speaking at the table, and several team members who are often selected because of their experience, expertise, and willingness to serve on the bargaining team.

At the first meeting, the teams decide the ground rules. These rules of procedure include maximum numbers of persons on the negotiation teams, the times and places of the meetings, and the method both will use to issue press releases. During that first meeting, the bargaining agent, or union, may present its initial proposal concerning wages, hours, wage-related benefits, and conditions of employment. This proposal may be piece meal or in a complete package.

The team representing the school board often presents a proposal that avoids the topics of wage and benefits. Items in a collective bargaining agreement that do not concern wages and wage-related benefits are normally referred to as *language items*. The initial proposal by the management team often contains language items that concern powers of the administration or *management rights*. At the first meeting both teams attempt to explain their proposal and the logic supporting its inclusion in the new agreement. Following the initial meeting both teams study the proposal of the other in preparation for the actual negotiations that begin at the next meeting.

216 Chapter 8 *Supervision, Evaluation, and the Law*

As the following meetings progress, each item in the master contract upon which both sides agree is marked *TA* for "*tentative agreement.*" The items are tentatively agreed upon because both sides know that negotiations concerning wages and benefits are the last to be discussed and during such discussion some of the items marked *TA* may be renegotiated. If agreement by both teams is finally reached concerning the entire collective bargaining agreement, it is presented to the members of the bargaining unit, union members and non-union members alike, for a ratification vote. Adequate notice for the vote must be given to all members of the bargaining unit. To do otherwise could be a breach by the bargaining agent of its duty to fairly represent all members of the bargaining unit.

If a majority of those voting accept the agreement, it is then presented to the school board for its ratification. If a majority of the school board votes to accept the agreement, it then becomes the working master contract that will govern the items and issues contained therein for the term specified.

If the two opposing negotiation teams fail to reach an agreement after a reasonable time, either may declare an *impasse* by written notification to the other team and to the designated state agency. When an impasse occurs either or both sides may act to appoint a *mediator* whose job is to assist in the resolution of the impasse and help the two sides arrive at an agreement. The mediator may be selected through the *Federal Mediation and Conciliation Service*, a federal government agency established in 1947 by the *Labor Management Relations Act* or the *Taft-Hartley Act*. Some states allow mediators to be selected in other manners. Furthermore, some states allow for the mediation process to be closed to the public. In such cases, the mediation process may be less formal than regular negotiations which are open to the public because of state *open door* or *sunshine laws*.

If the mediator is unsuccessful in resolving the impasse, either side may request that the designated state agency appoint a *special master* or *fact finder* who will conduct hearings to determine facts that are in dispute. These hearings are in many states open to the public, and therefore, quite formal. Within a predetermined number of days of the close of the final hearing, the fact finder will issue a report including a recommended decision to each team and the employee relations agency specified by state statute. The fact finder considers factors including comparative wages with others in the area, hazards of employment, physical qualifications, educational qualifications, intellectual qualifications, job training and skills, retirement plans, sick leave, job security, and the interest and welfare of the general public. Each side in the negotiations has a specified number of days from the receipt of the report and recommendations to reject in writing any or all recommendations along with their reasons. They transmit these to the designated agency such as the *Public Employment Relation Commission*.

Chapter 8 *Supervision, Evaluation, and the Law* **217**

Within a specified time from the rejection by either side in whole or in part of the report by the fact finder, the chief executive officer or school superintendent must submit a copy of the findings to the school board with recommendations for resolving the impasse. In most states the members of the bargaining unit will work under the language of the old contract until the impasse is resolved.

The role of the supervisor in the collective bargaining process is to acquire a clear and accurate understanding of the language contained within the master contract. It is important for supervisors to obtain official interpretations concerning language that is written ambiguously. It is not uncommon for principals and other persons serving as personnel supervisors to be called upon to provide input and recommendations for changing language provided in the master contract. It is recommended that personnel supervisors maintain a copy of the master contract throughout the term of the contract to mark problem areas for input before the collective bargaining process. The marked areas should include additional comments that describe in detail the problems and actual circumstances related to the language and possible solutions to the problem.

Because the negotiation process is often viewed as adversarial, persons serving in school-level supervisory positions should exercise caution towards their participation as members of the management negotiation team. School-level climate and trust levels can be negatively influenced following meetings where unresolved conflict has frayed nerves and tested the most docile of temperaments. What is more important, supervisors should recognize that the negotiating process is here to stay. This should not become a personal issue. It can be a positive experience when personnel are treated as professionals rather than subordinates to various positions of power.

Figure 8-4 describes strategies that cause adversarial relationships between bargaining unit members and management team members. Supervisors should:

1. become aware of potential adversarial relationships and not become intimidated by them
2. avoid personalizing the conflict
3. emphasize trust building and moral supervisory practices

Past Practice and Unfair Labor Practices

Johnson (1984) found that principals who functioned from a source of power related exclusively to the position of the principalship were more likely to have faculty who were alert to the contract language. Teachers operating under such an autocratic style of

218 Chapter 8 *Supervision, Evaluation, and the Law*

leadership typically are more contract conscious, and therefore, file substantially more grievances. Two general reasons for filing a grievance include the claim of a violation concerning a *past practice* or a claim of a violation of the *master agreement*. Past practice is an event that has had significant historical meaning.

Adversarial Bargaining Unit Strategies				
Strategy	**Rationale**	**Timeline**	**Target Group**	**Building Principal Response**
Provide incorrect information and communication that teams are dissatisfied with each other	Gain support through sympathy to draw side together	Outset of bargaining process	The side which initiates this strategy	If management team initiates— "No comment" If Unit initiates— provide factual information
Go public concerning school board expenditures for bargaining, such as salary for negotiator	Intimidate school board members and prevent hiring a professional negotiator and to gain sympathy from public	Early in the bargaining process and when school board discusses hiring such an outsider	Teachers, building personnel and the community	"No comment"
Divide the superintendent and school board members from negotiation team	To prevent hiring an outside negotiator and to foster distrust in negotiation team	When negotiations are not progressing	Superintendent, school board members and building personnel	Little or no comment Just factual information

Initiate negative publicity from unit members, alleging poor working conditions, disrepair of buildings, lack of safety and administrative support	To receive increase in dollars by placing pressure on the school board to avoid negative publicity	Throughout the bargaining process	Community	Little or no comment— only factual information
Undermine building level administrators and superintendent	To remove them from the bargaining process and to redirect the focus of the school board	Throughout the bargaining process	Community and school board	Positive factual information
Personally contact each school board member to solicit them to take leadership role in the bargaining process	To redirect the focus of the school board and to separate the members	When the bargaining process reaches a stalemate	School board members	"No comment" but inform the superintendent
Attack the school board for refusing to bargain in good faith	To create a "trump card" to trade for something else	Throughout the bargaining process	Community and other school personnel	Little or no comment— only factual information
Seek increased publicity such as picket lines, leaflets, news conferences, parent association support and media releases	To gain sympathy and support from community	When the bargaining process is not progressing in the desired direction	Community, school personnel, and school board members	Little or no comment— only factual information

220 Chapter 8 *Supervision, Evaluation, and the Law*

Job action such as work slow down, working to the contract, using personal or sick days, not speaking to building level administrators	To gain more publicity and to send a not-so-subtle message that a strike may be forthcoming	When the bargaining process is not progressing in the desired manner	Community and teachers	Little or no comment—only factual information and assurances that students are safe and being served as well as possible
Creating a community nuisance by boycotting businesses owned by school board members or supporting the school board	To gain support of community and to punish those not supporting the teachers	When bargaining is not progressing as desired	School board and anyone supporting the school board	Little or no comment—reinforce the definition of professional behavior—education is to serve children
Spread rumors of strike or even take a strike vote	To intimidate the school board and frighten the community	Late in the bargaining process when stalemate has been reached	Community and school board	Assure the community of the safety of their children and that their education is the priority of the administration
Solicit community members to attend school board meetings	To pressure the school board	Throughout the bargaining process	School board and superintendent	"No comment"
Call for binding arbitration or intervention by the State Employment Relations Board	To pressure the school board	Throughout the bargaining process	School Board	"No comment"

Figure 8-4

Elkouri and Elkouri (1989) describe the elements that must be present in order for a practice to be recognized as having an historical significance, which in essence becomes as enforceable as the actual contract: 1) the practice must be widely recognized by the unit members, 2) the practice must be absent of ambiguity, and 3) the practice must be administered over a period of time to warrant being labeled "past practice."

Unfair labor practices are, in essence, violations of the rules of collective bargaining as specified in the enabling statute. Murray and Murray (1994) list the Florida rules concerning unfair labor practices as mandated by *The Public Employees Collective Bargaining Act*. The rules include the following.

- The public entity may not encourage or discourage union membership of employees. Such pressure includes discrimination in hiring, assignment, dismissal, tenure, or working conditions of employees. The public entity may not dominate, interfere with, or assist the formation or administration of an employee organization. Neither the public entity nor the employee organization as the bargaining agent may refuse to bargain collectively in good faith.

- The public entity may not refuse to discuss an employee grievance in good faith. This law also prohibits the public entity from retaliating against an employee who exercises his or her rights within the grievance procedure.

- The employee organization as the bargaining agent may not interfere with or coerce employees in the exercise of their rights under the Public Employees Collective Bargaining Act.

- The employee organization may not participate in a strike.

- The employee organization and any of its members may not solicit support from students in grade school, high school, or higher education.

- The employee organization may not cause or attempt to cause the governmental entity or any of its representatives to discriminate against employees because of their membership or nonmembership in the employees' organization. (pp. 160-1).

While the above rules are specific to Florida, they generally represent items commonly found in other states.

The Grievance Procedure

The master collective bargaining agreement serves as the school district's blueprint for the hours, wages, and other working conditions of the employees in the bargaining unit. The agreement also stipulates the rights and responsibilities of the school board and its representatives such as building principals and other supervisors. When a member of the bargaining unit believes that a school board representative has or continues to violate a provision of the master agreement, the employee can seek redress through the *grievance procedure*. Some state laws require that the grievance procedure culminate in *binding*

222 Chapter 8 *Supervision, Evaluation, and the Law*

arbitration. That is the final step whereby a third and neutral party hears the complaint and renders a decision binding upon the bargaining unit and the school board.

Murray and Murray (1994) describe a typical grievance procedure as follows:

A typical negotiated grievance procedure normally provides an initial step which is an informal voicing of the grievant's concern to his or her immediate supervisor—normally the principal. Most grievances are settled at this point without further proceedings. If, however, the grievance is not settled at the initial step, the normal procedure is to reduce the complaint to writing. This writing must include the section of the master collective bargaining agreement alleged to have been violated. It must also contain the redress sought and must be submitted to the same immediate supervisor.

Within a specified period of time the supervisor must answer the grievance by either satisfying the grievant or by denying such. If the grievance is denied, it will proceed to the next step of the procedure which normally requires the complaint to be forwarded to a higher level administrator such as an assistant school superintendent. Assuming the grievance is not satisfied in step two of the procedure, the third step normally provides that the complaint be considered by the superintendent and then culminates into a final step of a third and neutral party binding arbitration. (pp. 158-9)

Some school district procedures provide for school board review prior to a grievance being forwarded to binding arbitration. The arbitrator usually is not allowed to add to, subtract from, or alter the terms of the collective bargaining agreement. Figure 8-5 shows an example of the information which appears on a grievance form.

Teacher Strikes

Many state laws preclude public school teachers from participating in strikes and allow for striking personnel to be court ordered back to work. In addition, heavy fines can be assessed against the organization and striking individuals can be terminated or placed on probation upon their return to work. The courts have uniformly held that strikes are illegal unless state statute specifically provides for such. In states where statutes permit strikes, procedures are often viewed as convoluted insofar as strikes are not considered ordinary.

Job actions such as slow downs, refusal to grade papers or record grades, and refusal to perform other duties have been looked upon by the courts with disdain. A work stoppage was ruled as a strike in Michigan (*Warren Education Association v. Adams, 1975*). A New Jersey case received a similar decision when the court ruled that refusal to perform extracurricular duties constituted a strike (*Board of Education of City of Asbury Park v. Asbury Park Education Association, 1976).* Generally, the courts have ruled that any

Chapter 8 *Supervision, Evaluation, and the Law* **223**

concerted absence from work, work stoppage, and other such attempts to interfere with the overall operations and purpose of the school are illegal.

Example Grievance Form
Sunshine School District
Sunshine Teachers Association
Appendix C: Grievance

I.
Grievant:

Name:_____   STEP 1 GRIEVANCE REPRESENTATIVE

School:_____   NAME: _____

Dept.:_____   MAILING ADDRESS:

Grievant school phone:_____   _____

If grievant is represented by union or legal council,   OFFICE PHONE:_____
all district communications should go to the
grievants' representative

Other address to which district mailings pertinent to grievance should be sent

_____

_____

_____

II: GRIEVANCE:
Provisions of Agreement allegedly violated (specify Articles and Sections):

_____

_____

_____

III: AUTHORIZATION
I will be represented in this grievance by: (Check one - representative must
sign on appropriate line):
___Union _____

___Legal Counsel _____

___Myself _____

I (do)____ (do not)____ want a postponement for up to 25 days to seek informal
resolution of this grievance.

I UNDERSTAND AGREE THAT BY FILING THIS GRIEVANCE, I WAIVE WHATEVER
RIGHTS I MIGHT HAVE UNDER CHAPTER XXX OF THE STATE STATUTES WITH
REGARD TO THE MATTERS I HAVE RAISED HEREIN AND UNDER OTHER SCHOOL
DISTRICT PROCEDURES WHICH MAY BE AVAILABLE TO ADDRESS THESE MATTERS

This grievance was filed with the Superintendent's office on _____
by (check one) mail (certified or registered; restricted delivery;
return receipt requested)_____; personal delivery _____

For administrative use only: Date Grievance Received by Superintendent's office_____
Immediate Supervisor's Decision: _____

_____

_____

Supervisor's Signature: _____   Date: _____

copies to: Supervisor/Principal
Association building representative
Grievance chairperson
Teacher

Figure 8-5

224 Chapter 8 *Supervision, Evaluation, and the Law*

In 1968, Florida experienced a state-wide teacher strike in which 25,712 teachers, approximately 40% of the teachers, within the state, walked out. Upon the conclusion of the strike and the return of the teachers some of the school districts elected to avail themselves of punitive remedies. In Lee County the school board conditioned the return of its 400 striking teachers upon each paying the district $100. The *National Education Association* filed suit in federal district court challenging the right of the school board to assess such a fine. The federal district court ruled the fine as violating *The 14th Amendment* guarantee of due process. The Lee County School Board appealed this decision to the federal circuit court of appeals which certified it to the United States Supreme Court.

The United States Supreme Court, as it often does in state matters, certified the case to the Florida Supreme Court. The Florida Supreme Court recognized the right of the parties to negotiate a back-to-work agreement and that the controversy centered on the use of the term "fine." Even though the Court referred to the school board's taking of broad discretion in this area as "Kentucky windage," it upheld the agreement and ruled in favor of the Lee County School Board by simply relabeling the "fine" as *liquidated damages* which is allowed under Florida Law. The court supported this decision by stating "that just because the cat had her kittens in the oven, does not make them biscuits."

The following includes suggestions for supervisors to prevent personnel from filing grievances.

1. Recognize that collective bargaining is a way of life, and that the master agreement serves as the guideline for dealing with personnel matters.
2. Maintain an appropriate level of flexibility by recognizing that there is more than one solution to many problems.
3. Reflect respect for personnel as the professional experts within the field and respective content areas.
4. Refrain from adversarial comments and behavior that erodes trust and overall working relations.
5. Practice being a good listener who maintains control and does not personalize complaints even in the most difficult of circumstances.
6. Exercise caution when allowing for practices which deviate from the language in the master agreement.
7. Do not engage in "under-the-table" or "off the record" agreements which may result in inconsistent treatment of personnel.
8. Prepare to receive the "heat" during the negotiating process by preparing factual information and developing ideas that may offer legitimate solutions to the problem.
9. Maintain silence when matters are not communicated in a reasonable fashion.
10. Remain calm and in control to convey the message that you will not be intimidated or manipulated.

Chapter 8 *Supervision, Evaluation, and the Law* **225**

Constitutional Legal Constraints

Section 1 of the 14th Amendment to the United States Constitution provides in part "nor shall any State deprive any person of life, liberty, or property, without due process of law. . . .." Public school districts are considered political subdivisions of the state. Teachers and administrators are considered state employees at least for the purpose of certain constitutional protections. Certain United States constitutional rights afforded to public school teachers and administrators as a result of the 14th Amendment in conjunction with the Bill of Rights of the United States Constitution include the following:

- Freedom of Expression
- Academic Freedom
- Freedom from Prior Restraint
- Freedom of Association
- Right to Privacy
- Right of Personal Appearance

Freedom of Expression

Freedom of expression is a right grounded in *The First Amendment* to the United States Constitution. It becomes a topic of concern when a school employee is dismissed or disciplined by a school district supervisor because of some out-of-classroom statement, writing or other communication made by the school employee. The right of public school employees to engage in such communications has been defined and qualified by three landmark decisions by the United States Supreme Court.

1. In the case of *Marvin L. Pickering v. Board of Education*, an Illinois school board dismissed a teacher who wrote a letter to a local newspaper admonishing the school board and superintendent for the way they had handled proposals to increase school revenues and taxes. The school board decided that the letter written by Pickering was detrimental to the district and required the dismissal of Pickering from his teaching position.

   The United States Supreme Court ruled that the teacher's right to speak on issues of public importance could not furnish the basis for his dismissal. The Court further noted, "where such comments do not interfere with the maintaining of discipline by immediate superiors or harmony among coworkers," such statements may not constitutionally furnish grounds for dismissal.

   Supervisors should understand the lessons to be learned from the Pickering case. School employees generally have the right to speak out on issues of public

226 Chapter 8 *Supervision, Evaluation, and the Law*

concern. The right is not absolute and may be restricted if the expression were to cause undo disruption to the organization's effectiveness or impair the teacher's classroom effectiveness. If disruption exists, the Court will balance the interest of the employee against the interest of the organization.

2. The second Supreme Court decision is that of *Mt. Healthy v. Doyle (1977)* about a nontenured teacher who had been involved in several disruptive incidents. He had engaged in arguments with other teachers and other school employees, made an obscene gesture to female students and had called a radio station and related the contents of the building principal's memorandum concerning faculty appearance. The school board refused to renew his teaching contract citing as the reason Doyle's lack of tact in handling professional matters. They specifically mentioned his gesture to the female students and contact with the radio station. Doyle brought suit against the school district and based his position on Pickering.

The United States Supreme Court held that Doyle's communication to the radio station was protected by the First and Fourteenth Amendments; but even though Doyle's communication was protected, such should not preclude his dismissal if the school board would have otherwise reached the same decision. The Court further stated that an exercise of one's right to freedom of speech should not place him in a worse or better position than he would be without such exercise and the issue of tenure was not a deciding factor in this case. Even though a nontenured teacher could be legally *nonrenewed* without reasons offered, such teacher could not be nonrenewed for constitutionally protected reasons.

Supervisors should understand that teachers working under an employment contract without permanent or tenure status, in most states, may be legally nonrenewed with no reasons given. The teacher may not be nonrenewed for statutorily or constitutionally prohibited reasons. It is wise in this case for supervisors to refrain from providing even well intended reasons. An example that might likely be overturned is, "We need a younger person for the position."

3. The third Supreme Court decision that has been used to define the limits of freedom of expression of public school employees involved the dismissal of an assistant district attorney. In *Connick v. Myers (1983)* an assistant district attorney was internally transferred by her supervisor to prosecute cases in a different section of the criminal court. Ms. Myers voiced her objection to no avail. She then solicited the views of coworkers in a questionnaire. The topics listed on the questionnaire concerned transfer policy, morale, confidentiality, the need for a grievance committee, and whether employees felt pressure to work in political campaigns. The district attorney ordered her dismissal for failure to accept the transfer and considered the questionnaire an act of insubordination.

The United States Supreme Court held that "a federal court is not the appropriate forum to review the wisdom of personnel decisions taken by a public agency." and "...except for one question regarding pressure upon employees to work in political campaigns, the questions posed were not of public concern." The Court held that the district attorney did not have to tolerate action which he believed would disrupt the office, undermine his authority and destroy close working relationships within the office.

The lesson for supervisors is that for public employees to enjoy freedom of expression they must prove two points: 1) The expression was of public concern and not merely an internal or personal concern; and 2) The First Amendment interests of the employee outweighs the interest of the organization.

Academic Freedom

A teacher normally has the discretion to select any teaching technique as long as the teacher has not otherwise been directed, and the selected teaching technique is one that is generally accepted among the teaching profession. The U.S. Supreme Court has emphasized that the right to teach, to inquire, to evaluate, and to study is fundamental to a democratic society. The right of academic freedom, however, is not absolute. In *Parducci v. Rutland (1970)*, the Court used a balancing test to determine if the objectionable conduct "materially and substantially interferes with the requirements of appropriate discipline in the operation of the school." In the *Parducci* case the Court found no convincing evidence that a *Vonnegut* reading assignment was inappropriate for high school juniors or that it created a significant disruption to the educational process of the school.

Supervisors should be careful not to cross ethical boundaries when engaged in teacher observations and evaluations and require teacher behavior that infringes upon academic freedom. It is important to remember that no single teaching technique works best during all situations and the final determination concerning teacher effectiveness should be based upon whether the students are learning.

Freedom from Prior Restraint

Prior restraint is described as the governmental preclusion of some expression prior to the expression being transmitted. In one case, *National Gay Task Force v. Board of Education of the City of Oklahoma City* (1985), the Tenth Circuit Court of Appeals invalidated an Oklahoma statute which allowed for the dismissal of a teacher for "advocating, soliciting, imposing, encouraging or promoting public or private homosexual

228 Chapter 8 *Supervision, Evaluation, and the Law*

activity in a manner that creates a substantial risk that such conduct will come to the attention of school children or school employees.

The Supreme Court looks upon prior restraint by governmental agencies very critically. The courts, however, allow for the agency to designate a reasonable time, place, and manner of certain expressions. Supervisors must understand that when attempting to determine time, place, and the manner of communication, any restriction may not be based upon the content of the expression. For example, efforts by the school administration to restrict the distribution of the teacher union newsletter, if challenged, will probably be unsuccessful.

Freedom of Association

The government or its agencies may not prohibit organizational membership as a condition of public employment. The general rule is that courts will veto any attempt to inhibit the constitutional rights of citizens unless the government is able to show a compelling public interest to justify its actions. Such memberships may include, but are not limited to, political parties and local teacher associations.

Right to Privacy

The right to privacy is not found in any specific area of *The United States Constitution* but rather from *The Bill of Rights* as included in the due process guarantee of *The Fourteenth Amendment* through judicial interpretation. This right to privacy is responsible for prohibiting school districts to designate where employees must send their own children to school. Most states have statutes often referred to as *open door* or *sunshine laws* that require school boards and other political entities to meet and make decisions in public meetings. The statutes often specify which information is open to public inspection. Supervisors should become familiar with state law and local school district policy so as not to find themselves in violation. These laws usually stipulate criteria necessary for inspection of personnel files, payroll information, and derogatory material placed into personnel files.

A second issue affecting supervisors is whether educators have a right to privacy in their offices, desks, filing cabinets, or other work areas. The general rule is that if areas have traditionally been treated as private places for employees, then employees probably enjoy protected privacy rights therein. A United States Supreme Court decision involving a publicly employed physician was based not upon the fact that the employee was a physician but rather upon the fact the he was a public employee. Therefore, the decision is considered to hold significance to all public employees including public school teachers and administrators. The Court reviewed two issues: whether the employee had a reasonable expectation of privacy in his office, desk, and filing cabinets; and whether the legitimate government interest in entering the premises in the particular situation outweighed the employee's interest in privacy. The Court noted:

Ordinarily such a search of a public employee's office, desk or files by a supervisor will be justified at its inception when there are reasonable grounds for suspecting that the search will turn up evidence that the employee is guilty of work-related misconduct, or that the search is necessary for a noninvestigatory work-related purpose such as to retrieve a needed file. The search will be permissible in its scope when the measures adopted are reasonably related to the objectives of the search and not excessively intrusive in light of the nature of the [alleged misconduct]. (O'Conner v. Ortega, 1987)

Right to Personal Appearance

The chosen dress, hair length, male facial hair, and appearance of a teacher are not subject to school board restrictions unless it can be shown that the appearance is disruptive to the overall purpose of education or to the school or is related to a governmental interest in public safety. Educators claiming that appearance reflects racial or religious beliefs are likely to enjoy more protection than those persons merely exercising personal preference.

Supervisors should exercise caution when challenging teaching and other school personnel concerning selected dress, hair style and general appearance. While some courts have supported related district policies, supervisors must realize that challenges of this type often result in more damage than benefit to the educational climate and learning environment. Supervisors may want to learn from the methods used by the courts when making decisions and balance whether placing restrictions on dress and eroding teacher morale deserves more supervisory time than supervisory practices that will improve upon teaching strategies and learning outcomes.

Due Process

The Fourteenth Amendment provides that a public school teacher or administrator may not be deprived of a property or liberty right without proper due process of law. A property right is described as a right of entitlement such as a right to a job. A liberty right is described as a right to be free from undo restraint. An example of an infringed liberty right might include a teacher who is dismissed improperly and accused publicly of something that hinders his or her chances of getting another job. Supervisors of personnel have the legal

230 Chapter 8 *Supervision, Evaluation, and the Law*

responsibility to use fair treatment concerning matters that relate to property and liberty rights of teachers.

The rights of the public school teacher during a dismissal proceeding are determined by the type of employment contract of the teacher. The teacher whose contract is permanent or of tenure status has a legal expectation of continued employment. Such permanent status has been looked upon by the courts as qualifying as a property right and therefore requires a substantial amount of procedural due process. A teacher who is working under an annual or impermanent contract does not have a legal expectation of continued employment and therefore does not enjoy the same process because the property right has not been established.

Although respective state statutes address circumstances and offenses for which permanent or tenured teachers may be dismissed, the following lists reasons.

- Immorality described as behavior counter to public standards.
- Misconduct in office defined as a violation of ethics or knowingly breaking the law that is so serious as to impair the effectiveness of the individual's performance.
- Incompetency (difficult to prove) described as the inability to discharge the educational duties deemed common to those practicing within the field.
- Gross insubordination and willful neglect of duty, generally described as a continuing refusal to obey a direct and reasonable order given by an individual with proper authority.
- Moral turpitude defined as a crime evidenced by an act of idleness which is in violation of the standards of the time.

Various statutes and court decisions indicate that the following steps are required in most tenured teacher dismissal proceedings.

1. The teacher is to receive notice by the statutory deadline concerning the school board's consideration for the decision to terminate the teacher's contract.
2. The teacher is to be provided evidence such as complete and detailed documentation by the supervisor in charge, usually the building principal, as to the reasons for the recommendation for dismissal.
3. The teacher is to be provided information concerning the hearing procedures including time frames and requirements for requesting an administrative hearing to present testimony that supports the side of the teacher and for receiving testimony by the school representatives on evidence that supports the views of the school district.
4. The teacher is entitled to an impartial hearing.
5. Following the hearing a decision is made by the school district based on factual information.
6. If state statute permits, an appeal process may be initiated.

Chapter 8 *Supervision, Evaluation, and the Law* **231**

Contractual Constraints

The master agreement serves as the blueprint concerning personnel matters. Supervisors should become familiar with the contents of the master agreement or master contract so as not to make incorrect decisions that could provide reasons for teachers to file grievances. Contract language is as varied as the school districts and teacher organizations which collectively bargain, and therefore, is not practical to discuss here. One example of contract language, however, which deserves attention is the *just cause provision.*

School principals and other personnel supervisors evaluate or supervise teachers on a daily basis but submit formally written evaluations of teachers twice per school year. Historically, the evaluator has enjoyed the position of dominance in the evaluator-teacher relationship. While trends toward the method of collegial supervision and the erosion of the dominant evaluator figure are supportable, contract language such as "just cause" should be looked upon critically for its impact on the evaluation process. The *just cause* provision generally recites some verbiage to the effect that any teacher discharge must be precipitated by a good reason or be for just cause.

To the average person, this provision simply states that no teacher is to be fired without the fairness of receiving a good reason. Frequently, the "just cause" provision is joined with additional language which states that the evaluator should offer assistance to any teacher experiencing performance difficulties. The premise seems reasonable, harmless, and supportive of most clinical supervision models. However, when such practices become a requirement of the contract language, school evaluators not only must have a good reason to discharge a teacher but most collective bargaining agreements allow for the teacher to grieve the discharge all the way to a third-party binding arbitrator.

Typically, timelines for such grievance procedures do not terminate with a decision from the arbitrator until well into the subsequent school year and, therefore, create complications concerning the selection and hiring of a replacement teacher. It is important to realize that the replacement teacher is also protected under the same collective bargaining agreement as the reinstated teacher.

The above seems to describe that which is fair for teachers discharged inappropriately. However, the federal Constitution and state statutes protect employees from unfair practices by requiring due process of law and the courts have been reluctant to become involved with making determinations which "second guess" professional decisions.

Grievance and arbitration proceedings most often focus on the adequacy of the written evaluations and any related documentation given to the teacher by the evaluator. The teacher organization will charge that the evaluations were not accurate, timely, did not offer

232 Chapter 8 *Supervision, Evaluation, and the Law*

appropriate or sufficient suggestions for improvement, did not clearly establish reasonable time limits for improvement and were not handled properly. In fact, the evaluator will be on trial during the grievance proceedings.

If the arbitrator finds in favor of, and reinstates, the teacher with an award of back salary, the school district may feel pressured to find a scapegoat to save face. It is unfortunate when such pressure is reflected in the evaluation of the evaluator. The real tragedy is that the typical evaluator is likely to respond to such treatment with future reluctance to recommend dismissal of any teachers (including first year teachers). This behavior can be misinterpreted as weak administration of the school. In such cases, it is unfortunate that evaluators fall victim to collective bargaining agreements when they have had little part in bargaining.

Friction-reducing Methods

The evaluator should learn and practice writing impeccable evaluations. Such evaluations should offer very specific suggestions for improvement along with a workable and reasonable timeline for completion. The teacher should receive written evaluative reports from several evaluations, not merely the number required by state law and local policy. The *management by objectives* model provides guidelines for developing effective steps and procedures.

The evaluator should begin by giving the teacher a memorandum expressing dissatisfaction with the teacher's performance. The evaluator should include documentation and a list of goals toward which the teacher should work. The goals are typically broad such as "to maintain better control over students" and should be accompanied by two or three related objectives. Objectives should be specific and clearly communicate specific tasks for the teacher to perform. Examples of such tasks are: 1) assign students to certain seats, 2) arrive at your classroom on time, and 3) develop and post a list of classroom rules.

The teacher should be given the memorandum in person, not through the school mail. The delivery of the memorandum along with all conferences should be documented. Do not give conflicting signals. If other supervisors or assistant principals are assigned to your building, it is wise to have separate evaluations from each concerning the teacher in question.

Following the above steps the evaluator should make his or her immediate supervisor aware of the situation. The school district superintendent and school board should also receive information to prepare for meetings for discussions concerning teacher nonrenewal. The school board should be made aware that unions have learned over the years that strategies attacking the evaluator go a long way to reduce the number of future recommendations for teacher non-renewal. If a grievance is initiated, school district administrative personnel should realize that even when the school district wins the

Chapter 8 *Supervision, Evaluation, and the Law* **233**

grievance, the administrator or supervisor in charge usually suffers a public verbal whipping in the process. The union representative will strive to focus upon the evaluator as the cause of the problem and depicting the "dedicated teacher" as one who is trying to teach in spite of your supervisory weaknesses and abuses.

While no one has created a method by which to predict the direction of an arbitrator's decision, meticulous documentation, detailed, clearly communicated suggestions and timelines will provide safeguards against supervisor ineffectiveness.

A Model for Documenting the Observation

Noyer, Finnegan, and Finn (1976) developed a functional approach to documenting teaching performance during an observation. This model, based upon positive reinforcement technique, separates written documentation into two parts: the *positive translation* and the *positive statement*.

Positive Translation

The *positive translation* is a statement made by the evaluator that focuses upon teacher performance in need of improvement. The *translation* is delineated into four components: the *key positive sentence*, *suggestion*, *example*, and *follow up statement*.

Key Positive Sentence. The first component, a *key positive sentence*, begins such as, "It is so natural to" or "Did you notice that?" Figure 8-6 shows examples of *key positive sentence* beginnings.

Key Positive Sentence Beginnings

☞ Be careful ...
☞ You may want to ...
☞ Good recovery when ...
☞ Maybe it would have been better to ...
☞ Next time you may want to ...
☞ I noticed that ...
☞ It's amazing how ...
☞ Did you think that ...
☞ Rather than _____ would you agree that _____ would be better?
☞ It's so natural to ...

Figure 8-6

234 Chapter 8 *Supervision, Evaluation, and the Law*

Suggestion. The second component includes a *suggestion* that is made by the evaluator concerning strategies for improving performance. Such suggestions might include, "You may want to close the distance between you and the students when teaching a lesson," and can be related to any teaching performance-related activities. Because suggestions are varied across teaching areas related to planning, instructional delivery, questioning techniques, praise, and student and program evaluation, the successful evaluator must be knowledgeable about effective practices within the respective content areas and field of education.

Example. The third component that is closely related to the second includes an *example* that is given by the evaluator to provide detailed support for the above suggestion. An example of a specific behavior that supports the above suggestion might be, "You may want to move Richard's desk so that he is closer to you during instructional time."

Follow-up Statement. The fourth component includes a follow-up statement by the evaluator providing a rationale for the suggested change in teacher behavior. Such a rationale is typically based upon research or successful practices proven over time. An appropriate rationale statement supportive of the above example and suggestion includes, "Close physical proximity to the instructor has proven successful as a technique to increase a student's on-task behavior."

A sample of the entire *translation* would read as follows.

Did you notice that Richard was off task during much of the lesson and playing in his desk? You may want to close the distance between you and the students when teaching a lesson. For example, you may want to move Richard's desk so that he is closer to you during instructional time. Close physical proximity to the instructor has proven successful as a technique to increase a student's on-task behavior.

Positive Statement

The *positive statement* is described as a statement by the evaluator about a teaching technique that is performed well. In this case the components are similar but do not need a suggestion for improvement.

The first component includes a statement that focuses on the successful technique. Such a statement might be, "You did a nice job of providing motivational materials to your students."

The second component to the Positive Statement includes the *Example*. An example includes a specific description of what was observed, such as "Posters of space travel, the shuttle and space station caused excitement among the students and encouraged interest in the materials."

The third component includes the *rationale* which like the *translation* provides reasons for continuing the behavior by giving supporting research and proven effective practices. A sample of rationale related to this case includes, "Promoting students' interest and involvement is a successful technique for increasing the level of learning."

The completed positive statement is as follows.

You did a nice job of providing motivational materials to your students. Posters about space travel, the shuttle and space station caused excitement among the students and encouraged interest in the materials. Promoting students' interest and involvement is a successful technique for increasing the level of learning.

The importance of writing detailed descriptions of teacher performance is emphasized throughout court decisions and grievance proceedings. Just as it is important for contract language to be clearly written, it is also important for evaluations to be written with specific information void of ambiguity. Figure 8-7 lists samples of ambiguous statements that commonly appear on teacher evaluations. Such statements when written without examples and rationale lack the detail necessary for administering the typical teacher dismissal proceeding, reflect upon an evaluator's knowledge or lack thereof concerning practices within the teaching field, and erode evaluator credibility.

Ambiguous Evaluation Standards

☞ ... relates well to parents ...

☞ ... rapport with students and staff is excellent ...

☞ ... has warm personality ...

☞ ... has good judgment ...

☞ ... is dependable ...

☞ ... is knowledgable in subject matter ...

☞ ... is to be commended for teaching ability ...

☞ ... demonstrates good classroom management ...

☞ ... maintains a classroom environment conducive to learning ...

☞ ... motivates students ...

Figure 8-7

236 Chapter 8 *Supervision, Evaluation, and the Law*

Principles and Practices for Success

- Understand the differences between evaluation and supervision.
- Recognize the dilemmas and conflicts which persons face when serving in positions that require both supervisory and evaluative practices.
- Understand the fundamental procedures of the principal's role concerning the teacher evaluation.
- Understand the process of collective bargaining and associated strategies.
- Identify teacher behavior protected under the Constitution and related to freedom of expression, academic freedom, freedom from prior restraint, freedom of association, right of privacy, right of personal appearance, and due process of law.
- Understand the implications of a contractual "just cause" provision.
- Develop a working models for writing evaluations that include detailed suggestions, examples, and rationale.

Summary

This chapter provided a definition of evaluation and discussed differences concerning characteristics of supervision and summative evaluation. The chapter addressed the dilemmas and conflicting roles which supervisors such as school principals face when acting as a collegial supervisor and transforming into the evaluator. The topic of collective bargaining was described along with ways in which the collective bargaining and negotiations process influence the evaluation process. Procedures for the roles of supervisors and principals were suggested. Teacher organization or union strategies were introduced to create an awareness among persons serving in positions that are responsible for teacher and other personnel evaluations. Legal and contractual constraints were provided and included constitutional rights of educators, case law, and contract language restrictions such as the just cause provision. The chapter concluded with suggestions for reducing evaluator-teacher friction and a model for writing useful and effective evaluations.

Case Problem: *Mrs. Anderson*

You recently have been appointed as principal of Saturn High School. Soon after your appointment you begin to receive complaints from parents and graduates enrolled in local universities that Mrs. Anderson, a senior English teacher, is not adequately preparing students for college and the job market. In addition, teachers complain that Mrs. Anderson's classes are out of control. Upon reviewing the teacher's personnel file you find evaluations

Chapter 8 *Supervision, Evaluation, and the Law* **237**

that contain many ambiguous statements. When walking throughout the school you casually observe Mrs. Anderson's classroom and find behavior that supports the received complaints. You know that Mrs. Anderson is in her last year as an annual contract teacher and will be placed on permanent or tenured contract status following renewal at the end of this school year. You are also aware that Mrs. Anderson received professional assistance during the previous school year to assist her in improving performance.

To further complicate matters, you are informed that Mrs. Anderson lost both of her parents during the last ten months and her husband recently left her with a two-year old son and four-year old daughter.

Identify the educational and legal issues related to Mrs. Anderson's performance along with other issues you deem important.

What procedures will you follow to correct what you define as the major problem? Justify your course of action with detailed examples, rationale, and law.

References

Board of Education of City of Asbury Park v. Asbury Park Education Association, 368 A.2d 396 (NJ Super 1976).

Duval County School Board v. PERC and Duval Teachers United, 353 So.2d 1244 (1st DCA 1978).

Elkouri, F., & Elkouri, E. (1989). *How arbitration works* (4th ed.). Washington, DC: The Bureau of National Affairs.

Exec. Order No.10,998, Fed. Reg. (1962).

Exec. Order No. 11,491. Fed. Reg. (1969).

F.S.A. § 447.203 (8).

Gorton, R. A. (1983). *School administration and supervision: Leadership challenges and opportunities*. Dubuque, IA: Wm. C. Brown Comapny Publishers.

Harry Connick v. Sheila Myers, 461 U.S. 138, 75 L.Ed.2d 708, 103 S. Ct. 1684 (1983).

Johnson, S. M. (1984). *Teacher unions in schools*. Philadelphia, PA: Temple University Press.

Marvin L. Pickering v. Board of Education of Township High School District 205, Will County, Illinois, 391 U.S. 563, 20 L.Ed.2d 811, 88 S. Ct. 1731 (1968).

McGreal, T. L. (1988). Evaluation for enhancing instruction: Linking teacher evaluation and staff development. In S. J. Stanley & W. J. Popham (Eds.), Teacher evaluation: *Six prescriptions for success* (pp. 1-29). Alexandria, VA: Association for Supervision and Curriculum Development.

Mount Healthy City School District Board of Education v. Fred Doyle, 429 U.S. 274, 50 L.Ed. 2d 471, 97 S.Ct. 568 (1977).

Murray, K., & Murray, B. (1994). *School law for the Florida educator*. Titusville, FL: IntraCoastal Publishing

National Education Association, Inc. v. Lee County Board of Public Instruction, 260 So2nd 206 (FL Sup. Ct. 1972).

National Gay Task Force v. Board of Education of City of Oklahoma City, 729 F.2d 1270, affirmed by an equally divided court, 105 S.Ct 1858 (1985).

Noyer, P., Finnegan, J., & Finn, N. (1976). *Supervision: A functional approach*. Columbus, OH: Author.

O'Conner v. Ortega, 480 U.S. 709 (1987).

Oliva, P. F. (1989). *Supervision for today's schools*. New York: Longman.

Parducci v. Rutland, 316 F. Supp. 352 (1970)

Schmidt, P. (1990, May). A vote for peer review. *Teacher Magazine*.

Sergiovanni, T. J., & Starratt, R. J. (1988). *Supervision: Human perspectives*. New York: McGraw Hill.

Warren Education Association v. Adams, 226 N.W.2d 536 (Mich. App. 1975).

Wise, A. E., Darling-Hammong, L., McLaughlin, M. W. & Bernstein, H. T. (1984). *Teacher evaluation: A study of effective practices*. Santa Monica, CA: The Rand Corporation.

Chapter 9

APPRAISING ADMINISTRATOR PERFORMANCE
Jeffrey S. Kaiser

Introduction

The purpose of appraisal is the improvement of performance. That purpose is much better understood in the field of education than it is in industry. Educators have well-defined methods of conducting formative appraisals of teacher performance. Boards of education, administrative teams, and teacher teams have cooperated over the years to develop clear, and reasonably objective techniques for measuring teacher performance.

The word *appraisal* is used here instead of *evaluation* because evaluation may have an inherently excessive summative connotation. It is not the person of teachers or subordinate administrators that is evaluated. It is the performance that is appraised. That difference in emphasis is often crucial to the success of the process.

While there is still great disagreement among educators as to which teacher behaviors are the most important, most educators agree on the various methods of observation and recording of those teacher behaviors. There has been, however, relatively little attention paid to developing standards for measuring *administrative performance*. To that extent, educational administration is, at best, on par with most of industry.

This chapter will provide an understanding of the most recent techniques used

---

Questions to answer after studying this chapter

✔ What is the purpose of appraisal?

✔ How is appraisal of teacher performance different from appraisal of administrator performance?

✔ What are some typical problems with performance appraisal?

✔ What steps can be taken by a supervisor to prepare to appraise a subordinate administrator's performance?

✔ How can a supervisor relate a subordinate's six month objectives to the district mission?

✔ What kind of data can be gathered on an administrator's performance?

✔ How can a supervisor help the employee prepare for a performance review?

✔ What are the four main components of a performance interview?

✔ How can a supervisor help to establish rapport during the assessment meeting?

✔ What are some proven ways to discuss the subordinate's performance during the review meeting?

✔ How are performance standards set for the subordinate?

✔ What are typical graphic methods of displaying performance?

✔ What are typical psychological errors made by evaluators?

✔ How can the supervisor and subordinate plan for the future?

✔ What are some good supervisor behaviors at the close of the review meeting?

-239-

240 Chapter 9 *Appraising Administrator Performance*

by companies and school systems in the planning for and appraisal of manager and administrator performance. The information is provided with the clear understanding that the appraisal of teacher performance has taken priority over the appraisal of administrator performance to date. This is not to suggest that it should have been this way. Instead, this material is presented with the understanding that nationally agreed upon methods have yet to be developed. Many states have now mandated district-level appraisal of administrator performance.

Teacher vs. Administrator Appraisal of Performance

It is more difficult to observe administrators doing their jobs than it is to observe teachers doing theirs. Supervisors of teachers can observe teachers in classrooms. Administrators are in their offices, out of their offices, talking with students in corridors, having meetings with parents, having meetings at central office, out of the building at community events, meeting with architects, police, food service personnel, contractors, lawyers, and plumbers. Administrators are on the phone, monitoring bus arrivals, attending football games, representing their district at city and county political hearings, presenting papers at national conferences, and processing computer data. They are writing reports for accreditation agencies, rewriting reports for state education department visitation teams, gathering teacher budget requests, submitting state reimbursement requests, and applying for federal grants. And, despite all this, they are charged with major responsibility for instructional leadership.

To observe administrators in their multifaceted roles would take more than an occasional visit to their offices. Yet administrators have their own supervisors. These supervisors have the responsibility of ensuring the community that subordinate administrators are performing well. In larger school districts, superintendents have direct supervisory responsibility for assistant superintendents, assistant superintendents for directors, directors for principals, principals for assistant principals, assistant principals for department or grade-level chairpersons, and chairpersons for teachers. All but chairpersons function as supervisors of subordinate administrators (see Figure 9-1). Some districts do not classify chairpersons as administrators.

It is generally impractical for supervisors of administrators to observe administrators for long periods throughout the day and to do so over many days. Other means of appraising administrative performance are more practical and usually more beneficial. Those means focus on: 1) rating scales of administrative attributes, and 2) administrative goal acquisition. Although an application of a model of formative and summative appraisals would be excellent, it is more usual for the appraisals to be a combination of 1) and 2) above, and to be scheduled as summative at the end of each academic year. These summative appraisals function as formative appraisals in preparation for succeeding years.

Chapter 9 *Appraising Administrator Performance* **241**

To that extent, administrators do not usually hold themselves to the same model of appraisal as the teacher model. This may be due to the difference in contractual relationships, the difference in venue of performance, and the more easily applied concepts of goal accountability to administrative performance. The idea that teachers might be held responsible for achieving goals related to student achievement has largely been criticized by its association with outcome-based education models, still controversial at this writing.

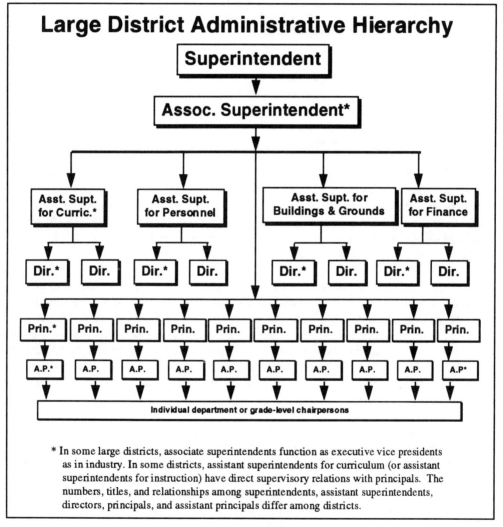

Figure 9-1

242 Chapter 9 *Appraising Administrator Performance*

Problems with Performance Appraisals

Performance appraisals rarely go smoothly. Although meetings with subordinate administrators ought to take place in quiet without the chance of disturbance, rarely is this guaranteed. Despite supervisors' attempts to prevent phone and personal interruptions during performance reviews, there is often an emergency call from a parent, a board member, a teacher, a secretary, or a superordinate administrator that cannot wait. Supervisors who prevent such interruptions secure the undivided attention of their subordinates and ensure that the subordinate understands the very important nature of such a session.

Performance appraisal interviews usually require the use of authority over those appraised. Although American administrators have come a long way toward creating a pluralistic-collegial environment in the school workplace, the appraisal of another's performance is usually met with at least a bit of anticipatory trepidation. Americans have grown up with a love for rugged individualism.

The John Wayne image of having the freedom to think and act as one desires without any annoying intervention carries over into the attitudes of many employees. The very idea that anyone, especially one's supervisor, could be able to understand what one should have done, could have done, or what one ought to do, is tantamount to a challenge. Indeed, in some cases, the performance appraisal interview is pictured as two gunmen in the middle of a dusty Western town, facing each other, ready to draw.

These attitudes are unnerving for both people involved. Neither want it to be that way, but when the discussion goes poorly, each may suspect the other of being too sensitive. Much of this attitude comes not from the inner workings of paranoid minds, but from a history of poor supervisory behavior on the current or previous job. To the extent that we reap what we sow, supervisors who use an autocratic leadership style should not expect subordinate administrators to enter performance appraisal interviews with a collegial-pluralistic mode of critical thinking. The use of authority over others requires responsibility for future behavior as well.

Performance appraisals can never be totally objective. Even the most objective checklist appraisal form requires a human to decide the placement of the checks, thus accounting for additional concern from subordinates who suspect that their supervisors are *against* them. A rating of *good* on a particular aspect of performance will not be well received by a subordinate believing that the rating should have been *very good*. Differences in steps between ratings of good, very good, excellent, and outstanding are subtle and usually subjective. Attempts to objectify those differences usually result in more steps on the rating scale which in turn have subtle, subjective differences.

More acceptable methods involving a review of goal achievement, although potentially less subjective, are yet replete with interpretive differences. In the end, our noble attempts at objectivity often break down at the borders of our decisions. Although striving for objective, agreed-upon goals should be a goal in itself, there will never be an escape from subjectivity.

That human, subjective element in decision making might be referred to as the reflection of reviewer *wisdom*. Any arguments over the subjectivity of wisdom are moot. A reductionist approach to the argument might be to view subjective wisdom as the objective decision making of an expert. See Figure 9-2 for a compilation of statements resulting from recent performance appraisal interviews.

Some Reactions to Most Recent Evaluation

Positive:
got recognition, wasn't surprised, accomplished goals, confirmed my relations with my supervisor, helped in planning, learned how to improve, helped with a personal goal

Indifferent:
always negative, too informal, going through the motions, wasn't detailed, never matters anyway

Negative:
wasn't written, not really evaluated, never know what he's going to find, rules change after the fact, he's a bas...., there is no way I can ever get a good evaluation

Figure 9-2

Supervisor Preparation for Appraising a Subordinate's Performance

Five steps in a supervisor's preparation for appraising a subordinate administrator's performance are shown in Figure 9-3.

---

5 Steps in Preparing For a Performance Review

1. Gather data

2. Assess employee performance

3. List points to be discussed

4. Determine objectives

5. Be sure employee is prepared

Figure 9-3

244 Chapter 9 *Appraising Administrator Performance*

Gathering Data

Gathering data regarding subordinate performance prepares supervisors for an objective approach to appraisal (see Figure 9-4). It is not advisable to hold subordinates accountable for responsibilities about which they have not been informed. Their written *job descriptions* contain basic documentation on the duties and responsibilities of the position incumbent. Copies of each subordinate's job description must be secured.

Gathering Data

* The job description
* Anecdotal record
* Organization's forms and guidelines

Figure 9-4

Anecdotal records on subordinate performance must be kept. These are formal and informal documents. These are notes supervisors make as reminders of specific incidents of subordinate performance. Documents may also include memos and letters regarding the subordinate's performance received from the subordinate and from others. Anecdotal records may be positive and negative. These records allow for an analysis of data related to more specific performance than that contained in a more general job description.

School districts often have approved *forms* and *guidelines* used as data for assessing performance. Forms such as subordinate appraisal checklists, rating scales, and attendance records are all useful data. Districts often have board-approved guidelines for performance assessment procedures. Supervisors are well advised to adhere to official guidelines to prevent improper appraisals and future litigation.

Assessing Performance

Assess a subordinate administrator's performance from the analysis of the data collected in step one.

Listing the Points to be Discussed

Rome was not built in a day. Neither can a supervisor change all aspects of a subordinate's performance in one performance appraisal meeting. Prudent supervisors select points to be discussed from careful analyses of data and with eyes toward accomplishing important objectives first (see Figure 9-5).

What Are My Objectives For This Interview?

* What do I want this employee to do more of? Less of?
* What do I want the impact of this meeting to be?
* Should I show appreciation?
* Should I show concern for low productivity?

Figure 9-5

Chapter 9 *Appraising Administrator Performance* **245**

Supervisors may at times focus not on production, but on satisfying a subordinate administrator's need for appreciation. The human element is often a strong driving force in productivity and may be more important than quantifying output. At other times, quantification or qualification of output is exactly what needs to be discussed. Therefore, supervisors must decide what objectives to emphasize far ahead of the performance appraisal meeting date. This is accomplished by deciding the objectives of the performance appraisal meeting (see Figure 9-5) and compiling a list of points to be discussed (see figure 9-6).

Keep a list of the subordinate's major successes during the current performance period. That list will prove to be very helpful in building subordinate cooperation during the meeting and subordinate motivation thereafter. Recognition for jobs well done is an important motivating factor.

A list of ways in which the subordinate might improve will act as a reminder to the supervisor of what needs to be discussed. Even more important, it will provide the supervisor with a list of items to which the *supervisor* must pay attention. The logic here is that if the subordinate administrator has not been sufficiently successful with a project or with the attainment of a goal, it is the supervisor's responsibility to help design plans for success. Those plans should be ready for subordinate discussion and modification during the performance appraisal interview.

Compile a List of Points to be Covered

* Major successes
* Needs for improvement
* Recommendations for future action
* Any other important points

Figure 9-6

Preparing the Subordinate

Subordinates must come to the performance appraisal interview well prepared (see Figure 9-7). A memo to the subordinate well before the meeting should specify the purpose of the meeting, the agenda, and whether this is a normal performance appraisal interview scheduled for every subordinate or whether this is being scheduled for any other specific reason. Be sure to provide them copies of the district guidelines and copies of any pertinent forms from your file. Require subordinates to complete appraisals of their own performances. This will provide an excellent vehicle for discussion. Encourage the subordinate to come to the meeting prepared with any pertinent

Prepare the Employee in Advance of The Meeting

* Send a memo including the date, time, place, points to be discussed
* Send a copy of any completed evaluation forms
* Send a copy of any regulated P.A. procedures

Figure 9-7

documentation related to performance.

The Performance Appraisal Meeting

Figure 9-8

The performance appraisal meeting is held between the superordinate administrator (supervisor) and the subordinate administrator. It is held not merely to begin and end an assessment of the subordinate's performance. Instead, it is held to review performance since the previous performance assessment meeting, discuss previously undiscussed performance, design interventions to improve performance, and set goals for future performance. (*Performance Review*, 1986). (See Figure 9-8.)

The meeting should be cooperative. Meetings where the subordinate sits respectfully in silence while the supervisor announces the evaluation and pronounces a resultant sentence are failures. They result in frustrated employees who usually become disillusioned and eventually withdraw (McGregor, 1957). If the purpose of assessment is performance improvement, every step should be taken to enhance the possibility that performance will indeed improve as a result of the meeting.

Establishing Rapport

The first moments of the meeting should be used to establish a good working rapport with the subordinate. Supervisors ensure meeting privacy, with no interruptions, and with an atmosphere of working comfort to enhance the likelihood of good communication. They arrange incoming phone calls to be forwarded to a third number or request their secretaries or another subordinate to receive the calls. They close the door for privacy. They choose the placement of chairs to aid in collegial problem solving. They remain behind their desks only if they feel it is necessary to create an obvious air of authority during extreme discipline problems.

Establish Rapport
• **Be sure the employee understands the purpose of the meeting**
• **Ensure privacy, be polite, act positive, respectful, and supportive**
• **Adapt your approach to the employee's needs**

Figure 9-9

It is often helpful to begin with what is commonly referred to as small talk about nonperformance-related activities. Brief chat about the condition of the parking lot, the new electronic mail network, the health of the subordinate's family, or this morning's news report about federal funding of education often break the ice, relax both the supervisor and subordinate, and provide for easier communication. Following a brief amount of small talk, a quick review of the purpose of the meeting is in order.

Spending too much time on small talk can have the opposite effect. It can appear that the supervisor is ill at ease and reluctant to move ahead with the purpose of the meeting. To an extent, supervisors do well to adapt their approach to the needs of the subordinate. Subordinates who appear nervous may need a bit more time to relax. Others may be quite eager to move ahead with the purpose of the meeting.

The appropriateness of a stern or more friendly approach is employee specific. Neither approach should be to the extreme. Pluralistic decision making is hardly enhanced by authoritarianism or immature behavior. This is not to say that the use of authority is never to be implemented. To the contrary, it may become necessary to override subordinate desires. When doing so, however, supervisors recognize the danger in subverting the pluralistic decision-making process. In no cases should supervisors be rude or disrespectful to subordinates. Subordinates have few ways of fighting back when treated rudely by a supervisor. Instead, subordinates often become resigned to such rude supervisor behavior and learn to disrespect the supervisor who has been so disrespectful of them. The result is lowered morale, antiorganizational behavior, and lowered productivity.

Discussing Performance

During discussion of the subordinate's performance, supervisors are careful to avoid language that might stifle the subordinate's desire to participate. Phrases such as "Don't tell me that you haven't been late" or "I am not an idiot, you know ..." quickly silence the subordinate's attempt to explain behaviors. It just could be that the subordinate was stopped by the superintendent on each occasion listed as a lateness. Without a chance to explain, communication is stopped and progress is curtailed.

Supervisors do well to come prepared for these meetings. Preparation includes the gathering of data, records, forms, guidelines and anecdotal files, the review of that information in light of the subordinate's goals for that time period, the objectives for the meeting, the tentative interventions, and the drafting of tentative objectives for the next period.

Discuss Performance
- Ensure 2-way communication
- Come prepared
- Avoid personal feeling
- Ask & listen effectively
- Try for concensus on each issue
- Keep discussion on track

Figure 9-10

Subordinates are not computers to be reprogrammed when their output fails. They are humans in need of more than mere directives. Supervisors must avoid the interpretation of subordinates' negative behaviors as personal affronts. Asking appropriate questions and listening effectively to the answers help supervisors and subordinates solve problems. Many problems are the result of personality clashes. The discussion of such problems is not to be avoided. Straightforward discussion of these issues is no different from straightforward discussion of mechanical breakdowns. These are all problems and all need to be solved.

A consensus on each issue will help ensure success. For example, if the subordinate has been unable to meet a specific performance standard, cooperatively determine the reason. Perhaps the subordinate can meet the standard in the future with the aid of additional secretarial services for the project. Once agreement is reached on the cause of the problem, a giant step will have been taken toward consensus on the solution. An intimidated subordinate will not likely be in a problem solving mode. Ensuring that the subordinate approaches problems in a nonthreatening manner will help ensure pluralistic problem solving. It will also set objective problem solving as a model for subordinate decision making.

Setting Performance Standards

Performance standards are goals written in measurable terminology. The following is an example of a goal and one possible set of its performance standards that might have been agreed upon by a supervising principal and subordinate assistant principal. The purpose of the setting of performance standards is to give the subordinate and supervisor a clear understanding of what is expected of the subordinate's performance. The development of the goals and standards should come from an agreement between the supervisor and subordinate. Standards should have a specified time frame with measurable behavior specifically related to the attainment of the goal. Standards should be realistic-they should not be so easily attained that the process disrespects the need to achieve, and they should not be so difficult to achieve as to result in programmed failure. (See Figure 9-11.)

Setting Performance Standards

- Is the performance standard as specific and precise as possible?
- Have you avoided ambiguous words?
- Have you specified a time frame?
- Have you focused on observable and measurable behavior that specifically relates to job performance?
- Is the performance standard realistic?
- Is the standard too easy to attain?

Figure 9-11

Goal: The assistant principal will lead the development of a discipline policy handbook for our junior high school. That policy will be in place by June 30.

Performance standards:

A) The assistant principal will form a committee consisting of two representatives from the PTA, six teachers (two from each grade level), the president of the student government, and the assistant principal to meet before October 15.

B) The October 15th meeting will have on its agenda, the following topics:
   1) A brief discussion of the need for a unified discipline policy for the school.
   2) The assignment of committee member responsibility for acquiring sample discipline handbooks from all five surrounding school districts or their component schools.

C) The committee will set a date of no later than November 3 for a second meeting of the committee. The meeting will include on its agenda:

250 Chapter 9 *Appraising Administrator Performance*

1) To peruse collected policy handbooks and agree on tentative categories for inclusion in our policy handbook.

2) To assign responsibility for the development of a memo to faculty, parents, and students briefly describing the progress of the committee's work, setting a tentative outline of topics for inclusion in the handbook, and inviting students, teachers, administrators, and parents to contribute their ideas on an enclosed one-page form for committee discussion. The draft of the memo and the form will be due back to the assistant principal by November 10. The assistant principal will send the final version of the memo and form to all students, teachers, parents, and administrators by November 20. The form will be due back to the assistant principal by November 30.

D) The committee will meet no later than December 4. The agenda will include:
1) A discussion of the ideas expressed on the returned forms.
2) The resultant agreement on topics for inclusion into the handbook.
3) An agreement on handbook format for each topic including a minimum of the following:
   a. Discipline infractions within each category
   b. Why the infraction is considered a discipline problem
   c. The consequence of the infraction and successive repeats of the infraction.
4) The assignment of individual committee member drafting responsibilities for each part of the handbook. These drafts will be due to the assistant principal by December 15.

E) The assistant principal will develop a first draft of the school discipline policy handbook for discussion by the committee at a meeting to be held before January 10. That meeting will have as its purpose the finalization of committee recommendations regarding the draft.

F) The assistant principal will complete the second draft of the handbook. This second draft will be word processed complete with cover page, table of contents, and all complete handbook sections for submission to the principal before January 25. It is understood that the principal will meet with the superintendent for any final revisions before the handbook is submitted to the board of education for approval.

Performance standards A—F above are illustrative only. They are not to be developed by the supervisor in isolation from the subordinate. To do so would be poor management. Supervisors need subordinates to participate in the development of long-term goals, shorter-term objectives, and performance standards for a very simple reason. Supervisors cannot know all aspects of a subordinate's job, the subordinate's time constraints, the project's time constraints, the supporting service constraints, or even the political contraints of a subordinate's job. Pluralistic decision making is not just a popular philosophy. It works well because a subordinate's expertise is necessary to supplement the supervisor's wisdom.

Management by Objectives and Curriculum Terminology

Whether one refers to the completed handbook as a *goal* or as an *objective* is of no consequence. The purpose is to complete the project. Curriculum specialists and *management-by-objectives* specialists have conflicting definitions of what constitutes a goal and what constitute an objective. Goals are usually considered longer term, a minimum of a year and sometimes up to five years. Objectives are shorter in term, a maximum of a year and usually much shorter. Missions of a school district (or any organization) are the longest term of all. A mission is often expressed as a never-ending purpose of the district. That purpose can only be actuated by continuous setting of goals and objectives that relate to the overall mission. The goals and objectives can be more easily achieved by the setting of performance standards to be reviewed during periodic performance assessment meetings. (See Figure 9-12.) When goals are reached, new goals are set for the next performance period.

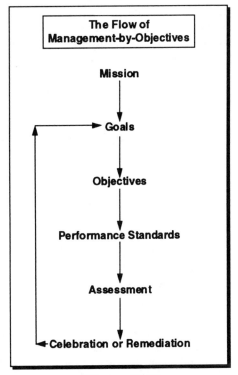

Figure 9-12

Figure 9-12 shows a loop back to the setting of goals for the next performance period. That the loop does not go back to the mission is meant to depict the usual lack of subordinate input into the organizational mission. Missions are usually set by the community through their boards of education. Certainly many communities ask for administrative and teacher assistance in the setting of the district's or school's mission, but the responsibility for the setting of a community's mission rests with the community, not with its hired educator.

Educators are hired to implement board policy to achieve district and school missions. For example, missions might differ among communities interested in the preparation of students for higher education and communities interested in preparing their children for post high school jobs in industry or farming. Missions are set by communities and their boards of education. The goals and objectives are methods for accomplishing the mission and are usually set by administrators and teachers.

252 Chapter 9 *Appraising Administrator Performance*

Performance Appraisal Display Methods

A performance appraisal meeting to review subordinate success in achieving agreed upon performance standards is made easier if the performance standards are clear, time related, unambiguous, and measurable. However, there are many ways to track or display levels of subordinate achievement (see Figure 9-13).

> ### P.A. Display Methods
>
> - **Graphic Scale**
> - **Behaviorally Anchored Rating Scale**
> - **Critical Incident**
> - **Free Form Narrative**
> - **Multi-person Comparison**
>   - **Ranking**
>   - **Paired with each**

Graphic Scales. Graphic scales are pictorial displays of changes in performance over time. A line graph showing a school's mean student achievement on standardized tests over a five-year period is an example of a graphic scale.

Figure 9-13

Behaviorally Anchored Rating Scales. Behavioral anchored rating scales refer to displays of changes in human behavior over time. The example of a graphic scale in the above paragraph is also an example of a behaviorally anchored rating scale. A rating scale that is not behaviorally anchored would be one that depicts changes in a supervisor's ratings of a subordinate's attitude over time. Subordinate attitude as rated by a supervisor over time is not behavioral. A more obvious example of behavior is subordinate attendance.

Critical Incident Technique. A record of critical incidences in subordinate performance may be as simple as a file folder containing any letters of thanks received from parents concerning a subordinate's performance, letters of reprimand, letters of accommodation, awards won, and supervisor's notes regarding specific performances during the period. The idea is that if the file folder is empty, the subordinate is simply doing an adequate job. Positive or negative variations from adequacy are evidenced by materials in the subordinate's critical incidents folder kept by the supervisor. One criticism of the critical incidents technique is that an empty file folder may not simply indicate adequacy. It may also indicate mediocrity (Posner & Schmidt, 1986).

Free Form Narrative. Free form narrative is a technique allowing for supervisors to write their observations and feelings about subordinate performance in paragraph format rather than forcing supervisors to rate subordinates on rating scales. Proponents of this technique argue that it allows for the introduction of supervisor wisdom into the process. One criticism is that such subjective judgment is prone to bias. The best free form narrative techniques require supervisors to focus their narrative on previously agreed upon performance standards.

Multi-person Comparison. Displaying a subordinate's performance in relation to other subordinates' performances is often useful. It lets subordinates see how they are performing compared to how others in similar positions are performing. An example of such usefulness might be a subordinate's low rating in multicultural awareness. If all other subordinates in similar positions receive similarly low ratings, supervisors would more easily recognize the need to arrange for staff development programs for the entire cadre of subordinate administrators at that level. Also, individual subordinates can easily see that their ratings do not necessarily disadvantage them among their peers.

Ranking of all assistant principals in the district on various behaviorally anchored rating scales can provide supervisors and subordinates with clear understandings of how they are performing in relation to peer performance.

Paired with each. A variation of a ranking system has each peer subordinate compared in pairs. An example would be to compare Bill with Judy on multicultural relations, Bill with Pete on multicultural relations, Bill with Jan on multicultural relations, and Bill with Barbara on multicultural relations. Besides the sensitive nature of rating someone on their multicultural relations, the *compared with each* method is often criticized as fostering unhealthy competition.

Norm vs. Criterion-Referenced Assessment

Supervisors are often unaware of the difference between norm-referenced and criterion-referenced assessment of subordinate performance. Norm-referenced assessment compares or rates subordinates in comparison with the mean ratings of their peers. Thus, an assistant principal in a large school district might be informed of receiving the highest rating of all assistant principals in the district on a specific aspect of expected performance.

Criterion referenced assessment is without regard to supervisors' assessments of others. Instead, each subordinate's performance is assessed by reviewing that subordinate's achievement of performance standards without regard to the achievement of other subordinates. (See Figure 9-14.)

Norm vs. Criterion Referenced Tests

Norm referenced

An individual's score is based on how others did (percental rankings).

Criterion referenced

An individual's score is based on a scale of mastery of the subject.

Figure 9-14

254 Chapter 9 *Appraising Administrator Performance*

Psychological Errors in Evaluation

Supervisors often make errors in assessing subordinate performance. Although some errors are based on erroneous data, some errors are the result of the psychology of the assessor. These psychological errors create erroneous assessments that can have a deleterious effect on future performance.

Halo Effect. The halo effect usually refers to a falsely positive assessment of a specific aspect of a subordinate administrator's performance when that assessment is affected by a positive assessment of another aspect of the subordinate's performance. Consider David's error in the case below:

Psychological Errors in Evaluation

• **Halo effect**
• **Central tendency**
• **Unconscious prejudice**
• **Contrast**
• **Inappropriate upgrading**

Figure 9-15

Sarah is an assistant principal with a fantastic personality. She is bubbly, very positive toward students, parents, faculty, and staff, works very hard for very long hours, volunteers for extra assignments, gets along with the principal and everyone in central office, and has developed a new student-mentoring program which has been extremely well received by everyone in the school and in the community.

However, Sarah is disorganized. Her office appears to be in chaos. Her desk is piled with papers and she can't seem to find things when she (or the principal) needs them. She is often late to meetings because of her intense involvement in an earlier activity.

Her principal, David, is responsible for completing an annual assessment of Sarah's performance. A copy of the written assessment must be filed in Sarah's personnel file after its reading by the superintendent of schools. David thinks the world of Sarah. He is thrilled to have her in his school and is extremely pleased with her overall performance. When it comes time for David to complete the portion of the assessment form devoted to *suggestions for improvement,* David leaves it blank. It never occurs to him that she needs to improve in anything. After all, Sarah is great!

In David's eyes, Sarah has a halo around her. This halo effect has caused David to make an error in her performance assessment. As a result, she and David never discuss her organizational skills and her skill level remains the same for the next performance period.

Central Tendency. A central tendency error occurs when a supervisor refuses to rate subordinates' performances as very high or very low. Consider Roger's error in the case below:

> As principal, Roger must assess the performance of two assistant principals and five department chairpersons each year. Roger does not believe that anyone in the world is perfect. On the form having a rating scale from one to five where one is low and five is high, Roger usually rates everyone as a two, three, or four. He never rates anyone as a one because he believes that no one is absolutely at the bottom and he does not want to be mean.

Roger is guilty of a central tendency psychological error. It has resulted in a change in the scale from that of five points to that of three points. Roger does not have the right to unilaterally change the scale. Neither does he have the right to deny everyone a chance at a high rating nor to force others with performance at the *two* level to be categorized the same as those at the *one* level. One of Roger's department chairpersons has been overheard as saying that Roger's psychological error is nothing more than an attempt toward politically safe bias, but bias all the same.

Unconscious Prejudice. Unconscious prejudice can take many forms but always exists in a supervisor who is completely unaware of its existence. It may be that the supervisor, for some unknown reason, feels very positively toward people having brown eyes. Perhaps the supervisor feels more comfortable supervising female subordinates than when supervising male subordinates. Perhaps race is an unconscious issue affecting supervisor ratings of subordinates. Consider Sandra's unconscious prejudice in the case below:

> Sandra is superintendent of an elementary school district having nine female administrators and two male administrators. The entire administrative team meets for a luncheon meeting once each month. Whenever either of the two male administrators sit at the lunch table where Sandra usually sits with five female administrators, Sandra becomes notably quieter. She has mentioned to her husband that she has a great relationship with the women on her staff. The two men are new and when they sit at her table, she feels that it stifles the conversation that she says usually involves friendly women talk. She swears that she has nothing against having men on her administrative team.
>
> Lately, the men have begun to sit at another table with three or four other administrative team members. Sandra has noticed this and does not know what to make of it. She knows for certain that she has never done anything to make the men feel uncomfortable. Perhaps they are interested in the women at the other table for private reasons. She will have to watch that carefully to be sure that it does not affect the organizational climate of her district.

256 Chapter 9 *Appraising Administrator Performance*

At assessment time, Sandra wrote that both of the men need to volunteer for more after school functions and spend more time socializing with all of their colleagues. Her district has a space on the form to rate subordinates as team players. She gave one a *two* and the other a *one* indicating the lowest of ratings. Her average ratings of subordinates on this dimension was a three.

Sandra may be unaware of it, but her assessment of the two men has been affected by unconscious prejudice. For whatever and however deep the reason, Sandra's own performance as an administrator is affected by this psychological problem unknown to her but keenly felt by her subordinates.

Contrast. Contrast error refers to the inappropriate rating of a subordinate's performance because of comparison of that subordinate with extraordinary peers. Consider Carol's error in the case below:

Carol is the principal of what is generally known to be the best school in her state. Her faculty are mostly in their late forties with Master's degrees. Eight percent of her faculty have Ph.D.s. Most of her faculty are involved with their national professional organizations.

Carol's former Social Studies chairperson was president of the National Council for the Social Studies before her recent retirement, and her Math Department Chairperson has organized a team of students for national mathematics competition each year for the past ten years. They have won four times.

Her English department has taken second place in national student poetry competition and first place in state debate competition for four years. Her tennis team consistently makes it to state competition and the school band was invited to Washington, DC last year to play at a luncheon for U.S. senators.

Ken is the new Social Studies chairperson. He is in his late twenties, already holds an M.Ed., and was lured away from a neighboring district where he was a social studies teacher. He has been well received by the faculty and is often seen working late into the evening at school on paperwork or student scheduling problems, a continuing problem over the years in all departments.

During Ken's first annual assessment, Carol expressed concern that Ken had yet to move the department into student activities and competition at the state or national level. She was sure to tell him that she did not expect his department to have begun and won such competition all in his first year as chairperson, however, she did want him to know that she was a bit disappointed that his movement into such areas was slower than expected. She rated him as a two on the five-point scale for "gets faculty involved with activities enhancing the image of the school in the community."

Carol has made a contrast error. She expects all of her chairpersons to perform at the same level as her extraordinary and most experienced chairpersons. This is unreasonable. Although there is nothing wrong with Carol setting high standards for her team, purposeful downgrading of high performing people, just because someone else has performed at an even higher level, is unfair and can hurt the future performance of those downgraded. Carol misunderstands the positive aspects of competition. She does not understand that athletes eventually lose to better athletes. Each athlete begins as a lower performer than those more experienced and ends as a lower performer than others. That does not suggest that the first person to break the four-minute mile should now be rated as less than excellent because his record has been surpassed. Carol needs to rate a person's performance against agreed upon performance standards, not against the performance of stars. She needs to also consider how she would rate an average performer among a group of below average performers. If she rates average performance as outstanding, the same type of contrast error occurs.

Inappropriate Upgrading. Many supervisors find all sorts of excuses for inappropriately upgrading the ratings of certain subordinates. Consider John's error in the case below:

John is a high school principal with a large faculty. Bill, a sixty-six year old assistant principal has decided to retire at the end of the year. Bill has lately been considered one of the most marginal administrators in the building. He comes to work one minute late and leaves one minute early. He refuses to serve on committees, rarely enforces the discipline policy, and sends even the most difficult students back to class if they promise not to do it again. He has been rude to teachers and more rude to parents. He openly laughs at schoolboard and central office directives.

Since Bill is retiring at the end of the year, John decides not to give him a poor performance assessment. John feels that since Bill is older and is retiring, he should get a nice final rating.

John feels the same way about new administrators, new teachers, and older teachers for that matter. John feels that new employees should get inappropriately high ratings to welcome them and to motivate them. He also gives inappropriately high ratings to anyone who has recently been ill or has had a death in the family. Some of his department chairpersons believe that the only people who do not get high ratings are those who deserve them. When John learned about their feelings, he felt badly and gave everybody high ratings the following year.

258 Chapter 9 *Appraising Administrator Performance*

John found himself caught in a never-ending spiral of well intentioned lies. Eventually, someone in central office will recognize his poor assessment technique and send him back to school.

Consider the statements in Figure 9-16. All are concerned with pressures upon supervisors. No one is immune from these pressures. However, to the extent that supervisors can control their own intentional or nonintentional distortions of reality, they can rise above their own human vulnerability and bring the performance assessment process to the height and purpose for which it exists—to improve subordinate performance. To the extent that supervisors fall victim to these errors. in their rating of others, subordinates' performance suffers. And, from another perspective, the supervisor's performance has been poor.

Supervisors have great responsibility for the performance of subordinates. They have an even greater responsibility not to disillusion, depress, or even destroy the emotional well being of others. Living up to such responsibility requires not only the proper attitudes, but the development of skills.

How about these statements?

- *Inaccuracy in performance ratings stems more from intentional distortion than from rating error.*
- *The 'halo effect': Well-liked people get rated favorably in all aspects of their work.*
- *Women working at traditionally masculine jobs receive lower ratings than men of comparable ability.*
- *False memories are particularly likely when supervisors must evaluate many people but rarely observe them on the job.*
- *Supervisors rate their friends higher than their enemies.*
- *Supervisors' ratings are influenced by economic pressures.*
- *Supevisors get tough with evaluations when pressured from above to do so.*
- *Politics do play a role in evaluations whether right or wrong.*

Figure 9-16

Rating Scales

Administrators are often graded on each aspect covered within a rating scale. Rating scales vary as to their content, layout, and scoring. Some are mere checklists for supervisors to attest to the adequate performance of criterion. Others require supervisors to grade the subordinate on scales from 1 to 4, 5, or 6, one end of the scale meaning unsatisfactory performance, the other end meaning excellent performance on each criterion. Older instruments emphasized simplistic behaviors such as *comes to work on time*. Some newer instruments specify behaviors more closely aligned to individual school missions. Figure 9-17 is an example of a rating form using a graded scale. It is not specifically goal oriented, but provides subordinates with a good idea of the values of the district and the perceptions of their supervisors.

Chapter 9 *Appraising Administrator Performance* **259**

Kosmoski Administrator Performance Instrument (API)

Circle one: SELF ASSESSMENT or ASSESSMENT BY SUPERVISOR

This is a performance assessment on (please print)_____
Person completing this form _____
Using the scale at the right, mark each item as it applies to the administrator whose name appears above.
This form will be seen only by the administrator whose name appears above and by the person completing
this form. Please be truthful, and forthright. Do not inflate scores.
1=poor and unsatisfactory; 2=barely satisfactory and below average; 3=satisfactory and average;
4=highly satisfactory and above average; 5=excellent and superior. SUPERIOR ◄——————► POOR

	5	4	3	2	1
1. Problem analysis - Ability to seek out relevant data, analyze complex information, & determine important elements of a problem situation.					
2. Judgment - Ability to reach logical conclusions & high quality decisions based on available information.					
3. Organizational ability - Ability to plan, schedule, & control the work of others.					
4. Decisiveness - Ability to recognize when a decision is required & to act clearly & quickly.					
5. Leadership - Ability to get others involved in problem solving, ability to recognize when a group requires direction, ability to interact effectively with a group, & ability to guide in the accomplishment of a task.					
6. Sensitivity - Ability to perceive & respond to the needs, concerns, & personal problems of others.					
7. Stress tolerance - Ability to perform under pressure & opposition.					
8. Oral communications - Ability to clearly verbalize ideas & facts.					
9. Written communications - Ability to express ideas clearly when writing for different audiences.					
10. Range of interest - Ability to discuss a variety of subjects & admit limitations.					
11. Personal motivation - Ability to show that work is important to operational satisfaction.					
12. Educational values - Expresses & demonstrates a clear, well-reasoned educational philosophy, along with a receptiveness to change to accommodate new ideas.					
13. Creativity - Ability to bring unique & effective approaches to the position.					
14. Supervision - Effective in instructional supervision & evaluation of instruction.					
15. Community relations - Fosters positive parent-community-school relations.					
16. Policy development - Engages in appropriate & effective policy development.					
17. Personnel - Engages in positive personnel management.					
18. Team work - Interacts well within the school system organization & acts as a team player.					
19. Action under stress - Copes & acts effectively with disorder, interruption, & crisis.					
20. Observation & feedback - Uses observation skills & provides appropriate feedback.					
21. Accessibility - Provides staff direction; is highly visible & available to staff.					
22. Planning - Engages in thorough planning to ensure appropriate & timely action.					
23. Student interaction - Interacts well with students; recognizes diversity, group, & individual needs.					
24. Professional development - Keeps up-to-date on effective school practices & literature & provides for staff development.					
25. Cocurricular - Engages in after hours student, parent, & community activities.					
26. Budget - Engages effectively in budget management & protects education during fiscal restraint.					
27. Labor relations - Interacts well with union representatives & during union negotiations.					
28. Climate - Fosters a positive school climate.					
29. Legal & SE issues - Deals effectively with legal & special education issues.					
30. Technology - Uses & encourages the use of technology.					

Source: contributed to this chapter by Georgia Kosmoski. Some items were adapted from NASSP's *12 Skill Dimensions* and from Gottfredson and Hybl's (1987) *Key Responsibilities of the Principal.*

Figure 9-17

260 Chapter 9 *Appraising Administrator Performance*

Some rating instruments require the supervisor to write a few lines called narrative, explaining why each grade was given on each criterion. The benefit is that supervisors are thereby required to individualize their thinking by focusing on specific behaviors attributable to each specific subordinate. Supervisors using that type of rating form are forced to spend a moment thinking about why their check marks are going into each gradation. It also helps the subordinate administrators better understand why they received each specific grade.

Recommendations for Future Action

Concentration on subordinate failures may serve to prevent future repetition of those failures, but does little to advance the subordinate toward newer goals. Supervisors prepare lists of recommendations for future action to provide themselves with ideas to discuss with subordinates during performance appraisal interviews. These performance assessment meetings not only provide the supervisor and subordinate with a vehicle for reflecting on past performance, they provide an excellent venue for planning future performance. (See Figure 9-18.)

Identify areas for improvement

Once the supervisor and subordinate have thoroughly discussed the subordinate's performance over the past performance period, they both can begin to plan for the next performance period. The first step in such planning is to identify areas for improvement.

> ## Plan for the Future
>
> - Identify areas for improvement & specify goals
> - Identify WHY this is necessary
> - Solicit employee input
> - Try for consensus on action

Figure 9-18

Identify the Rationale for Goals and Priority Shifts

The development of a clear understanding of those areas will have come partially from the discussion of the previous performance period. However, older areas that have formerly been rated quite well may now have a different priority and higher expectations because of changes in district mission. It is through mutual agreement that the best goals are set and the best performance is achieved. It has long been understood that subordinates perform better when they have a clear understanding of why newer goals and changes in priorities are necessary.

Solicit Employee Input

The forming and firming of goals and objectives come as a result of the discussion of recommendations brought to the meeting by both supervisor and subordinate. Usually, subordinate administrators have an excellent understanding of how to improve their departments. They may be reluctant to share these ideas because of previous relationships with supervisors or because of a fear that their responsibilities may increase without the necessary support services increase. Supervisors must encourage employee input. A history of supervisors withholding support services while increasing subordinate responsibility will limit a subordinate's desire to contribute.

Strive for Consensus

It does little good for supervisors to assign all subordinate goals without a willingness of the subordinate to achieve them. The process of goal specification includes the need for supervisor and subordinate to agree on what can be done and how to do it. The setting of performance standards in a management-by-objectives process (see Figures 9-11 and 9-12) provides the best means of assuring that supervisors and subordinates are allowed and encouraged to participate in the process.

Closing the Meeting

The proper ending of a meeting is as important as the start (see Figure 9-19). Just as the pleasantries of the first moments of the meeting allow the supervisor and subordinate to move into the meeting mode, so does the closing provide a smooth transition from the meeting to the separation of the subordinate and supervisor.

The encouragement of subordinate participation continues through the closing of the meeting. Once it appears that all points in the planning phase have been discussed, it is advisable to ask the subordinate if any other matters need to be discussed. Those matters pertinent to the purpose of the meeting should be discussed. Those more appropriate for another venue might be better scheduled for another time.

Close the Interview
• **Any other matters to bring up?**
• **Summarize the main points**
• **Agree on follow-up dates**
• **Thanks and encouragement**

Figure 9-19

Once assured that all matters have been discussed, a summary of the main points of the meeting is advisable. It is here where a supervisor orally lists all major agreements and reiterates any settled controversies with the subordinate. Responsibilities are enumerated including deadlines. Consider the case below:

OK, Steve, let me make sure I have everything straight. We have agreed that you will be able to get the state reports to me by noon on September 12 this year so long as I can get the attendance figures to you by September 9. Also, you are going to get back to me before next Tuesday on

262 Chapter 9 *Appraising Administrator Performance*

your estimate of the labor and materials costs in painting that north wing corridor. I am going to have this year's goals and objectives we just agreed upon word processed and in your e-mail by next Friday so we can finalize all this by the following Tuesday during 3rd hour here in my office. Is that right?

Oh yes, one more thing. We both are going to work on communicating a bit more. That means that I will check with you before I assign any short deadline projects to you while you are swamped with other projects. And, you will become more familiar with the new e-mail system so that you can check with me before you rush ahead into too many projects with no supporting staff. Great! See you next Tuesday, August 22, here in my office at the start of third hour.

Other Important Points

Other important points may be discussed which do not relate directly to the individual's past performance or future goals and objectives of the school district. An example may be the desire of the subordinate to move up the hierarchy. These subordinate desires are important to supervisors in the planning for subordinate experiences to ready them for advancement. It may be important to discuss the need for further university coursework, involvement with staff development programs, and even to recommend a good self-improvement book. It may also be important to solicit subordinates' expert opinions on projects not directly related to the subordinate's job description. These discussions are quite appropriate during the discussion portion of the meeting and during the portion devoted to future planning. However, care must be taken not to usurp too much time from a subordinate's performance appraisal meeting on items better suited to a separate meeting. The planning of next year's budget for the subordinate administrator's department is better suited to a separate meeting.

External Assessment

The 1980s brought a period of growth in the use of external agencies to assess administrative potential. This allows districts to send their administrators or potential administrators to external assessment centers to evaluate their administrative abilities. Assessment centers use a variety of techniques including written exams, administrative simulations, in-basket case problems, and group interactions to assess participant performance. While nonbiased objectivity is certainly one of the goals (Johnson & Douglas, 1986) in the use of outside assessors, the use is often time consuming and expensive (Notar, 1993). Its benefits come when used in conjunction with personal interviews and assessment techniques administered by the district.

Chapter 9 *Appraising Administrator Performance* **263**

Principles and Practices for Success

- Understand the purpose of appraisal
- Be sensitive to typical errors in performance appraisal
- Relate objectives to mission
- Gather appropriate data for analysis
- Prepare the subordinate administrator
- Learn techniques for establishing rapport
- Treat the process as collaborative
- Try for consensus on plans for action
- Set follow-up dates

Summary

This chapter provided the framework for appraising administrative performance. It emphasized the collegial aspect of the appraisal process based on goals and de-emphasized the older checklisted trait approach. It provided a stepwise approach to the process from planning during one performance period through assessment in the next. Rater bias was discussed. Methods of gathering objective data and of writing tight performance standards were presented.

Straight talk between subordinate and supervisor is mandatory. The use of hidden agendas or the use of assessment meetings for other than assessment purposes is discouraged. The use of performance assessments for political purposes or for vengeance does little to further the purpose of assessment—to improve performance.

Case Problem: *Martin Mobile's Decision*

Martin had been a principal for three years. During that period, he had gained respect from the faculty, students, and community. He had also completed a doctoral program in educational administration and been elected to an officer's position in the state-wide association of school administrators. His faculty often spoke of him as the sole reason their school had been transformed from one of chaos to one of order. The students referred to him simply as "a great guy."

During his tenure as principal, he had never had a formal appraisal of his performance. He set his own goals and scheduled his own tasks toward achieving objectives.

His superintendent's management philosophy was to leave his subordinate administrators alone until something bad happened. If there were any complaints from the community concerning any principal, the superintendent would come down hard on the principal involved. Rarely would the principal be given a chance to explain. The superintendent would simply say:

Trouble is trouble! It is your school and you are responsible. Now fix it!

Martin often found himself conferring with more experienced principals from other districts regarding questions of policy development. His attempts to discuss such things with his superintendent always resulted in rushed and rescheduled meetings. Eventually, Martin and his faculty developed a long-range plan for his school. He presented it to his superintendent with a note attached asking for a meeting within the month to discuss the plan. The superintendent never responded.

At the state-wide conference of school administrators, Martin had lunch with a friend who had become a superintendent in another district. His friend offered him a principalship in his district. Martin thanked him for the offer and went home to discuss it with his family.

References

Gottfredson, G., & Hybl, L. (1987). *An analytical description of the school principal's job. (Report #13).* Baltimore: Center for Research on Elementary and Middle Schools, Johns Hopkins University.

Johnson, M., & Douglas R. (1986, January*)*. Assessment centers: What impact have they had on career opportunities for women? *NASSP Bulletin.*

McGregor, D. (May-June 1957). An uneasy look at performance appraisal. *Harvard Business Review,* 89-94

NASSP. (1985). NASSP's 12 skill dimensions. In J. Kaiser (1993). *Educational Administration (2nd ed.).* Mequon, WI: Stylex Publishing Co., Inc.

Notar, E. Assessment of Administrators In J. Kaiser (1993). *Educational administration, 2nd ed.)* Mequon, WI: Stylex Publishing Co., Inc.)

Performance Review (1986). (a film). New York: NY: DSI Micro, Inc.

Posner, J. & Schmidt, N. (1986). *Instructor's guide for performance appraisal: The human dynamics.* Del Mar, CA: CRM/McGraw-Hill.

Chapter 10

SUPERVISION AND CURRICULUM
Georgia J. Kosmoski

Curriculum Management

A primary task of school supervision is the management of curriculum (Harris, 1985). How and what students learn are major concerns for all educators. Ultimate responsibility and accountability for curriculum processes rest with the school supervisor as he or she assumes the role of curriculum leader. The supervisor needs to understand the meaning of curriculum, curricular controversy, and influences that affect the decision-making processes. As curriculum leaders, supervisors must have expertise in development, implementation, and evaluation. Successful completion of curriculum tasks requires the same high level of leadership skills as other administrative functions.

Questions to answer after studying this chapter

✔ How do constituents and specialists define curriculum?

✔ What is the planned and unplanned curriculum?

✔ What is an acceptable working definition for curriculum?

✔ What are the major curricular roles of the supervisor?

✔ How do the two curriculum screens affect development?

✔ What are the six stages of curriculum development?

✔ What is the role of the supervisor in development?

✔ How does the supervisor facilitate curriculum implementation?

✔ What is the supervisor's role in curriculum evaluation?

✔ What are the three major influences on curriculum decisions?

✔ Which local, state, and national spheres of power affect a given school?

✔ How does background influence curriculum decisions?

✔ How does political conflict affect curriculum?

Blood (1993) explained that curriculum leadership involves the ability to work with group process and committees. Curriculum leaders should work toward teacher empowerment and ownership of the curriculum. Only through teacher ownership will development, implementation, and evaluation result in processes that have genuine meaning. The attitudes of the leader toward curriculum have a dramatic effect on teachers' views of that curriculum.

Curriculum Defined

The Community's Perception of Curriculum

Most Americans think they know what the curriculum is at their neighborhood school. Ronald Doll (1992) conducted a poll of people's beliefs regarding the meaning of the word

-265-

266 Chapter 10 *Supervision and Curriculum*

curriculum. Some people think that curriculum is what is taught, pupils' in and out-of-school experiences, materials used by students and teachers, and combinations of these items.

Others offer more sophisticated definitions. To some, the curriculum consists of modes of inquiring about the events and phenomena of our world. Other people think the curriculum is the accumulated tradition of organized knowledge found in school and college subjects. Still others feel curriculum represents something enduring and pervasive—the collection of experiences of the society. Few people in the United States believe the curriculum is a mandated document distributed by the district central office, the state, or the federal government. See Figure 10-1.

Curriculum Defined

- What is taught
- Pupils' school experiences
- Learning/teaching materials
- Accumulated organized knowledge
- Collection of society's experiences
- Mandated document

Figure 10-1

Specialists' Perception of Curriculum

Like the general population, curriculum specialists disagree on concepts or semantics as they attempt to define the term. An examination of three such definitions illustrates the disagreement.

Taba (1962) combines the broad definition of "experiences" with a scientifically measurable view. Her definition is an attempt to find a compromise "somewhere in between the two extremes." She proposes:

A sharp distinction between method and curriculum seems unfruitful, but some distinctions need to be drawn between aspects of learning processes and activities that are of concern in curriculum development and those that can be allocated to the realm of specific methods of teaching. Only certain objectives can be implemented by the nature of curriculum content, its selection and organization. Others can be implemented only by the nature and organization of learning experiences. Thinking, for example, is one of the latter objectives. It would appear, then, that the criteria for the decisions about learning experiences necessary to implement major objectives belong in the realm of curriculum design. (p. 214)

Twenty-two years later, Glenys and Adolph Unruh (1984) suggested a more pragmatic and compartmentalized definition.

Curriculum is defined as a plan for achieving intended learning outcomes: A plan concerned with purpose, with what is to be learned, and with the results of instruction. Curriculum is comprised of several elements: learning outcomes, selection, and structure. Learning outcomes include knowledge, attitudes, and skills. Knowledge encompasses facts, information, principles, and generalizations that help an individual understand his or her world better. Attitudes include values, beliefs, interpersonal feelings, creative thinking, appreciations, self-esteem, and other aspects of affective growth. Skills are techniques, processes, and abilities that enable the individual to be versatile in using knowledge and physical resources effectively to extend the horizons of his or her world. (p. 96)

A number of curriculum definitions were offered in the 1990s. Among the noteworthy is that proposed by Oliva (1993). He specifically separates the in- and out-of- school elements that encompass this process. Oliva writes:

Curriculum . . . those experiences of a child that come under the supervision of the school. Included in the concept of curriculum described . . . are
(1) all in-school experiences, including classroom learning experiences, student activities, use of the library, use of learning resource centers, assemblies, use of the cafeteria, and social functions, and (2) out-of-school learning experiences directed by the school, including homework, field trips, and use of community resources. (pp. 266-267)

Planned and Unplanned Curriculum

A brief examination of definitions proposed by scholars in the curriculum field suggests the existence of two general levels of curriculum. Every school has a planned, acknowledged, and formal curriculum and, simultaneously, an unplanned, hidden, and informal one. The planned curriculum includes content which is usually categorized into subjects or fields of study. The unplanned curriculum encompasses various experiences ranging from working cooperatively within groups to learning how to out-smart or defend oneself from the class bully.

For some students, unplanned experiences are the most meaningful and memorable in their school careers. Students often verbalize these occurrences to their families and, in turn, color parent and community perspectives of the school. Every school administrator in America is held

268 Chapter 10 *Supervision and Curriculum*

responsible for the curriculum—both the formal and informal experiences that pupils have in school (Doll, 1992).

A Working Definition of Curriculum

In the final analysis, one's definition of curriculum is determined by personal perception. However, for purposes of clarity in future discussion, this working definition is offered.

School curriculum is both the formal and informal processes and content experienced by the learners. Under school direction, curriculum includes student cognitive growth, skill development, affective and value changes.

This definition is broad enough to include both the formal and informal aspects of curriculum. What is taught (content) and how it is taught (process of instruction) is specified. Content and instruction enjoy equal status in this view of curriculum. When deemed appropriate, change and improvement for either content or instruction is possible for both the planned and unplanned curriculum. Refer to Figure 10-2.

The Renewed Dilemma

When engaged in curriculum activities supervisors wrestle with the dilemma of what students should learn and what and how the school should teach. Two recently published best-selling books and a widely disseminated national report sparked renewed interest in these age old questions.

The first to initiate controversy was E. D. Hirsch, Jr. in his book, *Cultural Literacy: What Every American Needs to Know* (1987a). Hirsch contended that the reason many students— especially those students from low-income homes—do not read well is not their lack of skills but their limited background in knowledge. He attacked curriculum workers for intentionally neglecting important subjects. Hirsch argued that curriculum should systematically teach information and ideas that are the basis of our national culture. He claimed most educators believe otherwise; hence their current interest in teaching thinking and their disdain for "mere facts" (Hirsch, 1987b). Kosmoski, Gay, and Vockell (1990) supported this position by demonstrating that student academic success is positively and significantly related to knowledge of the culture.

In *The Closing of the American Mind*, Allan Bloom (1987) provided a scathing critique of higher education and indirectly indicts elementary and secondary schools. He contended that American students arrive at college with much less "book learning" than their European counterparts. By suggesting that American students leave the public school system as unprepared "native savages," Bloom condemned the educational system that produced them.

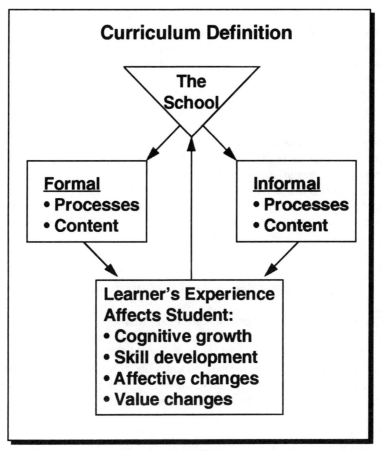

Figure 10-2

Writing in *What Do Our 17-Year-Olds Know? A Report of the First National Assessment of History and Literature*, Diane Ravitch and Chester Finn, Jr. (1987) reported that numerous adolescents could not tell the half century in which the Civil War occurred or who wrote *Leaves of Grass*. They concluded that "our eleventh graders as a whole are ignorant of much of what they should know" and strongly condemn this "shameful performance." Ravitch and Finn demanded more time for instruction in literature and history.

These critics exemplify the turmoil that exists among educators regarding the essential elements of curriculum. They serve as catalysts to encourage renewed debate in the "what and how" of teaching and learning. Rather than expending precious time and energy to solve this

270 Chapter 10 *Supervision and Curriculum*

dilemma, curriculum supervisors would be well advised to follow the suggestions of Ronald Brandt (1988) who stated:

> *It may be true that some educators are so concerned with skills and processes that they consider content "irrelevant," but most probably believe that both are important, and that stating the issue that way creates a false dichotomy. . .Educators do hold varying views about the purpose of education and the way curriculum should be organized to achieve them. In all fairness, however, these difficulties can be ascribed not to laziness or cowardice, but to deeply held convictions about what is best for children.*

> *Rather than responding in kind, educators should conserve their energies for the curriculum struggle of deciding what schools should teach. Curriculum leaders do not make organizational decisions by personal decree; they manage a give-and-take political process in which the views of teachers, board members, parents, and others are heard and considered . . . Most existing school programs are an amalgam of progressive and traditional practices, the best that can be achieved under the circumstances but not fully satisfactory to anyone. (p. 3-4)*

Curricular Roles of the Supervisor

With the national movements toward more building autonomy, empowerment of building staff, and various forms of restructuring, the building administrator finds that he or she is expected to assume more, if not most, of the duties of curriculum leader. Decreased funding prompts many districts to rely on the building administrator to perform functions that were once given to specialists. In the case of curriculum management, many building supervisors, replacing central office directors or assistant superintendents, now serve as the curriculum leader for their building.

The three major roles of the curriculum supervisor are *curriculum development*, *implementation*, and *evaluation*. In curriculum development the supervisor oversees and guides the staff as they work through the six stages of development. These are needs assessment, educational philosophy, goals and objectives, content, methodology, and evaluation.

The supervisor, acting as curriculum leader, serves as a facilitator to teachers as they implement the curriculum. Some activities which facilitate implementation are the timely and effective provision of learning materials, equipment, facilities, and positive climate.

The third role of the supervisor is that of leader and facilitator in curriculum evaluation. Student achievement and the curriculum need to be examined both formatively and summatively in order to determine the effectiveness and worth of the program. Refer to Figure 10-3.

Curricular Roles of the Supervisor		
Curriculum Development	**Curriculum Implementation**	**Curriculum Evaluation**
1. Clarify and focus committee on educational philosophy.	1. Provide facilities and resources.	1. Help select ongoing curriculum evaluation tools.
2. Facilitate needs assessments.	2. Provide learning/teaching materials.	2. Serve on the evaluation team.
3. Help determine goals and objectives.	3. Monitor teacher implementation.	3. Help select and organize student assessment.
4. Collegially select and organize content and methodology.	4. Serve as a resource for teachers.	4. Serve as an expert in test interpretation.
5. Guide evaluation efforts.		

Figure 10-3

Supervision and Curriculum Development

Schools find it necessary to constantly develop or revise curriculum to match changing philosophy, goals, objectives, and needs of the constituency. Most often curriculum is developed by committees of teachers led by an administrator serving as the curriculum supervisor. This collegial structure has generally replaced the independent work of the central office administrator common through the early 1980s. Within this framework, the supervisor (based at the central office or more often at the building) provides leadership, organization, and structure.

In the task of curriculum development the supervisor acts as a change agent or catalyst. The supervisor helps teachers identify curriculum problems and aids in the search and study for solutions. It is the curriculum leader who stimulates teachers to examine the existing curriculum and suggest recommendations for improvement. He or she sparks dissatisfaction with the present condition and causes teachers to embrace change.

The curriculum supervisor accomplishes the task of development as a member and participant of a cooperative group. The supervisor is not the sole developer and should not behave as an independent author. It takes at least two people to develop curriculum. The supervisor's authority and respectability is not predicated on status alone but rather on the level of credibility perceived by fellow curriculum workers.

272 Chapter 10 *Supervision and Curriculum*

Oliva (1993) suggested that to achieve credibility the supervisor must possess specialized skills. He listed a firm grounding in curriculum theory, knowledge of attempted solutions and how they fared, and cognition of current national and international curricular developments as necessary skills.

In addition, the supervisor needs expertise in research, proposal construction, analysis of research and subsequent biases, and the interpretation of findings. The supervisor's role includes knowledge of learning theory and a sensitivity to societal problems. Among necessary skills, Oliva cited the supervisor's ability to manage work groups and to facilitate their efforts.

The Curriculum Development Process

The supervisor must understand the general components involved in development and revision. Each step is sequentially accomplished and is dependent upon and related to other steps. Tyler (1949) and other curriculum specialists included the following as essential curriculum development components: *educational philosophy, needs assessment, goals and objectives, content selection and organization, selection of methodology, and evaluation.*

Supervisors must conceptualize this process as continual and cyclical. The completion of the evaluation step, for example, is a return to the step of re-examination and development of new and appropriate goals and objectives. Figure 10-4 visually represents this process.

The supervisor must provide leadership, organization, and the structure necessary to accomplish each step in the process.

Philosophy of Education Screen

All schools and districts have a philosophy of education. Educational philosophy is the general view or basic beliefs of education. It is sometimes written in the form of a philosophy, mission, or vision statement. Occasionally, the philosophy is not formalized in any specific document, but rather is an informal group or individual view. Regardless of the form, philosophy influences and shapes all school practices and policies.

In curriculum, the educational philosophy of the constituents serves as a screen for acceptance or rejection (Tyler, 1949). All processes pass through the philosophy screen before being accepted in the school. Using the philosophy screen, a school that generally believes in mental discipline and traditional academic excellence would probably welcome the addition of an advanced course in calculus and trigonometry, but might shun expanded independent student course work.

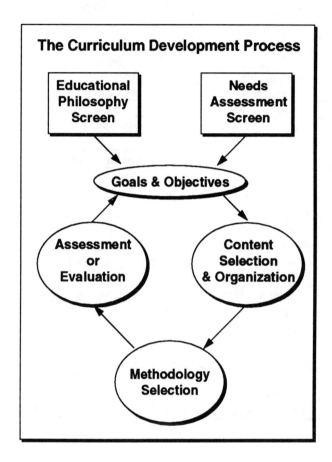

Figure 10-4

Curriculum supervisors must provide codevelopers with honest information about the past and existing school philosophy, facilitate the formulation of a current consensus philosophy, and insure that selected curriculum components match the philosophy. They should deliberately articulate this philosophy throughout the development process. These actions provide the curriculum committee with an appropriate filter necessary for curriculum selection. Supervisors must insure that the committee constantly checks the compatibility of their curriculum design with their philosophy or mission statement. Understanding the school's mission brings focus to the development process. Figure 10-5 describes the generally accepted educational philosophies and respective characteristics.

274 Chapter 10 *Supervision and Curriculum*

Basic Philosophies and Their Application to Education	
Philosophy	**Applied to Education**
Idealism	The mind is the central element of reality.
	Knowledge is absolute and there is one correct way to learn and behave.
	Emphasis is on concepts and theory.
	Administrators and teachers act as role models.
Realism	The mind learns through contact with the physical world.
	The basic tools of learning are observation and measurement.
	Knowledge is discovered.
	Content and methodology are based on current data.
	Administrators and teachers serve as resources and facilitators.
Essentialism	An educated person must possess a core of information and skills to live well.
	Administrators and teachers are authorities and motivators.
Pragmatism	Knowledge is relative and constructed.
	Content and methodology emphasize the practical.
	Administrators and teachers favor whatever works.
Existentialism	Content and methodology are determined by the learner.
	Administrators and teachers guide students and stress student questioning and value clarification.
Behaviorism	Knowledge, appreciation, and wisdom are replaced by actions, conduct, and skills referred to as observable behavior.
	Centered around behavioral objectives, learning is accomplished in short rewarded steps toward a goal.
	Administrators/teachers are trainers or engineers of human behavior.

Figure 10-5

The Needs Assessment Screen

The second screen used to select curriculum is the needs assessment. A needs assessment is any procedure used to identify, confirm, and prioritize the needs of the school's constituents. It is a device or tool used for identifying gaps between "what should be" and "what is" in current practice (Dillon-Peterson, 1981). The assessment may be at the micro or macro level. Micro is specific and deals with areas such as the classroom teacher's examination of topics which might improve performance for selective students within the class or content of a specific unit within a given area. Macro assessment is general assessment of the needs of the entire constituency that must be met by the curriculum under consideration. Whether the needs assessment is micro or macro, findings should be relative and pertinent to the curriculum which is developed or revised for the specific population (Blood, 1993).

Shepard and Ragan (1982) emphasized that an effective needs assessment must involve input from all members represented in the constituency or school community. Unsuccessful curriculum implementation was most often attributed to lack of teacher involvement in development and the lack of a local needs assessment prior to design.

To meet the needs of the community, specific needs must first be identified through opinion and factual data. Pratt (1980) recommended that the school directly ask the constituents what should be taught. Sources of data include students, teachers, administrators, parents, taxpayers, social and political leaders, business and industry, recent graduates, and community service agencies. These sources provide the information necessary to determine the needs which should be addressed by the adopted curriculum.

Needs assessment data is gathered in numerous ways, including surveys or questionnaires, public meetings or forums, individual and group interviews, local newspapers, and observations. The most common is the survey or questionnaire. Pratt (1980) recommended using more than one data-collecting tool for cross-checking the results to increase accuracy. Figure 10-6 lists a sample of appropriate items that could appear on a parent questionnaire regarding middle school social studies.

Goals and Objectives

Goals and objectives are those statements that define, direct, and channel the desired curriculum. They provide continuity of curricular implementation by teachers at different cites. While both goals and objectives set the course or direction of curriculum, they do so in different ways. A goal is a broad general statement which outlines the course the learner should follow. Goals are not necessarily observable or measurable.

Objectives, however, are narrow, short-range statements which specifically designate learner behaviors. The objective clearly gives the conditions under which the learner will be evaluated, designates the student behavior to be evaluated, and indicates the minimum level at which the learner must perform in order to be rated acceptable (Weigand, 1971). Briefly stated the objective should have three components: the situation, the behavioral term, and the acceptance level. A goal is not attained until its objectives are accomplished.

When writing objectives special attention is given to the selection of observable verbs which clearly describe exact learner behavior. Verbs such as write, select, state, list, analyze, synthesize, and evaluate clearly identify learner behavior, while verbs such as know, understand, and appreciate are unacceptable because of ambiguity. Figure 10-7 gives several examples of goals and the accompanying acceptable objectives.

276 Chapter 10 *Supervision and Curriculum*

Parent Social Studies Questionnaire

Your Name: _____

Your Child's Name: _____ Grade: _____

School: _____

Do you feel this current program satisfactorily teaches conservation? Environment? Explain.

_____

_____

_____

_____

Some concepts or ideas I would like to see added to the program are:

_____

_____

_____

_____

Some concepts I feel are no longer needed in the social studies program are:

_____

_____

_____

_____

I feel the current textbook is:

_____

_____

_____

Figure 10-6

Chapter 10 *Supervision and Curriculum* **277**

Sample Goals and Objectives

Goal A

The student will learn the addition facts.

Objective 1

Given a worksheet of 50 addition facts 0-20, the student will write 90% correctly.

Objective 2

Using the "Math is Fun" computer drill program, the student will successfully choose 90% correct responses for the 0-20 addition facts.

Objective 3

Given a 5 second audio time test for addition facts, the student will write the correct sums for 90% of the items.

Goal B

The U. S. History class will learn about the U. S. Constitution.

Objective 1

With 95% accuracy, the student will be able to recite the Preamble to the U. S. Constitution.

Objective 2

To the satisfaction of the instructor, the student will be able to write a one-page essay tracing the history of the Constitutional Convention.

Objective 3

Given a sheet of 20 possible amendments, the student will select the 10 amendments composing the Bill of Rights with 90% accuracy.

Goal C

The students will recognize the main character in a story.

Objective 1

Given 10 separate short stories, to read silently, the student will be able to underline the name of main character for 90% of the stories.

Objective 2

After the teacher orally reads a short story, the student will be able to write the name of the main character with 100% accuracy.

Figure 10-7

A second consideration when writing objectives is the use of a taxonomy or hierarchy to insure various levels of difficulty. With current emphasis on higher level thinking skills a taxonomy helps the development committee to incorporate various cognitive levels into the adopted curriculum. A conscious effort to write objectives at more difficult levels will encourage students to expand their higher-order thinking skills. Two taxonomies that facilitate this process

Chapter 10 *Supervision and Curriculum*

are Bloom's (1967) *Taxonomy of Educational Objectives* and Gagne's (1965) *The Conditions of Learning*. For a visual representation of these taxonomies refer to Figures 10-8 and 10-9.

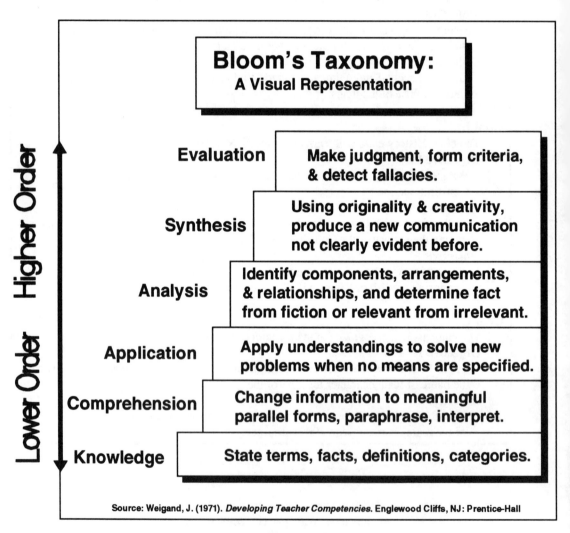

Figure 10-8

Chapter 10 *Supervision and Curriculum* **279**

Gagne's Ascending Learning Taxonomy:
A Visual Representation

Problem Solving — Solving a new problem to achieve a goal by applying one or more rules. Example: Find three similarities between car and lion.

Rule Using — Relating two or more concepts. Perform an action based on a rule or chain of concepts. Example: Give an operational definition for a spider.

Classifying — Ability to form a class, group, generalize. Example: Assign all the adjectives to a given group and the adverbs to another given group.

Multiple Discrimination — Recognizing physical differences and different responses according to them. Example: Remembering the names of flowers in the garden.

Verbal Chaining — Combining words to form verbal responses. Example: Stating a descriptive sentence about swimming.

Motor Chaining — Learning motor skills. Example: Print the capital letters.

Stimulus-Response Learning — Giving a response after a specified stimulus. Example: Say "seashell" after the teacher has said "seashell".

Source: Weigand, J. (1971). *Developing Teacher Competencies*. Englewood Cliffs, NJ: Prentice-Hall

Figure 10-9

280 Chapter 10 *Supervision and Curriculum*

The supervisor can facilitate the development of appropriate and meaningful goals and objectives by providing the development committee with proper space and time. Adequate and pleasant surroundings allow the group to concentrate on the task rather than personal needs or comfort. Some even suggest the setting should be away from the school to avoid distractions and interruption. The curriculum supervisor should provide release time for the development committee to work. If this is impractical or physically impossible, the supervisor may arrange extra pay for extra work for the developers who toil after regular school hours.

Because useful goals and objectives require proper form, supervisors must have expertise in writing skills. They should use these skills to guide the committee to use accepted terms, succinct language that reflects their intentions, and proper grammatical structure.

Throughout the curriculum development process, supervisors need to remind their co-workers to filter all decisions and choices through the philosophy and needs assessment screens. Personally, or through designees, supervisors should periodically review committee progress.

Content

The fourth stage of curriculum development is the selection and organization of content. Content is that body of information, concepts, ideas, generalities, and principles, that is to be learned (Zais, 1976). Selection should be based upon the developed goals and objectives. It should provide the learner with the tools necessary to achieve goals and objectives. Content is not a text book. Rather, it is the activities chosen to meet the goals and objectives. Texts, worksheets, and manipulatives are only tools or vehicles of the content.

To organize the content, most curriculum committees use the framework of scope and sequence. Scope refers to the horizontal organization of the material. It delineates the breadth and depth of the content. Scope defines "what" and "how much" is to be learned in a given course or grade level. Sequence is vertical organization and refers to the order in which the curriculum is taught. Doll (1992) listed numerous methods to establish sequence. Among them are chronological order, simple to complex, and part to whole.

The supervisor's role in the selection and organization of content is similar to the role in developing goals and objectives. The supervisor should serve as a resource, provide leadership, and give direction. To accomplish this, the supervisor should become familiar with available source materials, understand preview procedures, and provide an acceptable process for group selection.

Methodology

Methodology, or the method of instruction, should be selected by the curriculum committee with due respect for academic freedom. Curriculum defined as "what and how" to teach and learn, demands attention be given to the type of instruction. Selection of instructional method is based upon the chosen objectives. Some objectives are best met by specific methodology or approaches. An objective that specifies group problem solving, for example, strongly implies that students need to work cooperatively.

In this stage of curriculum development, the supervisor needs a strong foundation and broad background in proven methodology and its application. The supervisor should possess and willingly share this expertise with colleagues.

Evaluation

The final stage in curriculum development is evaluation or assessment. Both student performance and all aspects of the curriculum should be assessed. Assessment of student performance provides feedback about how well actual performance matches planned performance. Are students achieving the goals and objectives set forth for them? To be most effective, evaluation of student performance should begin with course implementation and continue throughout the learning process. Some potential assessment tools for gathering data on student success are *norm-referenced* achievement tests, *criterion-referenced* tests, observational checklists, and teacher-made tests.

All areas of the curriculum itself should be evaluated to determine if it accomplishes the intended purpose. Questions that should be addressed are: Is this goal appropriate? Should this concept be added to the content? Would this method of instruction improve student learning? Students, teachers, and supervisors should be formally queried during the learning cycle.

The supervisor must work with teachers to ensure appropriate evaluation in the classroom and the school. Results should be analyzed to 1) identify level of student achievement and, 2) determine curriculum effectiveness. Although this should be a group task, the ultimate responsibility rests with the curriculum supervisor.

Supervision and Curriculum Implementation

The role of the central office or building supervisor in curriculum implementation involves obtaining adoption, facilitating, and ensuring delivery. After the work of the curriculum committee is complete, the supervisor, along with the superintendent of schools, recommends to

282 Chapter 10 *Supervision and Curriculum*

the board of education the adoption of the new or revised curriculum. Once approved, the supervisor assumes a number of implementation duties.

Foremost among these facilitation duties are allocating funds for the purchase of needed materials and resources, providing staff development, employing and directing staff and consultants, and providing suitable facilities. These responsibilities encompass the school and individual classroom (Unruh and Unruh, 1984). After basic materials are purchased and dispersed it is possible that an individual teacher requires specialized material. Successful staff development might entail more in-service training than was predicted. For these and other incidences, the supervisor should be flexible and proactive.

To ensure that teachers are effectively implementing the adopted curriculum, the supervisor needs to be familiar with everyday classroom activities. Classroom observations and informal visitations are excellent methods for acquiring first-hand information regarding implementation. Effective supervisors are often in the classroom.

Two additional techniques for ensuring implementation are periodic review of teacher lesson plans and feedback. Although the regular reading of lesson plans is tedious, it is also beneficial. From thorough review, the supervisor gains information about teacher implementation, organization, and time on task. A second method for checking implementation is direct feedback from teachers and students. Asking, either verbally or in writing, helps the supervisor determine which staff members need additional support.

Supervision and the Evaluation of Curriculum

Evaluation of curriculum is twofold. It includes the assessment of student achievement and scrutiny of the curriculum. The curriculum leader should view evaluation as a positive process that will lead to improvement and success. According to Tyler (1949), evaluation is the process for discovering if the learning experiences are actually producing the desired results. This assessment process includes identification of the strengths and weaknesses of the plan. Tyler added that evaluation checks the validity of basic aims and goals of the developed curriculum. He concludes that evaluation makes it possible to pinpoint areas which are effective or in need of improvement.

The role of the supervisor in assessing student growth and achievement is thoroughly discussed in Chapter 5: *Teaching Teachers About Testing*. Review of essential supervision roles in Chapter 5 is recommended.

Evaluation of the curriculum is an ongoing and collegial process accomplished by the supervisor and the teachers. Working together as an evaluation committee, these educators conduct formative and summative evaluation. *Formative evaluation* is prescriptive. Its purpose is to identify and formulate appropriate revision. The supervisor aids the staff in determining what information should be gathered to analyze the existing curriculum. One method of gathering information is periodic use of teacher and student surveys. Results from these surveys are examined and revisions are made. *Summative evaluation* is a statement of the perceived value or worth of the curriculum. This form of evaluation often serves as the basis for retaining or rejecting the existing curriculum.

Influences on Curriculum Decisions

Unruh and Unruh (1984) pointed out that curriculum design and implementation decisions are influenced by spheres of power, background, and existing political conflict. They argued that curricular tasks are complex and exist within a complex political milieu. While making curriculum decisions the school supervisor needs to be cognizant and sensitive to these influences. Figure 10-10 outlines the conditions that influence curriculum decisions.

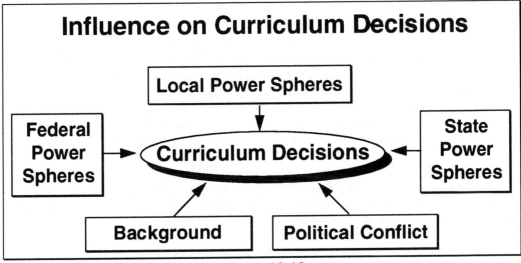

Figure 10-10

Spheres of Power

The spheres of power that influence curriculum decisions are found at the local, state, and national levels. These influences often shape or determine who will be the decision makers in curriculum formulation or selection.

284 Chapter 10 *Supervision and Curriculum*

Local Influence

Local influences include the various stake-holders: students, parents, teachers, other community members, business and industry, administrators, and Boards of Education.

Student involvement in curriculum planning and implementation should be encouraged. At the building or district level older students serve successfully on design and assessment teams. The most common type of student participation occurs in the classroom. Many teachers solicit student opinions, even from very young children, through classroom discussions, opportunities to vote on programs, and individual conferences. In middle and high school, cooperative learning group projects, oral presentations, school/community projects, study tours, and student exchange programs are examples of student involvement in curriculum planning in which they assume joint responsibility with the teacher.

Parents, nonparent community residents, and local business and industry are potentially powerful influences. Partnership is a key concept in the successful involvement of these individuals.

Kenney and Perry (1994) identified two trends which increase parent involvement. These are volunteerism and the expansion of school directed parenting classes. Volunteerism that influences curriculum decisions in the school includes such activities as participation on advisory or policy-making committees, helping children with class activities or special projects, sharing expertise as a resource person, and tutoring special needs students. Parenting classes urge parents to assume their responsibilities in matters of child health, nutrition, discipline, and intellectual development. Both trends encourage home-school partnerships in curriculum implementation.

The 25th Annual Phi Delta Kappa Gallop Poll (Elam & Gallup, 1993) of the Public's Attitudes Toward the Public Schools indicated that 64% of adult Americans have no children in school and 71% have no children in the public school system. As eligible voters, this large majority greatly influences school operations. Recognizing this fact, many school districts reach out to these individuals in hopes of positively involving them in school projects. Involvement will make the participant a stake-holder who is positively disposed toward the project or organization.

Corporations, business organizations, and schools are now forming partnerships which extend far beyond the traditional contributions to vocational education. New involvement includes contributions in curriculum design and fiscal management. Business seeks this active role because of the dramatic change in the nation's work place caused by the rapid evolution of computer technology and the worker's need to think, listen, and communicate well with others. Toch (1982) illustrated this involvement by describing the *adopt-a-school* programs and the *school-business partnerships*, where corporations encourage employees to become active in the schools. Lectures, career counseling, and contributions of equipment and services were encouraged.

Teachers are a dynamic influence in all curriculum decisions. A comprehensive study by the National Science Foundation in 1979 reported that the curriculum reform programs of the 1960s failed because teachers were not involved in development and were not properly supported by administration during implementation. As early as 1980, the National Education Association issued a position paper on the necessity and desirability of strengthening teacher roles in all aspects of curriculum decision-making. Most educators in the late1990s continue to hold these beliefs.

The body of effective school research of the 1980s demonstrated the importance of the role of the *school administrator*, namely the principal, in all school decisions. While performing supervisory tasks the principal makes critical decisions concerning curriculum development, implementation, assessment and renewal. Curriculum supervisors find that they are a key influence. Theodore Sizer (1984) commented that administrators are largely responsible for the quality of school programs and climate. If schools have a large number of behavior problems, their climate may be at fault. This requires administrators to look to revitalization. In *Schools Without Failure*, William Glasser (1969) wrote that instead of stressing success, schools led by narrow-minded principals, emphasize failure. He observed that children enter school in successful and optimistic frames of mind and that the school pins labels of failure on some students. He concluded that shattering children's positive outlook is the most serious problem in elementary schools.

As schools become more site-based, principals' responsibilities dramatically increase. When districts understand the uniqueness of each of their schools and allow for site-based decisions, principals become prime directors of curricular advancement.

Central office administrators and board of education members also influence district curriculum. Many districts have central office curriculum supervisors and specialists whose responsibilities are to direct all curriculum processes for an entire district. They report directly to the superintendent who is the school executive ultimately responsible for curriculum decisions. *Board of Education members* make all final decisions regarding curriculum. The influence of these board members varies among districts, but must always be regarded as important.

A major local influence is the existing district philosophy, usually expressed in the form of a vision or mission statement with accompanying goals and objectives, identified needs, and the demographics of the district as a whole. In highly bureaucratic districts and districts engaged in strategic planning, district goals, needs, and demographics strongly influence curriculum processes.

286 Chapter 10 *Supervision and Curriculum*

State Influence

State influences that affect the curriculum processes can include the *governor, state legislature, court case decisions,* and *state boards of education.* Supervisors working on curriculum tasks should remain knowledgeable of state influences swaying or dictating local decisions.

Governors, acting both independently and collectively on panels, commissions, and advisory boards, frequently utilize their influence over curriculum. They are often highly visible members of national investigative and policy making groups such as the National Commission on Excellence in Education which issued the famous report, *A Nation at Risk: The Imperative for Educational Reform* (1983). President Bush and fifty governors wrote *America 2000: An Education Strategy (U.S. Department of Education, 1991).* Curricular areas addressed by governors include at-risk programs, early childhood initiatives, technology, national standards and assessments, and tax waivers.

Throughout the nation, state legislatures seem to be writing more and more legislation to deal with daily school operations. By exercising their power and addressing historically local issues, legislatures depart from their traditional *hands-off* curriculum role. Bills are passed to regulate equal educational opportunity, due process procedures, minority and gender equity, and course offerings. Nearly all states have enacted mandates to school districts to develop and implement competency-testing and to produce local plans for student academic improvement. These and other statutes directly influence what is taught in the classroom.

Unruh and Unruh (1984) explained that, like state legislatures, courts are increasing their involvement in school issues. Although courts and lawyers claim no expertise in professional education they are called upon to resolve school problems. Usually, these problems relate to the basic rights of citizens set forth in the First and Fourth Amendments of the United States Constitution and those parallel provisions provided in state constitutions. These problems resolved by state courts are classified as matters pertaining to separation of church and state, distribution of wealth to schools, race, equity, and freedoms. Many rulings affect the development and implementation of curriculum.

Finally, state departments of education influence school curriculum. State supervision is often of an administrative nature, rather than instructional, as in checking compliance with state-mandated programs or goals. Faced with administering newly created statutes and court rulings, state boards are actively engaged in developing interpretations and regulations for compliance. These actions directly influence local curricular decisions.

National Influence

National influences that affect curriculum include *federal laws, programs,* and *funding.* Influences of state and regional federal offices, national teacher training trends, professional interest groups, and special interest groups also affect curriculum (Campbell et al.,1990).

Although the Tenth Amendment of the U.S. Constitution reserves the area of public education to the states, the federal government has always had a hand in public education. The United States Congress enacts many laws strongly influencing local curriculum decisions. Title IX on sex discrimination in education and PL 94-142 on education for the handicapped are but two examples. Schools must comply with these federal statutes and follow the regulations prepared by the U.S. Department of Education or federal agencies. Federal courts exercise increasing civil rights-related involvement and control in matters of sex discrimination and desegregation.

Most federal monies designated for public education are in the form of categorical grants. These include grants for aid to disadvantaged students, vocational education, preschool and handicapped students, and many others. The existence of these funds constitutes control since local schools must use these monies for no other purposes and within the guidelines dictated by the grant.

Often federal legislation includes provisions for inservice and preservice training for teachers. The training is intended to provide additional understanding and skills in funded fields such as special education, preschool education, and vocational education.

Nationwide professional and special interest groups also exercise control of federal dollars and often set standards and policy (Elmore & Fuhrman, 1994). By awarding large categorical grants such organizations as the National Institute of Education, the National Center for Vocational Education, the National Science Institute, and the National Assessment of Educational Progress wield great influence over what is taught. For an overview of the spheres of power that influence curriculum processes refer to Figure 10-11.

Spheres of Power Influencing Curriculum Decisions		
Local	State	National

- Students
- Teachers
- Parents
- Other Community Members
- Business & Industry
- Administrators
- Boards of Education
	- Governors
	- State Legislatures
	- Courts
	- State Boards of
	  Education
		- Federal Laws and Courts
		- Programs
		- Funding
		- State/Regional Federal
		  Offices
		- Teacher Training
		- Professional & Special
		  Interest Groups

Figure 10-11

288 Chapter 10 *Supervision and Curriculum*

Background

To make successful decisions, modern supervisors need to know the national, state, and local trends in curriculum design, development, and implementation. This knowledge provides supervisors with invaluable tools in quality decision making.

1. Supervisors acquire national information through reading, attending conferences, and participating in organizations devoted to supervision and curriculum. Numerous journals, books, and newspapers are published which specialize in curricular issues. *Educational Leadership, Phi Delta Kappan, Urban Educator*, and *Education Week* are a few examples of what is readily available. Organizations such as the Association for Supervision and Curriculum Development (ASCD) provide practitioners with research materials, resource services, and regional and national conferences with curricular emphasis.

2. Virtually all states disseminate update bulletins; provide copies of state codes, regulations, and directives; and conduct education sessions for local supervisors. This vital information facilitates curricular decisions at the school level.

3. Finally, the supervisor needs to be familiar with local forces. This is most often accomplished by communication with other practitioners, veteran administrators, teachers, and community leaders. The review of the longitudinal demographics of the school and community is also most helpful in acquiring background knowledge.

After examining the many factors influencing curriculum decisions, it should be obvious that supervisors have a difficult task. However, it is one which is essential for developing and implementing quality curriculum.

Political Conflicts

Continuing changes in political conflicts nationally, state-wide, and locally also influence curriculum decisions.

1. Changes in political power at the national level eventually influence local curriculum programs. The conservative attitudes of former President Reagan's administration led to trends such as the return to a *back to basics* movement and the withdrawal of federal control and financial support to many school programs across the country. The more liberal viewpoints of President Clinton's administration encourages and funds numerous child welfare programs such as the expansion of early start education.

Chapter 10 *Supervision and Curriculum* **289**

2. State politics strongly affect curriculum decisions. Historically, traditionally liberal states have more innovative programs than do states with a tradition of conservative politics. A comparison of two states illustrates this concept. Over the last decade, the historically progressive and liberal state of California mandated a form of *site-based management* (SBM) for all schools. This policy encourages supervisors to make curriculum decisions at the building level. Indiana, to the contrary, is historically considered a conservative state. Few Indiana public school districts engage in SBM and most curriculum decisions are made at the central office.

3. Another influence in political conflict occurs at the local level. All communities encounter occasional political conflict. Any curriculum issue may become controversial. Curriculum supervisors are wise to explore general population attitudes and the positions of various local power spheres prior to initiating curriculum change. Supervisors must also remain cognizant that the move to more shared decision-making increases independent thinking which makes consensus more difficult.

Principles and Practices for Success

- Recognize that the management of curriculum is a primary task of school supervisors.

- Acknowledge the existence of planned and unplanned curriculum in the school.

- Formulate a personal working definition for curriculum.

- Assume a leadership role in development, implementation, and evaluation of curriculum.

- Be proactive in incorporating the curriculum development changes resulting from screens of educational philosophy and constituent needs.

- Understand and be able to initiate the six stages of curriculum development.

- Facilitate curricular implementation and evaluation.

- Recognize and be sensitive to local, state, and national power spheres, background, and political conflicts that affect the curriculum.

290 Chapter 10 *Supervision and Curriculum*

Summary

Curriculum encompasses both the formal and informal processes experienced by the learner. Under the school's direction, curriculum includes student cognitive growth, skill development, and changes in attitude and values. The school supervisor must constantly grapple with the task of how and what should be taught to successfully prepare students for the future.

Three major curriculum responsibilities are *development, implementation,* and *evaluation.* Curriculum supervisors act as change agents and facilitators in these processes. In development, supervisors cooperatively participate in formulations of educational philosophy and in needs assessment. They provide leadership in the design of goals, objectives, content, methodology, and evaluation processes.

Supervisors are facilitators for teachers as they implement and evaluate the curriculum. Finally, supervisors understand that internal and external forces affect curricular decisions. Using this knowledge, supervisors help ensure that curriculum decisions are appropriate and successful.

Case Problem: *Dusty Chalk*

Dusty Chalk, Principal of Fernwood Middle School, is reading the memo that arrived in the school mail from his superintendent for the third time. He can't believe his eyes. The memo reads.

October 3

At last night's meeting, The Board and I agreed that our district math curriculum is outdated and no longer meets the needs of our students and the new state requirements for higher order learning skills. We feel that review and revision are in order and set this as a district priority during the coming school year.

Dusty, no one in the district knows the middle school math curriculum better than you and your faculty. I am asking you to assume this responsibility and spearhead this curriculum development project at the middle school level. I realize that this is a big job, but I'm sure you can do it and do it well. I would like to set May 1st as the date for school board approval. I'll send over a tentative budget and a copy of the new state guidelines. If you need anything else, call.

Dusty Chalk has a major curriculum job ahead. If Dusty asked you for advice, what steps would you recommend. Help him prepare an activity time line to successfully complete this supervision task.

Chapter 10 *Supervision and Curriculum* **291**

Case Problem: *A Class Act*

As principal of Horizon High School, Sheila Class is reviewing the list of volunteer names for forthcoming English Curriculum Development Committee membership. She is surprised to see the name, Cheryl Payne, on the list. Cheryl is the teacher's union grievance representative at Horizon. She has been strongly opposed to teacher participation in committee work during the school day. She often complains about the state's demands for change and the school's willingness to comply. Cheryl feels that curriculum work, like so many other duties, is the responsibility of the administration and that shared decision-making is a ploy to "get more work out of the teachers." In short, Ms. Payne does not favor change, building-based curriculum development, or committee participation.

Principal Class is aware of Ms. Payne's attitudes and must decide if Ms. Payne should be seated as a curriculum committee member. What should she do? Why? How would you convince Mrs. Class to follow your suggestion? Be specific.

References

Blood, D. (1993). The role of the administrator in curriculum. In J. Kaiser (Ed.), *Educational administration*. (2nd ed.).. Mequon, WI: Stylex Publishing Company.

Bloom, A. (1987). The closing of the American mind. New York: Simon and Schuster.

Bloom, B. (1967). Taxonomy of educational objectives. Handbook 1: Cognitive domain. New York: David McKay.

Brandt, R. S. (1988). Introduction: What should schools teach. In R. S. Brandt (Ed.), ASCD yearbook: Content of the curriculum. Alexandria, VA: Association for Supervision and Curriculum Development.

Campbell, R., Cunningham, L., Nystrand, R., & Usdan, M. (1990). The organization and control of American schools (6th ed.). Columbus, OH: Merrill.

Dillon-Peterson, B. (Ed.). (1981). ASCD yearbook: Staff development/organization development. Alexandria, VA: Association for Supervision and Curriculum Development.

Doll, R. C. (1992). Curriculum improvement: Decision making and process (8th ed.). Boston: Allyn and Bacon.

292 Chapter 10 *Supervision and Curriculum*

Elmore, R. F., & Fuhrman, S. H. (Eds.). (1994). The governance of curriculum: 1994 yearbook of the association for supervision and curriculum development. Alexandria, VA: Association for Supervision and Curriculum Development.

Elam, S., Rose, L. C., & Gallup, A. (October 1993). The 25th annual Phi Delta Kappa Gallup poll of the public's attitudes toward the public schools. Phi Delta Kappan, 137-152.

Gagne, R. M. (1965). The conditions of learning. Chicago: Holt, Rinehart, Winston.

Glasser, W. (1969). Schools without failure. New York: Harper & Row.

Harris B. M. (1985). Supervisory behavior in education (3rd ed.). Englewood Cliffs, NJ: Prentice-Hall.

Hirsch, E. D. (1987a). Cultural literacy: What every American needs to know. Boston: Houghton Mifflin.

Hirsch, E. D. (1987b). Restoring cultural literacy to the early grades. Educational Leadership, *45* (4), 63-70.

Kenney, E., & Perry, S. (1994). Talking to parents about performance-based report cards. Educational Leadership, *52* (2), 24-27.

Kosmoski, G. J., Gay, G., & Vockell, E. (1990). Cultural literacy and academic achievement. Journal of Experimental Education, 58 (4), 265-72.

National Commission on Excellence in Education. (1983). A nation at risk: The imperative for educational reform. Washington, DC: U.S. Government Printing Office.

National Education Association. (1980). Curriculum issues for the eighties: Structure, content, context. Washington, DC: National Education Association.

National Science Foundation. (1979). What are the needs in precollege science, mathematics, and social science education? Views from the field. Washington, DC: National Science Foundation.

Oliva, P. F. (1993). Supervision for today's schools (4th ed.). New York: Longman.

Pratt, D. (1980). Curriculum design and development. New York: Harcourt Brace.

Ravitch, D. & Finn, C., Jr. (1987). What do our 17-year-olds know? A report of the first national assessment of history and literature. New York: Harper and Row.

Sizer, T. R. (1984). Horace's compromise: The dilemma of the American high school. Boston: Houghton Mifflin.

Shepherd, G., & Ragan, W. (1982). Modern elementary curriculum. New York: Holt, Rinehart and Winston.

Taba, H. (1962). Curriculum development: Theory and practice. New York: Harcourt Brace Jovanovich.

Toch, T. (1982). New activism marks corporate role in schools. Education Week, 2.

Tyler, R. (1949). Basic principles of curriculum and instruction. Chicago: University of Chicago Press.

Unruh, G., & Unruh, A. (1984). Curriculum development: Problems, processes, and progress. Berkely, CA: McCutchan.

U.S. Department of Education. (1991). America 2000: An education strategy. Washington, DC: Government Printing Office.

Weigand, J. (1971). Developing teacher competencies. Englewood Cliffs, NJ: Prentice-Hall.

Zais, R. S. (1976). Curriculum: Principles and foundations. New York: Harper and Row.

Chapter 11

SUPERVISION AND STAFF DEVELOPMENT
Georgia J. Kosmoski

Staff Development: A Supervision Function

Most of today's supervision specialists agree that staff development is a key function of the school supervisor (Oliva, 1993). Harris (1985) explained that staff development and teacher evaluation are two vital developmental tasks performed by supervisors.

Not all specialists conceptualize staff development in the same way. Some maintain that staff development is a broad term that includes any work with groups or individuals in both formal and informal settings and situations. Others view staff development as training to develop new knowledge and skills. Still others contend that staff development is an organized program to aid teachers to feel better about themselves and their jobs, to develop personal skills, or to provide training in new curricula and pedagogical skills (Oliva,1993).

Specialists often distinguish inservice education from staff

Questions to answer after studying this chapter

✔ What is an acceptable working definition for staff development?

✔ How does staff development differ from in-service education?

✔ Why do school employees need staff development?

✔ Who benefits from staff development opportunities?

✔ Where do staff development programs occur?

✔ According to Tanner and Tanner (1987), what are the functions of staff development?

✔ What does Johnson (1990) list as staff development purposes?

✔ What is the role of the supervisor in staff development?

✔ What are some of the administrative responsibilities associated with staff development?

✔ What are eleven characteristics of effective staff development programs?

✔ What are the five steps in the staff development model?

✔ What are the basic tasks of staff development planning?

✔ What are indicators of effective staff development implementation?

✔ What are the characteristics of adult learning?

✔ Which are the most common staff development activities?

✔ When should staff development evaluation occur?

✔ What is meant by staff development evaluation/ application/reevaluation?

development. Thomas J. Sergiovanni and Robert J. Starratt (1988) suggested that staff development focuses on teacher growth while in-service education is concerned with overcoming deficiencies. Orlich (1989) held that staff development is a broad and comprehensive term that includes all personal development while in-service education deals only with those aspects that meet immediate training needs.

296 Chapter 11 *Supervision and Staff Development*

Harris (1989) made a firm distinction between staff development and in-service education. He held that in-service education is but one component of staff development. He divided staff development into the two categories of staffing and training. Harris explained that the training portion of staff development included in-service education and advanced preparation.

The difference between staff development and in-service education is based on whether an activity has been designed to address a perceived deficit in professional knowledge or performance level, or to promote long-term improvement. In-service education includes those activities directed toward remediation of a perceived lack of understanding or skill. Staff development refers to a continuous process promoting professional growth, rather than remediation. Professional development is yet a broader term that includes the subsets of in-service education and staff development (Daresh, 1989).

Other specialists in supervision equate staff development and in-service education and use these terms synonymously. Lloyd Dull (1981) suggested that modern practitioners use these terms interchangeably. Regardless which terms are used—staff development, in-service education, or professional growth opportunities—this learning process is designed to assist the school staff in carrying out their duties more effectively, thereby helping children learn better.

Staff Development Defined

Numerous specialists have attempted to define staff development. Oliva (1993) agreed that staff development and in-service education were identical and defined it as:

A program of organized activities of both a group and individual nature planned and carried out to promote the personal and professional growth of staff members, in this case, teachers. Staff development is in-service education, or put another way, the staff is developed through in-service education. In-service education may be either remedial or developmental, corrective or enriching. p. 351.

Stated more succinctly, Burden (1990) wrote:

Staff development programs are often designed to change the on-the-job behavior of the participants. p. 11.

Taking a much broader view, Dale (1982) held that staff development is:

The totality of educational and personal experiences that contribute towards an individual's being more competent and satisfied in an assigned professional role. p. 31.

Kimble Wiles and John Lovell (1975) took a more specific and narrow view when they offered:

Continuing staff development is an attempt to increase the competency of the present staff through courses, workshops, conferences, study groups, interschool visits, lectures, and staff improvement days. p. 160.

Drawing from the diverse views of present supervision specialists, this text will define staff development as follows:

Staff development is a planned program of activities designed to promote personal and professional growth or remediation of staff members. In-service education is one vehicle for accomplishing the goal or purpose of staff development.

This definition encompasses the purposes of *growth and enrichment* and *prescriptive and remedial.* It includes programs that address staff members personal and professional needs. This definition does not limit its scope to teachers, but recognizes the staff development needs of all staff members. In-service education is identified as one of a number of possible methods or tools used to accomplish staff development.

The Need for Staff Development

Although staff development programs are relatively new to American schools, all schools and school districts need these planned and organized activities. Staff development:

- serves as a vehicle for purposeful organizational change
- supplements and expands initial formal teacher training
- insures staff maintenance and growth
- combats complacency and satisfaction with the status quo

Over the last fifty years, American industry has learned that survival and success are related to improving employee performance. In today's global economy, profit-seeking companies search for advancements that will give them an edge in production, marketing, and sales. These advancements often include acquiring new technology or improving employee capabilities to use the technology already acquired (Kowalski & Reitzug, 1993).

Enlightened educators, like their business counterparts, recognize that purposeful organizational change is a slow and difficult process. Yet, school supervisors face mounting pressure to reshape or restructure American schools (Guskey, 1985). Connor and Lake (1988) believed that organizational change is enhanced when leaders (1) identify the employees who have a great need for change and (2) provide these employees with opportunities for growth. Staff

298 Chapter 11 *Supervision and Staff Development*

development provides the supervisor with an apparatus to meet the organizational needs for change and growth.

Most college teacher-education programs consist of four-year plans that include twenty to thirty courses dedicated to work in pedagogy or methodology. These programs culminate with the *hands on experience* of student teaching which usually lasts from eight to sixteen weeks. Although much knowledge and skill are taught to preservice teacher trainees, college training programs are only a beginning—hence, the need for continuing staff development programs throughout teachers' careers.

Staff development programs that focus on instruction provide opportunities for teachers to expand the knowledge and skills learned in a rudimentary fashion at the college or university. This type of staff development also provides new skills and knowledge for teachers in areas that were developed after their college training was completed. Such staff development programs prepare teachers for their present teaching assignments and situations. Joyce (1990) made a strong case for the need for staff development by reminding educational leaders that humans, like equipment, need maintenance and development or their value diminishes.

Madeline Hunter (1990) noted that the final criterion of any profession is that its practitioners never stop learning better ways of providing service for their clients. She suggested that continuous examination and modification of practice are essential to professional growth.

Finally, staff development is necessary to combat complacency and satisfaction with the status quo (Kowalski and Reitzug, 1993). Staff development programs serve to motivate or provide avenues to rectify areas of dissatisfaction. They allow one to explore new or alternative options.

Who Benefits From Staff Development?

Staff development activities benefit all employee groups within the organization. School supervisors and administrators, certified staff, support personnel, clerical, and custodial workers need these activities to upgrade efficiency, maintain skills, and dispel stagnation. To deny staff development opportunities to any group will inevitably weaken the entire organization (Brown, 1987). A visual representation is presented in Figure 11-1.

Supervisors should not underestimate their own and other administrators need for professional development. One reason for continuing professional development is that no two administrative positions are identical. Positions vary in terms of work groups, scope of responsibility, and constituent expectations. This suggests that administrators must continue to learn on the job to maintain effectiveness in their specific and unique situation.

Those Who Benefit From Staff Development
• Supervisors and administrators
• Professional certified staff
• Support personnel
• Secretarial and clerical staff
• Custodial and maintenance workers

Figure 11-1

Chapter 11 *Supervision and Staff Development* **299**

A second reason for administrators to engage in staff development activities is that they often experience changes in position or change in environment and location. Changing conditions demand that the administrator seek and acquire additional knowledge and skills.

Another reason for pursuing continuous growth is that the knowledge base in education and administration is expanding. The educational leader must remain current to be a successful resource and in-house expert for his or her superordinates and subordinates.

Finally, supervisors should recognize that, like all humans, they need revitalization and stimulation. Staff development programs provide such opportunities.

Administrative professional development has been largely an individual responsibility. Each administrator or supervisor must identify personal needs and the staff development activities that will meet those needs. Some sources include:

- colleagues with specific expertise
- professional organizations
- outside speakers and workshops
- local colleges and universities (Campbell, Cunningham, Nystrand, & Usdan, 1990)

Where Does Staff Development Occur?

Staff development programs and activities may take place within the school or district or may occur outside the organization. Internally provided programs are often referred to as in-service or in-house. They may serve the entire staff, groups with special interests or needs, and individuals. An in-service workshop on conflict management or a training session on cooperative learning techniques exemplify appropriate total organization-wide staff development programs. A workshop to incorporate hand calculators into the curriculum would be an example of a staff development activity for a special interest group, in this case the mathematics department. New staff orientation meetings, clinical supervision experiences, and peer coaching are some possible individual staff development opportunities.

Meaningful and successful in-service staff development requires much effort by the supervisor and the staff. The processes, components, and activities for these programs will be specifically addressed in future sections of this chapter.

In some instances, the organization cannot effectively meet the staff development needs of specific members or teams internally. In this case, outside sources may be utilized. These sources include:

- university advance degree programs or sponsored activities

300 Chapter 11 *Supervision and Staff Development*

- professional organization conferences or workshops offered at the local, state, or national level
- programs offered by private providers
- activities sponsored by state educational agencies

In these circumstances, the supervisor's major responsibility is to provide the participants with encouragement and financial support where appropriate. For a list of some internal and external staff development programs refer to Figure 11-2.

Internal and External Forms of Staff Development	
Internal Staff Development Programs	• Total staff in-service • Special group in-service • Clinical supervision • Mentoring • Peer coaching • Orientations
External Staff Development Programs	• University advanced degree programs • University courses, sponsored workshops, lecture series, etc. • Professional organization conferences, workshops, and training sessions • Privately provided (for profit) conferences, workshops, and training sessions • State sponsored opportunities • Round tables • Discussion and literature review groups

Figure 11-2

Functions of Staff Development

To successfully select, plan, and implement staff development programs, the supervisor must understand the basic purposes of staff development. A clear understanding of purpose aids the supervisor in making appropriate and meaningful decisions. Before initiating a staff development effort the supervisor should identify its purpose and value.

Tanner and Tanner (1987) held that it is advisable to approach the concept of staff development as continuously developmental. Dale Mann (1984) supported this position by explaining that a key to the professional behavior of teachers is to treat teachers as professionals. The belief that staff development is developmental dictates four basic functions. These are:

1. Developing the ability to solve classroom problems.
2. Improving curriculum.
3. Helping individuals learn what they need to know to reach their own professional goals.
4. Providing the stimulation for continuous learning (Tanner and Tanner, 1987).

Three years later, Johnson (1990) also identified four basic purposes of staff development. These differ markedly from the Tanner and Tanner (1987) list. His purposes were predicated upon teacher needs. He stated that teachers need to acquire:

1. **Information:** Updating teachers in areas of expertise establishes a staff with knowledge of current practices and paradigms.
2. **Skills:** Providing teachers the tools or methods to deliver knowledge to students.
3. **Competencies:** Acquiring new skills and information directly increases teacher competence.
4. **Behavioral Change:** Growing in abilities leads to behavioral change.

The Role of the Supervisor

One of the most important responsibilities of the proactive supervisor is to promote continuous growth and professional development of all those who work toward the goals and objectives of the school. To accomplish this task, the supervisor needs to be aware of current and effective staff development practices (Daresh, 1989).

Staff development within the organization entails a myriad of activities. As a staff development leader, the supervisor must be directly and intimately involved in all aspects of the process. Supervisory behaviors include participation, guidance, assistance, encouragement, facilitation, and provision of resources. Glickman (1990) pointed out that supervisors need to redefine their duties from those of the omnipotent manager to that of the facilitator who involves staff in decisions related to self-improvement.

302 Chapter 11 *Supervision and Staff Development*

Oliva (1993) identified a number of supervisory responsibilities. Supervisors must first *identify staff needs* through surveys, teacher requests, and observations. They participate in the planning, implementation, and evaluation of the staff development program. Supervisors are responsible for development of master plans, information sharing, and facilitation of use, and documentation of participation and successes.

Schmidt and Jacobson (1993) went one step further and concluded that the supervisor must assume certain administrative duties to ensure a successful staff development program. These specific administrative responsibilities are outlined in Figure 11-3.

Supervisors' Administrative Responsibilities for Staff Development

• Establishing the staff development program
• Providing program guidance, direction, and support for the program
• Providing presenters
• Maintaining timetables
• Participating in the staff development teams: planning, implementation, evaluation
• Allocating human, material, and financial resources to the program
• Providing follow-up materials and activities

Source: Kaiser, J. (1993). *Educational Administration,*, (2nd ed.) Mequon, WI: Stylex Publishing Co., Inc.

Figure 11-3

Characteristics of Effective Staff Development Programs

Eleven characteristics of effective staff development programs have been identified by staff development specialists (Sergiovanni and Starratt, 1988; Burrello and Orbaugh, 1982; Jamison, 1981). Effective staff development programs are:

• Integrated into and supported by their organization, including design and funding.
• School-based with teacher participants actively engaged.
• Individualized with differentiated experiences for different teachers.
• Teacher focused. Teachers assume an active rather than strictly receptive or passive role.
• Collaborative. All school constituents may be involved.
• Cooperative. Teachers share and provide mutual assistance. Teachers do not work separately.
• Driven by program participants. An assessment of their needs and interests is used to plan and develop the staff development program.
• Centered upon the teacher's choice of goals and activities.
• Responsive to changing needs. Conditions and emerging research change the existing plans.
• Accessible. Important factors for success are timing, location, and facilities.
• Evaluated frequently to ensure compatibility with existing educational philosophy.

Chapter 11 *Supervision and Staff Development* **303**

Staff development programs vary greatly between school districts in both quantity and quality. Some operate on a casual, informal, and trouble-shooting basis, while others are structured, long term, and highly planned. Factors or conditions that apply to the quantity and quality of all staff development opportunities are teacher motivation, supervisory leadership, financial resources, and support (Oliva, 1993).

A visual representation of the characteristics of effective staff development programs and the factors that affect quantity and quality is found in Figure 11-4.

Effective Staff Development Factors and Characteristics Which Affect Quantity and Quality	
Factors	
Teacher Motivation	**Supervisory Leadership**	**Funding**
Characteristics	
• Integrated and funded by the organization	• Mutually assisted
• Accessible	• Individualized
• Evaluated and found compatible with philosophy	• Responsive to change
• School-based	• Teacher chosen
• Teachers are active participants	• Needs driven program
• Collaborative	

Figure 11-4

One Staff Development Model

This staff development model is collegial with definite activities or processes. It is applicable at the department or division, the school, or the district level. The major components of this model are planning; providing the staff development program; evaluating the program; having participants apply new knowledge, skills, or behaviors; and evaluation of the application. This model is cyclical. Each phase naturally flows into the next and the final evaluation of the application component leads directly back to the first phase of planning, thus to begin another cycle. See Figure 11-5.

Collegiality

As many staff members as possible should be involved in the staff development program. Involvement ensures valuable input and provides relevance to the program. For success to occur, staff need to feel that they *own* the program (Schmidt & Jacobson, 1993). Staff may successfully serve on the planning team, participate in the implementation phase, and engage in application and evaluation activities.

Research shows that programs in which teachers participate as planners are more successful than programs organized without teacher input and involvement. Programs established at the central office and announced to staff demonstrate poor success. These programs are virtually "owned" by administrators rather than emerging from the needs of particular staff (Berman & McLaughlin, 1977).

Staff Development Planning

The planning process is the first and unquestionably the most crucial phase in establishing a meaningful, relevant, and timely program. Tasks most usually addressed in this phase are establishment of a staff development planning team or committee, identification and prioritizing of staff needs, topic selection, development of a master plan which includes goals and objectives, scheduling, and selection of a provider (Oliva, 1993; Schmidt & Jacobson, 1993).

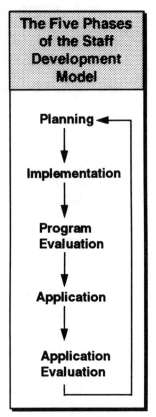

Figure 11-5

The Planning Team

The supervisor begins the planning process by creating a staff development team. This should not be a haphazard activity but rather a thoughtful action. Members should be fairly representative of those who will participate in the staff development program. The team must be a workable number (5 to 12 members) to ensure representation and efficiency.

The supervisor should serve and is advised to chair this planning committee. The staff should then have input into the selection of all other team members. McCoy (1970) holds that if a staff is given the opportunity to select the planning team, they will feel that the members represent their needs and interests. Two-way communication regarding staff development matters is enhanced by the team's establishment. After the team is established, all future planning tasks become their joint responsibility.

Chapter 11 *Supervision and Staff Development* **305**

Identifying and Prioritizing Staff Needs

The planning team begins by identifying staff development needs or interests through a process called *needs assessment*. Peter Williamson and Julia Elfman (1982) defined a needs assessment as a process that identifies the needs of the school, ranks the needs, and then designs a plan of action based upon the results.

Most literature on in-service education recommends the use of a staff survey, questionnaire, or request sheet to determine interests and needs (Oliva, 1993). Caution suggests that not all genuine needs will be identified in this manner. Staff are often too close to the situation to accurately judge. It is therefore suggested that the planning team use more than one source or tool to gather data. The supervisor's observations and professional experience are excellent avenues for discovering additional staff needs. The supervisor should be well acquainted with educational philosophy, mandates and policies, effective educational research, and current trends. This relevant information must be shared with the team before completing a final needs list.

After the plan team has gathered the needs and interests information, prioritizing the list is necessary. The committee might rank order the items themselves or they may request, through a second survey, that the entire staff rank order the list. Results become the basis for topic selection and should be shared with all involved parties.

Topic Selection

The selection of staff development topics naturally flows from the needs assessment.. The planning team must examine the needs list and consider each item's time constraints, cost, and scope. They select those topics that are feasible and might be successfully presented. After the topic selections are finalized the team members should convey their choices and the reasons for those choices to the staff.

Developing a Master Plan

Master teachers often construct a long-range lesson plan spanning up to one year for a given subject or course. They do this to have a guide and timetable for all future activities. So too, the staff development team must design a long range plan to ensure success. This plan is called the staff development *master plan*.

The master plan is a blueprint or outline of the desired staff development activities that will compose their staff development model. The master plan usually spans a period of one year and includes each step in the process necessary to guarantee successful implementation and evaluation. The commonly included plan components are program goals and objectives, a detailed timetable and schedule of events, location, presenter, projected costs, and evaluation procedures.

306 Chapter 11 *Supervision and Staff Development*

The plan begins with goals and objectives for the entire program and for each specific topic addressed in the program. To ensure quality in goals and objectives, they must be constructed with care (Tyler, 1949). For examples and construction tips for goals and objectives refer to Chapter 10.

After the goals and objectives are in place, the next components are more easily completed. Goals and objectives help identify those staff members with legitimate needs and interests, time requirements for achievement, appropriate expenditures, qualified presenters, and necessary resources and facilities.

While constructing the master plan, the plan team may choose to work as a total group or may delegate specific areas of the plan to individuals who do the work independently and then report back to the group. Since all components must fit with the goals and objectives, components should not be finalized until the goals and objectives are in place.

The final master document may take various forms. No format is inherently superior to another. If all the essential components are included, the form is a matter of preference. The completed document should be disseminated to the entire staff ideally several months before implementation. This allows the staff time to make individual plans for their own personal development and reaffirms the staff's ownership of staff development efforts. For an excerpt from a simulated master plan refer to Figure 11-6.

Selective Section from a Hypothetical Master Plan

p. 2

Topic: Cooperative Learning
Goal: The participants will learn cooperative learning techniques for use in the classroom.
Objectives: (1) Participants will construct a minimum of two lesson plans containing cooperative
                learning techniques.
            (2) Participants will discuss, then role play, at least three cooperative learning techniques.

---

p. 3

Presenters: Ms. Carol Clark, 3rd grade teacher, Washington School
             Mr. John Kooch, teacher, Orchard Hill High School
             Dr. Sandra Ester, Curriculum Coordinator, District Office

Cost: None
Incentive: $100 stipend
Date
  and Times: Saturday, January 17th 9:00 AM-2:30 PM
             Saturday, January 24th 9:AM-11:30 AM
             Saturday, February 1st 9:00 AM-11:30 AM

Location: District Office, Rooms 126, 127, and 128
Open to: Administratrators, teachers, other certified personnel, and paraprofessionals

---

Figure 11-6

Scheduling

Scheduling staff development activities often poses some of the greatest difficulty for planning. Today, many states have increased the number of student attendance days and the length of the school day. Consequently, many local school districts are operating close to or at the minimum legal time requirements. Therefore, the supervisor and plan team find they have far less flexibility to schedule activities. Long time blocks that could be devoted to staff development are rapidly vanishing or are already a thing of the past (Schmidt & Jacobson, 1993).

There appears to be no one definite solution to this dilemma. Rather, the team must use creative combinations of time blocks to schedule staff development. Dodd (1987) noted that a combination of a full staff development day followed by a series of shorter follow-up activities yield measurable benefits for the participants. One-time presentations and half-hour activities should be limited to topics that can be adequately covered in such time periods. The goal should be a comprehensive and meaningful program.

Some alternative uses for time are:

- Reschedule district release days to match program needs. Many schools have traditionally provided staff development release days just before the start of the school year. Although this is common practice, this schedule is usually not mandated by law. Often the start of school, when staff are rushed and frenzied, is an inappropriate time to conduct staff development opportunities. The supervisor and team should seriously consider using release days at times that would enhance rather than hinder staff development efforts.

- Use time normally assigned to administrative information sessions (e.g., faculty meetings) for staff development activities. In this incidence, the administrator, as staff development supervisor, demonstrates commitment to the process. As Sievert (1983) commented, the principal must make time for what is important. If the supervisor sincerely values improvement of instruction and staff growth, using administrative time for staff development becomes a viable alternative.

- After gaining staff cooperation, a creative supervisor may juggle individual schedules during the regular school day. Arranging mutual preparation time for staff with similar interests and assignments facilitates staff development activities. Other alternatives include providing substitutes for specific personnel who need specific training or temporarily rescheduling students into special activities, thereby "freeing up" the teachers.

- Conduct staff development programs outside the regular school day. The creative planning team should seriously consider utilizing evenings, weekends, and vacations

308 Chapter 11 *Supervision and Staff Development*

for staff development. Successful programs appeal to the staff's sense of professionalism (Odden & March, 1987). Dedicated professionals are often willing to use personal time for self improvement. Staff incentives for such behavior is highly desirable. Thomas Sergiovanni and Robert Starratt (1988) stated:

Staff development is not something the school does for the teacher but something the teacher does for himself or herself. p. 391.

Numerous alternative uses for time exist. The supervisor and planning team should set aside time to brain-storm this topic for their particular circumstance. Individual organizations present unique opportunities that should be explored. When formulating any schedule, remember that immediate follow-up is crucial to success (Kaiser, 1995).

A final consideration of scheduling is the selection of an appropriate location or facility. The program and its goals set the parameters for choosing the proper location. The facility must accommodate the needs of both participants and presenter. It must provide adequate space, furnishings, creature comforts, and equipment to ensure positive implementation. Before making a final selection, the planning team should include the requests of the presenter.

Selecting a Provider

The staff development team is responsible for selecting a program provider. The necessary qualities of any provider are expertise in the topic, credibility, skill in delivery, and a willingness to meet goals and objectives outlined in the master plan.

Citing earlier research, Schmidt and Jacobson (1993) affirmed that staff development has a greater positive effect if provided by a fellow staff member. Since teachers attribute more credibility to those most like themselves and "closer to home," they propose an order for selection of qualified presenters. The order moves step-by-step from in-house to most distant. This order is:

1. Members of the staff.
2. District personnel outside of the school.
3. Experts from other districts.
4. University personnel.
5. Professional staff development providers.

To locate potential internal presenters, the planning team should rely on their intimate knowledge of colleagues' areas of expertise. Experienced supervisors possess a wealth of information regarding the staff. To identify outside presenters, the planning team may query colleagues, local universities, and professional organizations. Flyers and advertisements may be consulted. School administrators receive a multitude of printed material advertising professional staff development programs and providers. Regardless of how a presenter pool is established, the

Chapter 11 *Supervision and Staff Development* **309**

planning team is advised, when possible, to directly observe final candidates in action and to directly ask them pertinent questions before making their final determination.

Other Planning Considerations: Cost and Incentives

Professional growth programs cannot be successfully provided without an investment of time and money. Staff development programs are funded from a variety of sources: local school districts, state funding, private grants, and the teachers themselves. A farsighted school district would emulate their business counterparts who perceive staff development as a prime responsibility and commit significant portions of their budgets to this pursuit (Oliva, 1993). Staff development should be viewed as a financially sound investment.

The planning team must also determine appropriate incentives for participants. Along with personal growth and satisfaction, the modern staff expects compensation for their participation and use of time. Some incentives used for staff development participation are release time, stipends, credits toward salary increments, and partial or full reimbursement for college course work.

In the staff development process, planning is most important and includes many vital tasks. Planning sets the tone for success or failure and should be executed with diligence and care. Led and encouraged by the supervisor, the usual tasks of the planning team are outlined in Figure 11-7.

Tasks of the Staff Development Planning Team
• Identifying and prioritizing staff needs and interests
• Selecting staff development topics
• Developing a master plan that includes:
• goals & objectives
• timetable
• location
• Selecting a provider
• Determining cost and participant incentives

Figure 11-7

Providing the Staff Development Program

Indicators of an Effective Program

When staff development is provided, a crucial concern is whether the program accomplishes the prime goal of positively changing participants' behaviors. To increase the chances for achieving this goal, staff development specialists suggest that certain features be observed. These features are indicators for successful presentation. The astute staff development

310 Chapter 11 *Supervision and Staff Development*

supervisor will continually check whether these indicators occur during the program implementation.

The first indicator of effectiveness is the subject matter or topic's value to the participants. It must truly provide professional improvement.

The program and activity goals and objectives drive the presentation. All involved are aware of these goals and objectives. Specific activities are geared to accomplish specific outcomes. At the conclusion of program activities, these goals and objectives have been achieved.

The program consists of a comprehensive initial presentation with immediate follow-up activities designed to allow for practice or to enhance internalization. Follow-up activities should occur no more than two weeks after the previous activity. They afford participants opportunities to ask questions after they have had time to practice, strengthen newly acquired knowledge and skills, and receive needed encouragement.

Another indicator of an effective program is the existence of continuous evaluation. The program, its individual activities, and application are constantly examined. Refer to the next section in this chapter for more detail.

The last indicator for success is an effective presenter. Effective presenters have expertise in the topic of the program. It is important that presenters have credentials in the area or the specific content studied (Zimpher, 1988). Presenters demonstrate preparation throughout the program. They have professional deliveries that are at appropriate comprehension levels, accommodate various adult learning styles, use varieties of instructional methods, and demonstrate positive human relations skills. A checklist of program presentation effectiveness is found in Figure 11-8.

Checklist of Effective Program
• Valuable topic and subject matter
• Goals and objectives drive the program
• Program goals and objectives are achieved
• Initial presentations have follow-up activities
• Continuous evaluation for program components and participants
• Effective presentation

Figure 11-8

Adult Learning

The ability of a presenter to accommodate adult learning styles should not be under-estimated. As early as 1970, Malcolm Knowles coined the word *andragogy* (the art and science of teaching adults) as distinct from *pedagogy* (the art and science of teaching children). He listed four principles for adult learning:

1. As a person matures, self-concept moves from dependency to self-direction.

2. The adult accumulates a growing reservoir of experience that provides a resource for new learning.
3. Readiness to learn becomes increasingly oriented toward the developmental tasks of his or her social role.
4. Learning shifts from subject-centered to problem-centered and time perspective changes from postponed application of knowledge to immediate application.

Later, Wood and Thompson (1980) identified nine characteristics of adult learning:

1. Adults learn when the goals of the activity are perceived by the learner as related, realistic, and important to the issue at hand.
2. Adults learn, retain, and use only what they perceive as relevant to their immediate needs.
3. Adults need accurate and frequent feedback about progress toward their goals. They need to see the results of their efforts.
4. Adult learning is highly ego-involved. The learner perceives lack of success of a given task as an indication of personal incompetence and failure.
5. Adults draw from a wide range of previous experiences, knowledge, skills, and competencies.
6. Adults want to be directly involved in the selection of learning goals and objectives, content, activities, etc.
7. Adults resist learning experiences that they perceive as attacks on their personal or professional competence.
8. Adults reject commands or prescriptions by others for their learning.
9. Motivation comes from the learner and not from external sources.

Common Implementation Formats

The most common formats used to present staff development are the workshop, institute, conference, course, and visitation. The *workshop* is a presentation where participants work together to find solutions to identified problems. The workshop emphasizes participant involvement and "hands-on" activities. It typically lasts two or three days, but may last as long as two weeks.

The *institute* is very similar to the workshop but differs in that it brings information and possible solutions to the participants. The institute may or may not provide opportunities for participants to work together to solve problems. Workshops and institutes usually do not require an exit content examination.

The *conference* is a group meeting of participants with similar needs and/or interests. Usually a variety of activities are available to the participants. Some of these activities are lectures,

312 Chapter 11 *Supervision and Staff Development*

workshops, symposiums, and panels. This format is designed to provide information and skills to a large group in a short time. Conferences are often offered by professional organizations. One such organization that holds conferences specifically for people interested in supervision is the *Association of Supervision and Curriculum Development.*

Perhaps the most common of all in-service activities is the college or *university course.* The course may be taught on the campus of a local university or college or off-campus in a local school. With expanding technology, telecourses or interactive video classes are viable options. Local districts and schools may request that these institutions provide a specific course for their staff (Oliva, 1993) to be offered with or without credit. When credit is given for completed coursework, an examination is usually required.

The *visitation* is a staff development opportunity where the participants individually or in small groups visit and observe a fellow teacher in action. The purpose of visitations is to learn new approaches and techniques, broaden the participants' horizons, and find solutions to individual problems.

Evaluation/Application/Reevaluation

To strengthen future programs and to assess the effectiveness of the staff development program, continuous evaluation is necessary (Oliva, 1993). The overall program, each activity, and the participant's achievement need to be evaluated. Summative and formative evaluation should be conducted. For accountability purposes an overall rating of the program under scrutiny is appropriate. More valuable is program information gathered for formative purposes. Formative evaluation provides feedback that will aid the staff development team in planning and providing future programs that will be more effective for their specific participants. Program evaluation should begin with the first activity and continue throughout the program's existence. Figure 11-9 is an example of a program activity evaluation.

Evaluation of participant behaviors provides feedback concerning needs fulfillment, personal and group growth, and assimilation of the knowledge or skills. Both cognitive and affective growth can be evaluated. What have the participants learned and how have their feelings changed? Staff evaluation should begin before any formal participation to provide a base line. Evaluation should be conducted after the initial presentation and after each follow-up activity. After participants have had time to apply their new founded knowledge and skill, evaluation should again occur. Three months and again six months after completion of the program are appropriate intervals to reevaluate participant application.

Arcadia Middle School
Cooperative Learning Program

Name _____

Date _____   Seminar Selected - Name _____

A. Value of seminar to me (circle one)

5	4	3	2	1
Very Much	Much	Average	Not much	Little

B. Quality of seminar presentation (circle one)

5	4	3	2	1
Very Much	Much	Average	Not much	Little

C. Comments regarding today's seminar: _____

_____

_____

D. Comments regarding overall workshop (today) _____

_____

_____

_____

_____

Figure 11-9

Evaluation should take a number of forms. Multiple tools will give a clearer perspective of what changes have occurred. The most commonly used forms of staff development evaluations are generally informal and include the survey, response sheets, one-on-one or group discussion, and observation by the supervisor or other administrators.

314 Chapter 11 *Supervision and Staff Development*

A combination of these evaluation tools should be analyzed for improvement purposes. It is suggested that the supervisor establish a staff development evaluation team to conduct these activities. Although the plan team may be used for this committee, if the staff is large enough to support a separate team, this is preferable. By establishing this group, more staff members will have an opportunity to participate and this in turn will increase staff ownership. See Figure 11-10 for an overview of the components of staff development evaluation.

Staff Development Evaluation Timetable		
Program Evaluation	**Participant Evaluation**	**Participant Reevaluation (to measure application)**
• Throughout or immediately following initial presentation • Immediately after each follow-up activity • Several months after completion of entire program	• Before initiation of all activities (establishing a base line) • After conclusion of initial presentation • Immediately after each follow-up activity	• Two to three months after program conclusion • Six months to one year after program conclusion

Figure 11-10

Principles and Practices for Success

- Recognize and accept that staff development is a primary task of school supervision.
- Formulate a personal working definition for staff development.
- Appreciate the need for and the purposes of a viable staff development program.
- Understand the benefits, beneficiaries and the various forms of staff development.
- Assume a leadership role in planning, implementation, and evaluation of staff development and its programs.
- Understand and facilitate the basic tasks of staff development planning.
- Assume an active role in providing the staff development program.
- Become knowledgeable in the formats available for staff development programs.
- Understand the basic principles of adult learning.
- Lead the efforts of the staff development evaluation team.

Chapter 11 *Supervision and Staff Development* **315**

Summary

Staff development is a primary function of school supervision. Staff development specialists have not always agreed on the scope or definition of staff development. An acceptable working definition for staff development is:

Staff development is a planned program of activities designed to promote personal and professional growth or remediation of staff members. In-service education is one vehicle for accomplishing the goal or purpose of staff development.

All school employees benefit from staff development. Schools need staff development for purposeful organizational change; for staff maintenance, expansion, and growth; and to combat complacency. Occurring internally or externally, staff development programs serve specific purposes. Those purposes, based on teacher needs, include acquiring information, skills, competencies, and behavioral changes.

The supervisor, serving as staff development leader, has many responsibilities. The supervisor should actively and willingly perform all duties as a guide, resource, and facilitator rather than as an authoritarian. Recognizing the characteristics of effective programs, the supervisor works diligently to achieve these qualities.

The cyclical collegial staff development model discussed includes the steps: planning, providing, evaluating, applying, and reevaluating. After establishing a planning team, a needs assessment is conducted from which topics are selected, goals and objectives are identified, a master plan is established, scheduling occurs, a presenter is selected, and cost and incentives are determined. After thorough planning implementation occurs. The astute supervisor monitors this process in noting the existence or lack of success indicators. Formative and summative evaluations are conducted throughout the staff development process. After ample time for personal and classroom application, reevaluation is conducted.

Case Problem: *Della Gate's Staff Development Program*

Two weeks ago, Ben completed the course work for an administrative certificate. He was sitting in his office writing lesson plans when his principal, Della Gate, entered. Della explained to Ben that she was giving Ben a chance to get some practical administrative experience. Della was going to let Ben chair the newly established school-wide *Staff Development Planning Team*. He stated that since she was personally so overworked in the springtime, Ben would have a free hand. After Ben agreed to accept the assignment, Della reminded Ben that a successful effort would be a "big feather in his cap" and a great experience to put on his resume.

316 Chapter 11 *Supervision and Staff Development*

That evening, Ben called you, his best friend and fellow student, seeking help. Ben asked your help in sorting out the requirements and tasks associated with the job. As the best student in your graduate course in school supervision, Ben was sure that you would know what to do. Ben was appreciative that principal Della Gate had allowed him to gain this experience.

Help Ben! Tell him what he should do!

Case Problem: *To the Rescue*

The Prairie Hill's School Board meeting had now lasted more than three hours. Members were still engaged in a heated discussion of where to cut funding so they could balance the budget as the law required. Five items were mentioned as possible cuts. For each potential cut Superintendent Peg Champion put up a successful defense and the discussion moved to the next possible victim. Although board members were frustrated and disgruntled they agreed to make one last attempt before adjourning for the evening.

After poring over the line item budget for the tenth time, member Sam Whinner, launched into a tirade on the cost incurred by the district for staff development. He voiced his disapproval of this "outrageous" expenditure. Several other members sided with Sam. Finally, Dr. Champion was asked to comment. She realized that what she said could rescue or destroy all her efforts to provide professional growth opportunities for the district staff.

Pretend you are Superintendent Champion defending the cost required to conduct the district staff development program. Remember that what you say could have major repercussions.

References

Berman, P., & McLaughlin, M. W. (1977). *Federal programs supporting educational change, Vol. VII: Factors affecting implementation and continuation.* Santa Monica, CA: Rand Corporation.

Brown, P. W. (1987). In-service education: Cultivating professional growth at your school. *Perspectives for Teachers of the Learning Impaired, 5* (5), 16-18.

Burden, P. (1990). Follow-up. *Journal of Staff Development, 11* (2), 11.

Burrello, L. C., & Orbaugh, T. (1982). Reducing the discrepancy between the known and unknown in in-service education. *Phi Delta Kappan, 63,* 385-386.

Chapter 11 *Supervision and Staff Development* **317**

Campbell, R. F., Cunningham, L. L., Nystrand, R. O., & Usdan, M. D. (1990). *The organization and control of American schools* (6th ed.). Columbus, OH: Merrill.

Connor, P. E. , & Lake, L. K. (1988). *Managing organizational change.* New York: Praeger.

Dale, E. L. (1982). What is staff development? *Educational Leadership, 40,* 31.

Daresh, J. C. (1989). *Supervision as a proactive process.* New York: Longman.

Dodd, A. W. (1987). Getting results from a one-day in-service program. *Principal, 66* (5), 57-60.

Dull, L. W. (1981). *Supervision: School leadership handbook.* Columbus, OH: Merrill.

Glickman, C. D. (1990). *Supervision of instruction: A developmental approach,* 2nd ed. Boston: Allyn and Bacon.

Guskey, T. R. (1985). Staff development and teacher change. *Educational Leadership, 42* (7), 57-60.

Harris, B. (1985). *Supervisory behavior in education* (3rd ed.). Englewood Cliffs, NJ: Prentice-Hall.

Harris, B. (1989). *In-service education for staff development.* Boston: Allyn and Bacon.

Hunter, M. (1990). Preface. *Changing school culture through staff development: The 1990 ASCD yearbook.* Alexandria, VA: Association for Supervision and Curriculum Development.

Jamison, P. J. (1981). *The development and validation of a conceptual model and quality practices designed to guide the planning, implementation, and evaluation of in-service education programs.* unpublished doctoral dissertation College Park: University of Maryland.

Johnson, R. (1990). Getting results from staff development. *The Developer, 1,* 1-6.

Joyce, B. (1990). Prologue. *Changing school culture through staff development: The 1990 ASCD yearbook.* Alexandria, VA: Association for Supervision and Curriculum Development.

Kaiser, J. (1993). *Educational Administration* (2nd ed.). Mequon, WI: Stylex Publishing Co., Inc.

Kaiser, J. (1995). *The 21st century principal.* Mequon, WI: Stylex Publishing Co., Inc.

Knowles, M. S. (1970). *The modern practice of adult education.* New York: Association Press.

Kowalski, T. J., & Reitzug, U. C. (1993). *Contemporary school administration: An introduction.* New York: Longman.

Mann, D. (1984). Impact II and the problem of staff development. *Educational Leadership,* 42, 44.

McCoy, D. L. (1970). In-service education—what does the teacher want? *Educational Resources and Techniques, 10* (2), 20-22.

Odden, A. & March, D. (1987). *How state education reform can improve secondary schools.* Berkeley, CA: University of California.

Oliva, P. F. (1993). *Supervision for today's school* (4th ed.). New York: Longman.

Orlich, D.C. (1989). *Staff development: Enhancing human potential.* Boston: Allyn and Bacon.

Schmidt, L. J., & Jacobson, M. (1993). In J. Kaiser (Ed.), *Educational administration* (2nd ed.).Mequon, WI: Stylex Publishing Co., Inc.

Sergiovanni, T. J., & Starratt, R. J. (1988). *Supervision: Human perspectives* (4th ed.). New York: McGraw-Hill.

Sievert, N. (1983). Staff development: The principal's role. *Thrust, 13,* 19.

Tanner, T., & Tanner, L. (1987). *Supervision in education: Problems and practices.* New York: Macmillan.

Tyler, R. (1949). *Basic principles of curriculum and instruction.* Chicago: University of Chicago Press.

Wiles, K., & Lovell, J. T. (1975). *Supervision for better schools.* Englewood Cliffs, NJ: Prentice-Hall.

Williamson, P. A., & Elfman, J. A. (1982). A common sense approach to teacher in-service training. *Phi Delta Kappan, 63,* 401.

Wood, F., & Thompson, S. R. (1980). Guidelines for better staff development. *Educational Leadership, 37,* 374-378.

Zimpher, N. L. (1988). A design for the professional development of teacher leaders. Journal of Teacher Education, *39* (1), 53-60.

Chapter 12

FUTURE SCHOOLS AND SUPERVISORS
Georgia J. Kosmoski

Supervisors and Vision

Effective supervisors are those with an ability to clearly define what is and what they believe should be. They seek to achieve goals that will benefit their students as they assume their future places as productive adults. To accomplish this task, supervisors who are true leaders will have a realistic view of the present, and have the vision to implement the internal and external changes to affect learning. They are able to lead staff as they develop and work toward a shared vision for their school.

Thomas J. Sergiovanni and Robert Starratt (1988) explained vision as follows.

Leaders have a vision of what they and their colleagues can accomplish. While that vision flows out of the core meanings which guide the leader's basic approach to life, it usually has many particular features to it which imply an organizational structure of some kind. By the word vision we do not mean some mystical fantasy. Rather, the leader's vision tends to be a fairly detailed picture of a social unit of some kind, functioning in certain ways which achieve and reflect those core meanings and values at the center of the leader's consciousnes. (pp. 202-203)

Questions to answer after studying this chapter

✔ What is school vision and why must supervisors develop a vision?

✔ What are the four steps necessary for formulating a credible school vision?

✔ How would one describe school change?

✔ What are the two major types of expected school change?

✔ What will be some predicted organizational changes found in the schools of 2010?

✔ What will be some predicted curricular changes found in the schools of 2010?

✔ Why should school supervisors analyze current events so as to predict future changes?

✔ How will changes in school funding affect schools?

✔ How will community involvement affect future schools?

✔ What are some of the needed qualities of an effective school supervisor?

How do effective supervisors formulate a credible and worthy vision for their school? Four steps are necessary. Supervisors must (1) realistically identify the current state, (2) select and apply the best practices for immediate needs, (3) analyze the present so as to predict future possibilities and challenges, and (4) utilize the analysis and basic beliefs and values to shape the desired vision.

-319-

320 Chapter 12 *Future Schools and Supervisors*

Beliefs, wishes, and dreams alone are not sufficient to shape a vision. Facts, knowledge, and reasoning must be an integral part of the process. Supervisors must have knowledge of current educational programs, paradigms, practices, and initiatives. This is readily accomplished when supervisors personally practice the professional development recommendations outlined in the previous chapter, Supervision and Staff Development. By reading professional journals and literature, attending seminars and workshops, and discussing issues and trends with fellow educators, supervisors can develop an accurate and realistic view of the current state of education, in general, and their own schools, in particular. An example is the junior high school supervisor who reads, attends seminars and conferences, and regularly communicates with other professionals concerning the possibilities and challenges of restructuring to a middle school concept.

Supervisors should apply this information to their present situation to implement the shared school vision. Vision requires time and step-by-step progress toward the ideal. When tending to the immediate needs and goals of the school, effective supervisors must keep in mind the vision of the future. By constantly recalling or mentally revisiting the desired vision, present choices and decisions become clear and more focused.

Events at Arcadia Elementary School, Olympia Fields, Illinois illustrate the importance of vision in decision making. The school's curriculum committee was split in its decision to adopt a daily sustained silent reading time. Pros and cons were debated in a heated discussion. Finally, the school principal asked if such a program would foster the school vision of encouraging life-long learning. Focus on that vision soon resulted in the obvious decision to pilot the program for at least one year and then reassess its value in light of the shared vision at the conclusion of the trial period.

This action suggests that groups should use a shared vision as a filter for innovation and decisions. Individuals can reach consensus and accept change when they are mindful of the vision. It takes courage for a supervisor and staff to suspend an initiative after time and energy has been committed, but it may be necessary when that initiative does not align with the vision.

The third step in developing vision is to analyze present practices and trends to determine future possibilities and challenges. When analyzing the present, astute supervisors should ask a number of questions. What current practices and conditions will exist ten or fifteen years from now? Which emerging trends will become established practice? What programs, models, structures, and processes will lose favor and/or vanish? What societal, political, and economic conditions and the subsequent trends will affect the schools?

A situation in Matteson, Illinois School District #162 illustrates the value of analyzing trends and initiating change to meet the needs of the future. In 1991, after reviewing the literature and numerous training and information sessions, the district supervisors and staff began a district-wide special education student inclusion program. The

Chapter 12 *Future Schools and Supervisors* **321**

process was well planned and introduced slowly and gradually over a three year period. Several years later when inclusion was mandated for all Illinois schools, District #162 was, not only in compliance, but operating a successful inclusion program.

Lastly, supervisors must use the knowledge and inferences acquired in the first three steps to shape their educational vision. Horace Mann had a vision that the public schools were the vehicle to meld immigrant groups into an enlightened citizenry of one nation. Martin Luther King had a vision of an America where black and white could live and learn in brotherhood (Sergiovanni and Starratt, 1988). Likewise, today's effective supervisors must develop and strive for a vision that meets the needs and aspirations of their students. They must, through example and statements, share the vision with their colleagues and subordinates. There are supervisors who can "walk the walk," and those who can "talk the talk," but there are few who can "walk the talk."

A visual representation of the steps for developing and establishing an educational vision is found in Figure 12-1.

Schools and Change

Educators can be sure that there will be change. Although change comes slowly in education, it eventually does occur. Schools are growing, viable organizations and change is a constant inevitability. Kaiser (1995) summarized the nature of school change by stating *"Change is a continual if not continuous part of organizational growth."* (p. 33)

Schools will experience both organizational and curricular changes. A review of the literature suggests that expected organizational changes include expanding collegial or democratic structures and processes, continuing restructuring efforts, an increase of women and minority leaders, entrepreneurial ventures, partnerships, and more independent and autonomous schools. Predicted curricular changes will include programs and practices that are more integrated, reflect social concerns, and meet individual and/or group needs. Accountability and measurable standards will expand and become more sophisticated and demanding.

Could educational changes in the next fifteen years be so dramatic so as to change the very nature of our schooling model? Probably not. Educators tend to inch, rather than leap, in the right direction when instituting positive change. Critics suggest that educational changes are only superficial with little substance. R. G. Des Dixon (1994) adamantly expressed the critics' view as he charged:

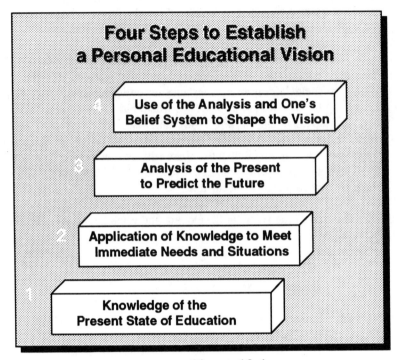

Figure 12-1

The changes proposed are too narrowly conceived to kill off old models of schooling, so it eventually kills or cripples them (changes).

The school as an organism routinely accepts cosmetic changes and even a bit of plastic surgery now and then for the sake of appearances. But it hemorrhages away transfusions of fresh blood and rejects transplants for its diseased vital organs. It remains forever alive on life-support systems, even though it is brain dead. If we want to change the school significantly, we must smother it with a critical mass of changes in rapid succession.

A "critical mass" implies so many changes as to constitute a new model of schooling. Unfortunately, nobody has the specs for such an entirely new model. Academics and innovators have been too busy with patches for the old model. Year in, year out, the education industry offers the public Band-Aids™ for whatever school wound is suppurating at the time. (p. 361)

Historically, changes in American education have been reactive rather than proactive. Our schools tend to reflect and react to the needs identified by our other national institutions. Social, political, and economic changes trigger changes in schools that try to identify, cope, and meet these new circumstances or attitudes. One recent example of this phenomenon is the addition of substance abuse prevention programs now found in the curriculum at all levels and in all areas throughout the country. This is education's response to the sky-rocketing increase of drug use by young people. Spin-off programs that followed substance prevention initiatives include value judgment or "good choice" programs and self-esteem curricula.

If change is expected and inevitable, effective supervisors, using higher order thinking skills themselves, must predict change and plan for implementation.

Schools in 2010

Education, like most institutions, is slow to change. The history of American education suggests that many practices, policies, and structures traditionally accepted and firmly established today will remain in place through 2010. Yet, the world is changing more rapidly now than at any other time in recorded history. These changes will inevitably affect our schools causing them also to change.

A close examination of today's social events, political climate, business initiatives, and trends provides clues to the future. First, in *Megatrends* and then *Megatrends 2,000*, futurist John Naisbitt (1982, 1990) examined American trends, used the information gleaned, and successfully predicted changes in population shifts, political swings, and economic conditions for the 1980s and 1990s. School supervisors should do likewise for educational issues in the early 2000s.

Changes expected in the school organization by the year 2010 (see Figure 12-2) include more school autonomy and accountability, expanding restructuring and renewal, increased entrepreneurship and competition between schools, expanding collegiality and democratic processes within the organization, and shifts in traditional roles. Curricular changes will include efforts to ensure a safe environment conducive to learning, a technology explosion, and additional content that reflects social needs.

324 Chapter 12 *Future Schools and Supervisors*

A reevaluation of some accepted practices is predicted. Educators will question the validity and merit of a number of "sacred cows." Changes in funding and community involvement will affect both the school organization and the curriculum.

School Organization Changes

School Autonomy and Accountability

┌─────────────────────────────────────┐
**Characteristics
of Educational Change**

- Continual and inevitable
- A continuous part of organizational growth
- Change will affect both the school organization and the curriculum
- Critics suggest that change is only superficial
- Historically reactive rather than proactive
- Usually a slow step-by-step process
└─────────────────────────────────────┘

Figure 12-2

The movement toward school autonomy and accountability is in full swing and will continue for at least the next fifteen years. All fifty states are requiring some form of competency testing and an individual school plan for student academic improvement. Increasingly, schools will have to stand alone as they report their successes and failures. The time when school districts garnered the lion's share of the praise or blame is gone. Educators' reputations, careers, and school funding will be directly affected by these mandates.

The state of Indiana, using a commonly accepted approach, serves as an illustrative model. In 1995, using the Indiana State Test for Educational Progress (ISTEP) (1992), the state required that all students in grades three, six, and nine be given a competency test. Those students who did not pass were successfully remediated in summer school or retained. Individual school scores and rankings were published in local and state-wide newspapers. Some state monies were allocated based upon test evidence of improvement. Indiana also required that all schools, under the guidance of a state facilitator, develop an individual school plan consisting of nine correlates, designed to improve student academic performance.

Under the conditions and regulations found in most states, what might be expected by the year 2010? Some predictions include:

- Expanded site-based management where the vision of creativity and excellence will be achieved after decentralization (Tanner and Tanner, 1987). Since schools are held accountable for student achievement, they are demanding that they have the final voice in curricular and organizational decisions and choices. Building supervisors will assume an ever-widening leadership role. Teachers will be empowered to exercise more control over learning practices.

Chapter 12 *Future Schools and Supervisors* **325**

- Contined restructuring and renewal. To renew schools, educators must transform them from rigid constraining institutions to inviting places that adjust to changing times and new challenges. Although these schools might use different strategies to achieve this end, they will all demand high professional standards, collegiality, questioning, and experimentation (Sagor, 1995). Successful school reform initiatives will recognize the interplay between the structure and culture found within that particular school (Fullan, 1994). Supervisors must maintain and expand their expertise in the area of reform, restructuring, and renewal. They must understand that restructuring is not a one-time event, but rather a never-ending journey.

- Emerging national standards and an accompanying testing program. Although there will be great opposition from local and state leaders to setting and monitoring a national standard, it is quite possibile that the strong public opinion for accountability and uniformity will result in legislative mandates (Cohen, 1995; Lewis, 1995). An outline of autonomy and accountability changes predicted by the year 2010 is found in Figure 12-3.

> **Future Changes in School Autonomy and Accountability**
>
> - Increased and various forms of site-based management
> - Individual school recognition of the interplay between school structure and culture
> - Continued restructuring and renewal efforts
> - Supervisors with expertise in the reform movement and leadership
> - Potential student testing for national standards
> - Potential setting of national standards

Figure 12-3

Competition and Entrepreneurship

With the emergence of state competency and possible national standard testing, schools will find themselves in the precarious position of having to compete with other schools. Rivalry between schools to acquire grants and awards, positive press, and lucrative school-business partnerships will increase. There is a genuine danger that camaraderie and cooperation between schools may be seriously damaged.

Unfortunately, school supervisors might find themselves in the unenviable roles of "field sales representatives" as they try to acquire additional community, state, and federal financial or service support. Particularly during times of fiscal constraints, building supervisors will be actively engaged in tasks to acquire needed resources historically reserved for central office administrators.

326 Chapter 12 *Future Schools and Supervisors*

Increased Collegiality and Leadership Role Shifting

Most organizational changes predicted for the future require strong building staff collegiality if schools hope to be successful. Since schools in 2010 are expected to have a solid collegial climate, the supervisor must develop a democratic leadership style. Mutual professional respect and shared leadership and decision-making will be necessary. Garston and Wellman (1995) described shared leadership roles and their importance to successful change as follows:

> *In an adaptive school, leadership is shared—all the players wear all the hats. All the players must have the knowledge and skill to manage themselves, manage students, or lead other adults. Leadership is a shared function in meetings, in staff development activities, in action research, and in classrooms. Recognizing the hats and knowing when and how to change them is shared knowledge within the organization, because when values, roles, and work relationships are clear, decisions about appropriate behavior are easy.* (p. 11)

A graphic representation of major organizational changes expected in future schools is found in Figure 12-4.

Organizational Changes Expected In Future Schools

- Increased building autonomy
- Increased and measurable school accountability
- Accelerated competition between schools
- Required entrepreneurship by school personnel
- Increased collegiality within the building organization
- Supervisors with expanded skills in democratic leadership, restructure and renewal, and public relations
- Shifts in leadership roles within the organization

Figure 12-4

Today's school administrators are primarily white males. A disproportionately low percentage of women and minority educators hold administrative positions. In 1993 Bell and Chase reported that although student gender is fairly evenly distributed at all educational levels for American K-12 public schools and both public and private postsecondary institutions, women administrators are underrepresented. They report the following percentages of female school supervisors: 11.3% postsecondary, 6.6% secondary, 23%

middle, and 37% elementary. The racial and ethnic stratification of leaders in schools is even more striking than gender. Educational administrators do not reflect the racial and ethnic diversity of the student population. The percentages of minority school administrators at the various levels are 8% postsecondary, 4.2% secondary, 11.3% middle, and 12.1% elementary.

However, present trends suggest that the schools of 2010 will experience a shift toward gender and racial equity of school leaders. Today school boards, representing the sentiments of their constituent citizens, are demanding the hiring of more representative administrators. This coupled with the fact that more women and minority educators are completing degrees and certification programs in educational administration supports the prediction that there will be more representative numbers in the future. The Educational Administration Masters and Certification Program at Governors State University, near Chicago, well illustrates this point. By 1995 the program included 63% women and 27% minorities. Schools of the future should reflect an increase in women and minority administrators if this trend continues (Wesson, 1995).

Curricular Changes

A Safe And Drug Free Environment

Since the mid-1980s, Americans have been outraged by the lack of security and the infiltration of drugs in our public schools. Addressing this issue in his State of the Union message in 1990, former president George Bush enumerated six goals for American education developed by the nation's governors. The sixth goal clearly emphasizes the national concern for this problem and a call for action. Goal six stated: *Every school in America will be free of drugs and violence and will offer a disciplined environment conducive to learning* (U. S. Department of Education, *America 2000*, p. 19).

The *Gallup Poll of the Public's Attitudes Toward the Public Schools* (Elam, Rose, & Gallup, 1994) lists school *fighting, violence, and gangs* as the number one school concern or problem for parents and nonparents, alike. It shows drug abuse as the third major problem existing in schools. The poll stated:

Two problems—the growth of fighting/violence/gangs and poor discipline—are by far the most serious problems facing U. S. public schools today. . . . Lack of financial support and drug abuse were also frequently mentioned. People cited a web of causes for violence in and around schools, including the abuse of drugs and alcohol by students, the growth of gangs, the easy availability of weapons, and the breakdown of the American family. Remedies for most of these problems may be beyond the direct control of the schools, but people would like to see stronger penalties for student

328 Chapter 12 *Future Schools and Supervisors*

possession of weapons and more training for school personnel in how to deal with student violence. (p. 42)

Clearly, American citizens are demanding strong measures to ensure a drug-free environment and safety for their children in schools. Further, common sense tells them that learning is impossible in a classroom where one or a few children receive 80% or more of the attention because of their disruptive or violent behavior.

Statistics indicate that the public's fear has merit. Almost two million teenagers are regular users of illicit drugs. In 1990, 81 percent of surveyed high school seniors reported using alcohol during the previous twelve months, while 27 percent reported using marijuana, and over 5 percent reported using cocaine (Education vital signs, 1991; Krantz, 1990).

Albert Shanker (1995), President of the American Federation of Teachers, expresses the frustration and concern of many by writing about the lack of learning in the classroom and education's approach to discipline. He wrote::

We are not doing our job as teachers. And the system is not doing its job, if we send youngsters that message that this (violence and disruption) is tolerable behavior within society. We are putting at risk the education of millions of other youngsters. Are we are doing something we wouldn't do as parents? Suppose a family had four or five kids, one of whom was emotionally disturbed and very dangerous. Most parents would separate that one youngster from the other three or four because they wouldn't want the others to be harmed. They would try very hard to help the disturbed child— indeed they'd probably do more for him than the other kids—but they would consider it their first responsibility to make sure he didn't hurt the others. They wouldn't say to themselves, "I have to trust this youngster with my other children to show him that I'm not separating him out or treating him differently. Otherwise I might damage his self-esteem." That kind of ridiculous talk is left to the schools, and the proper response to it is outrage—outrage that we have a system willing to sacrifice the overwhelming majority of children for a handful, without even doing the handful any good. (p. 11)

Public education and state legislatures are responding to these concerns. Over the next fifteen years supervisors will encounter a number of roadblocks to instituting the desired change. Parent opposition to severe and strict regulations imposed upon "their child" will be tested at the local level and undoubtedly in the courts. The fear of sullying a school's or community's reputation by admitting that the school has a problem makes dealing with gangs, drugs, and violence more difficult for the school supervisor. Administrators, teachers, and community constituents must be convinced that honest reporting of these problems is the first step in rectifying the situation. Regardless of the opposition to change, change will come and the school supervisor will be actively engaged in initiation, implementation, and monitoring of these new measures.

Schools in 2010 will institute practices and policies which are designed to keep out drug dealers, weapons, gangs, and perpetrators of violence, and to ensure student discipline on and around the school campus. Measures most likely established will include:

- Security systems will be in place for admittance such as: locked doors, buzzer alarms at the "day time" entrance, metal detectors, guards, sign-in procedures for visitors, student and staff identification badges, and closed campus lunch periods.
- Written policies which outline procedures for dealing with intruders (calling the police).
- Student "get tough" codes of conduct with zero tolerance. These will specifically prohibit drug use, possession, and drug sale, weapon possession, and physically violent acts committed against students and staff. Punishments for violations will be explained in advance and strictly enforced. Enforcement will be the responsibility of all staff, and where appropriate, representative students.
- Schools will work closely with the law enforcement agency when dealing with criminal behavior.
- Class disruption such as yelling, cursing, and throwing objects will not be tolerated and predetermined consequences will be enforced. Written codes of discipline will be developed by schools and/or districts.
- Staff training and professional development will be provided.
- At all levels, curriculum will be expanded to include content that deals with interpersonal skills, drug prevention, values and ethics, etc.
- Active parent and community involvement in developing and maintaining these measures will be in place. (Odden, 1995; Shanker, 1995; Stover, 1986; Brooks, 1985; & Bauer, 1984) See Figure 12-5.

A Technology Explosion

During the last decades of the 21st century, America has changed from a manufacturing base to an information base (Cetron & Rocha, 1988). Schools will try diligently to adjust to this phenomenon. Technology will finally start to fulfill its promise by the year 2010. For years educational innovators and futurists have predicted that technology would revolutionize schools. Finally, their projections will come true. Low cost, compact size, and a huge variety of both hardware and software will make technology practical and accessible to even the most financially disadvantaged districts. Radical technological changes will take place in the classroom and in the administrator's office.

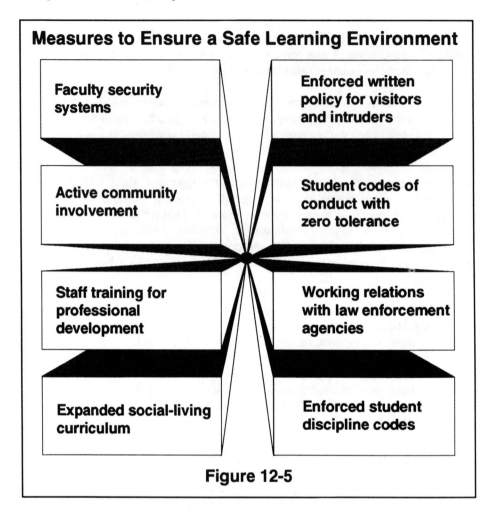

Figure 12-5

Classroom technology shall affect student and teacher. Beginning in the elementary school and continuing through higher education, students will replace the notebook and ballpoint with the computer. Teachers shall see chalkboards replaced with dust free wipe-off boards. In numerous situations, computers will replace the dictionary, thesaurus, and encyclopedia. Students carrying laptop computers to and from school and between classes shall become common sights. Computers will be accessible to all students in the regular classroom, making the computer lab, as we know it today, obsolete. CD-ROMs, interactive classrooms, and satellite hook-ups will be commonplace in the public schools of 2010.

Computers will shape the pedagogy and methodology used by the classroom teacher. Gwen Solomon (1992), director of the School of the Future, explaineds that computers allow students to discover learning for themselves. She pointed out that computers provide hands-on activities that enable students to create real products that demonstrate knowledge and ability, thereby, serving as the perfect tool for mastery learning. Means and Olsen (1994) confirmed the link between technology and authentic learning by empirically demonstrating that technology is a powerful performer when students are asked to perform complex authentic tasks. Early forms of drill and practice computer programs, or electronic ditto pages, will be replaced by interactive programs that promote inference, analysis, and synthesis.

Computers will change adult-directed pedagogy to student-centered learning. Students will use computers to directly contact researchers for information regarding a current project or will be able to write a social studies paper with video and sound. Computers will combine the imagination of students and teachers in ways seldom considered possible (Raker, 1995).

Technology will shape the planned curriculum in 2010. David Dwyer (1994) reported findings, from an in-depth study of students and teachers who used technology extensively for a minimum of three years, that teachers' behaviors change as they use technology. Teachers who use technology team teach more regularly, work across disciplines, modify schedules to accommodate ambitious class projects, and more frequently integrate several kinds of media in the same lesson. These teachers, more often than their traditional counterparts, serve as facilitators rather than as lecturers. Students who use technology extensively demonstrate better attendance patterns, longer attention spans, increased cooperation skills, and leadership behaviors compared to pupils who do not regularly use computers. Teachers of the future will be using proven strategies from *effective schools* research as they use their technology tools.

School supervisors and their office staff will use microcomputers extensively. The microcomputer enables the supervisor to have instant access to records and allows for creative or analytical administrative applications. Use will ensure increased productivity and efficiency of all personnel. Some administrative uses of computers include: a myriad of writing, budgeting, various forms of scheduling, financial projections, visuals such as graphs and charts, and personnel records and files (Blood & Kaiser, 1993). Supervisors will also use computers for communications. E-mail, modem hookup to the central office mainframes, and on-line information networks will be standard in the supervisor's office.

Building supervisors must also understand that as computers do more, the number of tasks that can be performed on the building level will increase. Supervisory responsibility and duties will increase. Leaders will also be faced with security of information decisions that were previously handled at the district office.

332 Chapter 12 *Future Schools and Supervisors*

Curriculum to Meet Social Needs

Watching the evening news, glancing at the headlines in the local newspaper, and a healthy dose of common sense makes it possible for one to predict some of the content additions expected by the year 2010. Added to the curriculum at the appropriate level, some expected additions include:

- Public school supported early childhood, early start, early care, and preschool classes will exist in most districts. These classes will be intended to prepare three- and four-year-old children for kindergarten. Early detection of special needs and swift intervention will be encouraged.
- Latch-key, after-school tutoring programs, and/or student clubs and interest groups will exist in most schools. As in the state of Indiana, many state legislatures will mandate these types of programs.
- Curricula will shift to include social and emotional behavior. Units and courses will exist that explore the topics of ecology, conflict resolution, sex education, parenting, interpersonal relations, ethics, vocational opportunities, diversity, quality choices, global studies, self-esteem, international politics and economy, drug prevention, personal safety, and the study of philosophy and religion.
- Citizenship, service, and democratic ideals studies will be resurrected. These areas will be expanded to include required out-of-school activities, necessary for grade advancement or high school graduation. Iowa and Minnesota have required a service credit requirement for graduation since the early 1990s.
- Technology and media proficiency programs will be instituted at all levels.
- High schools in cooperation with local colleges will offer or allow students to attended some classes for college credit.
- Physical fitness programs, not to be confused with sports, will be required for all students.
  (Clinchy, E., 1995; Martin, J., 1995; Banks, J., 1994; Caldas, S., 1994; Katz, L., 1994; Kohn, A., 1994; McNergney, R., 1994: Pang, V., 1994; Shepard, L., 1994; Yaffe, E., 1994)

Glasser (1969) reminded educators that school curriculum must be relevant to the student's life, and the student's life must be relevant to the curriculum. These expected changes are an attempt to realize this rubric.

Figure 12-6 gives a visual overview of these curricular additions expected in the schools of 2010.

Chapter 12 *Future Schools and Supervisors* **333**

Future Programs to Meet Emerging Social Needs
• Public school classes for three- and four-year olds
• Curriculum to address social behavior, i.e., parenting, drug prevention, ecology
• Expanded citizenship, service, and democratic ideals studies
• College credit courses
• Latch-key and after school programs
• Curriculum to address emotional needs, i.e., conflict resolution, self-esteem, diversity
• Technology and media proficiency programs
• Required physical fitness programs at all levels

Figure 12-6

Reexamining the Sacred Cows

Some educational beliefs and practices traditionally seem to be beyond question. It is inconceivable that anyone could doubt the truth and wisdom of these "sacred cows" or "untouchables." However, rapidly changing times and dire or serious conditions cause thinkers and leaders to reexamine all past ideas and behaviors in order to solve pressing problems. By the year 2010, a number of sacred cows will be questioned, reexamined, and if found wanting, discarded. Untouchables that will not exist in their present form in 2010 include tenure for teachers, total inclusion programs for gifted and special needs students, strict superordinate evaluation, and due process practices.

To illustrate this notion, consider the climate of the library. Children growing up in the 1950s knew without question that a library was a silent place where one individually read or researched. It was a place of work where frivolity was frowned upon. Today's youth would find that idea ludicrous. What happened to change this once sacred cow? Notions of effective learning changed, and library scientists and educators accepted the concept that libraries should be learning centers. This new belief led to encouraging a library climate that fostered learning—fun, group activities, and cooperation. The names of these facilities typify the change—first the library, later the media, resource, or learning center, to most recently, the information center.

• Tenure. Tenure and academic freedom are supported by the National Education Association and the American Federation of Teachers as a way of protecting the

334 Chapter 12 *Future Schools and Supervisors*

freedom of speech of public school teachers. Many states adopted tenure laws for the express purpose of protecting teachers' rights. Court decisions extended academic freedom for all teachers (Spring, 1991). Tenure seemed a secure practice that would never be questioned.

Today, state legislatures are challenging the wisdom of teacher tenure. They argue that tenure promotes sub-quality performance by protecting uncaring, lazy, and irresponsible teachers with few incentives for continued growth. The public cry is for accountability and the dismantling of barriers to accountability. Tenure is viewed as a barrier to accountability, and therefore, should be abolished. Educators should take notice when conservative states, such as Indiana and Illinois, introduce legislation (to date unsuccessful) to abolish teacher tenure. By the year 2010 teacher tenure might be considered an archaic discarded custom.

- Inclusion. Special (integrated or alternative) programs for disabled students and gifted students are areas of heated controversy. Should these students be fully mainstreamed into the regular heterogeneous classroom, should they be assigned to a regular class but pulled out for special services, or should they be served in their own self-contained environment?

Since the passage of P. L. 94-142 interpretation of special education placement has been questioned. Inclusion refers to a philosophy that students with disabilities have the right to be members of classroom communities with nondisabled peers, whether or not they can meet the traditional expectations of those classrooms. Inclusion is based upon the idea that all students make valuable contributions to a class. Inclusion has yet to be firmly established across the country. Its effectiveness and value have come under scrutiny, suspicion, and debate. Legitimate sincere cases are made for and against full inclusion (Sapon-Shevin, 1994/1995; Savitch and Serling, 1994/1995; Tomlinson, 1994/1995).

Expressing the view of many educators, Bill Thomas (1994) opposed inclusion and argued that full-time inclusion in a regular classroom denies special needs students the crucial services to which they are entitled. He further suggested that nonclassified students in such a class are deprived of many hours of instruction time that the teacher must devote to the special needs student.

Mara Sapon-Shevin championed the view that favors inclusion and argued that educators need not defend inclusion, but rather, should make others defend exclusion. She suggested that there is little evidence that some children require segregated settings and that the real world is an integrated place. She reasoned that educators must provide "real world" or integrated settings for all students and that all students will benefit from this configuration (O'Neil, 1994/1995).

Chapter 12 *Future Schools and Supervisors* **335**

A parallel controversy exists for the placement of gifted students. Educators debate the merits of inclusive, pull-out, separate, and alternative programs (Sapon-Shevin, 1994/1995; Tomlinson, 1994/1995).

In the year 2010 educators should expect that these highly controversial and high budget placement decisions will still be debated. The popularity of the viewpoint will likely depend upon

Traditional Beliefs and Practices Challenged in The Future
✓ Teacher Tenure
✓ Inclusion for Special Needs Students
✓ Inclusion for Gifted Students
✓ Teacher Evaluation Procedures
✓ Due Process Interpretation

Figure 12-7

the prevailing national ideology, court rulings, and fiscal condition. Expect the pendulum to swing between these opinions in the future.

- Due Process Interpretation. Since the creation for federal and state laws and guidelines to ensure due process, interpretation has shifted between the rights of the individual and the rights of the organization. With the heightened public concern for school safety, discipline, accountability, and order, it appears that the courts and federal and state agencies will tend to favor the rights of the organization or group over those of the individual. While educators of the 1970s, 1980s, and 1990s complained vehemently that most interpretations favored the individual and often tied their hands, educators of tomorrow might expect more support from the courts.

One case in point is the interpretation by the state of Illinois of a one-year student expulsion. In the 1980s and early 1990s, a one-year student expulsion meant expulsion for the rest of the school year after the infraction. If the student offense occurred in November, the expulsion lasted for six months and the student lost a year of credit. However, if the same infraction happened in April the expulsion lasted for six weeks and the student lost one semester of credit. In Illinois today the one-year expulsion is interpreted to mean one year from the time of the expulsion. A student expelled in May would not be reinstated until the following May. This stricter interpretation obviously favors the schools and gives them more power when disciplining student offenders. In the future, expect to see more such interpretations across the country. Figure 12-7 illustrates the changes educators might expect regarding the sacred cows.

Exclusive Subordinate Examination

As discussed in Chapter 8, the movement toward alternative forms of teacher evaluation is under way and will not be turned back. The days when administrators hand teachers a summative report card with no feedback will end. In 2010 expect that, within a framework of collegial decision-making, schools will employ a variety of evaluation procedures. Most often used will be formative, performance-based evaluation based upon predetermined goals

336 Chapter 12 *Future Schools and Supervisors*

and standards. These will be jointly produced by the teacher and supervisor. Other noteworthy forms of evaluation will be teacher self-evaluation and peer evaluation. For an overview of predicted curricular changes expected by the year 2010, see Figure 12-8.

Curriculum Changes Expected in Future Schools

- Measures to insure a safe and drug-free school environment

- A technology explosion in the classroom and school office

- Expanded curriculum to meet social needs

- Re-examination of long-held beliefs and practices

- Funding reduced and state controlled

- Active community participation in school organization and curriculum

- Additional student service requirements

Figure 12-8

Major Additional Changes

Two factors that will affect the school organization and the curriculum are 1) changes in funding, and 2) increased community involvement. These circumstances will be responsible to some extent for reshaping future schools.

- Funding. Financial trends that will have long term ramifications for schools are the amount of federal monies allocated to education and the restructuring of the administration of federal funds. With a national push by Congress to balance the budget, spending cuts to schools and educational research is predicted. Dismantling or reorganizing of some sections of the U. S. Department of Education and federal education agencies will mean a change in the control of educational dollars. People holding the purse strings largely determine program existence or demise. With the federal government expected to turn over still more administration and monitoring of federal categorical grant programs to the states, the states will have increased responsibility and power.

In 2010 schools should expect fewer federal dollars. Those few dollars may likely be controlled by the state. Categorical grants must be applied for by districts or individual schools that meet predetermined requirements. Since the funds must be used for programs related to the specific category and are often competitively awarded (Small, 1993), school supervisors must become efficient in the mechanics of writing and

Chapter 12 *Future Schools and Supervisors* **337**

managing grants. School organization and curriculum will be affected as they attempt to fulfill the grant requirements.

- Community involvement. Today many services required by students and families are available to some degree, but their delivery is greatly inefficient and fragmented. In 1993, California had 160 programs residing in thirty-five agencies which were designed to help children and young adults. Kowalski and Reitzug (1993) suggested a logical solution to this dilemma by writing:

> *Schools are the logical choice for the structural center of coordination efforts since they are the only agency or institution through which all children pass, and they have more extensive contact with children than any other agency or institution. Schools also embrace the developmental perspective (as opposed to the acute-care perspective of many agencies) that is required to solve the problems of children.* (p. 272)

Community organizations, businesses, and agencies will become increasingly involved in schools. They will work as partners with educators to provide not only material resources, but services and expertise.

It will be commonplace for schools to house after hours or summer school programs run by the park district or Y.M.C.A., to entertain "guest teachers" with credentials in a desired field of study, or to jointly sponsor (with local social agencies) family counseling on school premises. In the future, schools working with health and service agencies might provide on-campus free immunization for students, driving tests, internships, and service opportunities. Curriculum will be expanded to include programs available through community groups and businesses. Examples of such programs are drug prevention programs sponsored by police departments, sexually transmitted disease programs or good health programs sponsored by local hospitals, and computer graphic designing programs taught by a local business professional. School supervisors must remain open, flexible, and actively engaged to take advantage of the numerous opportunities that await schools in the future.

Closing Thoughts

These are very exciting, rewarding, and demanding times for education and the school supervisor. The future holds great promise and challenge. Changes, such as those mentioned in this chapter and others, such as increased numbers of women and minority leaders, should be expected and welcomed. Effective supervisors must be true democratic leaders. They must be secure in the knowledge of the present; develop a clear vision of a desired future; and have the courage, tenacity, and wisdom to try.

338 Chapter 12 *Future Schools and Supervisors*

Principles and Practices for Success

- Supervisors must develop a personal vision of education. They should share their vision verbally and by example with staff.

- Supervisors must recognize that change is an inevitable and continual part of organizational growth. Change should be welcomed and positively addressed.

- Supervisors should understand that school change is usually slow, reactive, and responsive to the society.

- Supervisors must understand and prepare for organizational changes such as more building-based autonomy and accountability, competition and entrepreneurship, collegiality, and shifts in leadership roles.

- Supervisors must recognize and prepare for curriculum changes such as providing a safe and drug-free environment conducive to learning, an explosion of technology both in the classroom and office, units and courses that serve social needs, and the reexamination and possible abolition of some sacred cows.

- Supervisors must understand that the amount and form of allocation of educational funds will affect school organization and curriculum.

- Supervisors should expect continued and expanded community involvement in the schools of the future. This involvement will reshape school organization and curriculum.

- Supervisors must remain vigilant of federal and state funding practices and procedures. They must develop skills necessary to secure and hold needed competitive funding.

- Effective supervisors must value and actively seek increased community involvement and participation. They should be open to joint ventures with business, public agencies, community organizations, and concerned citizens.

Summary

Effective supervisors should strive to develop their own personal vision of the ideal school of the future. They will readily accomplish this by realistically identifying the current state of affairs, applying the best principles and practices to meet present school needs, analyzing the present to predict future possibilities and challenges, and using the previous

Chapter 12 *Future Schools and Supervisors* **339**

information to shape a desired vision. Personal vision must be translated into a shared vision with the staff. Vision must be the driving force that moves decision making.

Supervisors should recognize that educational change is continuous, inevitable, and usually slow and persistent. By planning for expected change, supervisors will become more effective leaders.

Some expected organizational changes that are predicted by the year 2010 are expanded building autonomy and accountability, competition between schools and building entrepreneurship, increased staff collegiality, and shifts in leadership roles. Expanded autonomy and accountability will be manifested through some form of site-based management. More demanding and sophisticated student testing will be mandated at the state and national levels. Schools will continue to improve through restructuring and renewal efforts.

Curriculum changes expected by the year 2010 include providing a safe and drug-free climate conducive to learning. Public outcry will result in written "get tough" policies, security systems, discipline codes with spelled out consequences for infractions, added staff development, and student courses. Agency, parent, and community support will be solicited. Technology will be used extensively in the school office and in the classroom where teacher and student behavior and performance will change dramatically. Curriculum will be implemented which serve and meet social needs.

Astute supervisors will use higher order thinking skills to apply current knowledge to plan and prepare for the future. Supervisors will use this information and skill to meet the challenge and promise of the future, and thereby, provide our future, the students, with the tools needed to be successful.

Case Problem: *Crystal Ball*

As people gathered for the monthly Administrators' Roundtable Luncheon, Will B. Brite, Assistant Principal of Middleberry High School, sat down at a table next to Dr. I. C. Little. Dr. I. C. Little is the superintendent of the most envied school district in the area and it was rumored that his district would have a principal's opening in the fall. Will B. would give his eye teeth to secure that position.

Conversation at the table was friendly and lively with various administrators taking part. After a few minutes, Dr. Little began to complain about an upcoming and pressing task. He explained that his school board wanted him to submit a plan for the future, outlining next years' goals and long range goals "to meet the challenges of the future, five or ten years down the road." Continuing, he added that to formulate immediate goals was simple but how

340 Chapter 12 *Future Schools and Supervisors*

was he supposed to predict long range future needs. Did he have a crystal ball? People laughed and shook their heads in sympathy. Surprisingly, I. C. Little turned to Will B. and said: "Seriously, what would you expect our schools to be like in the future?"

Will B. Brite immediately recognized that this question could very well be most important to his own career. How he answered would say much about himself—his vision and his leadership ability.

If you were Will B. Brite, how would you answer Dr. I. C. Little's question? Support your prognostications with present information and logical inferences. There are many possible changes not mentioned in this chapter. Include some in your response.

References

Banks, J. A. (1994). Transforming the mainstream culture. *Educational Leadership, 51*(8), 4-8.

Bell, C. S., & Chase, S. E. (1993). The under representation of women in school leadership. In C. Marshall (Ed.), *The new politics of race and gender.* Washington, DC: Falser Press.

Bauer, G. L. (1984). *Disorder in our public schools.* Washington, DC: White House Cabinet Press.

Blood, D., & Kaiser, J. (1993). Microcomputers in educational administration. In J. Kaiser (Ed.), *Educational administration (* 2nd ed.). Mequon, WI: Stylex Publishing.

Brooks, D. (1985). Order in the classroom - Forget the fire - Just keep teaching. *National Review, 37,* 25-30.

Caldas, S. J. (1994). Teen pregnancy: Why it remains a serious social, economic, and educational problem in the U. S. *Phi Delta Kappan, 75*(5), 402-406.

Cetron, M., & Rocha, W. (1988). *Into the 21st century: Long term trends affecting the United States.* Bethesda, MD: World Future Society.

Clinchy, E. (1995). Learning about the real world: Recontextualizing public schooling. *Phi Delta Kappan, 76*(5), 400-404.

Cohen, D. (1995). What standards for national standards. *Phi Delta Kappan, 76*(10), 751-757.

Dixon, R. (1994). Future schools and how to get there from here. *Phi Delta Kappan, 75,* 360-365.

Dwyer, D. (1994) Apple classrooms of tomorrow: What we've learned. *Educational Leadership, 51*(7), 4-10.

Education Vital Signs. (1991). *Executive Educator, 13*(12), A1-A27.

Elam, S. M., Rose, L. C., & Gallup, A. C. (1994). The 26th annual Phi Delta Kappa/ Gallup poll of the public's attitudes toward the public schools. *Phi Delta Kappan, 76*(1), 41-56.

Fullan, M. (1994). An interview by Dennis Sparks. National Staff Development Council Audiotape. Oxford, OH: National Staff Development Council.

Garston, R. & Wellman, B. (1995). Adaptive schools in a quantum universe. *Educational Leadership. 52*(7), 6-12.

Glasser, W. (1969). *Schools without failure.* New York: Harper & Row.

Indiana Department of Education. (1992). *Indiana State Test of Educational Progress (ISTEP).* Indianapolis, IN: Indiana Department of Education.

Kaiser, J. S. (1995). *The 21st century principal.* Mequon, WI: Stylex Publishing Co., Inc..

Katz, L. G. (1994). Perspectives on the quality of early childhood programs. *Phi Delta Kappan, 76*(1), 200-205.

Kohn, A. (1994). The truth about self-esteem. *Phi Delta Kappan, 76*(4), 272-283.

Kowalski, T. J., & Reitzug, U. C. (1993). *Contemporary school administration: An introduction.* New York: Longman.

Krantz, P. (1990, February). Is your child hooked on drugs or alcohol? *Better Homes & Gardens,* 41-43.

Lewis, A. C. (1995). An overview of the standard movement. *Phi Delta Kappan, 76*(10), 744-750.

Martin, J. R. (1995). A philosophy of education for the year 2000. *Phi Delta Kappan, 76*(5), 355-359.

McNergney, R. F. (1994). Videocases: A way to foster a global perspective on multicultural education. *Phi Delta Kappan, 76*(4), 296-298.

342 Chapter 12 *Future Schools and Supervisors*

Means, B., & Olsen, K. (1994). The link between technology and authentic learning. *Educational Leadership, 51*(7), 15-18.

Naisbitt, J. (1982). *Megatrends: Ten new directions transforming our lives.* New York: Warner Books.

Naisbitt, J. (1990). *Megatrends 2,000: Ten new directions for the 1990s.* New York: Warner Books.

Odden, A. R. (1995). *Educational leadership for America's schools.* New York: McGraw-Hill, Inc.

O'Neil, J. (1994/1995). Can inclusion work? A conversation with Jim Kauffman and Mara Sapon-Shevin. *Educational Leadership, 52*(4), 7-11.

Pang, V. O. (1994). Why do we need this class? Multicultural education for teachers. *Phi Delta Kappan, 76*(4), 289-292.

Raker, D. (1995). Current computer use in schools. *Streamlined Seminar: National Association of Elementary Principals Bulletin, 13*(6), 1-4.

Sagor, R. (1995). Overcoming the one-solution syndrome. *Educational Leadership, 52*(7), 24-27.

Sapon-Shevin, M. (1994/1995). Why gifted students belong in inclusive schools. *Educational Leadership, 52*(4), 64-67.

Savitch, J., & Serling, L. (1994/1995). Paving a path through untracked territory. *Educational Leadership, 52*(4), 72-74.

Sergiovanni, T. J., and Starratt, R. J. (1988). *Supervision: Human perspectives* (4th ed.). New York: McGraw-Hill, Inc..

Shanker, A. (1995). Classrooms held hostage. *American Educator, 19*(1), 8-13.

Shepard, L. A. (1994). The challenge of assessing young children appropriately. *Phi Delta Kappan, 76*(1), 206-213.

Small, R. (1993). Legal and financial aspects of school administration. In J. Kaiser, *Educational administration* (2nd ed.). Mequon, WI: Stylex Publishing Co., Inc..

Solomon, G. (1992). The computer as electronic doorway: Technology and the promise of empowerment. *Phi Delta Kappan, 74,* 327-329.

Spring, J. (1991). *American education: An introduction to social and political aspects* (5th ed.). New York: Longman.

Stover, D. (1986). A new breed of youth gang is on the prowl. *American School Board Journal, 173*(8), 19-24, 35.

Tanner, D., & Tanner, L. (1987). *Supervision in education: Problems and practices.* New York: Macmillan.

Thomas, B. (1994). Education should be special for all. *Phi Delta Kappan,* 74(9), 716-717.

Tomlinson, C. A. (1994/1995). Gifted learners too: A possible dream. *Educational Leadership, 52*(4), 68-69.

United States Department of Education. (1990). *America 2000 - An educational strategy.* Washington, DC: United States Government Printing Office.

Wesson, L. H. (1995). Women and minorities in educational administration. In J. Kaiser (Ed.). *The 21st century principal.* Mequon, WI: Stylex Publishing.

Yaffe, E. (1994). Not just cupcakes anymore: A study of community involvement. *Phi Delta Kappan, 75(9), 697-705.*

INDEX

#s

14th Amendment, 224
1872 Teachers' Rules, 6
1872 Teachers Rules, 5
1872 Teachers' Rules, 6
1915 Rules for Teachers, 5, 7
1915 Teachers' Rules, 7
2010 (Schools in), 323
26th Annual Phi Delta
    Kappa/Gallup Poll, 165
3 Phase Model, 203
5 Stage Model of Clinical
    Supervision, 203
8 Phase Model of Clinical
    Supervision, 203

-A-

A Class Act, 291
Academic Freedom, 227
Accountability, 324
Acheson, 4, 20, 13, 17, 25,
    182, 183, 188, 190, 192,
    199, 203
Achievement Tests, 142
ACT, 142
Adler, 174
Administrator Performance
    Instrument, 259
Adolescence, 36
Adult Learning, 310
Adulthood, 36
Adversarial Bargaining Unit
    Strategies, 218
Affective aspects of the
    classroom, 166
Affective Domain, 102
Albert, 172, 173, 174
Alfonso, 34
America 2000, 327
American College Testing
    program, 142

American Federation of
    Teachers, 214
American Federation of
    Teachers, 333
American perspective, 3
Analysis & strategy, 185
analytical observer, 19
Analyzing the teaching-
    learning process, 188
Anastasi, 139
ANCE, 144
Anderson, 85, 112, 114, 121,
    168
Anecdotal records, 244
Anticipated Normal Curve
    Equivalence, 144
Application, 170
Appraisals, 239
Appraising, 239
Argyris, 17, 20
Armstrong, 124
Artistic approach to teaching,
    95
ASCD, 288
Aspirations, intentions,
    purposes, & plan, 194
Assessing the current
    condition, 78
Association for Supervision &
    Curriculum Development,
    288
Attention, 170, 173
Austin, 20
Ausubel, 105, 114
Authority, 51
Autocratic, 20
Autonomy, 324
Avoidance of Failure, 174

-B-

Baker, 76
Bands, 144
Bandura, 43, 170
Banks, 332

Bans, 144
Bargaining process, 215
bargaining unit, 214
Barnard, C., 4
Barnard, H., 5
Barriers to quality supervision,
    24
Bates, 39, 126
Bauer, 120, 329
Beehr, 88
Behavior, Concepts of, 173
Behaviorism, 43
Beliefs & Practices, 98, 335
Benis, W., 20
Benjamin Franklin Philidelphia
    Academy, 4
Benne, 57
Bennis, 17
Berliner, 85, 143
Berman, 304
Berne, 174
Berschied, 46
Bill of Rights, 228
Blanchard, 55
Blood, 75, 265, 274, 331
Bloom, 101, 109, 114, 268,
    278
Blumberg & Adimon, 22
Board of Education of City of
    Asbury Park v. Asbury Park
    Education Association, 222
Borg, 85
Boyd, 45
Brandt, 270
Bray, 48
Brooks, 329
Brophy, 73, 74
Brown, 298
Bruner, 107
Building based curriculum
    development, 26
Burden, 296
Bureaucratic Management Model
    for Schools, 8, 9
Burrello, 302
Burton, 15

Bush, President George, 286
Butler, 124

-C-

Caldas, 332
Campbell, 4, 48, 287, 299
Campbell, Corbally, & Nystrand, 13
Canner, 151
Career stages, issues & dissatisfiers, 38
Carrier, 120
Carriere, 167
Case Problems:
  Della Gate's Staff Development Program, 315
  Dusty Chalk, 290
  Effective Mentoring, 178
  Finding Waldo, 160
  Martin Mobile's Decision, 263
  Mrs. Anderson, 236
  New Broom Sweeps In, 161
  Newfangled Ideas, 204
  Out of Step, 204
  Perplexed Professor, 204
Cegela, 76
Center for Applications of Psychological Type, 40
Certified personnel, 60
Cetron, 329
Change, 321, 324, 326, 327, 336
Characteristics of a good teacher (Acheson & Gall), 199
Charlottesville, 165
Checklists, 199
Chicago, 138
Christopher, 171, 172
Classroom management techniques, 117
Classroom observation, 188
Classroom rules, 177
Clawson, 120
Clements, 166
Climate, 157

Climate, Academic, 157, 167
  Classroom, 166
Clinchy, 332
Clinical Supervision, 14, 17, 181, 192
Closing the meeting, 261
Cogan, 3, 14, 16, 17, 20, 182, 183, 187, 203
Cognitive Ability Test, 142
Cognitive Domain, 102
Cognitive Theory, 44
Cohen, 37, 325
Cohort groups, 19
Collaboration, 12, 19
Collective bargaining Act, 221
  agreement, 214
Collegial, 11, 304, 326
  supervision, 19
Coloroso, 175
Commitment, 194
Committee of 10, 4
Communication practices, 59
Comparison of Operational Models of School Supervision, 19, 20
Competencies, principal, 49
Competency tests, 142
Competition, 325
Comprehensive Test of Basic Skills, 142
Compressed Outline (for a Written Unit Plan), 87
Conference, 188
Conflict, 212
Connecticut, 5
Connick v. Myers, 226
Connor, 297
Constitutional Legal Constraints, 225
Constraints, Contractual, 231
Construct Validity, 140
Content (in Curriculum), 280
  Validity, 140
Contingency leadership, 22
Contrast, 256
Coons, 48
Cooper, 73, 74, 85

Cooperative curriculum development, 12
Cornett, 123
Corrective feedback, 170
Criterion referenced, 253
Criterion Validity, 140
Criterion-reference tests, 144
Criterion-referenced tests, 145
Critical incident technique, 252
Crystal ball, 339
CTBS, 120, 142
Cunningham, 299
Curriculum, 332
  defined, 265, 268
  supervisor roles, 270
  evaluation, 281, 282
  implementation, 281
  perception, 266
  planned & unplanned, 267
  spheres of power, 283
  development process, 15, 272
Curwin, 175

-D-

Dale, 296
Daresh, 296, 301
Daresh, 4, 11
Daresh, 84
Data Gathering of, 244
Democratic, 11, 20
  supervision, 12
Demonstration, 170
Denny, 123
Designing & writing goals, 80
Developmental supervision, 18
Dillon-Peterson, 274
directive, 19
Discipline
  problems, 165
  profiles, 174
Discussing Performance, 247
Display Methods, 251
Diverse Workforce, 60
Dixon, 321
Dodd, 307
Doll, 80, 265, 268, 280

-346-

Dreikurs, 174
Drug Free, 327
Duck, 167
Due process, 229
Dull, 296
Dunn, 124
Durea, 119
Dwyer, 331

-E-

Early childhood, 36
Education summit, 165
Education vital signs, 328
Education Week, 288
Educational leadership, 288
Effective teacher
    characteristics, 72, 74, 199
Eidell, 123
Eisner, 20
Elam, 165, 284, 327
Elfman, 305
Elkouri, 220
Ellis, 174
Elmore, 287
Encouraging teachers, 71
Entrepreneurship, 325
Environment, orderly, 168
Equity theory, 46
Erikson, 35
Essay Tests, 147
ESTJ, 40
evaluation, 71, 84, 209, 239
    of instruction, 15
    of student progress, 117
Evertson, 168
Executive Order 10988, 213
Expectancy theory, 46
Experienced meaningful, 23
Experienced responsibility, 23
External assessment, 262
External forms, 300

-F-

Facilities, 148
Fact finder, 216

Fayol, H., 4, 8
    Five Basic Functions, 10
Federal Mediation &
    Conciliation Service, 216
Feedback
    conference, 190
    to students, 152
Fiedler, F., 22
Finn, 233, 269
Finnegan, 233
Firth, 34
Fisher, 85
Florida, 49, 128, 214, 224
    Constitution, 214
    Performance Measurement
    System, 127, 128
    Statute §447, 214
follow up statement, 233
formative evaluation, 209
Fourteenth Amendment, 228
FPMS, 127
Franklin, B, 4
Franseth, J., 13
Free form narrative, 252
Free schooling, 5
Freedom
    of association, 228
    of expression, 225
French, 52
Friction-reducing methods, 232
Fuhrman, 287
Fullan, 325
Fuller, 37
Furst, 73, 74
Future, planning for, 260

-G-

Gage, 143
Gagne's, 278
Gall, 182, 183, 188, 190, 192,
    199, 203
Gallop Poll, 165, 284, 327
Gardner, 124
Garman, 194
Garston, 326
Gay, 268

General achievement tests, 142
General supervision, 14
Gibson, 34
Glasser, 174, 285, 332
Glatthorn, 19
Glenn, 185
Glenys, 267
Glickman, 18, 20, 193, 301
Goals & objectives, 80, 100, 275
Goldhammer, 3, 17, 20, 85,
    183, 184, 185, 203
Goldstein, 114
Good, 114
Goodlad, 4
Gorden, 119
Gorton, 23, 211
Governmental forces, 99
Grade equivalence., 143
Graduate Record Examination,
    142
Grant, 48
GRE, 142
Grievance
    preventing, 224
    procedure, 221
Grissmer, 45
Gronlund, 144
Grouius, 114
Group alerting, 172
Guskey, 297

-H-

Hallinger & Murphy, 28
Halo effect, 254
Harris, 105
Harris, 26, 265, 295, 296
Harris, B., 15
Harrow, 103
    psychomotor domain, 104
Havighurst, 37
Hemphill, 48
Herman, 112
Hersey, 55
    & Blanchard, 22
Herzberg, 45
Hierlmeier, 46

-347-

Hirsch, 268
Historical perspective, 3
Hoffman, 121
Hornstein, 97
House, 46
Hoy, 123, 193
Human relations, 11
Human resources supervision, 11, 17
Hunter, 20, 298

-I-

IDEA, 100
Identify areas for improvement, 260
IEP, 111
Illinois, 334
Impact teacher, 57
Impasse, 216
Implementation, 71
Inadequate funding, 25
Inappropriate upgrading, 257
Indiana, 334
    State Test for Educational Progress, 324
Individualized instruction, 107
Individuals with Disabilities Education Act, 100
Industrial revolution, 5
Infancy, 35
Inquiry & Discovery, 106
Inservice education, 15, 194
Instructional
    delivery, 105, 113
    design, 77
insufficient time, 25
Intelligence Tests, 142
Internal & external barriers to effective supervision, 27
Internal forms, 300
Involvement by parents, 284
Iowa Test of Basic Skill, 142
Ishler, 167, 168, 170
ISTEP, 324

-J-

Jacobson, 122, 302, 304, 307, 308
Jamison, 302
Job descriptions, 244
Johnson, 217, 301
    & Douglas, 262
Jones, 60, 175
Joyce, , 80298
Judgmental evaluation, 211
Jung, 39

-K-

Kaiser, J., 8, 17, 46, 47, 60, 76, 302, 308, 321, 331
Kalamazoo, 5
Katz, 332
Kenney, 284
Kentucky windage, 224
Kerlinger, 139
Key positive sentence, 233
Kibber, 76
Kids are Worth It, 175
Kiersey, 39, 126
Kindsvatter, 167, 168, 170
Kingdoms, 12
Kirby, 45
Kirkpatrick, 88, 140
Kleinfeld, 78
Knowledge of the results, 24
Kohn, 332
Kosmoski, G., 3, 19, 137, 181, 259, 265, 268, 319
Kounin's Techniques, 116, 171, 172
Kowalski, 5, 297, 298, 337
Krajewski, 85, 185
Krantz, 328
Kratwahl, 102
Krey, R. & Burke, P., 13
Kurtz, 46

-L-

Labor Management Relations Act, 216
Lack of trust, 24
Laissez faire, 21
Lake, 297
Latham, 88
Leader
    traits, 52
    member relations, 22
Leadership, 48, 326
    style (elements for shaping), 57
Leading in a diverse environment, 54
Learning, 113
    process, 43
Lee County School Board, 224
Lefrancois, 107, 118, 123
Legal & contractual constraints, 25
Lerner, 35
Levin, 167
Lewin, Lippitt, & White, 20
Lewis, 88, 140, 325
Lezotte, 167
Lifespan development, 35
Likert, 57
Linn, 144
Lipsitt, 35
Liquidated damages, 224
Little, 138
Local Influence in Curriculum, 284
Long, 167
Love, 88
Lovell, 182
Lovell, 297
Lowry, 125
Lunenberg, 89
    & Ornstein, 24

-M-

MacArthur Foundation, 138
Mackenzie, A., 27
MacQueen, 167

Management by Objectives, 251
Management Style Indicator Test, 53
Mann, 4, 5, 300
Marland, 115
Marlow, 46
Marsh, 121, 308
Marsh, 308
Martin, 185, 332
Marvin L. Pickering v. Board of Education, 225
Maslow, 44
Massachusetts, 5
Master agreement, 218
Master contract, 214
Mastery
    learning, 109
    level, 56
MAT, 142
Maturity, 36
Maugham, 167
McClelland, 45
McCoy, 304
McGraw Hill, 144
McGreal, 211
McGregor, 17, 20, 55, 246
McLaughlin, 304, 308
McNergney, 332
McQueen, 121
Means, 331
Mediator, 216
Meister, 150
Mendler, 175
Mentoring, 19
Messick, 124
Methodology, 83
    in Curriculum), 281
Methods of instructional delivery, 105
Meyers, 171
Michigan, 5, 222
Miles, 76
Miller Analogies Test, 142
Miskel, 193
Modern perspective, 11
Momentum, 172
Montenegro, 60

More of the Same, 91
Mortimore, 167
Mosher & Purpel, 12, 17
Motivation, 44
Mt. Healthy v. Doyle, 226
Mullis, 138
Multi-person comparison, 252
Murnane, 45
Murray, 33, 95, 209, 215, 221, 222
Myers-Briggs, 39

-N-

NAEP, 138
Naisbitt, 323
Nation at Risk, 167, 286
National Assessment Initiatives, 138
National Assessment of Educational Progress, 138, 287
National Center for Educational Statistics, 138
National Education Association, 214, 224, 285, 333
National Gay Task Force v. Board of Education of the City of Oklahoma City, 227
National Influence, 287
National Science Foundation, 285
National Science Institute, 287
NC, 144
Needs assessment screen, 274
Needs theory, 44
negative attitudes, 25
Neville, 34
New Jersey, 222
New Standards Project, 138
Noncertified personnel, 60
nondirective, 19
Nonstandardized Tests, 142
Norm referenced, 143, 145, 253

Normal curve equivalence, 144
Normal schools, 5
Noyer, 233
NPS, 138
Number of students tested., 148
Nunnally, 139
Nuthall, 114
Nystrand, 299

-O-

O'Conner v. Ortega, 229
O'Neil, 334
Objectives, 80, 100
Observation 17, 184, 187, 198
    of instruction, 95
Odden, 138, 329
Oklahoma, 227
Old Deluder, 4
Oliva, 4, 12, 17, 20, 76, 86, 90, 183, 200, 211, 267, 272, 295, 296, 302, 303, 304, 305, 309, 312
Olsen, 331
Open door, 228
Operational models, 20
Orbaugh, 302
Organizing
    for instruction, 15, 86
    the classroom, 166
Orientating new staff, 16
Orlich, 295
Ornstein, 89, 139, 140, 142, 149, 150, 152, 170
Osler, 119
Osteen, 37, 38, 45, 48
Ouster, 167
Outline (for a written lesson plan), 87
Overlapping, 171
Owen, 138

-349-

-P-

Page, 121
Paired with each., 253
Pang, 332
Pankratz, 114
Parducci v. Rutland, 227
Parent Social Studies
  Questionnaire, 276
Participant misperception, 25
Past practice, 217
Pawlas, 165, 171
PCI, 123
Pedagogy, 82
Peer coaching, 12, 19
Percentiles, 143
Perceptions, 41
Performance
  appraisal meeting, 246
  assessment, 150
  characteristics, 150
  review, 246
  standards, 249
Perry, 284
Personal appearance, 229
Personality styles, 39
Pew Memorial Trust, 138
Phi Delta Kappa, 165
Phi Delta Kappan, 288
Philadelphia, 138
Phillips, 138
Philosophy of education screen,
  272
Physical aspects of the classroom,
  166
Piaget, 100
Pickering v. Board of
  Education, 225
Pilgrims, 4
Planning, 71, 76, 77, 100, 188
  conference, 188
  considerations, 84
  for the lesson, 187
  micro & macro, 75
  of successful activities, 82
  team, 304
  of conference strategy, 188
  of observation strategy, 187

Platforms, 41, 98
Play age, 36
pluralistic, 11
Political conflicts, 288
Position power, 22
Positive statement, 234, 235
Positive supervisory practices,
  86
Positive testing practices, 152
Positive translation, 233
postconference analysis, 185
postobservation conference, 17,
  200
Power, 51, 173
Practice, 170
Pratt, 275
Preassessment Tool, 81
Predictive Validity, 140
Prejudice, 41
Preobservation conference, 17,
  184, 195
Principal competencies, 49
Prior restraint, 227
Privacy, right to, 228
Professional, 19
Providing
  facilities, 15
  materials, 15
  staff, 15
Psychological errors in
  evaluation, 254
Public Employees Collective
  Bargaining Act, 214
Public Employment Relation
  Commission, 216
Public relations, 16
Pupil Control Ideology Scale,
  123

-R-

Race/ethnic stratification, 61
Ragan, 80, 275
Raker, 331
Ranking, 253
Rapport (establishing), 247
Rating scales, 258

Rationale, 235
Raven, 52
Ravitch, 269
Reddin, 47
Redfern, 19
Reese, 35
Reitzug, 5, 297, 298, 337
Relating special pupil services,
  16
Reliability, 139
Report: A Nation at Risk: The
  Imperative for Educational
  Reform, 286
Revenge, 173
Reynolds, 137
Right to privacy, 228
Rocha, 329
Rochester, 138
Rogosin, 121
Role shifting, 326
Roles & responsibilities of
  Supervisors, 176
Rose, 327
Rosenshine, 73, 74, 83, 114,
  150
Rosenthal, 122, 170
Rowe, 114
Rushton, 43
Russell & Hunter, 18
Rutter, 167
Ryan, 73, 74
Ryff, 35

-S-

Sacken, 19
Sacred Cows, 333
Safe, 327
Sagor, 325
Sapon-Shevin, 334, 335
SAT, 142
Satan, 4
Savitch, 334
Schein, 37, 38
Schmidt, 55, 212, 302, 304,
  307, 308
Scholastic Aptitude Test, 142

School age, 36
Science Research Associates, 111
Scientific
approach to teaching, 95
management, 5
Screen
needs assessment, 274
philosophy of education, 272
Seating chart observational records, 198
Selecting the methodology, 83
Selective verbatim, 198
Selectmen, 4
Sergiovanni, 4, 20, 34, 41, 62, 97, 98, 182, 185, 211, 302, 308, 319, 321
& Starratt, 13, 23
Serling, 334
Shakeshaft, 60
Shanker, 328, 329
Sheats, 57
Shepard, 80, 275, 332
Shipman, 26
Shirk, 121
Short Answer Tests, 147
Showers, 80
Sievert, 307
Singer, 45
Site-based management, 289
Situational leadership, 22
Sizer, 285
Slesinger, 97
Small, 336
Smith, 97, 139
Smoothness, 172
Snoopervision, 23
So Fresh, 90
Social
learning theory, 43
needs, 332, 333
Soliciting Employee Input, 260
Solomon, 331
Special education testing, 157
Special master, 216
SRA, 111
Staff development, 295, 296, 297, 298, 299, 302

Cost & incentives, 309
Evaluation, 312
Factors of effective, 303
Formats, 311
Functions of, 300
Indicators of an effective
Master plan, 305
Planning, 304
Program, 309
Responsibilities, 302
Scheduling, 307
Selecting a provider, 308
Tasks of the planning team, 309
Topic selection), 305
Staff needs, 305
Standardized Tests, 142
Standards, high, 167
Stanford Achievement Tests, 142
Stanford-Binet, 142
Stanines, 143
Starrat, 17, 34, 41, 62, 97, 98, 182, 211, 295, 302, 308, 319, 321
State Influence, 286
Steele, 88
Stogdill, 48
Stover, 329
Strategies (for effective teaching), 112
Strikes, 222
Striving for consensus, 261
Student assessment, 137
Student differences, 122
Success, 169
Suggestion, 233, 234
Summative evaluation, 211
Sunshine laws, 228
Supervision, 3, 33, 265, 295
Broad based, 35
By avoidance, 21
Clinical, 14
Defined, 12, 14
Direct style, 22
General, 14
Indirect style, 22
Models, 16, 97

Style, 20, 22
The need for, 23
Types of, 14
Supervisor's readiness, 192
Supervisor-teacher
relationship, 97, 187
Supervisory behavior plan, 34
Supervisory tasks, 15
Surber, 121
Survey Achievement Tests, 142

-T-

Taba, 266
Taft-Hartley Act, 216
Tannenbaum, 55
Tanner, 12, 83, 144, 300, 301, 324
Task,
Developmental, 15
Operational, 15
Preliminary, 15
Structure, 22
Taylor, F. W., 4, 5
Teacher
Differences, 125
Dropout, 19
Made Tests, 146
Opposition, 24
Personality, 25
Planning, 71
Rotation, 19
Skill., 148
Supervisor Relationship, 97, 187
Teaching,
in Style-Summary, 126
Kids Responsibility, 174, 175
Technology, 155, 329
Technology, 329
Test
Administration Practices, 150
Anxiety, 153, 156
Criteria, 139

-351-

Purpose, 148
Types, 119, 141
Testing Climate, 154
Theory X, 55
Thomas, 334
Thompson, 311
Time periods, 4
Time, 148
Timeline coding, 199
Titus, 120
To the Rescue, 316
Toch, 284
Tomlinson, 334, 335
Translation, 233, 235
Traymontana, 112
Trentham, 120
Trust relationship, 193
Tuckman, 125, 149
Turner, 123
Tyler, 77, 272, 282, 306
U. S. Department of Education, 327
Unconscious Prejudice, 255
Understanding History, 3, 265
Unfair Labor Practices, 217
Unfocused worker, 19
United States Supreme Court, 224
Unprepared supervisor, 25

-U-

Unruh, 80, 267, 282, 283, 286
Urban Educator,, 288
Usability, 139, 140
Usdan, 299

-V-

Validity, 139
Vision, 319
Vockell, 268
Vonnegut, 227
Vroom, 46

-W-

Walden, 185
Walster, 46
Warren Education Association
v. Adams,, 222
Weber, M., 4, 8
Webster, 116
Weigand, 275
Weiss, 45
Wellisch, 167
Wellman, 326
Wesson, 60, 327
Whittrock, 124
Wide lens, 198
Wigdor, 46
Wilen, 167, 170
Wiles, 182
Willet, 45
Willower, 123
Wilson, 168
Wise, 211
Withitness, 171
Wood, 311
Worsham, 166
Wright, 114
Writing Instructional Plans, 86

-Y-

Yaffe, 332
Yekes, 20
Yerian, 78
Young Adulthood, 36
Youssef, 114
Yukl, 52

-Z-

Zais, 280
Zimpher, 310